RETHINKING IMPLICIT MEMORY

RETHINKING IMPLICIT MEMORY

Edited by

JEFFREY S. BOWERS

Department of Experimental psychology
University of Bristol
UK

and

CHAD J. MARSOLEK

Department of Psychology
University of Minnesota
USA

OXFORD
UNIVERSITY PRESS

OXFORD
UNIVERSITY PRESS

Great Clarendon Street, Oxford OX2 6DP

Oxford University Press is a department of the University of Oxford.
It furthers the University's objective of excellence in research, scholarship,
and education by publishing worldwide in

Oxford New York

Auckland Bangkok Buenos Aires Cape Town Chennai
Dar es Salaam Delhi Hong Kong Istanbul Karachi Kolkata
Kuala Lumpur Madrid Melbourne Mexico City Mumbai Nairobi
São Paulo Shanghai Taipei Tokyo Toronto

Oxford is a registered trade mark of Oxford University Press
in the UK and in certain other countries

Published in the United States
by Oxford University Press Inc., New York

A catalogue record for this title is available from the British Library

Library of Congress Cataloging in Publication Data
(Data available)

ISBN 0 19 263233 7 (Hbk)
ISBN 0 19 263232 9 (Pbk)

10 9 8 7 6 5 4 3 2 1

Typeset by Integra Software Services Pvt. Ltd, Pondicherry, India
www.integra.india.com

Printed in Great Britain
on acid-free paper by Biddles Ltd, Guildford and King's Lynn

CONTENTS

Priming and memory

Commentary

PREFACE

Long-term priming has been one of the most thoroughly studied phenomena in cognitive psychology during the past 20 years. Excitement in this area was initially inspired by the observation that densely amnesic patients show robust (sometimes normal) memory for pictures and words when items are presented in a fragmented format at test and memory is tested indirectly. This occurs despite poor (sometimes chance) performance on recall and recognition tasks (e.g., Warrington and Weiskrantz, 1974). These findings led to important claims regarding the nature of amnesia, and more generally, opened up research to the experimental study of 'unconscious' or 'implicit' memories. Later work showed that this memory—now called long-term priming—can be studied in people with normally functioning memories (e.g., Jacoby and Dallas, 1981; Tulving *et al.*, 1982), making unconscious memory still more accessible to empirical study.

Within this tradition, a primary question has been how priming (and more generally implicit memory) relates to recall and recognition. One of the central debates from this perspective is whether priming and episodic memory should be explained within a single memory system or through qualitatively different memory systems. An underlying assumption in this perspective, then, is that priming is mediated by a system whose main function is memory—although the specific function of this system is rarely described.

An alternative framework for understanding priming was developed by researchers in psycholinguistics (e.g., Morton, 1979; Scarborough *et al.*, 1977) and object recognition (e.g., Bartram, 1974; Biederman and Cooper, 1991), and was modeled by researchers investigating concept formation (McClelland and Rumelhart, 1985). On this perspective, priming is a natural by-product of memory or learning processes embedded within systems designed to support perception (or conceptual processing). That is, the main function of the systems that support priming is pattern recognition (or conceptual understanding), not episodic memory, and the key to theoretical progress is to develop explicit links between priming and perceptual (conceptual) systems, rather than to debate functional similarities/dissimilarities between priming and episodic memory.

This shift from a 'memory' perspective on priming to a 'perception' or 'learning' perspective is not just a semantic point, as it likely entails important implications. For example, the long-standing debate of whether multiple memory systems are needed to account for episodic memory versus priming phenomena is no longer the central question. Indeed, given that priming is thought to be supported by systems that mediate visual and auditory word identification, object identification, etc., it is unclear whether it is helpful to label these systems 'memory systems', unless all systems that encode and recognize information are called memory systems. More appropriate would be to label the systems orthographic, phonological, object recognition systems, etc.

In addition, by characterizing priming as a natural consequence of perceptual and conceptual processing, theories of priming should be constrained by a large body of research not previously considered relevant in the memory literature, that is, research in visual and auditory word identification, object identification, concepts and categorization, sensory–motor control, and other areas of perception and cognition. Indeed, if this view is correct, priming research from the memory literature should provide important constraints on theories of perception and other abilities. For example, the internal learning mechanisms of perceptual systems should be capable of supporting various priming phenomena.

These two frameworks for studying priming have developed within the memory and psycholinguistic/perception literatures relatively independently, with little reference made across the two literatures. And although research in the memory perspective has been highly active, producing hundreds of articles in the past two decades, it is only recently that the perceptual approach has developed some momentum, with a growing number of authors employing long-term priming to address questions in these domains. Accordingly, we believe it is an auspicious time to explicitly consider the underlying assumptions and frameworks that guide research on priming.

In order to highlight the relevant perspectives, we asked leading researchers to contribute a chapter that would either directly address these issues or establish a view firmly within one of these traditions. By collecting a series of such chapters, we hoped to better characterize the different perspectives and illuminate bridges between them. This should serve to highlight important aspects of one approach for researchers working in the other. We think the chapters have succeeded nicely in this endeavor.

The first section includes three chapters (Bowers, Marsolek, and Roediger) that take a 'big-picture' view on priming, its possible functions, and how implicit memory may be delineated from other forms of memory. The chapters in the next section adopt the view that priming is embedded within systems that support word and object recognition, and employ priming phenomena in order to further our understanding of these systems. But the chapters take varied perspectives, with some authors assuming (at least implicitly) that perceptual and episodic memory systems are distinct (with priming a more relevant tool in studying perception; the chapters by Feldman, Marsolek and Burgund, Rueckl, and Wagenmakers *et al.*), and others (instance theorists, e.g., Goldinger *et al.*, Lachs *et al.*, Luce *et al.*) assuming that the perceptual systems themselves are embedded within a general episodic memory system, such that priming, perception, recall, and recognition are manifestations of a common memory system. But the common theme amongst all these chapters (rarely adopted in the past literature) is that priming is an important tool to understand word and object perception, with a close linking between the memory, perception, and psycholinguistic literatures.

The chapters in the third section (Kinoshita, Uttl *et al.*, Whittlesea, and Zeelenberg *et al.*) consider priming from a more traditional memory perspective, using priming to address questions about memory *per se*, but in ways that highlight new directions. This is not to say that these chapters have no implications for theories perception and language (e.g., Whittlesea's approach clearly takes a strong stand on this issue, not unlike some of the instance theories noted above). But the theories are primarily designed to explain memory phenomena, with constraints largely drawn from the memory literature itself and with perceptual and psycholinguistic phenomena considered less relevant.

Finally, the last chapter provides an authoritative commentary on the whole enterprise. Our hope is that this collection forms an important guidepost for contemporary views on priming and that it sparks new thoughts in the reader toward ultimately understanding implicit memory.

References

Bartram, D. J. (1974). The role of visual and semantic codes in object naming. *Cognitive Psychology*, **6**, 325–56.

Biederman, I. and Cooper, E. E. (1991). Priming contour-deleted images: Evidence for intermediate representations in visual object recognition. *Cognitive Psychology*, **23**, 393–419.

Jacoby, L. L. and Dallas, M. (1981). On the relationship between autobiographical memory and perceptual learning. *Journal of Experimental Psychology: General*, **110**, 306–40.

McClelland, J. L. and Rumelhart, D. E. (1985). Distributed memory and the representation of general and specific information. *Journal of Experimental Psychology: General*, **114**, 159–88.

Morton, J. (1979). Facilitation in word recognition: Experiments causing change in the logogen models. In *Processing of visible language* (ed. P. A. Kolers, M. E. Wrolstad, and H. Bouma), Vol. 1, pp. 259–68. New York: Plenum Press.

Scarborough, D. L., Cortese, C., and Scarborough, H. (1977). Frequency and repetition effects in lexical memory. *Journal of Experimental Psychology: Human Perception and Performance*, **3**, 1–17.

Tulving, E., Schacter, D. L., and Stark, H. A. (1982). Priming effects in word-fragment completion are independent of recognition memory. *Journal of Experimental Psychology: Learning, Memory, and Cognition*, **8**, 336–42.

Warrington, E. K. and Weiskrantz, L. (1974). The effect of prior learning on subsequent retention in amnesic patients. *Neuropsychologia*, **12**, 419–28.

CONTRIBUTORS

Tamiko Azuma Department of Speech and Hearing Science, Arizona State University, Tempe, Arizona, 85287–1104, USA

Jeffrey S. Bowers Department of Experimental Psychology, University of Bristol, Bristol BS8 1TN, UK

E. Darcy Burgund Department of Radiology, Washington University, School of Medicine, 4525 Scott Avenue, St. Louis, MO, 63110, USA

Jan Charles-Luce Language Production Laboratory, University at Buffalo, Buffalo, NY, USA

Stephanie Cosentino Psychology, Sociology, and Anthropology Department, Drexel University, 33rd Chestnut Sts., Philadelphia, PA, 19104, USA

Fergus I. M. Craik Rotman Research Institute, Baycrest Centre for Geriatric Care, 3560 Bathurst St., Toronto, ON M6A 2E1, Canada

Laurie Beth Feldman SS 112, The University at Albany, SUNY, Albany, NY 12222, USA, and Haskins Labs, New Haven, CT, 06510, USA

Stephen D. Goldinger Department of Psychology, Arizona State University, Box 871104, Tempe, Arizona 85287–1104, USA

Peter Graf Department of Psychology, University of British Columbia, Vancouver, BC, V6T 1Z4, USA

Virginia M. Holmes Department of Psychology, School of Behavioural Science, 12th Floor, Redmond Barry Building, The University of Melbourne, Victoria 3010, Australia

Dave Huber Department of Psychology, University of Colorado, Campus Box 345, Boulder, CO, 8030–0345, USA

Sachiko Kinoshita Department of Psychology, Macquarie University, Sydney, NSW 2109, Australia

Heather M. Kleider Department of Psychology, Arizona State University, Box 871104, Tempe, Arizona, 85287–1104, USA

Sid Kouider Laboratoire de Sciences Cognitives et Psycholinguistique, EHESS / CNRS, 54 Boulevard Raspail, 75270 Paris Cedex 06, France

Lorin Lachs Indiana University Bloomington, Speech Research Laboratory, Bloomington, IN, 47405, USA

Paul A. Luce Language Perception Laboratory, Department of Psychology, University at Buffalo, Buffalo, NY, 14260, USA

Chad J. Marsolek Department of Psychology, University of Minnesota, 75 East River Road, Minneapolis, MN, 55455, USA

Conor McLennan Language Perception Laboratory, Department of Psychology, University at Buffalo, Buffalo, NY, 14260, USA

Kipp McMichael Indiana University Bloomington, Speech Research Laboratory, Bloomington, IN, 47405, USA

Diane Pecher Department of Social and Organizational Psychology, Utrecht University, PO box 80. 140, 3508 TC Utrecht, The Netherlands

David B. Pisoni Indiana University Bloomington, Speech Research Laboratory, Bloomington, IN, 47405, USA

Jeroen G. W. Raaijmakers Faculteit der Psychologie, programmagraen Psychonomie, Universiteit van Amsterdam, Roetersstraat 15, 1018 WB Amsterdam

Henry L. Roediger, III Department of Psychology – Box 1125, Washington University, One Brookings Drive, St. Louis, MO, 63130–4899, USA

Jay G. Rueckl Department of Psychology, University of Connecticut and Haskins Laboratories, Storrs, CT, 06269, USA

Lael J. Schooler Department of Psychology, Penn State University, 622 Moore Building, University Park, PA, 16802–3106, USA

Richard M. Shiffrin Psychology Building, Room 350, Indiana University, Bloomington, IN, 47405–7007, USA

Bob Uttl Psychology Department, Oregon State University, 204C Moreland Hall, Corvallis, OR, 97331–5303, USA

Eric-Jan M. Wagenmakers Department of Psychonomics, University of Amsterdam, Roetersstraat 15, 1018 WB Amsterdam, The Netherlands

Bruce W. A. Whittlesea Department of Psychology, Simon Fraser University, Burnaby, BC V5A 1S6, Canada

René Zeelenberg Psychology Building, Indiana University, Bloomington, IN, 47405–7007, USA

GENERAL VIEWS ON PRIMING

CHAPTER 1

RECONSIDERING IMPLICIT MEMORY

HENRY L. ROEDIGER, III

In some sense, the idea underlying the concept of implicit memory is quite old. Schacter (1987) traced the history of the concept back to the beginnings of psychology (and even before), although the topic was considered under different names and studied mostly with anecdotal methods. However, the work of these early scholars did not impinge much on the conscious thoughts of experimental psychologists studying human memory throughout most of the 20th century. These researchers were preoccupied with other matters: serial learning, chaining, the serial position effect, paired-associate learning, interference, free recall, retrieval cues, organization, transfer, and on and on. To paraphrase Ebbinghaus's famous quote about psychology, the concept of implicit memory may have a long past but its real history of experimental study is short.

The use of modern methods that would today qualify as implicit (or indirect) tests of memory may be traced to the studies of Warrington and Weiskrantz (1968, 1970). They introduced techniques referred to by contemporary workers as word stem completion, word fragment completion (although their fragments were different from the type most researchers use today), and picture fragment naming. They showed that when memory performance of amnesic patients was probed by these techniques, there did not seem to be much if any impairment in performance relative to control subjects. This outcome shocked the field and debate about these early findings swirled through the 1970s, but mostly in neuropsychological circles. It was not really until the early 1980s, with famous papers by Jacoby and Dallas (1981) and Tulving *et al.* (1982) (and then later many others) that at least some experimental psychologists started to take note of this new type of inquiry and this new way of measuring a form of memory. The new area struggled for a name until Graf and Schacter coined the term *implicit memory* (1985), although even that name is not without controversy. (Some researchers prefer the term *indirect tests of memory* to implicit tests, for various reasons, e.g., Richardson-Klavehn and Bjork, 1988.) Still, whatever these studies are called, research in the past 20 years has produced a robust new area of inquiry that has caused psychologists to think hard about the concept of memory, to debate the existence of systems and processes that underlie performance on these new tests, and to open the field to questions that would have remained beyond the ken of experimental psychologists in 1975. The area captured by the term *implicit memory* changed the way cognitive psychologists conceive of their task and mission.

The study of implicit memory poses challenges to the whole concept of memory, challenges with which the field has struggled ever since. How are we to define *memory* and *implicit memory* without at once being too broad or too narrow? What are the appropriate contrasting terms for implicit or indirect memory tests? (Explicit memory and direct memory test?) How does the study of implicit memory fit into (and change) the broader picture? In this chapter I continue reflections on these matters begun earlier (Roediger, 1990a, b; 1993; Roediger *et al.*, 1999). However, the conclusion I come to is that the term *implicit memory* may have outlived its usefulness and that we gain no conceptual advantage from using this term that could not be obtained simply by calling the phenomena of interest long-term priming effects.

Defining memory

Memory can be defined in many different ways. In the first chapter of *Elements of episodic memory*, Tulving considered the issue of defining memory and suggested that 'Memory has to do with the after-effects of stimulation at one time that manifest themselves subsequently at a later time...' (1983, p. 7). He went on to say that this suggestion may be too broad, but let us stick with it for the time being because it is helpful for considering implicit memory. Explicit memory occurs, by the standard definition, when people attempt to recollect events from their past. The process is intentional, volitional. On the other hand, 'Implicit memory refers to manifestations of memory that occur in the absence of intentions to recollect' (McDermott, 2000, p. 231). (Definitions by others are similar in character and would not change the argument advanced here.)

If we put together Tulving's broad definition of memory with McDermott's definition of implicit memory, we might say that 'implicit memory refers to all after-effects of stimulation that do not involve explicit or conscious recollection'. When I have tried this broad definition of implicit memory on researchers who study this topic, many have nodded in approval and told me that they liked it. I am not surprised; they should like it. If we define implicit memory in these terms, then much of empirical psychology becomes a subfield (or a minor branch) of the study of implicit memory! Researchers from psychophysics to animal learning to social psychology are interested in 'after-effects of stimulation' as expressed on a tremendous variety of measures that do not require conscious recollection. If a surveyor asks about your opinion of gun control on a 1–7 scale, then surely you are expressing your past experience in an ongoing behavior—your current rating—and recent events or messages may prime your response one way or the other.

The case is similar for many (but certainly not all) standard dependent measures in the major fields of psychology. After all, the most common experimental technique in psychology is to manipulate some independent variable and to measure how it affects some dependent variable. Unless the dependent variable is recall, recognition, or another measure that reflects conscious recollection, then the dependent measure probably may qualify as an implicit memory measure by the definitions discussed above (and most other common definitions of implicit memory).

The foregoing consideration points to an obvious problem: If the concept of implicit memory (or indirect tests of memory) points to nearly everything, then there is a sense in which it points to nothing. The category is too broad and needs to be better specified. This point, which seems incontestable to me, has not been debated in the literature, although an exception exists in a chapter by Tulving (2000, pp. 38–40) in which he considers such fundamental problems. I consider why researchers have rarely worried about the breadth and scope of the concept of implicit memory in the next section.

Implicit memory research

Although the general definition of implicit memory may be quite broad—after-effects of stimulation that occur in the absence of attempts at conscious recollection—the study of implicit memory employs a rather limited range of actual measures. Borrowing a tip from Jacoby (1983), Roediger and Blaxton (1987) suggested that most verbal implicit memory tasks could be classified as data-driven (or perceptual) tests or conceptually-driven (or conceptual) tests. The idea is that some tests strongly involve the perceptual system in identifying or resolving ambiguous perceptual clues, whereas for other tasks seem to draw on meaning or concepts. Roediger *et al.* (1989) proposed converging measurement operations that would identify tests as perceptual and conceptual. Some tests might be difficult to classify, of course, either because the measuring operations could not be applied to the test or because the results of the tests would turn out ambiguously, with some markers pointing to the test as conceptual and others as perceptual. The distinction between perceptual and conceptual tasks works to a first approximation, given these limitations in measurement, but problems have arisen (see McDermott and Roediger, 1996; Roediger and McDermott, 1993 for examples and discussion).

I would estimate that 80% of all implicit memory research conducted from 1980–2001 used perceptual or data-driven implicit memory tests. A common example is shown in Figure 1.1. The ambiguous picture there can be named quite quickly by practically every cognitive psychologist, although if the same figure were shown to an equally intelligent group of chemists, their responses would be very variable and (like introductory psychology students) many of the chemists would take minutes rather than seconds to resolve the figure (and then only with verbal clues). Cognitive psychologists have seen the figure dozens of times and so are primed to name it quickly, even if it is presented in a new context (Roediger and Srinivas, 1993). I suspect that even if I were not to see R. C. James' fragmented figure for another 20 years, I would have no trouble in quickly naming it. In short, psychologists' ability to name the figure quickly and easily is a manifestation of long-term perceptual priming. The fragmented elements of the scene coalesce rather easily into a figure due to prior practice that transfers well to this task when it is presented again, even in an unexpected context.

The most common perceptual implicit memory tasks are verbal in nature (although pictorial tasks like that of Figure 1.1 have been used, too). In all cases subjects are told to name or to complete the fragmented form or brief glimpse of some stimulus, typically a word. The tasks include word stem completion (ele_____), word fragment completion (e_e_h_n_), word identification (naming the word from a very brief glimpse), anagram solution (rearranging the letters in *phelante* to form a word), and other variants of these tasks. Prior study of a word such as *elephant* will produce priming on these tasks relative to a non-studied baseline. However, studying a picture of an elephant produces little or no priming on these same verbal tasks despite activating the same concept in semantic

Figure 1.1 The fragmented form of a picture taken by R. C. James. Novices (those who have never seen the picture before) often take several minutes to identify the figure—a Dalmatian with his nose to the ground. However, cognitive psychologists who have practiced seeing the figure many times show almost instant recognition of the figure even when it is shown unexpectedly and after long periods of time. This kind of perceptual priming is the most commonly studied form of implicit memory.

memory (Rajaram and Roediger, 1993; Srinivas, 1993; Weldon and Roediger, 1987). These tasks are deemed perceptual (in part) because prior presentation of the word-form is necessary to produce priming on these lexical implicit memory tests. As already pointed out, perceptual implicit memory tasks can also be non-verbal, such as picture fragment naming (somewhat like the task in Figure 1.1), or naming pictures from brief displays, or naming pictures as they are gradually clarified from very small amounts of information. (In this last task, the measure is how much of the fragment is required to name the picture.) Once again, if subjects have recently seen words naming these concepts, then little or no priming occurs on these pictorial tasks (Srinivas, 1993; McDermott and Roediger, 1994). (References that provide examples of all these tasks can be found in Roediger and McDermott's 1993 review chapter.)

Although most of the implicit memory literature is based on perceptual implicit memory tests, perhaps 10% of the tasks used are conceptual implicit tests. If a subject had studied the word elephant or seen a picture of an elephant in a study phase, the conceptual tests could be of at least three types. One is the answering of general knowledge questions, such as 'What animal helped Hannibal in his attack on Rome?' (Blaxton, 1989). Another is a free association task, such as providing the first five words that come to mind in response to a cue such as *tusk*. A third task is naming category instances, so that subjects would be given a*nimals* and asked to list as many as possible in 30 seconds. These three tasks are just a subset of many possible conceptual tests, but they are the most common ones. All have been used in at least a handful of experiments. These tasks behave differently as a function of independent variables than do perceptual implicit tests. For example, prior study of pictures and words produces equivalent priming on conceptual implicit memory tests (McDermott and Roediger, 1996; Weldon and Coyote, 1996) rather than showing the sharp specificity found on perceptual tests.

If it is true, as I estimated, that 80% of all implicit memory tests are perceptual in nature and 10% are conceptual, then what about the other 10%? I would place in this class a few tasks that have been dubbed procedural in the sense used by Squire (1987). These are tasks such as mirror tracing and pursuit rotor tracking that defy classification as perceptual or conceptual (the measuring operations cannot be applied to ask the question), but the tasks are classified as implicit because even deeply amnesic patients can learn them. However, some researchers might question whether tasks such as pursuit rotor tracking and mirror tracing are implicit tasks in the same way as are the perceptual and conceptual tasks. Rather, some theorists might classify them as belonging to a somewhat separate area of inquiry referred to as implicit learning (see Stadler and Frensch's 1998 handbook with many chapters summarizing work on this topic). Implicit learning tasks often are spread out over time and involve subjects learning a subtle rule that affects their performance, although the subjects often seem unaware of the nature of the rule or even the fact that there is one. (However, this claim of 'unawareness' has been responsible for much research in this area, weighing in on each side of the issue.) The relation between studies of implicit memory and those of implicit learning have been rarely considered (although see Stadler and Roediger, 1998 for an exception). This relation will not be considered here, either, but should be considered more fully in the future.

The point being made here is that despite the wide scope of the definition of implicit memory, the actual range of tasks studied in this field of inquiry (narrowly defined) is relatively small. Although the study of implicit memory has been rightly championed as opening up the concept of memory to new tasks and new insights, the surface has barely been scratched once one pauses to consider the totality of possible tasks and possible measures that qualify as 'implicit memory tasks' under most definitions. Some type of memory is involved in practically every measure psychologists take.

Priming

The hallmark of all the implicit memory tasks—perceptual and conceptual—is that they show priming. 'Priming refers to facilitative effects of an encounter with a stimulus on subsequent processing of the same stimulus (direct priming) or a related stimulus (indirect priming)' (Tulving *et al.*, 1982, p. 336).[1] All the tasks listed above reveal priming, and for practically all these tasks an important dissociation has been observed. Severely

---

[1] Some people have referred to indirect priming as 'false priming' (e.g., McKone and Murphy, 2000), but of course there is nothing false about it. Priming from indirectly related experiences is as valid as any other kind of priming. Veridicality of memory (is the recollection true or false?) is only an issue in declarative memory tests, if we use Squire's (1987) framework, that is, in episodic or semantic memory.

memory-impaired (amnesic) patients who show greatly reduced performance on tests of explicit (episodic) memory, such as free recall, cued recall, and recognition, often show perfectly intact priming (just like that of healthy college students) on both perceptual and conceptual implicit memory tests.

The dissociation of priming from other forms of memory (chiefly episodic memory) underlies the discovery of other memory systems besides episodic memory. One defining characteristic of a new system is to show a strong dissociation between performance on standard explicit memory tests and a measure reflecting some other putative system. Intact priming on some new measure in subjects who reveal greatly impaired performance on explicit tests reveals two things: first, the task reveals memory (priming shows that) and second, the form of memory is different from that displayed on explicit memory tests. We will use this logic here in an effort to uncover other memory processes and systems in the body that have not yet been much discussed in the literature (but see Roediger, 1993 for a start). In the famous hierarchical representation in Squire's (1987) theory, there was a place for 'other' memory systems. Tentative evidence for them is forwarded in this chapter.

Memory and the body

Proponents of memory systems have concentrated their attention on the central nervous system. There is good reason for that, of course. Conscious recollection (episodic recollection) is supported by structures and processes arising in the central nervous system, particularly areas in and around the hippocampus and certain regions of the frontal lobes. However, other bodily systems also display a form of memory, as is shown on some procedural memory tasks. Let us first consider a thought experiment: the amnesic weightlifter.

Suppose a young man, W. L., is involved in a tragic accident that causes a brief period of anoxia. The loss of oxygen to the brain causes damage to regions in and around the hippocampus that seem to be responsible for certain forms of episodic memory. W. L. recovers from his accident and has reasonably normal general intelligence, but displays classic signs of amnesia—poor recall of recent events after a brief delay. He is mostly confined to his home, cared for by his family. One day he discovers weight-lifting equipment in his basement, left there by a previous owner of the home. He sets it up, with some help, near the television. He spends considerable time each day watching television, so now he finds that whenever he is near the television, he begins lifting weights.

W. L.'s mother, a retired psychologist, begins measuring his performance. She measures repetitions per minute and plots changes. She discovers an orderly growth in the number of repetitions (of bicep curls) and other easily measured aspects of his performance. He shows procedural learning. When she asks him over dinner if he has ever lifted weights since his accident, he thinks for a while and says no. Nonetheless, he continues to practice as he watches television and he gets better and stronger.

In a sense there is nothing remarkable in this hypothetical example—just another case of motor/procedural learning in the absence of explicit or episodic recollection of the episodes that gave rise to the learning. But this case has another interesting feature: the man's body shows profound changes. His biceps are enlarged; his neck and chest become thicker; his legs increase in size. In a very real sense, these changes are 'memory traces' of the experiences the man has had. He might not be able to read out these traces to know about the experiences, but others looking at him can. From observing the visible traces of W. L.'s past experience—his bulging muscles—others would know (if not remember) that he had been lifting weights, or at least engaging in strenuous physical activity. There is a sense that overt physical changes in an individual can signal their past experiences, as when adults who have had happy lives spent smiling have upturned mouths in their old age while perpetual naysayers have permanent frowns when they become old. These outward changes are 'traces of past experience manifested in current behavior' or, in this case, appearance. Therefore, they are memory traces, of a sort we usually don't consider.

The foregoing example is hypothetical, but not farfetched; it gives a new meaning to the phrase 'body memories'. Our past experiences can change our bodies in many ways—not just changes in the c.n.s.—that then change our behavior. However, other bodily systems besides the muscular/procedural system display forms of memory that are not so easily encompassed under current theory.

The immune system

The clearest case of a bodily system that exhibits the primary property characteristic of implicit memory, viz., priming, is the immune system (see Roediger *et al.*, 1999). Indeed, immunologists have recognized this fact for years and have uncovered many of the mechanisms that endow the immune system with memory, although knowledge remains incomplete in some critical areas. A recent paper on the immune system in *Science* is entitled 'T cell death and memory' and it is not atypical (Sprent and Tough, 2001). (Because studies of behavioral psychology so rarely intrude on the pages of *Science*, I would hazard the guess that as many 'memory papers' appear in that journal on the immune system as on the central nervous system.)

The immune system responds to antigens that invade it. If a pathogen's effect is too great, death of the organism results. However, if a person's immune system can ward off the pathogen, the immune system is changed and is more likely to fight off future infections. Ahmed and Gray (1996) began another *Science* article on this topic with this sentence: 'The immune system can remember, sometimes for a lifetime, the identity of a pathogen' (p. 54). A contemporary psychologist might quibble with the word *remember* in that sentence, but nonetheless their paper and much other work documents the fact that the immune system changes as a function of experience and that these changes are retained for a long time. This change is recorded in the immune system in what are called 'memory cells'—the immune system's memory traces—and the effect of these memory cells are expressed later in behavior of the immune system when a new pathogen invades the system. The concept of immunological memory is well established and the quotes below are the accepted explanation from a standard biology textbook by Chiras (1993):

> The first time an antigen enters the body, it elicits an immune response, but the initial reaction—or *primary response*—is relatively slow and of small magnitude…During the primary response antibody levels in the blood do not begin to rise until approximately the second week *after* the intruder has been detected…If the same antigen enters the body at a later date, however, the

immune system acts much more quickly and forcefully...This greatly fortified reaction constitutes the *secondary response*...[and] during a secondary response antibody levels increase rather quickly, only a few days after the antigen has entered the body. The amount of antibody produced also greatly exceeds quantities generated during the primary response. Consequently, the antigen is quickly destroyed, and a recurrence of the illness is prevented. (p. 360)

Researchers interested in implicit memory will immediately recognize the underlying concept described in the previous paragraph as priming. The introduction of the antigen into the body the first time leads to changes in the immune system that causes priming later, the second time the antigen is introduced. Note that the two measures reflecting priming in the immune system—magnitude of the response and speed of the response—are the same ones that cognitive psychologists measure in other systems. Although I do not know of research relevant to the issue, I would be willing to bet a large sum of money that amnesic patients such as H. M. or K. C. show intact priming in their immune systems. Priming in the immune system is, almost surely, independent of episodic/declarative memory (and, for that matter, other forms of implicit memory such as perceptual priming).

As noted above, the mechanism by which such priming is thought to occur is through creation of what are called memory cells, the memory traces of the immune system. To quote Chiras (1993) again:

During the primary response, some lymphocytes divide to produce memory cells. Memory cells are immunologically competent B cells that do not transform into plasma cells. Instead, they remain in the body awaiting the antigen's reentry. These cells therefore create a relatively large reserve force of antigen-specific B cells. When the antigen reappears, memory cells proliferate rapidly, producing numerous plasma cells that quickly crank out antibodies to combat the foreign invaders...during the secondary response, the memory cells also generate additional memory cells that remain in the body in case the antigen should appear at some later date.

Immune protection afforded by memory cells can last 20 years or longer and explains why once a person has had a childhood disease, such as mumps or chicken pox, it is unlikely that he or she will contract it again. Resistance to disease that is provided by the immune system is known as immunity. From an evolutionary standpoint, this adaptation serves us extremely well, greatly reducing the incidence of infectious disease. Without it, humans would probably not be able to survive.

Recent articles make it clear that the textbook description given above is somewhat simplistic and that many mysteries remain in immune system functioning (Fearon *et al.*, 2001; Lauvrau *et al.*, 2001; Sprent and Tough, 2001). Although the immune system clearly exhibits characteristics of memory and in some sense its operation depends on its being (or having) a memory system, the immune system never gets mentioned in discussion of non-declarative memory systems in the psychological literature.

Of course, the fact that a system shows priming does not necessarily indicate that it is a memory system (Schacter and Tulving, 1994). However, both the visual and auditory perceptual systems show priming that is independent of conscious, episodic recollection. Indeed, it is this independence of perceptual priming from episodic recollection that is the primary evidence leading to postulation of various perceptual representation systems (PRS). These perceptual representation systems are deemed memory systems. However, in principle, why shouldn't the immune system be said to have a memory system for the same reasons the auditory and visual systems do—both show priming independent of conscious recollection. Priming in perceptual systems probably evolved to help sharpen our recognition of frequently perceived sights and sounds. Priming in the immune system serves a critical evolutionary purpose, too, in helping us to ward off disease. These considerations lead to the hypothesis that perhaps many bodily systems have a kind of memory built into them that brings adaptive advantage. Many systems of the body profit in some way from past experience and help the organism to cope with the environment.

Other memory systems

Are there other bodily systems that display memory, like the immune system and the perceptual systems? My knowledge of biology is not great enough to answer this question with regard to respiratory, circulatory, and digestive systems, although clearly certain types of conditioning processes can affect these systems and classical conditioning (such as learning of taste aversions) is clearly a sign of a memory system.

There is at least one other system that shows a clear example of priming that is (probably) independent of conscious recollection and other implicit memory measures, too: the female reproductive system (Roediger, 1993). The birth process is extremely dangerous (as well as painful) for women. However, if women survive the birth of a first child, priming in the FRS (female reproductive system) helps facilitate the birth process for later children. Roediger (1993) summarized data reported by Friedman (1978) documenting priming in the FRS and these data are presented here in Table 1.1. Labor can be divided into a latent phase (dilation of the cervix) and an active phase (the rapid end to dilation and the descent of the fetus). Averaged over thousands of births, the mean times for these two phases were 6.1 and 3.4 hours, for a total of 9.5 for the birth of a first baby. However, for later-born children the numbers drop precipitously, to 4.5 and 2.1 hours for the two phases of labor, respectively, for a total of 6.6 hours. So, we see nearly three hours of priming for later-born than for first-born children. For psychologists used to measuring priming in a matter of milliseconds, the size of these priming effects in the FRS are staggering—a 10,440,000 ms effect (2.9 hours) of priming! These data for later-born children are collapsed over second-, third-, fourth-(etc.) born children. We can wonder if priming increases with the number of prior births, but I have been unable to find the relevant data.

Table 1.1 Selected data on duration of labor for first-born and later-born children during labors in which there were no medical complications (mean data are presented in hours, with standard deviations in parentheses)

	Phase of labor		
	Latent	Active	Total
First born	6.1 (4.0)	3.4 (1.5)	9.5
Later born	4.5 (4.2)	2.1 (2.0)	6.6
Savings	1.6	1.3	2.9

Adapted from Friedman (1978), data in Table 3 (p. 49).

Now, as with the immune system, I know of no evidence relevant to the issue of whether priming in the FRS is independent of episodic recollection. The relevant evidence would have to come from the case of a woman who became amnesic as a result of brain damage and who was impregnated more than once. I would predict that she would show intact priming in the FRS despite poor episodic recollection. Indeed, in the most dramatic case, she might show massive priming in the FRS but complete amnesia for the fact that she had had children. I also expect that priming in the FRS would be independent of priming in the PRS and the immune system.

It may well be that other bodily systems are already known to have forms of memory that have escaped my attention. As already noted, the muscular system and the skin system can show after-effects of prior experience that are visible to outsiders as well as to the person having had the experience, due to external memory traces. A person having spent a life working in the outdoors can easily be distinguished from one who has rarely seen the sun simply based on qualities of the skin on the face.

The notion that some type of memory is a general bodily function, characteristic of many systems, may seem new and odd given the recent preoccupation of researchers studying both implicit and explicit memory on a relatively narrow range of tasks (albeit a much wider range than in the 1960s or 1970s). However, this broader conception of memory really takes the field back to an earlier time because thinkers in the last part of the 19th century considered the concept of memory to apply more grandly to living matter.

On May 30, 1870 Ewald Hering (best remembered for a theory of color vision and for an illusion he discovered) addressed the Imperial Academy of Science in Vienna 'On memory as a function of organized matter'. Hering's conception of memory was much broader than even the examples given in this chapter. Edgell (1924) summarized Hering's approach this way:

> Memory is not merely a term used to denote a given collection of facts, but is used as an explanatory principle. Advance of the race, reproduction of one generation by another, material growth, increase in skill, recollection of the past, they are all explained by that function which is universal in organized matter: memory. If one tries to generalize these very diverse facts and regard them as a class one may term them each and all 'after-effects of stimulation' (Edgell, 1924, p. 7).

Behaviorists who studied various types of conditioning, verbal learners who examined serial and paired associate learning, and contemporary neurobiologists who study long-term potentiation have all considered (albeit for different reasons) the processes of learning and memory to be broadly generalizable throughout many systems and species. Therefore, in the historical sweep of ideas, it is only relatively recently that memory has become specialized again. Even modern theorists of memory systems typically consider only a few of the many systems that display memory-like qualities.

Implications

The definitions typically given for implicit memory (or for indirect tests for memory) are quite broad, even though as instantiated in 'implicit memory research' they have been considered rather narrowly. Implicit memory research today focuses on maybe a dozen tasks, only a few of which have been carefully investigated. The conceptual definition of implicit memory is much broader, so broad that it is in danger of encompassing much of the experimental study of behavior. As noted above, almost all researchers in psychology are interested in how the after-effects of experience affect current behavior. Only studies directed at explicit (conscious) recollection and a few others would be eliminated by the standard definition. However, if implicit memory encompasses so much, it may be too general to be a useful scientific term. Tulving (1983) remarked that having a general theory of memory would be like having a general theory of locomotion—difficult to achieve except at the most vague and vacuous level. Like locomotion, there are simply too many ways to instantiate the term *memory* to provide a meaningful general theory or framework.

Implicit memory is a term that has the same drawback. Priming occurs in many biological systems—perceptual, conceptual, motor, immune, female reproductive, and probably others. The fact that priming occurs in all these systems probably serves a useful biological function. The first time a system has to process an event, whether perceiving an object, reacting to an antigen, or having a baby, certain processes are brought into play to accomplish the goal. The after-effects of this first experience create changes in the system which in turn prime the system to perform the same task more quickly and efficiently the next time the need arises. This is probably the general adaptive reason for priming in its many forms, but of course the specific mechanism creating priming will differ dramatically across the bodily systems. Any commonalities would exist only at the level of a general principle, as stated a few sentences above, and not in specific mechanisms.

Psychologists interested in the study of implicit memory have considered a relatively narrow set of tasks, primarily perceptual implicit memory tests that involve identifying objects and words from degraded representations. Even within the perceptual systems, priming of words in the visual system occurs from different processes and mechanisms than priming of these same words in the auditory system, although the fact of cross-modal priming implies that some common mechanisms are involved, too (see Church and Schacter, 1994; Pilotti *et al.*, 2000). Priming of concepts from pictures provides little or no transfer to verbal tests of those same concepts and vice versa (e.g., Srinivas, 1993). Tulving and Schacter (1990) proposed that there were several perceptual representation memory systems, presumably one for audition, one for vision, one for pictures, and so on. However, even within the visual word-form system, Hayman and Tulving (1989) argued that priming was 'hyperspecific' because the amount of priming of a word depended on the exact fragment that was used to test the concept. Changing the type of fragment between two test occasions changed the amount of priming. (On the other hand, in examining a different kind of evidence, Bowers, 1996 proposed that the visual word-form system at least generalizes across graphemic characteristics.)

One solution to the problem of the broad general definition usually used for implicit memory would be to sharpen the concept so that it more accurately represents the tasks and measures that are studied. I will not propose such a solution here because that course may not be wisest. Is it possible to define implicit memory in a sensible way that will include the perceptual systems responsible for word and object priming and exclude other, presumably more far-flung, systems such as the immune system and the female reproductive system? Even if it were possible, would it be advisable? I think not. Priming in the immune, reproductive, and perceptual systems occurs as a function of past experience to prepare the body for similar experiences in the future—transfer appropriate priming. If we narrow our definition in such a way to include perceiving but to exclude immune function, the division would probably be arbitrary. For example, we could define 'memory' as processes relying on the central nervous system. Such 'neural chauvinism' seems unwise to me. Nature, via evolution, has endowed numerous bodily systems with forms of memory. Why consider only those represented by one bodily system as 'memory', except that we are psychologists and that is what we mostly care about? Immunologists would surely disagree with our categorizations and their study of their implicit memory system through immune priming is no less valid than our study of perceptual priming.

If we were to question some forms of priming as representing implicit memory, we would quickly be led to the issue of whether we should even consider perceptual systems as memory systems. The basic function of the perceptual systems is to take in information about the environment in various modalities (tastes, touches, smells, sights, and sounds). Priming in the perception of particular objects or words exists to improve the identification process after an initial occasion. Just as we may not want to consider the female reproductive system 'a memory system' just because it displays priming, so we need not consider the perceptual systems 'memory systems' because they show priming, either. The system exists to perceive the world and priming is just one feature of the system, as with the FRS or the immune system.

An alternative way of thinking about these issues seems more appropriate to me and calls into question whether the perceptual systems and other systems should be deemed memory systems. I would suggest that we rightly conceive of priming in various biological systems as an interesting fact. However, we should not use this fact to call these systems 'memory systems'. This point might seem mere semantics, but as usual, words and their meanings serve an important point here. Perceptual, reproductive, and immune systems exist to perform important biological functions. They exhibit characteristics of memory (that is, some of their operations show priming from past experience), but this 'memory' function may frequently be incidental to operation of the system which subserves a different basic function.

In short, these systems exist for some purpose and they should not be deemed memory systems just because they show priming in carrying out that purpose. The fact of perceptual priming that is independent of conscious recollection no more means that the perceptual systems are memory systems than the fact of reproductive or immune priming indicates that the reproductive or immune systems are memory systems. The perceptual, immune, and reproductive systems serve basic biological functions. Priming sharpens those functions. The fact of priming shows that the systems display a form of memory to enhance their operation, but does not necessarily show that they are memory systems. We should reserve this last term for systems whose primary function is to remember or to know the past, not for those systems in which memory is one component of the system's operation and the system exists for some other purpose. These systems evolved to serve some other biological purpose and they have a dash of memory tossed in to help the system profit from experience. Hence, calling them memory systems stretches the term too far.

Conclusion

The argument here is that the term implicit memory may be too broad, encompassing not only the traditional study of what are thought of as 'implicit memory tasks' but also many other processes—all those due to the 'after-effects of experience as expressed in behavior'. Assuming others see this issue as a problem that deserves attention, we may consider several solutions.

One strategy discussed above is to narrow our definitions of implicit memory to more appropriately capture the phenomena we study. The postulation of perceptual and conceptual implicit memory tests (Roediger and Blaxton, 1987) went some distance in this direction, but obviously many more categories exist than those two and need to be elucidated. Also, some tasks, such as priming of anagram solutions, are difficult to classify by the suggested criteria (Srinivas and Roediger, 1990). Even assuming we could achieve more exact definitions that would work, a danger exists with this strategy of defining a few tasks precisely. As discussed above, we may eliminate too much from the concept that should be saved. If we define implicit memory very narrowly, to (say) encompass only perceptual identification tasks, then why have this new term? Why not just discuss findings in terms of perceptual priming? However, the concept *implicit memory* is appropriately intended to cover more territory than perceptual priming.

Another strategy for solving these conceptual problems, and the one I prefer, is to welcome the diversity and the generality forced upon us by the general definitions of memory and to revel in them. Yes, perceptual priming reflects a form or memory, and so do does immune priming, reproductive priming, conceptual priming, motor learning, classical conditioning, and so on. All these phenomena are examples of memory and then our task is to classify them appropriately and study them in various ways. As Hering (1870) advocated 130 years ago, memory can serve as a unifying construct, with many manifestations. The trick is to appropriately conceptualize the many varieties of memory and study them appropriately (see Roediger *et al.*, 2002, for one attempt). If we take this approach, I would suggest that we not refer to all priming phenomena within the rubric of implicit memory, as the term would be stretched too broadly. Rather, we need to consider other concepts in our classification schemes and apply them more rigorously.

The primary intent of this chapter is to propose that we need to rethink and reconceptualize how we define the term *implicit memory* if it is to be of scientific use. Implicit memory may serve as a useful term, but it will take a considerable amount of further thought and writing to clarify the murky situation outlined in this chapter. It will also take a change of attitude. As Tulving (2000) has noted, psychologists interested in learning and memory have typically not been concerned with careful examination of the terms they use. However, in order to avoid the dangers discussed here regarding the breadth of the concept of implicit memory, we will need to devote considerable effort to developing conceptual clarity. If we do not make the effort to gain this conceptual clarity through further inquiry, then we could probably simply eliminate the term *implicit memory* and refer to 'long-term priming effects' to cover the phenomena of interest. Nothing much would be lost at this point, although we can hope that the situation will be different in the future.

Acknowledgments

Readers of earlier drafts of this chapter helped to improve it. The chapter still wanders a bit, mostly because in some places I was not always clear on what message I wanted to communicate. Still, the chapter would be worse if it were not for the comments of Jeff Bowers, Chad Marsolek, David Gallo, Beth Marsh, and Endel Tulving. Conversations with Kathleen McDermott helped, too.

References

Ahmed, R. and Gray, D. (1996). Immunological memory and protective immunity: understanding their relation, *Science*, **272**, 54–60.

Blaxton, T. A. (1989). Investigating dissociations among memory measures: Evidence for a transfer appropriate processing framework. *Journal of Experimental Psychology: Learning, Memory, and Cognition*, **15**, 657–68.

Bowers, J. S. (1996). Different perceptual codes support priming for words and pseudowords: Was Morton right all along? *Journal of Experimental Psychology: Learning, Memory, and Cognition*, **22**, 1336–53.

Chiras, D. D. (1993). *Biology: the web of life*. West Publishing, St. Paul.

Church, B. A. and Schacter, D. L. (1994). Perceptual specificity of auditory priming: Implicit memory for voice intonation and fundamental frequency. *Journal of Experimental Psychology: Learning, Memory, and Cognition*, **20**, 521–33.

Edgell, B. (1924). *Theories of memory*. England: Oxford University Press.

Fearon, D. T., Manders, P., and Wagner, S. D. (2001). Arrested differentiation, the self-renewing memory lymphocyte, and vaccination. *Science*, **293**, 248–50.

Friedman, E. A. (1978). *Labor: Clinical evaluation and management*. New York: Appleton-Century-Crofts.

Graf, P. and Schacter, D. L. (1985). Implicit and explicit memory for new associations in normal and amnesic subjects. *Journal of Experimental Psychology: Learning, Memory, and Cognition*, **11**, 501–18.

Hayman, C. A. G. and Tulving, E. (1989). Is priming in fragment completion based on 'traceless' memory system? *Journal of Experimental Psychology: Learning, Memory, and Cognition*, **14**, 941–56.

Hering, E. (1870/1910). On memory. Address given in 1870. Reprinted in *Unconscious memory* (ed. S. Butler). London: A. C. Fifield, 1910.

Jacoby, L. L. (1983). Remembering the data: Analyzing interactive processes in reading. *Journal of Verbal Learning and Verbal Behavior*, **22**, 485–508.

Jacoby, L. L. and Dallas, M. (1981). On the relationship between autobiographical memory and perceptual learning. *Journal of Experimental Psychology: General*, **3**, 306–40.

Lauvrau, G., Vijh, S., Kong, P., Horng, T., Kerksiek, K., Serbina, N., et al. (2001). Priming of memory but not effector CD8 T cells by a killed bacterial vaccine. *Science*, **294**, 1735–9.

McDermott, K. B. (2000). Implicit memory. *The encyclopedia of psychology* (ed. A. E. Kazdin), pp. 231–4. New York: American Psychological Association and Oxford University Press.

McDermott, K. B. and Roediger, H. L. (1994). Effects of imagery on perceptual implicit memory tests. *Journal of Experimental Psychology: Learning, Memory, and Cognition*, **20**, 1379–90.

McDermott, K. B. and Roediger, H. L. (1996). Exact and conceptual repetition dissociate conceptual tests: Problems for transfer appropriate processing theory. *Canadian Journal of Experimental Psychology*, **50**, 57–71.

McKone, E. and Murphy, B. (2000). Implicit false memory: Effects of modality and multiple study presentations on long-lived semantic priming. *Journal of Memory and Language*, **43**, 89–109.

Pilotti, M., Gallo, D. A., and Roediger, H. L. (2000). Effects of hearing words, imaging hearing words, and reading on auditory implicit memory tests. *Memory and Cognition*, **28**, 1406–18.

Richardson-Klavehn, A. and **Bjork, R. A.** (1988). Measures of memory. *Annual Review of Psychology*, **39**, 475–543.

Roediger, H. L. (1990a). Implicit memory: Retention without remembering. *American Psychologist*, **45**, 1043–56.

Roediger, H. L. (1990b). Implicit memory: A commentary. *Bulletin of the Psychonomic Society*, **28**, 373–80.

Roediger, H. L. (1993). Learning and memory: Progress and challenge. In *Attention and performance XIV: A Silver Jubilee* (ed. D. E. Meyer and S. Kornblum), pp. 509–28. Cambridge, MA: MIT Press.

Roediger, H. L. and **Blaxton, T. A.** (1987). Retrieval modes produce dissociations in memory for surface information. In *Memory and learning: The Ebbinghaus Centennial Conference* (ed. D. S. Gorfein and R. R. Hoffman), pp. 349–79. Hillsdale, NJ: Erlbaum.

Roediger, H. L. and **McDermott, K. B.** (1993). Implicit memory in normal human subjects. In *Handbook of neuropsychology* (ed. F. Boller and J. Grafman), Vol. 8, pp. 63–131. Amsterdam: Elsevier.

Roediger, H. L. and **Srinivas, K.** (1993). Specificity of operations in perceptual priming. In *Implicit memory: New directions in cognition, development and neuropsychology* (ed. P. Graf and M. E. J. Masson), pp. 17–48. Hillsdale, NJ: Erlbaum.

Roediger, H. L., Weldon, M. S., and **Challis, B. H.** (1989). Explaining dissociations between implicit and explicit measures of retention: A processing account. In *Varieties of memory and consciousness: Essays in honour of Endel Tulving* (ed. H. L. Roediger and F. I. M. Craik), pp. 3–39. Hillsdale, NJ: Erlbaum.

Roediger, H. L., Buckner, R. L., and **McDermott, K. B.** (1999). Components of processing. In *Memory: Systems, process or function?* (ed. J. K. Foster and M. Jelicic), pp. 31–65. Oxford, UK: Oxford University Press.

Roediger, H. L., Marsh, E. J. and **Lee, S. C.** (2002). Varieties of memory. In *Stevens' handbook of experimental psychology, 3e* (ed. D. L. Medin and H. Pashler), pp. 1–41. New York: John Wiley and Sons.

Schacter, D. L. (1987). Implicit memory: History and current status. *Journal of Experimental Psychology: Learning, Memory, and Cognition*, **13**, 501–18.

Schacter, D. L. and **Tulving, E.** (1994). What are the memory systems of 1994? In *Memory systems 1994* (ed. D. L. Schacter and E. Tulving), pp. 1–38. Cambridge, MA: MIT Press.

Sprent, J. and **Tough, D. F.** (2001). T cell death and memory. *Science*, **293**, 245–8.

Squire, L. R. (1987). *Memory and brain.* New York: Oxford University Press.

Srinivas, K. (1993). Perceptual specificity in nonverbal priming. *Journal of Experimental Psychology: Learning, Memory, and Cognition*, **19**, 582–602.

Srinivas, K. and **Roediger, H. L.** (1990). Classifying implicit memory tests: Category association and anagram solution. *Journal of Memory and Language*, **29**, 389–412.

Stadler, M. A. and **Frensch, P. A.** (ed.) (1998). *Handbook of implicit learning.* Thousand Oaks, CA: Sage Publications.

Stadler, M. A. and **Roediger, H. L.** (1998). The question of awareness in research on implicit learning. In *Handbook of implicit learning* (ed. M. A. Stadler and P. A. Frensch), pp. 105–32. Thousand Oaks, CA: Sage Publications.

Tulving, E. (1983). *Elements of episodic memory.* Oxford: Clarendon Press.

Tulving, E. (2000). Concepts of memory. In *The Oxford handbook of memory* (ed. E. Tulving and F. I. M. Craik), pp. 33–57. Oxford: Oxford University Press.

Tulving, E. and Schacter, D. L. (1990). Priming and human memory systems. *Science*, **247**, 301–6.

Tulving, E., Schacter, D. L., and Stark, H. A. (1982). Priming effects in word-fragment completion are independent of recognition memory. *Journal of Experimental Psychology: Learning, Memory, and Cognition*, **8**, 336–42.

Warrington, E. K. and Weiskrantz, L. (1968). New method of testing long-term retention with special reference to amnesic patients. *Nature*, **217**, 972–4.

Warrington, E. K. and Weiskrantz, L. (1970). Amnesic syndrome: consolidation or retrieval? *Nature*, **228**, 629–30.

Weldon, M. S. and Coyote, K. C. (1996). Failure to find the picture superiority effect in implicit conceptual memory tests. *Journal of Experimental Psychology: Learning, Memory, and Cognition*, **22**, 670–86.

Weldon, M. S. and Roediger, H. L. (1987). Altering retrieval demands reverses the picture superiority effect. *Memory and Cognition*, **15**, 269–80.

CHAPTER 2

DEVELOPING THEORIES OF PRIMING WITH AN EYE ON FUNCTION

JEFFREY S. BOWERS AND SID KOUIDER

Long-term priming has been one of the most extensively studied phenomena in cognitive psychology during the past 20 years, with literally hundreds of papers devoted to this topic (for reviews, see Bowers, 2000a; Roediger and McDermott, 1993; Tenpenny, 1995). For the most part, this research has been carried out within a memory framework in which priming is understood as a form of implicit memory that is compared and contrasted with recall and recognition. Within this framework, one of the central debates has been whether implicit and explicit memories are supported by common or separate systems, but whatever case, it is agreed that priming is mediated by a memory system whose central function is, presumably, memory. As a consequence, the constraints used in developing theories of priming are largely the priming data themselves along with related memory phenomena, and theories are judged a success to the extent they account for these data.

Although this framework has been successful in generating a rich database, we think it mischaracterizes the underlying function of the system(s) that supports priming. On our view, priming is a behavioral manifestation of learning processes embedded within perceptual (and sometimes conceptual) systems whose main function is to identify (or interpret) perceptual inputs. An implication of this approach is that theoretical progress can only be achieved by embedding theories of priming within theories of perception, and cognition more generally. Indeed, on this view, it is a mistake to develop a theory of long-term priming *per se*, but rather, theories of perception (semantics) need to be developed that support learning, with single-trial learning manifesting itself as priming in various tasks.

In the present chapter we highlight the role that functional considerations can play in improving our understanding of priming. We organize the chapter in four parts. First, we argue that priming is best explained as a by-product of learning within perceptual systems, with particular focus on visual word priming within the orthographic system. Although a number of authors have made similar functional claims, their theories are often unconstrained by these considerations, and as a consequence, develop relatively independently of the large literature on word and object perception. Second, we consider an alternative approach, according to which priming and perception are embedded within a more general theory of memory—so-called instance theories of memory. Although this framework also emphasizes the adaptive function of the system that supports priming, we review evidence that we take to be problematic for this approach. Third, we outline an initial attempt to model visual word priming as an incidental by-product of learning within the orthographic system using a standard connectionist model of word recognition. Although limited in important ways, we argue that the model's success demonstrates the promise of this general approach. And fourth, we discuss how long-term priming techniques should be used as a tool to constrain theories of reading. The standard view in psycholinguists is that long-term priming is mediated by episodic rather than lexical processes, and as a consequence, it is considered an inappropriate tool to study visual word recognition processes. Indeed, masked priming techniques were introduced in order to eliminate these episodic effects (Forster and Davis, 1984). This characterization of long-term priming, in our view, is a mistake.

Orthographic learning as the basis for visual word priming

The conclusion that long-term visual word priming is mediated by lexical–orthographic knowledge is based on numerous parallels between the structure of orthographic knowledge on the one hand and priming results on the other. Consider the following three attributes of orthographic knowledge that have been proposed on the basis of various empirical results other than long-term priming. First, orthographic knowledge is coded in an abstract and modality-specific format. So for instance, the visual patterns 'r' and 'R' map onto a common abstract letter identity r^*, which in turn maps onto abstract lexical–orthographic codes, such that 'read' and 'READ' map onto an abstract word representation read* (e.g., Besner et al., 1984; Bowers et al., 1998; Coltheart, 1981; McClelland, 1976; McConkie and Zola, 1979). Second, orthographic knowledge encodes frequency information, with high-frequency words identified more quickly than low-frequency words (e.g., Forster and Chambers, 1973). And third, orthographic knowledge encodes morphological structure, such that the words CARS and CAR contact common orthographic codes, whereas the visually similar word CARD maps onto a separate lexical–orthographic representation (e.g., Caramazza et al., 1988; Rapp, 1992).

Now, consider the following predictions that directly follow from the hypothesis visual word priming is mediated by orthographic representations—all of which have been supported. First, priming should be reduced for items heard at study and viewed at test, or between pictures and the corresponding words, as in both cases, the orthographic representations are not fully accessed at study. This has been repeatedly obtained (e.g., Jacoby and Dallas, 1981; Rajaram and Roediger, 1993). Second, and for the same reason, little or no priming should be obtained between synonyms and translation equivalents in bilinguals since these items share different orthographic representations, and again, this is obtained (e.g., Durgunoglu and Roediger, 1987; Roediger and Challis, 1992). Third, priming should be unaffected by study-to-test changes in the visual format of words when words are presented in familiar formats that allows the orthographic system to be engaged in the normal way. Although the story is somewhat complex, as discussed below, this is the standard result (Carr et al., 1989; Clarke and Morton, 1983; Feustel et al., 1983; Scarborough et al., 1977; for review of these findings, see Bowers, 1996, 2000a). Indeed, a pattern of abstract and modality-specific priming is obtained even when the perceptual changes are substantial, for example, between visually dissimilar upper- and lower-case words in English *READ/read* (Bowers, 1996) and between Hiragana/Kanji scripts in Japanese (Bowers and Michita, 1998).

Forth, assuming that visual word priming is mediated by *lexical*–orthographic knowledge, priming should be constrained by morphological structure, such that priming is obtained between form related morphological relatives (e.g., *cars/car*), but not between items that are unrelated morphologically (e.g., *card/car*). Again, this is what is obtained (e.g., Napps and Fowler, 1987). And fifth, assuming additive factor logic, priming should be sensitive to frequency, with more priming obtained for low- compared to high-frequency words. This is the case for the modality-specific and non-specific components of priming (Bowers, 2000b).

It is important to emphasize that all of these predictions follow directly from an orthographic account of long-term priming. This is not the case, however, for many memory-based theories. For example, according to a transfer-appropriate processing approach, priming is obtained to the extent that the same processes are engaged at study and test (e.g., Blaxton, 1989). Although this account can be reconciled with the above findings, it does so in an *ad hoc* manner. In order to account for case-insensitive priming effects, for instance, it can be assumed that the visual processing of upper- and lower-case words is effectively the same, resulting in robust cross-case priming. But the theory could just as well predict priming to be sensitive to study-to-test changes in letter case, and indeed, early reports of case-specific priming were taken as supportive of this approach (e.g., Roediger and Blaxton, 1987). Similarly, it is not at all clear that modality-specific priming should be constrained by morphological status, although it can always be argued that similar visual processes are engaged when processing CARS and CAR, but not when processing CARD and CAR. The fact that the theory is consistent with a variety of possible outcomes highlights the lack of constraints on the theory.

As noted above, the hypothesis that priming is a by-product of learning or memory processes within orthographic and related systems is not new, and indeed, Marsolek *et al.* (1992), Morton (1979), Schacter (1990), and more recently, Ratcliff and McKoon (1997) among others have made similar claims. Nevertheless, relevant constraints that follow from this assumption are often ignored in the development of these theories. In the case of Morton (1979), priming was embedded in a model of word recognition that ignored issues of learning, and as a consequence, the model was hand-wired (fair enough, as it was developed over 20 years ago). On this model, identifying a word reduces the threshold of its corresponding logogen, and as a consequence, less information is required to identify the word when later presented—that is, priming is obtained. Reducing logogen thresholds is not a form of learning that increases the efficiency in perceiving repeated words, but rather, it lowers the standard of evidence required in order to identify repeated words. That is, priming is a product of bias rather than a change in sensitivity.

The issue of bias versus sensitivity is currently an active topic of debate (see Bowers, 1999; McKoon and Ratcliff, 2001; Ratcliff and McKoon, 1997), although there is growing consensus that priming does reflect, in part, a change in sensitivity (although see Wagenmakers *et al.*, Chapter 5). If indeed sensitivity does change as a consequence of priming, then Morton's account of priming would be falsified. But a more fundamental problem is that the model does not include any learning mechanisms that could support the acquisition of orthographic knowledge in the first place. Not only is this a limitation of the model as a model of word identification, but it also leads to difficulties in accommodating key priming phenomena; in particular, the finding that priming extends to various novel materials, including pseudowords (e.g., Bowers, 1994). Indeed, this is the main reason the model is so frequently rejected as a plausible theory of priming (e.g., Schacter, 1990).

Like Morton, Schacter (1990) has argued that visual word priming is the product of memory processes embedded within the orthographic system (what Schacter called a visual word-form system). However, on this latter account, priming is assumed to improve the processing of repeated items (rather than cause bias), and priming is assumed to be mediated by new and highly specific memory traces encoded at study in addition to the possible contribution of abstract orthographic codes. The latter claim was based on the finding that priming extends to various unfamiliar materials, and that under some circumstances, is reduced following various changes in the format of words presented at study and test (e.g., Graf and Ryan, 1990). Schacter garners evidence from various neuropsychological populations in order to support this view (e.g., Schacter *et al.*, 1990), and the related claim that heard word priming and visual object priming are mediated by auditory word-form and structural description systems that support the identification of spoken words and objects, respectively (Schacter, 1992).

Schacter's approach is very much in line with our own. The main criticism we would raise is that Schacter has proposed a structural rather than processing theory of priming, and as a consequence, it is disconnected with processing theories of reading. In our view, the next key step is to explicitly link theories of priming with processing theories of word identification, such that priming is explained as a by-product of learning within these systems. In addition, we can't resist one quibble. That is, Schacter continues use of the terms 'implicit memory' and 'memory system' to describe long-term priming and the visual word-form system, respectively. This in our view obscures the claim that priming is mediated by a system whose primary function is visual word identification, not memory.

A more recent and computationally explicit account of visual word priming was proposed by Ratcliff and McKoon (1997)—the counter-model of priming. As in the Morton model, priming is understood within the context of a processing model of word identification. And like the logogen model, it assumes that each word is represented by an abstract logogen-like unit—so-called counters—and that word identification is achieved when the activation of a counter (measured in counts) passes some threshold. Furthermore, these counters are organized by similarity such that counters of similar words are close together within a cohort whereas counters of dissimilar words are far apart. As a consequence, similar items can be confused in the model, such that the presentation of *died* results in some counts being assigned to other items in its cohort, such as *lied*, especially under conditions in which *died* is flashed quickly so that the perceptual information is degraded.

Priming in the counter-model is due to the fact that counters act as attractors. That is, exposure to a word at study causes the word's counter to attract a few counts more than it otherwise would, stealing them away from counters of other similar words. This attraction leads to a benefit in identifying repeated words since the counter 'steals' counts that might otherwise have been mistakenly assigned to related words, and leads to costs when the study and test words differ, since the counter of the study word now steals counts away from the counter of the flashed word. In the original model (Ratcliff and McKoon, 1997), benefits equaled costs, and accordingly, the model was a pure bias model of priming. But based on the more recent evidence that priming for low-frequency words is not all bias, McKoon and Ratcliff (2001) revised the model by changing a parameter so that priming for low-frequency words also reflects an improvement in processing. In both the original and the updated models, the authors also assumed that the attractive force that mediates priming only extends to words within cohort. So for example, the prior study of *died* would result in extra counts being stolen from *lied*, but not *sofa*. This can account for a counter-intuitive finding obtained in a forced choice task in which participants identify briefly flashed targets by selecting one of two alternative choice words. That is, bias is eliminated when the alternatives are dissimilar, such that studying *died* did not facilitate the identification of *died* when the alternatives are dissimilar, such as *died* and *sofa*. It is important to note, however, that relevant data on this latter point are mixed: Bowers (1999, unpublished) and Neaderhiser and Church (2000) have found priming under these conditions, whereas McKoon and Ratcliff (2001) and Masson (2000) do not. The basis of these discrepancies are unclear.

Regardless of the ultimate resolution of this latter dispute, there are problems with the updated theory. Although the model is computationally precise and can account for a wide variety of word priming data in perceptual identification tasks, the model was constructed around these data, and it is not clear to what extent it can explain other findings. And even within this domain, the failure to consider functional or empirical constraints from the psycholinguistic domain results in the model providing *post hoc* rather than principled explanations of many of their findings. For example, as noted above, the authors initially obtained evidence that priming was pure bias, and accordingly, they did not include learning mechanisms in their model. When evidence was obtained that priming includes a change in sensitivity for low-frequency words, the authors changed a parameter that supported learning for low-frequency words. The latest version of the counter-model is now in the position in which it only includes learning mechanisms for pre-existing low-frequency words, and as a consequence, the model has to be hand-wired, much like the Morton (1979) model. It therefore inherits its chief weaknesses as a theory of priming, namely, it cannot support pseudoword priming.

In a similar way, the claim that priming is mediated by attractive forces between words within a cohort was solely based on their priming data. There is no obvious adaptive function for this claim, and the authors could change this parameter as well if subsequent work demonstrates that priming is obtained under conditions in which the alternatives are dissimilar. Indeed, because McKoon and Ratcliff (2001) now assume that priming for low-frequency words is mediated by a change in sensitivity, the authors should expect priming for these items regardless of the similarity of the alternatives—contrary to their claim and their observations (although consistent with Bowers, 1999; Neaderhiser and Church, 2000). More generally, even within the limited scope of word identification in the perceptual identification task, without some principled constraints, the authors are free to vary parameters to accommodate whatever specific set of priming results are obtained.

According to Ratcliff and McKoon (1997), one of the key advantages of their theory over previous theories of priming is that it is implemented in a computational model. But contrary to the common claim, there is no intrinsic virtue of implementing a theory in computer-code, nor of modeling a restricted data set with great precision (Roberts and Pashler, 2000). Computational modeling is only a virtue when it allows predictions to be made that are too difficult to calculate without the aid of simulation. The crucial test of their theory is whether it can accommodate the large psycholinguistic database on visual word identification (making it a competitor to various other theories of visual word identification), and whether it makes novel and non-trivial predictions regarding priming and/or reading. Otherwise, the authors have made the mistake of building a model of visual word priming in a particular task rather than building a theory of word identification in which priming is a incidental by-product of learning (or bias).

In contrast with the above theories, we would argue that a number of predictions concerning visual word priming can be derived from a theory that is primarily designed around constraints associated reading written words. For example, there is now strong evidence that phonological codes are quickly (some would say automatically) activated following the visual presentation of words (e.g., Stone *et al.*, 1997), and accordingly, we should predict phonological contributions to visual priming tasks. Indeed, phonological codes would provide an obvious candidate for cross-modal priming, and consistent with this hypothesis, priming effects obtained between homophones (which are presumably phonologically based) are approximately the same size as cross-modal priming (Rueckl and Mathew, 1999; Ziemer and Bowers, 1998). Similarly, phonology is often thought to play a larger role in visual word identification in languages with a regular grapheme-phoneme correspondences—the so-called orthographic depth hypothesis (e.g., Frost *et al.*, 1987). Consistent with this hypothesis, cross-modal priming is greater in Serbian, a language with a shallow orthography (Havelka *et al.*, submitted). In addition, various evidence suggests that orthographic and phonological representations are more strongly interconnected than visual object representations on the one hand and phonological and orthographic representations on the other (in fact, it is generally assumed that object and word knowledge are completely unconnected, with semantics intervening; e.g., Levelt, 1989). Accordingly, priming between pictures on the one hand and written or spoken words on the other should be reduced compared to cross-modal priming. Indeed, Rajaram and Roediger (1993) found that picture-to-written-word priming was reduced compared to spoken-to-written-word priming across four different tasks, and a similar finding is predicted when picture-to-spoken-word priming is compared to written-word-to-spoken-word priming. Numerous other predictions follow, and below, we describe a surprising prediction that has recently been confirmed. None of these predictions follow from standard memory-based accounts, nor from previous theories that have embedded priming within processing models of word identification.

Instance theories of perception and priming

There is another approach to understanding priming that also explicitly links theories of perception to theories of priming, but which is at odds with many of the claims made above. In contrast with the view that priming is best understood within the context of a more general theory of word and object perception, it is argued that theories of perception, semantics, and priming should all be embedded within a more general theory of episodic memory. On this approach, each experience is stored in detail as a separate memory trace, and the different ways this information is retrieved determines whether perception, semantics, episodic memory, or priming is expressed. On the strong version of this hypothesis, all of these diverse phenomena are seen as manifestation of different processes within a single episodic memory system. This obviously contrasts with the view described above in which written words are represented in terms of abstract logogen units, and where the orthographic system should be distinguished from related systems, such as phonological, semantic, and episodic systems. For more detailed accounts of instance approaches, see the chapters by Goldinger *et al.*, Lachs *et al.*, Luce *et al.*, and Whittlesea, this volume.

Despite the profound differences between 'instance' accounts of priming and the 'abstractionist' approach we've outlined above, they do share some fundamental properties. On both accounts visual word priming reflects a form of learning mediated by a system that supports visual word identification. On the instance view, however, learning (sometimes called skill acquisition within this framework) is mediated by the acquisition of new episodic instances within memory, making memory retrieval more efficient (Logan, 1990). In addition, because priming is mediated by a system that serves various functions, including object and word perception, both accounts are constrained by findings and theories outside the priming domain.

For example, if the abstractionist theory of object recognition advanced by Biederman, Hummel, and colleagues (Biederman, 1987; Hummel and Biederman, 1992) is correct, instance theories of priming would be falsified. On this account, objects are coded in memory in terms of abstract 'structural descriptions' specifying an object's parts in terms of categorical 3D shape primitives (e.g., brick, cones, etc.) and their categorical relations to one another (e.g., on-top-of). So a table might be represented as a horizontal slab on-top-of four vertical posts. The abstract nature of these representations allows the model to categorize familiar and novel objects at a basic level since members of the category typically share the same description—i.e. most tables will be represented as a horizontal slab on-top-of four vertical posts, regardless of viewing angle. But as noted by critics of this approach, the categorical nature of these representations leads to problems when trying to distinguish between two different tables that share the same structural description (but see Hummel and Stankiewicz, 1998).

On the other hand, if 'view-based' models of object recognition are correct, abstractionist views of priming would be compromised. On this approach, objects are coded as holistic two-dimensional patterns as they appear from specific views, and identification consists in comparing holistic visual input patterns to these holistic memory representations (Tarr and Bulthoff, 1998). Because these visual codes represent the precise metrical information of the 2D views, view-based models show promise in explaining exemplar-specific object recognition (i.e. recognizing the same objects from different viewpoints), but they have not been tested extensively on basic level categorization. Indeed, according to Hummel (2000), this approach utterly fails at basic level categorization, as well as various other functions.

Similar conclusions follow from an ongoing debate regarding spoken word recognition. As detailed by Lachs *et al.* (Chapter 10), standard theories tend to assume that lexical–phonological codes are coded abstractly, and the task of word recognition is to discard the idiosyncratic acoustic details associated with a given spoken word in order to match it onto its stored abstract memory trace. The alternative is that words are stored in memory with all their details, and these details serve to facilitate identification rather than being regarded as noise. Again, a resolution to this debate speaks directly to theories of priming, and indeed, a wide range of non-priming phenomena provide key sources of constraint for theories of priming.

Despite the very different processing and representational assumptions of abstractionist and instance-based approaches, it remains difficult to identify a critical experiment to distinguish between these views. Nevertheless, there are, in our view, empirical and theoretical reasons to prefer abstractionist accounts.

First, consider the priming data themselves. A number of authors claim that priming phenomena are sensitive to various study-to-test changes in the surface form of items, such as changing font or case of written words, or changing the voice of spoken words, and this is said to show that detailed perceptual memory traces support priming, and perception more generally. That is, the priming data are claimed to support instance-based theories of cognition (e.g., Tenpenny, 1995). However, as argued in detail elsewhere (Bowers, 2000a), the data are more compatible with abstractionist approaches. The story is most straightforward in the visual domain, in which priming effects are often strikingly abstract. For example, using the perceptual identification task, Bowers (1996) assessed priming for words that are composed of letters that are visually dissimilar (A/a, B/b, D/d, E/e, G/g, L/l, and Q/q) in upper- and lower-case (e.g., *DREAD/dread*). Similar priming was obtained for study/test items presented in the same case (17% improvement over baseline) and different case (16% improvement), and at the same time, little priming was obtained when words were spoken at study (5% improvement). More striking, in two studies using the lexical decision task, similar priming was obtained for Japanese words studied and tested in the same script (Kanji–Kanji or Hiragana–Hiragana) or different script (Kanji–Hiragana or Hiragana–Kanji) despite the fact that the scripts are completely unrelated in the visual format (Bowers and Michita, 1998). Averaging across the two studies, same script priming was 28 ms and cross-script priming was 24 ms, a difference that did not approach significance. Once again, little priming was obtained when items were spoken at study (6 ms averaging across studies), suggesting that cross-script priming was mediated by abstract orthographic codes (also see Brown *et al.*, 1984; Feldman and Moskovljevic, 1987). It is difficult to see how an instance-based theory can account for modality-specific priming effects obtained between unrelated visual forms. And although advocates of instance-based accounts have emphasized reports in which priming is reduced following study-to-test changes in visual format (e.g., Tenpenny, 1995), these effects are largely restricted to conditions in which the study or test words are presented in unusual formats (e.g., words presented upside down and mirror reversed). Given that these items are unlikely to be processed in the normal way within an orthographic system, abstractionist theories of word priming are not challenged by these findings (although the results do show that specific visual information is indeed coded in memory).

Priming results obtained with spoken words would seem to provide stronger evidence in support of instance-based theories, as study-to-test perceptual changes more often influence priming (see Lach *et al.*, this volume, for one characterization of this literature). But again, we would argue that the data are more compatible with abstractionist accounts. Luce and Lyon (1998), for instance, assessed spoken word priming in an auditory lexical decision task in which items were repeated in the same or different voice. The authors chose this task because test items are not degraded (as is required in perceptual identification, or completion tasks) and response latencies are brief (reducing any effects of explicit memory strategies). Under these conditions, no voice change effects were obtained despite robust priming effects. Recognition memory, by contrast, however, was sensitive to voice changes, showing again that perceptually specific information is encoded somewhere in memory. Consistent with this analysis, Schacter *et al.* (1995) used an identification task in which words were degraded with a low-pass filter at test, and they observed voice-specific priming in a group of participants with normal memory, whereas robust priming in the absence of voice-specific effects was obtained in a group of amnesic patients. Accordingly, the voice effects in the normal group may have been due to explicit contamination. Pilotti *et al.* (2000) found spoken word priming to be completely insensitive to voice changes in the stem- and fragment-completion tasks, whereas priming was sensitive to voice change in an identification task that masked words with either noise or low-pass filtering. It is not clear why different results were obtained across tasks, but again, it shows that spoken word priming is often insensitive to large perceptual changes.

More recently, Pallier *et al.* (1999, 2001) have provided compelling evidence in support of an abstractionist approach using a different logic. The authors took advantage of the existence of two populations of Spanish–Catalan fluent bilinguals who share a common lexicon but have slightly different phonetic systems. In particular, Catalan-dominant speakers distinguish between certain phonemes (for instance, the consonantal contrast /s/ – /z/) whereas Spanish-dominant bilinguals, even if they started learning Catalan as early as six years old, are unable do so. Participants performed lexical decisions to spoken Catalan words that were repeated verbatim or to words repeated with one phonetic feature changed (*casa–casa* versus *casa–caza*, meaning '*marry*' and '*house*'). The results revealed that the priming effects are modulated by abstract linguistic rather than the acoustic similarity. That is, the phonetic change eliminated priming for the Catalan-dominant speakers (they were perceived as different words), but for Spanish-dominant speakers, priming was equivalent to repetition priming (the two items were perceived as the same word).

To summarize, priming effects are often abstract, but specific visual and auditory information are encoded in memory and can affect priming and recognition memory under some conditions. What can be concluded from this? In deciding whether the data support abstractionist or instance theories, it is important to note that abstractionist theories do not reject the view that specific perceptual information is coded in memory—indeed, the information must be coded somewhere, as we can tell the difference between an upper- and lower-case letter, and perceive and remember differences between subordinate level items (although in the case speech perception, phonetic changes can be difficult to detect). Indeed, Spanish-dominant bilinguals have a difficult time distinguishing between the phonemes /s/ and /z/ that are represented in Catalan but not in Spanish (Pallier *et al.*, 1997). Thus, demonstrations of specific priming effects (or perceptually specific recognition memory) are not sufficient to rule out abstractionist views. It must also be shown that instances memories can support the various abstract results.

And indeed, advocates of instance theories claim that these theories can accommodate the abstract priming results (e.g., Tenpenny, 1995), as well as object recognition across changes in orientation (Tarr and Bulthoff, 1998) and spoken word identification regardless of voice (e.g., Goldinger, 1998). But in the case of object recognition, there is almost no research concerned with how basic level identification can be achieved, and as noted above, Hummel (2000) argues that they fail on this basic function. And with regard to priming, it is not at all clear that these theories can support priming between visually dissimilar study/test items. In order to explain abstract priming within an instance framework, each input is thought to retrieve all similar memories stored in memory, creating an 'echo' in which all instances blend together, producing a virtual abstract code in the absence of any abstract codes stored in permanent memory. This approach may indeed support abstract priming when the study/test words differ in font, size, etc., because in these cases, there is some similarity between items so that the test item can retrieve the studied word amongst other related items. However, these approaches cannot accommodate modality-specific priming effects between words that are arbitrarily related, such as READ/read (Bowers, 1996) and Hiragana and Kanji Japanese scripts (Bowers and Michita, 1998). The echo generated from a Kanji word at test will not be affected by the prior study of a Hiragana word, as there is no perceptual overlap. An echo could occur in semantics or phonology based on the similarity of these items in these domains, but it cannot account for the abstract priming results that are modality specific.

So how can abstractionist theories deal with the specific effects? A number of theorists have argued that the set of processes that support the effective categorization of items into basic level categories are incompatible with the goal of distinguishing different exemplars of the same category. On this view, different perceptual systems (or subsystems) support these two functions, so that both abstract and instance representations are encoded in memory separately (for different versions of this hypothesis, see Hummel and Stankiewicz, 1998; Marsolek *et al.*, 1992). Assuming both systems learn through experience, both should support priming. Specific priming effects would reflect priming within the specific system.

Of course, it might be objected that by advocating an abstractionist approach in which specific information can support priming makes the theory unfalsifiable. And indeed, this is a danger. The burden of this approach is to develop a theory in which the relation between abstract and specific information is well understood, allowing strong predictions to be made. Although this is not yet the case, it is interesting to note that there is some evidence that abstract and specific information is coded separately. For example, in the auditory modality, a number of studies indicate that patients with right hemisphere lesions show deficits in voice recognition (e.g., Van Lancker and Kreiman, 1987) and in processing prosodic aspects of speech (e.g., Coslett *et al.*, 1987), whereas word identification disorders result from left hemisphere lesions (e.g., Schacter *et al.*, 1993). Along the same lines, dichotic listening studies with non-brain damaged individuals have found a left ear (right hemisphere) advantage for processing aspects of voice information, whereas identifying words (irrespective of voice) is best accomplished in the left hemisphere (e.g., Kimura, 1973). Further converging evidence has been reported using brain imaging technologies. Using PET, Zatorre *et al.* (1992) reported that the left hemisphere is more active than the right when participants identified phonemes in spoken syllables (conditions in which surface details of the words were irrelevant), and the right hemisphere was more active than the left when participants made pitch discriminations to the same items (conditions in which surface details were critical). Schacter *et al.* (1993) reported a patient with a large left hemisphere lesion that led to *pure-word deafness*, such that he was able to repeat spoken words, but was unable to understand the meaning of these words. The patient showed robust priming for words repeated in the same voice (29% improvement over baseline) but minimal priming for words repeated in a different voice (4% improvement). One interpretation of this finding is that the patient's intact right hemisphere mediated his ability to repeat words and supported same voice priming, but damage to abstract phonological codes in the left hemisphere (that normally serve as access codes to semantics) prevented him from understanding the meaning of spoken words, and reduced priming following the study/test voice change. Consistent with this hypothesis, control subjects showed much more abstract priming (23% same voice versus 16% different voice), suggesting that the left hemisphere is indeed important for supporting priming following voice changes (see Church and Schacter, 1994, for additional evidence in support of this view). So in all cases, abstract and specific information appear differentially lateralized. Marsolek and colleagues make similar claims for visual materials (e.g., Marsolek *et al.*, 1992; but see Bowers and Turner, submitted who have obtained contrary evidence). The story is complicated by the finding that abstract and specific information often interact in word processing tasks (e.g., see Lach *et al.*, Chapter 10, this volume), and these important findings will also need to be explained. Also, there is some evidence that attention can modulate the degree of abstraction, as Stankiewicz *et al.* (1998) only found abstract priming between mirror inverted pictures when study items were attended, whereas repetition priming did not require attention. Despite these complications, as long as abstract information is encoded somewhere in perceptual (and semantic) systems, instance theories are falsified.

A second argument in support of abstractionist views is more fundamental. One of the virtues of positing abstract (and localized) mental representations is that they can be incorporated into generative systems that allow the construction of complex mental representations from simple representations—that is, they can support *compositional* representations (Fodor and Pylyshyn, 1988). This in turn allows visual, phonological, and lexical–semantic (that is, linguistic) systems to represent information that extends beyond past experience. This is not to say that abstract representations are sufficient to support these functions, but they play a necessary role in neural networks models of object identification (e.g., Hummel and Biederman, 1992) and semantics (e.g., Hummel and Holyoak, 1997) that implement these functions. By contrast, it is not clear how generative systems can be supported in an instance model of memory. Thus far, instance models have largely been applied to remembering or perceiving single words, with little consideration of how virtual abstract codes (e.g., echoes) could be fed into a language processor that must construct complex representations from simpler parts. Of course, it is not reasonable to rule out instance models because they currently fail to realize these high-level objectives, but it should at least be possible to *imagine* how such a model could scale up to achieve these functions. But thus far, there are not even speculations.

Finally, as a more general point, it is often claimed that instance models are more parsimonious, as they do away with multiple memory systems in favor of a single episodic system that serves various functions, from visual and spoken word identification, episodic memory, etc. And indeed, we agree that it is not helpful to attribute these different functions to separate *memory* systems. But in our view, the claim that all these functions are mediated by a single system loses sight of some basic distinctions. Not only do vision, audition, semantics, episodic memory deal with different types of information, they serve different functions, and they need to process information in qualitatively different ways. For example, in the case of vision, information is distributed over space, whereas in audition, information is distributed across time. It seems unlikely, at least to us, that these different demands are performed by a single system. To describe these as different processes within a single system amounts to the claim that we have different processes within a single brain—certainly true, but not particularly informative.

Modeling visual word priming within a theory of word identification that supports learning

In order to lend some plausibility to the claim that word priming is an incidental by-product of learning processes embedded within system(s) whose function is to identify words, Bowers *et al.* (2002) attempted to simulate priming in the distributed, developmental model of word recognition and naming put forward by Seidenberg and McClelland (1989). At first, this might seem an odd choice given the above discussion: The model does not include abstract orthographic representations that could cross-case or morphological priming (although connectionist models have been developed that can learn abstract letter codes, Polk and Farah, 1997; and some forms of morphological relations, e.g., Plaut and Gonnerman, 2000), and the model does not include localist representations that could be fed into a generative system (although connectionist models with localist representations can be developed with this properties as well, Hummel and Holyoak, 1997). Indeed, as noted by Bowers (in press (a)) models with distributed representations cannot even represent two things at a time, despite the obvious need to do so in semantic, phonological, and related systems.

However, we were not interested in evaluating the merits of this model as a model of reading, or as a model of priming. Rather, we were simply interested as to whether a model that learns by back-propagation—a learning rule common to many connectionist models—could in principle support long-term priming following a single study episode. Surprisingly, word priming has not previously been simulated within a model trained for reading a large set of words, and it was not at all obvious to us that they would be successful. Learning with back-propagation is subject to a phenomenon called the stability–plasticity problem (often called 'catastrophic interference') in which new information erases old information (Grossberg, 1987; McClosky and Cohen, 1989). In order to avoid this interference so that large vocabularies can be acquired, it has been necessary to reduce the learning rates, and to introduce an interleaved study regimen in which all the words in the vocabulary are acquired in parallel. This solution works fine for some purposes, but it raises the question as to whether this slow learning can support long-term priming that occurs following a single-study trial. Indeed, Ratcliff and McKoon (1997) argued that the Seidenberg and McClelland (1989) model was incapable of supporting long-term priming because of its slow learning rates. And even if the learning rates are found to be sufficient to support priming for a short duration, the interference effects due to learning unrelated words processed between study and test may be incompatible with the longevity of priming.

We used the fully trained Seidenberg and McClelland (1989) model in order to simulate word priming, without changing any of its parameters. In order to follow standard procedures in behavioral studies, we ran the simulations numerous times for each experiment, with each simulation corresponding to a single participant. In the study phase of each simulation, the model was presented with the study words, and the connection weights were modified to the same degree as the trials on which it was originally trained. That is, the study words were simply the most recent words the model was trained on. As in behavioral studies, study words were rotated through the various conditions, and at test, all target words were presented. Priming was computed by comparing the orthographic error scores for words in the repeated and baseline conditions, averaging across all simulations. These error scores were then translated to estimates of the reaction time using a formula described by Seidenberg and McClelland (1989, p. 532). Note, these estimates were not derived to fit long-term priming data, but were based on various naming and lexical decision studies the authors reported. Nevertheless, robust priming effects were obtained in the model, and the pattern of priming mirrored priming in various experiments.

For example, priming was greatly reduced for a set of high- compared to low-frequency words, typical in experimental studies (e.g., Bowers, 2000b). Furthermore, these priming effects persisted when thousands of unrelated learning trials were interposed between study and test, indicating that the priming effects were long-lasting. In addition, and contrary to our expectations, priming effects were largely word specific. In our simulation study, a robust repetition effect was observed that contrasted with a small form-related effect (e.g., prime = *boast*, target = *toast*), consistent with a large number of behavioral studies (e.g., Napps and Fowler, 1987; Ratcliff and McKoon, 1997). In trying to understand why a model with distributed representations only produced small form-priming effects, we discovered that form priming in the model was slightly larger for pairs that rhymed, and slightly inhibitory for pairs that did not rhyme. We subsequently ran a behavioral study (Bowers *et al.*, 2002), and found a similar pattern. So here, the model made a novel and counter-intuitive prediction that was subsequently confirmed.

The finding that facilitation and cost is obtained in the model for the rhyme and non-rhyme form-related words has another implication. In a number of recent reports, it has been claimed that changes in sensitivity result in no costs, for example, Keane *et al.* (2000) wrote 'According to a sensitivity account, by contrast, only the benefit, and not the cost, should be observed: If priming improves the ability to extract perceptual information from a stimulus, then identification of a word should be enhanced by prior exposure to that word and should not be harmed by prior exposure to its orthographic mate' (p. 318), and it has been proposed that separate mechanisms underlie benefits and costs in priming (e.g., McKoon and Ratcliff, 2001). Although the latter claim may turn out to be true, the present findings highlight the fact that both benefits and costs can be the product of a single learning system whose function is to improve processing. A particularly compelling example of costs associated with learning can be found in a related language domain. At a few months, babies are able to perceive and produce the phonemes of all the languages of the world, but as they are exposed and learn the phonology of their particular language, they become insensitive to key phonetic distinctions in other languages while becoming more adept in identifying the phonemes within their own language (Kuhl *et al.*, 1992). A familiar example is that Japanese speakers have great difficulty in perceiving and producing the phonemes 'l' and 'r' in English (Goto, 1971). It seems unlikely that a separate bias mechanisms underlies this deficit, just as there are no bias mechanisms underlying the costs we observed in these simulations. Learning systems that improve processing do not rule out cost in performance, although the benefits outweigh costs in the domain in which they function.

So in sum, a connectionist model that learns to pronounce individual words not only supports various long-term priming effects, but it also made a novel prediction that was confirmed experimentally. Although we do not take these findings as providing support for this particular model of word identification, or indeed, models that learn distributed representations using back-propagation, we do take these findings as providing general support for the view that visual word priming is best understood within the context of a model that is designed to identify words. On this view, theoretical advances in theories of word identification will improve our understanding of priming, and priming may provide important data concerning the types of learning that should be incorporated in models of reading.

Using long-term priming as a tool to address psycholinguistic questions

Although we think that there are compelling reasons to view long-term word priming as a by-product of learning within the orthographic system, this phenomenon is rarely used by psycholinguists interested in word identification processes. Instead, researchers interested in visual word recognition have relied heavily on masked priming paradigms in which a pattern mask (e.g., ######) is replaced by a prime word that is briefly flashed (e.g., 50 ms), which in turn is replaced by the target. Under these conditions, primes are typically unnoticed by the participants, but these items nevertheless facilitate processing of targets when prime and target are the same compared to different.

Although masked and long-term priming share many features (e.g., Bowers, 2000a, in press (b)), three particular attributes of long-term priming are often cited as reasons to reject this procedure as a useful psycholinguistic technique. First, Forster and Davis (1984) noted that long-term priming is reduced for high-frequency compared to low-frequency words, what the authors called the *frequency attenuation effect*. By contrast, a frequency attenuation effect generally does not occur in masked priming (but see Bodner and Masson, 1997). Given that recognition memory is generally better for low-frequency words (e.g., Balota and Neely, 1980), the discovery of this qualitative difference led Forster and

Davis (1984) to claim that the '…long-term priming effect is totally mediated by episodic factors, whereas the short-term effect is an automatic consequence of repeated access of the same lexical entry' (p. 694). The masking procedure was presumed to eliminate this episodic involvement in priming, suppressing the frequency attenuation effect. If in fact the authors are correct, then it follows that long-term priming is not a suitable technique to study abstract orthographic codes (unless of course episodic memories support lexical access, as assumed by instance theorists).

However, there are problems with this conclusion. Forster and Davis have considered the frequency attenuation effect to be an indicator of episodic influences whereas several studies have provided a dissociation between episodic recognition and the frequency attenuation effect (Rajaram and Neely, 1992; Duchek and Neely, 1989; Scarborough *et al.*, 1977). For instance, Rajaram and Neely (1992) addressed this issue by using a modified episodic recognition task in which stimuli are presented under conditions identical to a primed lexical decision task. Whereas they found the classical frequency attenuation effect for long-term priming, they found an advantage for high-frequency words in the recognition task, exactly the opposite to priming. Rajaram and Neely concluded that these data pose a serious challenge to the Forster and Davis claim. Further evidence for a dissociation between long-term priming and recognition memory effects comes from the memory literature. For instance, densely amnesic patients show robust (sometimes normal) priming despite poor (sometimes chance) performance on explicit recall and recognition tests (Warrington and Weiskrantz, 1974). These dissociations between priming and episodic recognition memory suggests that the Forster and Davis conclusions regarding long-term priming were premature. And as described above, the simulation study by Bowers *et al.* (2002) demonstrated that a frequency attenuation effect can be produced by learning processes embedded within an orthographic system.

A second criticism of using long-term priming to investigate psycholinguist questions put forward by Forster and Davis (1984) and others (e.g., De Groot and Nas, 1991) is based on findings reported by Oliphant (1983). Oliphant contrasted repetition effects in two conditions. In the first, participants performed a lexical decision both to the prime and target (as is common in this paradigm). In the second, they read prime words embedded in running sentences during the instruction session and then at test performed lexical decisions to repeated target words. Oliphant failed to obtain priming in this latter condition and concluded that participants have to be aware that target words are repeated for priming to occur. This awareness was assumed to result from overt responses on prime words and was supposed to be eliminated (along with priming) when words were embedded in text, leading him to support an episodic account.

Note, however, that a reduction in priming for words presented in the context of sentences is not surprising from an abstractionist position that attributes priming to the strengthening of abstract orthographic codes. Under these condition, there is no guarantee that prime words are perceptually processed to the same extent as when they are presented in isolation. Indeed, there is no reason to presume that structural changes occur automatically each time a word is identified, and there are many circumstances in which it is plausible to assume that the relevant changes do not take place. For example, when reading text, people tend to fixate on each specific word for only a brief moment, with an average fixation of approximately 200–250 ms (Rayner and Sereno, 1994). This may not be sufficient time to support the long-term modification of orthographic codes, particularly when multiple words are processed in running sentences. Consistent with this general analysis, Subramaniam et al. (2000) recently reported a failure to obtain any priming for pictures presented up to 31 times in an RSVP sequence when items were displayed for between 72–126 ms/picture. At the same time, the pictures could be identified at these durations, and accordingly, the authors argued that priming requires participants to attend to an item for a period of time after the item has been identified. But in any case, Oliphant (1983) assessed priming for high-frequency words. When MacLeod (1989) replicated Oliphant's (1983) study using lower-frequency words, priming was obtained.

A third criticism is that long-term priming often extends to nonwords (e.g., Besner and Swan, 1982; Kirsner and Smith, 1974; Scarborough et al., 1977) whereas nonword priming is reduced or eliminated in the masked priming procedure introduced by Forster and Davis (1984) in which participants make lexical decisions to targets. The finding that long-term priming extends to nonwords is often taken as evidence that episodic memory mediates these effects, and masking the prime is presumed to eliminate episodic involvement, reducing the nonword priming. However, subsequent work has found a close parallel between the masked and long-term priming for nonwords. In particular, when participants make lexical decisions to the targets, nonword priming tends to be absent in both long-term and masked priming procedures (for long-term results, see Bentin and Moscovitch, 1988; Bowers, 1994; Fowler et al., 1985; for masked results, see Forster, 1998; Forster and Davis, 1984), although exceptions are obtained in both tasks (for long-term results, see Besner and Swan, 1982; Kirsner and Smith, 1974; Scarborough et al., 1977; for masked results, see Bodner and Masson, 1997; Sereno, 1991). As argued by Feustel et al. (1983) and by Humphreys et al. (1990), the failure to obtain nonword priming in these two paradigms is due to an idiosyncratic property of the lexical decision task. That is, subjects have a bias to respond 'word' to the repeated nonwords since familiar letter strings tend to be words. This bias counteracts the improved perceptual processing of the nonwords, resulting in no priming. Consistent with this argument, when this response bias is eliminated by using an identification task, nonword priming effects are consistently obtained in both long-term and masked priming tasks (for long-term priming, see Bowers, 1994; Carr et al., 1989; Feustel et al., 1983; Kirsner and Smith, 1974; Rueckl, 1990; Salasoo et al., 1985; Whittlesea and Cantwell, 1987; for masked priming, see Humphreys et al., 1990; Masson and Isaak, 1999, among others). Accordingly, there is no reason to prefer masked over long-term priming techniques based on the nonword results.

Despite these considerations, the original arguments of Forster and Davis (1984) continue to be widely accepted in psycholinguistic circles (e.g., Frost et al., 2000). The irony of this is that long-term priming has been one of the major sources for the development of single-word processing theories. In particular, Morton's logogen model has been one of the most influential models of word recognition, and its development was mainly driven by long-term priming data. Consider the evolution of the model from its first 1969 version until its final and more elaborated 1980 version. Based on long-term priming data showing reduced cross-modal repetition between words and pictures or between written and spoken words, the model was constrained to include different modality-specific logogen systems. Although not all current models include logogens, the majority of current activation models of visual word recognition include these modality-specific distinctions (see, for instance, Coltheart *et al.*, 2001, for an historical review of how the logogen model evolved and how its last version influenced the Dual-Route Cascaded model introduced by Coltheart *et al.*, 1993). On our view, long-term priming techniques can contribute once again to the development these models.

Note, we do agree with Forster and Davis that masked and long-term priming are supported by two different mechanisms but, contrary to their conclusion, we claim these different mechanisms act onto the *same* abstract orthographic representations. Regarding masked priming, pre-existing abstract lexical codes are temporally activated (or opened) with no systemic structural change resulting. Thus, this form of priming has only short-term consequences and for those reasons it lasts only a few seconds. But on our view, long-term priming reflects structural changes (learning) in the orthographic system that affect the later processing of the repeated items, with larger improvements associated with lower-frequency words (e.g., Bowers, 2000b). On this later view, long-term priming should provide constraints to theories of word recognition, particularly those concerned with the issue of learning.

Summary

Although long-term priming has been extensively studied during the past 20 years, there are relatively few detailed theories of priming, and even fewer theories that have paid careful attention to the underlying function of priming. We would suggest that word priming is best understood as a by-product of learning within orthographic and phonological systems, and as such, it is a mistake to develop a theory of priming *per se*. Rather, it is important to develop theories of perception (and perhaps semantics) that learn. Such an approach leads to novel and counter-intuitive predictions, some of which we have already confirmed.

References

Balota, D. A. and Neely, J. H. (1980). Test-expectancy and word-frequency effects in recall and recognition. *Journal of Experimental Psychology: Human Learning and Memory*, **6**, 576–87.

Bentin, S. and Moscovitch, M. (1988). The time course of repetition effects for words and unfamiliar faces. *Journal of Experimental Psychology: General*, **117**, 148–60.

Besner, D. and Swan, M. (1982). Models of lexical access in visual word recognition. *Quarterly Journal of Experimental Psychology Section A: Human Experimental Psychology*, **34**, 313–25.

Besner, D., Coltheart, M., and Davelaar, E. (1984). Basic processes in reading: Computation of abstract letter identities. *Canadian Journal of Psychology*, **38**, 126–34.

Biederman, I. (1987). Recognition-by-components: A theory of human image understanding. *Psychological Review*, **94**, 115–47.

Blaxton, T. A. (1989). Investigating dissociations among memory measures: Support for a transfer-appropriate processing framework. *Journal of Experimental Psychology: Leaning, Memory, and Cognition*, **15**, 657–68.

Bodner, G. E. and Masson, M. E. J. (1997). Masked repetition priming of words and nonwords: Evidence for a nonlexical basis for priming. *Journal of Memory and Language*, **37**, 268–93.

Bowers, J. S. (1994). Does implicit memory extend to legal and illegal nonwords? *Journal of Experimental Psychology: Learning, Memory, and Cognition*, 20, 534–49.

Bowers, J. S. (1996). Different perceptual codes support word and pseudoword priming: Was Morton right all along? *Journal of Experimental Psychology: Learning, Memory, and Cognition*, 22, 1336–53.

Bowers, J. S. (1999). Priming is not all bias: Commentary on Ratcliff and McKoon (1997). *Psychological Review*, 106, 582–96.

Bowers, J. S. (2000a). In defense of abstractionist theories of word identification and repetition priming. *Psychonomic Bulletin and Review*, 7, 83–99.

Bowers, J. S. (2000b). The modality specific and non-specific components of long-term priming are frequency sensitive. *Memory and Cognition*, 28, 406–14.

Bowers, J. S. (in press). Challenging the widespread assumption that connectionism and distributed representations go hand-in-hand. *Cognitive Psychology*.

Bowers, J. S. (in press). An abstractionist account of masked and long-term word priming. Book chapter to appear in *Masked priming: State of the art*.

Bowers, J. S. and Michita, Y. (1998). An investigation into the structure and acquisition of orthographic knowledge: Evidence from cross-script Kanji-Hiragana priming. *Psychonomic Bulletin and Review*, 5, 259–64.

Bowers, J. S. and Turner, E. L. (submitted). In search of abstract and specific visual form systems in the left and right hemispheres.

Bowers, J. S., Vigliocco, G., and Haan, R. (1998). Orthographic, phonological, and articulatory contributions to masked letter and word priming. *Journal of Experimental Psychology: Human Perception and Performance*, 24, 1705–19.

Bowers, J. S., Damian, M., and Havelka, J. (2002). Can distributed orthographic knowledge support word specific long-term priming? Apparently so. *Journal of Memory and Language*, 46, 24–38.

Brown, H. L., Sharma, N. K., and Kirsner, K. (1984). The role of script and phonology in lexical representation. *Quarterly Journal of Experimental Psychology*, 36A, 491–505.

Caramazza, A., Laudanna, A., and Romani, C. (1988). Lexical access and inflectional morphology. *Cognition*, 28, 297–332.

Carr, T. H., Brown, J. S., and Charalambous, A. (1989). Repetition and reading—perceptual encoding mechanisms are very abstract but not very interactive. *Journal of Experimental Psychology: Learning, Memory, and Cognition*, 15, 763–78.

Church, B. A. and Schacter, D. L. (1994). Perceptual specificity of auditory priming—implicit memory for voice intonation and fundamental-frequency. *Journal of Experimental Psychology: Learning, Memory, and Cognition*, 20, 521–33.

Clarke, R. G. B. and Morton, J. (1983). Cross modality facilitation in tachistoscopic word recognition. *Quarterly Journal of Experimental Psychology*, 35A, 79–96.

Coltheart, M. (1981). Disorders of reading and their implications for models of normal reading. *Visible Language*, 3, 245–86.

Coltheart, M., Curtis, B., Atkins, P., and Haller, M. (1993). Models of reading aloud—dual-route and parallel-distributed- processing approaches. *Psychological Review*, 100, 589–608.

Coltheart, M., Rastle, K., Perry, C., Langdon, R., and Ziegler, J. (2001). DRC: A dual route cascaded model of visual word recognition and reading aloud. *Psychological Review*, 108, 204–58.

Coslett, H. B., Roeltgen, D. P., Rothi, L. G., and Heilman, K. M. (1987). Transcortical sensory aphasia: Evidence for subtypes. *Brain and Language*, 32, 362–78.

De Groot, A. M. B. and Nas, G. L. J. (1991). Lexical representation of cognates and noncognates in compound bilinguals. *Journal of Memory and Language*, **30**, 90–123.

Duchek, J. M. and Neely, J. H. (1989). A dissociative word-frequency X levels-of-processing interaction in episodic recognition and lexical decision tasks. *Memory and Cognition*, **17**, 148–62.

Durgunoglu, A. Y. and Roediger, H. L. (1987). Test differences in accessing bilingual memory. *Journal of Memory and Language*, **26** (4), 377–91.

Feldman, L. B. and Moskovljevic, J. (1987). Repetition priming is not purely episodic in origin. *Journal of Experimental Psychology: Learning, Memory, and Cognition*, **13**, 573–81.

Feustel, T. C., Shiffrin, R. M., and Salasoo, A. (1983). Episodic and lexical contributions to the repetition effect in word identification. *Journal of Experimental Psychology: General*, **112** (3), 309–46.

Fodor, J. A. and Pylyshyn, Z. (1988). Connectionism and cognitive architecture: A critical analysis. *Cognition*, **28**, 3–71.

Forster, K. I. (1998). The pros and cons of masked priming. *Journal of Psycholinguistic Research*, **27** (2), 203–33.

Forster, K. I. and Chambers, S. M. (1973). Lexical access and naming time. *Journal of Verbal Learning and Verbal Behavior*, **12**, 627–35.

Forster, K. I. and Davis, C. (1984). Repetition priming and frequency attenuation in lexical access. *Journal of Experimental Psychology: Learning, Memory, and Cognition*, **10**, 680–98.

Fowler, C. A., Napps, S. E., and Feldman, L. (1985). Relations among regular and irregular morphologically related words in the lexicon as revealed by repetition priming. *Memory and Cognition*, **13** (3), 241–55.

Frost, R., Katz, L., and Bentin, S (1987). Strategies for visual word recognition and orthographic depth: A multilingual comparison. *Journal of Experimental Psychology: Human Perception and Performance*, **13**, 104–15.

Frost, R., Deutsch, A., Gilboa, O., Tannenbaum, M., and Marslen-Wilson, W. (2000). Morphological priming: Dissociation of phonological, semantic, and morphological factors. *Memory and Cognition*, **28**, 1277–88.

Goldinger, S. D. (1998). Echoes of echoes? An episodic theory of lexical access. *Psychological Review*, **105**, 251–79.

Goto, H. (1971). Auditory perception by normal Japanese adults of the sounds 'l' and 'r'. *Neuropsychologia*, **9**, 317–23.

Graf, P. and Ryan, L. (1990). Transfer-appropriate processing for implicit and explicit memory. *Journal of Experimental Psychology: Learning, Memory, and Cognition*, **16** (6), 978–92.

Grossberg, S. (1987). Competitive learning—from interactive activation to adaptive resonance. *Cognitive Science*, **11**, 23–63.

Havelka, J., Bowers, J. S., and Jankovi, D. (submitted). Cross-alphabet and cross-modal long-term priming in Serbian. *Psychonomic Bulletin and Review*.

Hintzman, D. L. (1986). Schema abstraction in a multiple trace model. *Psychological Review*, **93**, 411–28.

Hummel, J. E. (2000). Where view-based theories break down: The role of structure in shape perception and object recognition. In *Cognitive dynamics: conceptual change in humans and machines* (ed. E. Dietrich and A. B. Markman). Mahwah, NJ: Lawrence Erlbaum.

Hummel, J. E. and Biederman, I. (1992). Dynamic binding in a neural network for shape-recognition. *Psychological Review*, **99** (3), 480–517.

Hummel, J. E. and Holyoak, K. J. (1997). Distributed representations of structure: A theory of analogical access and mapping. *Psychological Review*, **104** (3), 427–66.

Hummel, J. E. and Stankiewicz, B. J. (1998). Two roles for attention in shape perception: A structural description model of visual scrutiny. *Visual Cognition*, **5** (1–2), 49–79.

Humphreys, G. W., Evett, L. J., and Quinlan, P. T. (1990). Orthographic processing in visual word identification. *Cognitive Psychology*, **22** (4), 517–60.

Jacoby, L. L. and Dallas, M. (1981). On the relationship between autobiographical memory and perceptual learning. *Journal of Experimental Psychology: General*, **110**, 306–40.

Keane, M. M., Verfaellie, M., Gabrieli, J. D. E., and Wong, B. M. (2000). Bias effects in perceptual identification: A neuropsychological investigation of the role of explicit memory. *Journal of Memory and Language*, **43**, 316–44.

Kimura, D. (1973). The asymmetry of the human brain. *Scientific American*, **228**, 70–8.

Kirsner, K. and Smith, M. C. (1974). Modality effects in word identification. *Memory and Cognition*, **2**, 637–40.

Kuhl, P. K., Williams, K. A., Lacerda, F., Stevens, K. N., and Lindblom, B. (1992). Linguistic experiences alter phonetic perception in infants by 6 months of age. *Science*, **255**, 606–8.

Levelt, W. J. M. (1989). *Speaking: from intention to articulation.* Cambridge, MA: MIT Press.

Logan, G. D. (1990). Repetition priming and automaticity: Common underlying mechanisms? *Cognitive Psychology*, **22**, 1–35.

Luce, P. A. and Lyons, E. A. (1998). Specificity of memory representations for spoken words. *Memory and Cognition*, **26** (4), 708–15.

MacLeod, C. M. (1989). Word context during initial exposure influences degree of priming in word fragment completion. *Journal of Experimental Psychology: Learning, Memory, and Cognition*, **15**, 398–406.

Marsolek, C. J., Kosslyn, S. M., and Squire, L. R. (1992). Form-specific visual priming in the right cerebral hemisphere. *Journal of Experimental Psychology: Learning, Memory, and Cognition*, **18**, 492–508.

Masson, M. E. J. (2000). Bias effects in repetition priming of masked word identification: Differential influences of modality. Manuscript submitted for publication.

Masson, M. E. J. and Isaak, M. I. (1999). Masked priming of words and nonwords in a naming task: Further evidence for a nonlexical basis for priming. *Memory and Cognition*, **27**, 399–412.

McClelland, J. L. (1976). Preliminary letter identification in the perception of words and nonwords. *Journal of Experimental psychology: Human Perception and Performance*, **3**, 80–91.

McClosky, M. and Cohen, N. J. (1989). Catastrophic interference in connectionist networks: The sequential learning problem. In *The psychology of learning and motivation* (ed. G. H. Bowers). New York: Academic Press.

McConkie, G. W. and Zola, D. (1979). Is visual information integrated across successive fixations in reading. *Perception and Psychophysics*, **25**, 221–4.

McKoon, G. and Ratcliff, R. (2001). The counter model for word identification: Reply to Bowers (1999). *Psychological Review*, **108**, 674–81.

Morton, J. (1979). Facilitation in word recognition: Experiments causing change in the logogen model. In *Processing models of visible language* (ed. P. A. Kolers, M. E. Wrolstad, and H. Bouma). New York: Plenum.

Napps, S. E. and Fowler, C. A. (1987). Formal relationships among words and the organization of the mental lexicon. *Journal of Psycholinguistic Research*, **16**, 257–72.

Neaderhiser, B. J. and Church, B. A. (2000, April). Priming in forced choice identification: Memory or bias? Paper presented at the 92nd Meeting of the Southern Society for Philosophy and Psychology, Atlanta.

Oliphant, G. W. (1983). Repetition and recency effects in word recognition. *Australian Journal of Psychology*, **35**, 393–403.

Pallier, C., Bosch, L., and Sebastian-Galles, N. (1997). A limit on behavioral plasticity in speech perception. *Cognition*, **64**, B9–17.

Pallier, C., Sebastian-Gallès, N., and **Colomé, A.** (1999). Phonological representations and repetition priming. Proceedings of Eurospeech '99, Budapest, Hungary, Sept. 5–9, 1999, Vol. 4, pp. 1907–10.

Pallier, C., Colomé, A., and **Sebastian-Gallés, N.** (2001). The influence of native-language phonology on lexical access: Concrete exemplar-based vs. abstract lexical entries. *Psychological Science*, 12, 445–9.

Pilotti, M., Bergman, E. T., Gallo, D. A., Sommers, M., and **Roediger III, H. L.** (2000). Direct comparison of auditory implicit memory tests. *Psychonomic Bulletin and Review*, 7, 347–53.

Plaut, D. C. and **Gonnerman, L. M.** (2000). Are non-semantic morphological effects incompatible with a distributed connectionist approach to lexical processing? *Language and Cognitive Processes*, 15, 445–85.

Polk, T. A. and **Farah, M. J.** (1997). A simple common contexts explanation for the development of abstract letter identities. *Neural Computation*, 9, 1277–89.

Rajaram, S. and **Neely, J. H.** (1992). Dissociative masked repetition priming and word-frequency effects in lexical decision and episodic recognition tasks. *Journal of Memory and Language*, 31, 152–82.

Rajaram, S. and **Roediger, H. L. III** (1993). Direct comparison of four implicit memory tests. *Journal of Experimental Psychology: Learning, Memory, and Cognition*, 19, 765–76.

Rapp, B. C. (1992). The nature of sublexical orthographic organization – the bigram trough hypothesis examined. *Journal of Memory and Language*, 31, 33–53.

Ratcliff, R. and **McKoon, G.** (1997). A counter model for implicit priming in perceptual word identification. *Psychological Review*, 104, 319–43.

Rayner, K. and **Sereno, S. C.** (1994). Eye movements in reading: Psycholinguistic studies. In *Handbook of psycholinguistics* (ed. M. A. Gernsbacher). New York: Academic Press.

Roberts, S. and **Pashler, H.** (2000). How persuasive is a good fit? A comment on theory testing in psychology. *Psychological Review*, 107, 358–67.

Roediger, H. L. and **Blaxton, T. A.** (1987). Effects of varying modality, surface-features, and retention interval on priming in word-fragment completion. *Memory and Cognition*, 15 (5), 379–88.

Roediger, H. L. and **Challis, B. H.** (1992). Effects of exact repetition and conceptual repetition on free-recall and primed word-fragment completion. *Journal of Experimental Psychology: Learning, Memory, and Cognition*, 18 (1), 3–14.

Roediger, H. L. III and **McDermott, K. B.** (1993). Implicit memory in normal human subjects. In *Handbook of neuropsychology* (ed. F. Boller and J. Grafman), Vol. 8, pp. 63–131. New York: Elsevier.

Rueckl, J. G. (1990). Similarity effects in word and pseudoword repetition priming. *Journal of Experimental Psychology: Learning, Memory, and Cognition*, 16, 374–91.

Rueckl, J. G. and **Mathew, S.** (1999). Implicit memory for phonological processes in visual stem completion. *Memory and Cognition*, 27, 1–11.

Scarborough, D. L., Cortese, C., and **Scarborough, H. S.** (1977). Frequency and repetition effects in lexical memory. *Journal of Experimental Psychology: Human Perception and Performance*, 3, 1–17.

Schacter, D. L. (1990). Perceptual representation system and implicit memory: Toward a resolution of the multiple memory debate. In *Development and neural basis of higher cognitive function* (ed. A. Diamond). Annals of the New York Academy of Science.

Schacter, D. L. (1992). Priming and multiple memory-systems—perceptual mechanisms of implicit memory. *Journal of Cognitive Neuroscience*, 4 (3), 244–56.

Schacter, D. L., Rapcsak, S. Z., Rubens, A. B., Tharan, M., and **Laguna, J.** (1990). Priming effects in a letter-by-letter reader depend upon access to the word form system. *Neuropsychologia*, 28, 1079–94.

Schacter, D. L., McGlynn, S. M., Milberg, W. P., and **Church, B. A.** (1993). Spared priming despite impaired comprehension: Implicit memory in a case of word meaning deafness. *Neuropsychology*, 7, 107–18.

Schacter, D. L., Church, B., and Bolton, E. (1995). Implicit memory in amnesic patients—impairment of voice-specific priming. *Psychological Science*, **6** (1), 20–5.

Seidenberg, M. S. and McClelland, J. L. (1989). A distributed, developmental model of word recognition and naming. *Psychological Review*, **96**, 523–68. Southern Society for Philosophy and Psychology, Atlanta.

Sereno, J. A. (1991). Graphemic, associative, and syntactic priming effects at brief stimulus onset asynchrony in lexical decision and naming. *Journal of Experimental Psychology: Learning, Memory, and Cognition*, **17**, 459–77.

Stankiewicz, B. J., Hummel, J. E., and Cooper, E. E. (1998). The role of attention in priming for left-right reflections of object images: Evidence for a dual representation of object shape. *Journal of Experimental Psychology: Human Perception and Performance*, **24**, 732–44.

Stone, G. O., Vanhoy, M., and Van Orden, G. C. (1997). Perception is a two-way street: Feedforward and feedback phonology in visual word recognition. *Journal of Memory and Language*, **36** (3), 337–59.

Subramaniam, S., Biederman, I., and Madigan, S. A. (2000). Accurate identification but no priming and chance recognition memory for pictures in RSVP sequences. *Visual Cognition*, **7**, 511–35.

Tarr, M. J. and Bulthoff, H. H. (1998). Image-based object recognition in man, monkey and machine. *Cognition*, **67** (1–2), 1–20.

Tenpenny, P. L. (1995). Abstractionist versus episodic theories of repetition priming and word identification. *Psychonomic Bulletin and Review*, **2**, 339–63.

Van Lancker, D. and Kreiman, J. (1987). Voice discrimination and recognition are separate abilities. *Neuropsychologia*, **25**, 829–34.

Warrington, E. K. and Weiskrantz, L. (1974). The effect of prior learning on subsequent retention in amnesic patients. *Neuropsychologia*, **12**, 419–28.

Whittlesea, B. W. A. and Cantwell, A. L. (1987). Enduring influence of the purpose of experiences—encoding-retrieval interactions in word and pseudoword perception. *Memory and Cognition*, **15**, 465–72.

Zatorre, R. J., Evans, A. C., Meyer, E., and Gjedde, A. (1992). Lateralization of phonetic and pitch discrimination in speech processing. *Science*, **256**, 846–9.

Ziemer, H. and Bowers, J. S. (1998, April). The role of tasks and strategies in phonological long-term priming. Paper presented at the 44th Annual Southwestern Psychological Association Meeting, New Orleans, LA.

CHAPTER 3

WHAT IS PRIMING AND WHY?

CHAD J. MARSOLEK

Open almost any cognitive psychology textbook and you find chapter titles like 'Perception', 'Language', 'Memory', and so on. Often the delineations are more specific (e.g., 'Memory encoding' versus 'Memory retrieval' chapters), but almost always the topic of memory is treated separately from the others. Of course, to some extent, this reflects the organization of different literatures and different groups of researchers in the field, an important goal for a textbook. However, an interesting aspect of this segregated organization of topics is that the brain does not appear to respect it very well, especially with regard to memory. Assuming that memory can be defined as changes in information processing due to previous information processing, and assuming that human memory is subserved by physical changes in the nervous system (e.g., modifications of synaptic efficacy, protein synthesis, etc.), all of the cognitive areas of the human brain appear to be involved in memory *per se*. That is, all areas instantiate physical changes of the sort that underlie the changes in information processing due to previous information processing (i.e. memory).

In this chapter, I suggest that most cognitive theories of memory are cast in a manner that does not satisfactorily posit both what repetition priming is and *why* it is that way. Often, theories are cast in terms of abstract entities that are more analogous to computer programming functions than to the functions of brain subsystems. In the abstract approach, theories concern broad functional concepts of the sort reflected by the typical organization of cognitive research topics in textbooks. Alternatively, theories can be cast in terms of neurocomputationally dissociable processing subsystems, the functions that they accomplish, their interactions, and the neurally plausible mechanisms that perform those functions and interactions. In this approach, theories can do more than organize past research findings and generate new questions; they can do so in a manner that highlights how the phenomena stem from independently derived properties and principles of how brains implement memory and how brain-like models simulate memory. In other words, such theories may also explain why mental phenomena exist in the manners that they do and not in some other plausible ways.

Admittedly, explaining why mental phenomena exist as they do is not critically import-ant according to some philosophical and scientific positions. However, we currently are in a position to theorize about memory in a manner that draws direct connections to scientific fields and levels of analysis outside of cognitive psychology, so failure to do so is a choice. In the 1940s and 1950s, Hull's (1943) *Principles of behavior* was perhaps the most influential text in experimental psychology (at least it was the most cited; see Ruja, 1956; Spence, 1952). Only 60 years later, very few researchers hypothesize about 'The symbolic construct $_sH_R$ as a function of the number of reinforcements' or 'Primary motivation and reaction potential' (chapter titles in that book). This is at least in part because the concepts did not make close connections to other fields and levels, especially the newly developing field of cognitive psychology just a few years after publication of that book. Such connections are needed to help explain why behavioral principles of learning work in one way and not in some other way. Will today's theories of [insert chapter title of contemporary cognitive text here] likewise fail to make the kind of connections that ultimately *explain*?

In this chapter, I will contrast what I call *theories of cognitive functions* against *theories of functions of neural processing subsystems*. In doing so, I will highlight the fundamental differences in their respective theoretical constructs and degrees of explanatory adequacy. After briefly delineating a memory phenomenon of interest in this book, long-term repetition priming, I will describe a theory of priming that is cast in terms of the architecture, functions, and mechanisms of neural processing subsystems. This theory will highlight the virtues of increased explanatory adequacy through mutually reinforcing constraints from qualitatively different kinds of computational, implementational, and behavioral evidence. Finally, I will exemplify theory development within this approach with a brief description of two additional neural subsystems relevant to visual-form recognition and priming.

Cognitive functions versus functions of neural subsystems

Cognitive phenomena can be understood in different ways through different kinds of theories. The following two theoretical approaches are distinguished in large part by the theoretical constructs that are used, but not by their level of explanation/analysis.

Theories of cognitive functions

In early cognitive psychology, the serial digital computer was extremely useful as a model of how to concretely conceptualize the operations of the human mind. Such a model was essential, especially when attempting to overcome the 'anti-mind' influence of behaviorism on psychology. It offered the notion that the mind could be thought of as analogous to computer software, a tractable and coherent entity, with the underlying brain being analogous to computer hardware, a quite distinct entity from the software.

This model led to what I will call *theories of cognitive functions*. Very often, different phenomena of cognition were understood as being accomplished by different 'programs' or mathematical functions, not unlike how distinct pieces of code are used as distinct sets of instructions for computers. Cognitive theorists built different theories for cognitive phenomena with seemingly different behavioral properties. The different phenomena typically had their own real world names in natural languages (perception, language, memory, etc.).

Theories in this approach did not necessarily have an *explicit* commitment to the serial digital computer as a model of the mind. Instead, perhaps the most critical characteristic of theories of cognitive functions was that the theoretical constructs were fairly *abstract* entities (in line with a kind of implicit commitment to the computer model). Whether the theories took the form of flowcharts of processing with only pseudo-code specification of algorithms or the form of more detailed specifications in operational computer code, the theoretical constructs were abstract in that they were functional entities that did not necessarily resemble qualitative aspects of how the underlying machinery implemented them. For example, the breakdown of different functional entities (e.g., two distinct sub-programs of a common program, or two distinct mathematical functions) did not necessarily reflect a spatial separation of the underlying hardware locations. Furthermore, any two hypothesized processes could take place in the same underlying hardware. The breakdowns among different theoretical constructs and their operating characteristics reflected only fairly abstract theoretical entities.

Theories of functions of neural processing subsystems

As it became clear that the human brain does not operate like the hardware of a serial digital computer, however, different approaches to understanding cognition developed. An alternative to theories of cognitive functions is an approach that I will call *theories of the functions of neural processing subsystems.* In this approach, the computer model of the mind is largely replaced by the *brain* and its neural computations as something like a 'model' of the mind. Perhaps the most critical characteristic of theories in this approach is that the theoretical constructs are less abstract and more closely tied to qualitative aspects of how the underlying machinery implements mental phenomena in neurocomputationally plausible ways. For example, the breakdown of different functions in this approach reflect the breakdown of anatomically separable brain areas responsible for neurocomputationally distinct processes, and the hypothesized processes reflect brain-like information processing (e.g., making use of distributed representations, parallel processing, etc.). The breakdowns among different theoretical constructs and their operating characteristics reflect decidedly less abstract theoretical entities compared with theories of cognitive functions.

It is important to note that functions of neural processing subsystems are cast at the same 'functional' level of explanation (i.e. level of analysis) at which theories of cognitive functions are cast (see Figure 3.1). Within Marr's (1982) framework, both kinds of theories are cast at a 'representation and algorithm' level, in which *functions* of systems are hypothesized in terms of representations of inputs, representations of outputs, and transformations of one to the other in the system. Neither kind of theory is cast *in terms of* implementational-level information alone (the underlying physical hardware information *per se*), nor *in terms of* the computational-level theory alone (the goal for the output of the system, what is available in the input to help achieve the goal, useful strategies for achieving the goal given the available input, etc.; see Marr, 1982). Although constraints from the implementational and computational levels can help to delineate and specify functions of neural processing subsystems, the theories of those functions are cast at the middle, functional level of explanation, one in which mental representations and processes *per se* are hypothesized, just like in theories of cognitive functions. The difference between the two kinds of theories is one of abstractness of theory within the same level of explanation (for related discussion, see Broadbent, 1985; Rumelhart and McClelland, 1985).

Long-term repetition priming

The focus of this chapter is on the cognitive phenomenon of long-term repetition priming (cf. Cofer, 1967). According to most usages, this term refers to a facilitation in processing a stimulus due to recent processing of that stimulus or a highly similar one (for reviews, see

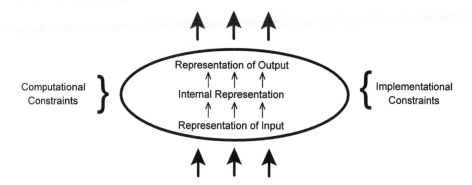

Figure 3.1 Computational-level constraints (from left) and implementational-level constraints (from right) can be brought to bear on a functional-level theory (depicted by the oval). In theories of cognitive function, functional-level theories tend to be cast in terms of abstract representations and processes. In this way, the oval depicts one of a set of cognitive entities analogous to stages in a flowchart or computer programs or subprograms. In theories of neural processing subsystems, the functional-level theory reflects mutually reinforcing constraints from both computational and implementational levels. In this way, the oval depicts one of a set of hypothesized processing subsystems that reflect the breakdown of neuroscientifically dissociable brain areas responsible for neurocomputationally distinct processes. Moreover, the hypothesized transformation from input to output in each subsystem is cast in terms of brain-like information processing.

Roediger and McDermott, 1993; Schacter, 1987; Tulving and Schacter, 1990). For example, the recent experience of naming an object has the effect of priming subsequent naming of that particular object (and, to a lesser extent, subsequent naming of different exemplars in the same category as that particular object), as measured by naming accuracy or response times (e.g., Bartram, 1974). Note that other phenomena such as short-term priming (e.g., Forster and Davis, 1984) or semantic/associative priming (e.g., Meyer and Schvaneveldt, 1976) may have properties similar to long-term repetition priming, but they also have different properties, and they lie outside the area of present focus.

Theories of long-term repetition priming

Theories of priming: cognitive function

Most contemporary theories of repetition priming and implicit memory are theories of cognitive function. This is relatively easy to discern in fairly abstract 'processing' theories of priming (e.g., Graf and Ryan, 1990; Jacoby, 1991; Roediger, 1990) whether or not they appeal to general principles for predicting memory performance (Morris *et al.*, 1977). It is also relatively easy to discern in highly abstract cognitive models of priming (e.g., activation in the logogen model, Morton, 1969; bias in the counter model; Ratcliff and McKoon, 1997) and in abstract mathematical models of priming (Wagenmakers *et al.*, this volume) within the global memory model approach (for review, see Clark and Gronlund, 1996). But, perhaps surprisingly, many 'systems' theories of priming should also be viewed as theories of cognitive function (e.g., Squire, 1994; Schacter and Tulving, 1994), at least when the proposed theoretical constructs (e.g., branches in a broad taxonomy of memory) do not correspond directly to the breakdown of neurocomputationally dissociable brain areas and do not propose distinct brain-like processes in some concrete detail. This point will be clarified later in the chapter.

Theories of priming that are theories of cognitive function posit fairly abstract explanations that are useful for some aspects of theoretical adequacy but not others. Such theories certainly are useful for providing the descriptive adequacy (cf. Chomsky, 1965) of organizing previous observations in a rational way and generating new questions and new observations, important goals for any scientific theory. However, they tend to provide relatively little *explanatory adequacy* (cf. Chomsky, 1965), in that they do little to show how the phenomenon stems from properties and principles that are independently motivated from other, different domains (for similar discussion, see Seidenberg, 1993).

Admittedly, some theories of cognitive function are aimed in the direction of providing explanatory adequacy. Many have the virtue of drawing connections to other domains of cognitive function (e.g., perceptual priming occurs due to normal processing and learning in perceptual recognition mechanisms; Bowers and Kouider, this volume; Schacter, 1990). Some also have the virtue of bringing mathematical tractability and other forms of computational constraint to bear on theories of priming (e.g., mathematical models of memory; Wagenmakers *et al.*, this volume), and others have the virtue of bringing neuroscientific evidence and other implementational constraints to bear on theories of priming (e.g., priming occurs independently of explicit/declarative memory and perhaps independently other forms of implicit/non-declarative memory; Squire, 1994; Schacter and Tulving, 1994). These theoretical moves are aimed in the right direction. However, in these theories, the set of additional, independently motivated constraints often does not suffice to explain why priming occurs in that way and *also* why it does *not* occur in other plausible ways. Theories with good explanatory adequacy are needed to make this important specification.

Explaining priming

A critical suggestion in this chapter is that the strongest set of independently motivated constraints from multiple domains is a set in which the theoretical constraints from all three levels of explanation of a processing entity (computational, functional, and implementational) *mutually reinforce* each other. Of course, using many different constraints is beneficial, whether they be multiple independent sources of evidence, methodological tools, or levels of explanation. Any one source, tool, or level has its limitations. But in addition, when the multiple constraints click together to *mutually* constrain a particular functional-level theory, they may form an additional, emergent constraint, to the extent that an integrated 'whole' constraint is greater than the sum of its 'parts'. A theory adhering to this kind of higher-order constraint not only offers descriptive adequacy but also a way to exclusively distinguish why the phenomenon occurs in that way and not in other plausible ways.

With today's methodological tools and theoretical concepts, this goal is better pursued from the perspective of theorizing about the functions of neural processing subsystems than from the perspective of theorizing about cognitive functions. Theoretical principles from biologically plausible computational models (McClelland, 1993; O'Reilly and Munakata, 2000) and neurocomputational tests of these models, combined with neuro-imaging and neuropsychological evidence from humans and neurophysiological and neuroanatomical evidence from other primates (in addition to cognitive/behavioral experimentation), can constrain theories of the functions of neural processing subsystems to a greater degree than theories of cognitive functions. This can lead to a theory of priming with explanatory adequacy.

Theory of priming: functions of neural processing subsystems

The desired theory of priming will posit a relevant set of neural processing subsystems at various levels of scale, their functions and processing mechanisms, and how they interact to accomplish relatively complex mental processes. Constraints from computational analyses and evidence, implementational evidence, and functional/behavioral experiments will converge to produce hypotheses of priming that attempt to provide explanatory adequacy.

Computational analysis

General architecture of subsystems   Computational reasoning has been offered for the general architecture of subsystems underlying consolidated memories and unconsolidated memories (McClelland et al., 1995). At a big-picture scale, the brain receives perceptual input, implements internal processing, and controls motoric outputs. In the internal processing, it is computationally useful to discover and store the structure that is common to various processing events, because this subsequently provides efficient ways to appropriately process similar but novel inputs. The structure contains the common information that is slowly abstracted from various previous events (e.g., that pianos can produce music), not the distinctive information about particular events (e.g., the distinctive information in an episodic memory of hearing music from a piano). Neurally inspired models with at least partially overlapping (superimposed) representations of knowledge naturally learn this kind of structure (e.g., Knapp and Anderson, 1984; McClelland and Rumelhart, 1985).

Of course, storing information about novel distinctive events is important as well. However, attempts to quickly store distinctive events in models with the superimposed representations that are useful for learning the common structure lead to a very significant problem: 'catastrophic interference' of the new learning on the retention of the old structure (McCloskey and Cohen, 1989). A computationally plausible solution to this problem is buffered storage of the new events in non-overlapping memories (using less superimposed representations) within a separate subsystem (McClelland *et al.*, 1995). This allows the new events to be stored quickly, without the catastrophic interference. Eventually, some of the new information (e.g., a novel musical instrument) can be integrated into the old-structure knowledge in the first subsystem, as long as slow learning of the new information is interleaved with reprocessing and 'relearning' of the old information (e.g., pianos). In this computational solution (validated through modeling studies reported by McClelland *et al.*, 1995), one subsystem stores the well consolidated common structure and another subsystem stores unconsolidated memories of recently encoded, distinctive information.

Mechanistic causes of priming   Computational reasoning also suggests what the mechanistic causes of priming may be. In the computational theory, 'relearning' of the old structure information must occur with some frequency, so it can be interleaved with new learning of novel information and avoid catastrophic interference from the new learning. Interestingly, processing events in everyday life provide just the opportunities needed to relearn the old information involved in those events. Another aspect of the computational theory is that both the relearning trials and the new learning trials must have relatively small effects on the structured knowledge in the consolidated memory subsystem (large changes create catastrophic interference). In neural network models, these changes are small modifications of the weights on connections between processing units in each training trial, for both relearning trials and new learning trials. In this way, the same weights that store the old structure can also integrate new information to update that structure with information from new experiences.

Therefore, a computationally plausible understanding of priming is that it occurs in the consolidated memory subsystem(s), and it is the memory effect produced by the small changes in this subsystem(s) due to relearning of old information and new integrations of unfamiliar information. For example, assuming visual object recognition requires a subsystem with consolidated visual object knowledge, perceptually recognizing a common object provides the opportunity for small changes to occur in the consolidated memory of that object's shape, which have the purpose of helping to avoid catastrophic interference. Such changes would have the effect of supporting the facilitation in subsequent recognition of that object that we refer to as repetition priming (for similar modeling approaches to priming and examples, see Becker *et al.*, 1997; Bowers *et al.*, in press; Marsdek and Burgund, 1997; McClelland and Rumelhart, 1985; Rueckl, 1990, this volume).

The effects of priming on subsequent processing   Computational reasoning also suggests important mechanistic effects of priming on the subsequent processing in the relevant subsystem. In network models that perform recognition or categorization of inputs, 'sparse distributed' patterns of activation are useful (e.g., O'Reilly and Munakata, 2000; Rolls and Milward, 2000) in the internal representations (i.e. in the activations of the units interposed between the input units and output units of the networks). Sparse distributed activations occur when only a small portion of the units (but more than one unit) is significantly activated (see Figure 3.2). These are patterns of activation that are intermediate between the extremes of local codes (only one unit activated) and densely distributed codes (all units activated), and they often are more useful in computational models than either of the two extreme versions of coding (see Földiák and Young, 1995). In networks that use sparse distributed activations, different units are sensitive to different features or portions of input patterns. Categorizations can be learned through discovering which features are almost always present in the inputs that belong to a particular category ('presence-diagnostic' features; e.g., the visual information in an object's shape that varies little across various viewings), which features are almost always absent for that category ('absence-diagnostic' features; e.g., visual information never found in an object's shape but found in other objects' shapes), and which features sometimes are and other times are not present for that category ('non-diagnostic' features; e.g., visual information specific to one

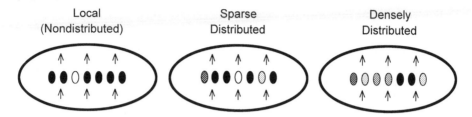

Figure 3.2 Depictions of a local (non-distributed) pattern of activation, a sparse distributed pattern of activation, and a densely distributed pattern of activation. The lighter the unit, the greater the activation of that unit.

viewing angle of an object but not another). In this way, a sparse distributed pattern of activation for a category would be strong activation of a small number of units in the internal representation (those representing the presence-diagnostic features for the category) and little or no activation of other units (especially those representing the absence-diagnostic features for the category). With representations like these, the weight changes that occur for relearning of old information and for new learning of unfamiliar information should take place as follows.

First, consider the relearning of *familiar information*: When a familiar input is recognized in everyday life, an input is accepted by the subsystem and an output representation is produced and sent to subsequent subsystems downstream. The degree to which the representation received by the subsequent subsystems is different from the representations received in the past for that category determines the degree to which the subsequent subsystems can categorize and hence make use of the information effectively (e.g., process the information in ways similar to before). Representations that are different from the norm for that category cannot be categorized or used as effectively as representations that are in line with the norm for that category. This degree of 'usefulness' can serve as feedback from the subsequent subsystems to the first subsystem to guide error-correction learning in the first subsystem (for biologically plausible forms of such error-correction learning, including backpropagation, see Mazzoni *et al.*, 1991; O'Reilly, 1996; O'Reilly and Munakata, 2000). Therefore, when a familiar input is recognized in everyday life, many of the units in the internal representation must be activated in the way that they have been during past successful recognition experiences (otherwise, the input would not be recognized). The connections to these units should *not* be associated with substantial weight changes, because the units are activated in a manner that is useful for the subsequent subsystems. However, many other units in the internal representation will not be activated in the way that have been in past successful recognition experiences. This is because recognition events since the last encounter with that familiar input will have changed the weights on connections to those units (to 'relearn' those other inputs). The connections to these units *should* be associated with small weight changes. Such units are responsible for producing a slightly different output representation compared with that produced in most of the past trials for the relevant category.

The important effects on the first subsystem are as follows. Activation of a subset of the units in a subsystem (especially presence-diagnostic units) should contribute to a categorization of the input that is much like the categorizations produced previously by members of that category. For this reason, few error-driven weight changes should occur on the connections to those units. In contrast, activation of another subset of the units (especially units that have not been learned to be absence- or presence-diagnostic) should contribute to a categorization that is not very similar to the categorizations produced previously by members of that category. As a result, error-driven weight changes should occur on the connections to those units in particular. These changes can be of two sorts. Units that contribute to decreases in the usefulness of the output should have associated weight changes that lead to a *lesser* likelihood of activation by that input (e.g., units that should be learned to be absence-diagnostic). Whereas, units that contribute to increases in the usefulness of the output should have associated weight changes that lead to a *greater* likelihood of activation by that input (e.g., units that should be learned to be presence-diagnostic). Because of such weight changes, repetition priming for that familiar stimulus would occur (cf. Desimone, 1996; Marsolek and Burgund, 1997).

At least two of the changes in the subsystem should be clearly discernible. First, in terms of the *activations* of individual units in the internal representations, many should not exhibit a discernible change in their likelihoods of activation due to priming. But, others should exhibit a discernible change, some becoming more likely and others becoming less likely to be activated subsequently. Second, in terms of the *weight changes* that occur in nearly every processing trial, fewer and lesser in magnitude weight changes should occur after processing a primed stimulus than after processing an unprimed stimulus. This is simply because a primed stimulus enjoys the benefit of recent weight changes that improved its processing, and because of this, subsequent processing of that stimulus leads to an output that should cause fewer and less substantial weight changes compared with a stimulus that has not been primed recently. These are critical hypotheses that will be revisited below.

Now consider the learning of *new information*. First, note that the new information considered at this point is not complex new event information (e.g., a new associative memory of the episode of hearing music from a piano or from a novel musical instrument); that would be the kind of information stored in the unconsolidated memory subsystem. Instead, the new information considered here is the simpler information relevant to a particular consolidated memory subsystem (e.g., the shape of a novel musical instrument for a visual-form recognition subsystem). Almost by definition, there is no differentiation between diagnostic and non-diagnostic information in an unfamiliar input, at least not until sufficient learning enables the diagnostic information to be abstracted from multiple inputs that should be categorized together (e.g., Knapp and Anderson, 1984; McClelland and Rumelhart, 1985). Instead, the units that happen to be activated and non-activated by an unfamiliar input are the initial candidates for representing the truly presence-diagnostic and the truly absence-diagnostic information for the relevant category, respectively (cf. Marsolek and Burgund, 1997; Marsolek *et al.*, 1996).

The effects of processing an unfamiliar input should be different from the effects of processing a familiar input. The first presentation of an unfamiliar input should elicit activation of units that happen to be sensitive to the features in that input. When this input is initially discerned to be novel (i.e. the output representation is substantially different from all past output representations), the weight changes should not be substantial. This is because no 'error signal' can be assessed in the subsequent subsystems; no pre-existing representations exist to allow a comparison between the output produced by the first subsystem against outputs produced in past trials. However, a new representation of that input may be stored quickly in the unconsolidated memory subsystem, and if so, subsequent processing of that input can lead to the kind of feedback from subsequent subsystems that signals weight changes in the first subsystem. Through this kind of process, the first subsystem eventually is able to abstract the diagnostic information for the relevant category via subsequent learning trials with additional, different inputs belonging to that category. Alternatively, the input may not be initially discerned to be novel, but instead may be misrecognized as belonging to the most similar familiar category. In this case, the first presentation of the 'unfamiliar' input should lead to the kind of repetition priming effect observed for familiar inputs (weights are adjusted—mistakenly in this case—on the connections to a subset of units in the first subsystem, as described above).

Thus, when unfamiliar inputs are discerned to be novel (not misrecognized as familiar), an important change in the subsystem should be clearly discernible. *Weight changes* should not be substantial for unprimed stimuli (stimuli never previously processed), but should be substantial for primed stimuli (stimuli previously processed once before). Thus, weight changes should be larger in number and magnitude for primed than for unprimed *unfamiliar* stimuli. This contrasts with how weight changes should be smaller in number and magnitude for primed than for unprimed *familiar* stimuli. This is a critical hypothesis that will be revisited below.

It is important to note that this understanding of priming stems from general computational constraints on mechanisms that could support human learning and memory. These are properties of learning and memory that are derived independently of behavioral or neuroscientific experimentation with repetition priming *per se*. Thus far, we have only considered computational constraints. To the extent that such constraints dovetail with independently derived evidence from other levels of explanation—in a mutually reinforcing way—the developing theory may have good explanatory adequacy. The next section summarizes implementational evidence of how the primate brain underlies learning and memory that integrates well with the computational reasoning.

Implementational analysis

General architecture of subsystems   Various neuroscientific findings are in line with the general architecture of memory subsystems hypothesized above. The hippocampal formation (and related areas) underlie unconsolidated memory—off-line from the neocortical areas underlying consolidated memory—according to evidence of selective impairment of unconsolidated memory in human amnesia (e.g., Milner et al., 1968), related animal models of amnesia (e.g., Zola-Morgan and Squire, 1990), and patterns of activation in neuroimaging studies with humans (e.g., Schacter et al., 1996). In contrast, neocortical areas underlie consolidated memory storage (e.g., Ungerleider, 1995) as well as priming effects, as evidenced by intact priming following medial temporal damage (for familiar information, e.g., Warrington and Weiskrantz, 1974, and for unfamiliar information under some conditions, e.g., Bowers and Schacter, 1993) and by neural changes during expression of priming in human neuroimaging studies (e.g., Buckner et al., 1995; Squire et al., 1992). A neuropsychological double dissociation between unconsolidated hippocampal memory and neocortical priming effects can be observed (Gabrieli et al., 1995). Moreover, properties of the organization of neocortical areas into perceptual and associative/conceptual areas reflects properties of priming effects. Priming of perceptual and conceptual information can be distinguished (e.g., Schacter, 1992), and neuroactivation patterns in human neocortex reflect this distinction (e.g., Blaxton et al., 1996; Gabrieli et al., 1996).

Mechanistic causes of priming   Neuroscientific evidence also integrates well with the hypothesized computational mechanism of priming. The hypothesis that priming is caused by small changes to the 'weights' on connections between processing 'units' fits well with evidence that modifications of synaptic efficacy occur between neurons in neocortex following recent activation. Long-term potentiation (LTP) and long-term depression (LTD) are synaptic modification effects that have been observed in cells from many areas of neocortex (for LTP, Artola and Singer, 1987; Komatsu et al., 1988; for LTD, Artola et al., 1990; Kirkwood and Bear, 1994), including the visual cortical cells that underlie shape recognition in human cortex (e.g., Chen et al., 1996). These synaptic changes very likely are involved in learning per se in the neocortex. Recent learning can be shown to induce natural synaptic changes in neocortex that affect subsequent measures of LTP and LTD saturation when LTP is electrically induced in slice preparations (Rioult-Pedotti et al., 2000). Furthermore, the properties of these synaptic changes are consistent with biologically plausible versions of error-correction learning in neural network models (O'Reilly, 1996; O'Reilly and Munakata, 2000).

The effects of priming on subsequent processing   Neuroscientific evidence also fits well with the hypothesized effects of priming on subsequent unit activations and on subsequent weight changes in computational models. First, sparse distributed coding is evidenced in neocortex (Vinje and Gallant, 2000), including in the temporal cortical neurons underlying visual shape recognition (Rolls and Tovee, 1995; Young and Yamane, 1992). These neurons are sensitive to visual shape, but it is often time-consuming to find which whole shape maximally activates a particular neuron (e.g., Gross et al., 1972), consistent with sparse distributed coding. Although the coding is relatively sparse, the representations of shape are at least partially superimposed (partially distributed). Different neurons are maximally sensitive to different critical features of larger whole objects (Tanaka, 1993). Such features are simple enough that they are present in multiple whole input shapes (indicative of overlapping, superimposed representations) but also complex enough that they are not present in very many whole input shapes (indicative of relatively sparse distributed activations). In addition, projection of feedback information from subsequently activated subsystems to previously activated subsystems occurs in all anatomically studied areas of visual neocortex (Felleman and Van Essen, 1991; Van Essen and DeYoe, 1995). Such feedback is the sort needed for the usefulness of categorizations in subsequently activated subsystems to influence changes in the previously activated categorization subsystems. Most important for present purposes, according to a series of studies (for review, see Desimone et al., 1995), the effects of repeated presentations of shapes on neuronal activations in temporal cortex fit well with the predicted computational effects of visual priming, both when the stimuli are familiar and when they are unfamiliar.

When *familiar* shapes are used in repetition studies (Miller *et al.*, 1991, 1993; Miller and Desimone, 1994), some cells, but not all, are affected by previous activation. About half of the cells are reactivated by repeated presentations of their 'preferred' stimuli to the same high level as during the preceding presentations. This is in line with the hypothesis that, when relearning old information, weight changes should not appreciably affect subsequent activations of many of the units (presence-diagnostic units). In contrast, the other half of the cells exhibit different levels of activation between the preceding and repeated presentations. Of the cells that exhibit a change, the majority show repetition suppression (see also, Baylis and Rolls, 1987; Brown *et al.*, 1987), in that lower activation is elicited by the repeated presentations. A minority show repetition enhancement effects instead. This is in line with the hypothesis that, when relearning old information, weight changes should have the effect of making some units less likely of being activated by a primed stimulus but other units more likely of being activated (units that are not yet learned to be absence- or presence-diagnostic). Moreover, several of the properties of such cellular repetition effects mirror behavioral properties of repetition priming for familiar shapes in humans (Desimone, 1996; Wiggs and Martin, 1998). For example, changes in object size or location do not substantially influence behavioral priming effects (Biederman and Cooper, 1992; Cooper *et al.*, 1992; but for evidence that task demands can alter this pattern, see Srinivas, 1996), and size or location changes do not influence cellular repetition effects appreciably (Lueschow *et al.*, 1994).

In addition, human neuroimaging evidence is in line with the computational predictions. When sets of familiar shapes are used, less activation typically is observed in occipital-temporal visual cortex for primed than for unprimed stimuli (for reviews, see Schacter and Badgaiyan, 2001; Schacter and Buckner, 1998; Wiggs and Martin, 1998). In addition, in a time-extended object-recognition task using functional magnetic resonance imaging (fMRI), the deactivation associated with priming has been shown to occur *after* the test object has been recognized but not before (James *et al.*, 2000). This is in line with the computational hypothesis that overall synaptic modifications should be less for primed than for unprimed familiar stimuli, in an effect that occurs after recognition of a stimulus and subsequent 'error-correction' computations.

A different finding is obtained with *unfamiliar* shapes. When a set of novel shapes is introduced after a set of familiar shapes has been presented many times previously (Li *et al.*, 1993), the cells that previously exhibited repetition suppression effects for the familiar stimuli typically are *activated* by the subsequent unfamiliar stimuli. This is in line with the hypothesis that, when learning new stimuli, the information in the input should produce activation in many of the units, because nearly all of the information in an unfamiliar stimulus is 'diagnostic' of its category (until truly diagnostic information can be gleaned from additional learning trials). In addition, human neuroimaging evidence fits this pattern. Unlike with familiar shapes, when unfamiliar shapes are presented, greater activation is observed for primed than for unprimed stimuli (Henson *et al.*, 2000; see also

Schacter *et al.*, 1995). This is in line with the computational hypothesis that new learning of unfamiliar stimuli is distinguished by weight changes that should be larger in number and magnitude for primed than for unprimed stimuli.

It is important to note that much of this implementational evidence provides independent constraints on understanding priming. With the exception of neuroimaging studies originally designed in part to investigate priming *per se*, the implementational evidence for the developing theory of priming stems from properties of the brain that were derived independently of interest in priming effects and independently of the computational reasoning for what priming may be. Nevertheless, both the computational and implementational constraints converge on a distinct functional-level understanding of repetition priming.

Functional theory

The theory of priming, cast in terms of functions of neural processing subsystems, is as follows. Neocortical subsystems store well consolidated knowledge. Everyday cognitive processing (such as perceptual recognition of objects) makes use of well-established structure in the knowledge in these subsystems. Priming occurs when processing of a stimulus causes small changes to the knowledge stored in these neocortical subsystems (to help avoid catastrophic interference), which has the effect of facilitating subsequent processing of the primed stimuli. The mechanism involves small structural changes to representations (different for familiar versus unfamiliar stimuli) that are analogous to weight modifications in neural network models and are actually instantiated by synaptic modifications that influence both subsequent cellular activation and subsequent weight changes.

Why?

This theory may be preferred over typical theories of cognitive function because it has stronger explanatory adequacy. It is true that some theories of cognitive function make effective use of computational or implementational constraints in addition to behavioral findings. But, unless they satisfy constraints from as many independently derived properties of learning and memory, from qualitatively different levels of explanation that all converge in a mutually reinforcing way, it can be argued that they offer a smaller degree of explanatory adequacy. In other words, such theories do a less effective job at explaining why priming works in one way and not in the other plausible ways.

For example, much neural evidence indicates that anatomically separate areas underlie priming versus learning of new episodes and explicit memory (e.g., Squire, 1994; Schacter and Tulving, 1994). But, why hypothesize that the neural evidence necessarily indicates that different subsystems underlie these forms of memory when a common memory system could account for the neuroscientific results (cf. Nosofsky and Zaki, 1998; Palmeri and Flanery, 1999)? Independently derived computational constraints (e.g., that interleaved learning of old and new information is needed to avoid catastrophic interference in the superimposed representations of consolidated memory) helps to choose between those two plausible alternatives.

In addition, many processing theories of priming are supported by findings that memory performance increases when the type of processing at encoding matches the type of processing at test (e.g., Graf and Ryan, 1990; Roediger, 1990). So why hypothesize that such a principle, as it applies to repetition priming, necessarily reflects mechanistic changes in a consolidated memory subsystem(s), when appeal to the more general principle of transfer appropriate processing (Morris *et al.*, 1977) or appeal to instance-based memory theories (e.g., Logan, 1990) may account for such results more parsimoniously? Again, independently derived computational constraints (e.g., that interleaved learning of old and new information is needed to avoid catastrophic interference in the superimposed representations of consolidated memory, whereas rapid learning of well-separated traces occurs in unconsolidated memory) helps to choose between these plausible alternatives.

Finally, other computationally explicit models can provide concrete explanations of priming; for example, priming may be due to a lowered criterion in an accumulator model of stimulus identification (Wagenmakers *et al.*, 2000a) or to changes in bias at a decision node following object identification in a neural network model (Rouder *et al.*, 2000). So why hypothesize instead that the models to be preferred are models that have superimposed representations, sparse distributed activations, and small changes to connection strengths that affect the relevant representations and activations? Independently derived implementational evidence that the relevant neurons compute activations that reflect superimposed representations, sparse distributed coding, and patterns of activation consistent with the proposed mechanistic understanding of priming all help to choose between plausible alternatives. Indeed, the proposed theory naturally accounts for the kind of main result that originally was offered to distinctively support bias explanations (Ratcliff and McKoon, 1997; but see also, Bowers, 1999; Wagenmakers *et al.*, 2000b): Priming of one object produces a bias effect that adversely affects subsequent recognition of a very similar unprimed object (Ratcliff and McKoon, 1996; see also Ratcliff and McKoon, 1995). Two very similar stimuli should produce very similar activations in the internal representations of a model with superimposed representations, thus weight changes that lead to a greater subsequent ability to produce one of the two outputs should also lead to a subsequent tendency to produce the primed output when the *other* stimulus is presented as input during a testing trial.

Abstract and specific visual-form recognition and priming

In this section, two additional subsystems are briefly described to exemplify theory development within the approach of theorizing about functions of neural subsystems. Stemming from the mechanistic theory of priming above, two critical subsystems of consolidated memory in the neocortex may be an abstract-category subsystem and a specific-exemplar subsystem. Both accomplish visual-form recognition and priming, but in different ways to subserve contradictory transformations and goals.

Computational analysis

Fundamental to visual-form recognition is the ability to recognize the abstract category to which an input shape corresponds (e.g., cup versus pen, etc.) as well as the ability to recognize the specific exemplar to which that same input shape corresponds (e.g., an individual pen). Post-visual feedback can help a visual subsystem to learn that multiple input shapes (even dissimilar ones; e.g., an upright piano and a grand piano) should be categorized together because they are associated with the same post-visual information.

Post-visual feedback also can help to learn that multiple input shapes (even similar ones; e.g., two highly similar upright pianos) should be distinguished because they correspond to different individual object entities in the world. Interestingly, mapping an input shape to its category representation and mapping that input to its exemplar representation involve contradictory computations when real world stimuli are considered.

Figure 3.3 helps to convey the computational analysis that leads to the theory of a two subsystems architecture. Object recognition can be conceptualized as instantiating a mapping from points in image space (retinotopically-mapped input representations for a visual-form recognition subsystem) to points in a long-term memory space (output representations from a visual-form recognition subsystem). First, dissimilar exemplars in a category reside in relatively distant points in image space, and they are mapped together for category recognition versus apart for exemplar recognition (Figure 3.3A). Such mappings are not contradictory; they can take place effectively in a common neural network model (Marsolek, 1992; Marsolek and Burgund, 1997). Second, similar exemplars in a category reside in relatively nearby points in image space, and they are mapped together for category recognition versus apart for exemplar recognition (Figure 3.3B). Such mappings also are not contradictory; they can take place effectively in a common neural network model (e.g., Hummel and Stankiewicz, 1998; Knapp and Anderson, 1984; Marsolek, 1992; Marsolek and Burgund, 1997; McClelland and Rumelhart, 1985). However, contradictory mapping solutions are demanded when categories contain *both* dissimilar exemplars and similar exemplars (as in most real world visual-form categories; e.g., pianos). Assuming a common internal representation for the mappings, the transformations useful for bringing together dissimilar exemplars contradict the transformations useful for separating similar exemplars (Figure 3.3C; Marsolek, 1994; Marsolek and Burgund, 1997). A computationally useful solution is to separate the mappings across different sets of weights and internal representations (i.e., implement separate, parallel subnetworks for the two mappings; see Figure 3.3D). Note that the same argument applies to learning of visual word-form categories and exemplars (e.g., the same word printed in different letter cases or fonts).

The internal representations that are most useful for abstract-category and specific-exemplar mappings may be qualitatively different, suggesting important mechanistic differences between the two subsystems. Both processors should utilize sparse distributed activations, of the sort hypothesized above, but the two may differ in the *degree* of sparseness that is most useful. For categorizing dissimilar exemplars in a category recognition subsystem, the presence-diagnostic features necessarily correspond to a small number of relatively simple features of whole input images, because little visual information is common to the dissimilar exemplars. Hence, very sparse distributed activations are useful in the internal representations. In contrast, for distinguishing similar exemplars in an exemplar subsystem, the diagnostic information for an exemplar corresponds to a large number of relatively complex features of whole input images, because so much visual information is common to the similar exemplars. Hence, less sparse distributed activations are useful in the internal representations. Indeed, a large number of units, each sensitive in different ways to information close to the whole of an input form, can be shown to represent extremely specific information (e.g., Ballard, 1986; Hinton *et al.*, 1986), as necessary for very fine-grained exemplar recognition (Marsolek and Burgund, 1997). Because a single,

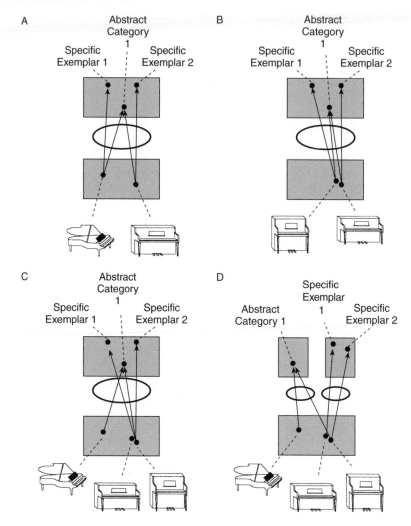

Figure 3.3 Abstract-category mappings and specific-exemplar mappings are not contradictory when categories contain either dissimilar exemplars (A) or similar exemplars (B), but they are contradictory when categories contain both dissimilar and similar exemplars (C). A computationally useful solution to the latter problem is to implement separate subnetworks for the two mappings (D). See text for explanation.

unified system cannot represent both very sparse and not very sparse distributed activations, separate subsystems are needed to accomplish both effectively. In line with these computational analyses, neural network modeling studies indicate that separate subnetworks accomplish abstract-category and specific-exemplar recognition (and priming) of objects in ways that mimic human performance in experiments with the same stimuli and the same priming procedures (Marsolek, 1999), but unified networks do not (Marsolek *et al.*, 1999). Also, the two subnetworks discover mapping solutions that make use of very sparse versus less sparse distributed representations, respectively (Marsolek *et al.* 1999).

Implementational analysis

Neuroscientific findings integrate well with the hypothesis that abstract-category and specific-exemplar visual-form recognition subsystems are dissociable and operate in parallel. Hemispheric asymmetries in normal human observers indicate that the pattern of priming that is characteristic of an abstract-category subsystem and the pattern of priming that is characteristic of a specific-exemplar subsystem are neurally dissociable (Marsolek, 1999; Marsolek and Burgund, this volume). In divided-visual-field experiments, participants name objects presented in the left or right visual field during a test phase. This occurs after they have viewed centrally presented same-exemplar objects, different-exemplar objects, and printed words that name other objects during an initial encoding phase. Priming is abstract yet visual (equivalent same- and different-exemplar primed performance, with both greater than word-primed performance) when test objects are presented directly to the left cerebral hemisphere. But, priming is exemplar-specific (greater same- than different-exemplar primed performance, with the different-exemplar primed performance being equal to word-primed performance) when test objects are presented directly to the right cerebral hemisphere. The evidence of abstract priming without accompanying specific priming in left-hemisphere presentations and specific priming without accompanying abstract priming in right-hemisphere presentations suggests that the two processors operate in parallel rather than in sequence. For a review of similar findings (including word-form priming effects) in normal participants as well as relevant results from brain-damaged patients and neuropsychological syndromes, see Marsolek and Burgund (1997).

Neuroimaging evidence also is in line with the proposed neural subsystems architecture. Deactivations associated with object priming in a rapid event-related fMRI study (using the same stimuli as in the divided-visual-field and neural-network modeling studies) indicate different neural locations for abstract-category priming and specific-exemplar priming, in both the left and right hemispheres (Marsolek *et al.*, 2001; for similar results, see also, Buckner *et al.*, 1998; Koutstaal *et al.*, 2001). Also, in line with different levels of sparse distributed coding, the abstract and specific areas differed in relative sizes and locations (Marsolek *et al.*, 2001).

Functional theory

The resulting functional theory is that two dissociable visual-form subsystems operate in parallel to accomplish abstract-category recognition and priming versus specific-exemplar recognition and priming. Both subsystems use sparse distributed activations in their internal representations, but they use different relative levels of sparseness to accomplish contradictory processes and goals. Both appear to operate in each hemisphere, but the abstract subsystem operates more effectively than the specific subsystem in the left hemisphere, and the specific subsystem operates more effectively than the abstract subsystem in the right hemisphere.

Of course, in typical real world situations, human observers recognize inputs in the center of vision with multiple fixations, such that the visual information is projected directly to both hemispheres. An interesting aspect of the subsystems theory is that task and stimulus demands are critical for hypothesizing whether one subsystem or the other will win the race to guide post-visual processing, and hence which one will be exhibited in performance following central presentations. For example, presenting visually degraded stimuli (which selectively affects very sparse coding mechanisms) and manipulating task demands so that recognition requires processing of relatively specific information both lead to decreased contributions from an abstract-category subsystem relative to a specific-exemplar subsystem in priming experiments (Burgund and Marsolek, 1997; Marsolek, 1999; Marsolek and Burgund, this volume; Marsolek and Hudson, 1999).

This theory also leads to interesting explanations for previously puzzling inconsistencies in the perception and memory literatures. For example, some experimental evidence indicates that visual object priming is not specific to particular viewing angles of the same object (e.g., Biederman and Gerhardstein, 1993), whereas other evidence indicates that it is (e.g., Tarr, 1995). This discrepancy may be due in part to tapping different abstract and specific subsystems, as viewpoint-invariant priming is observed in left-hemisphere presentations and viewpoint-specific priming is observed in right-hemisphere presentations (Burgund and Marsolek, 2000). Similarly, experimental results both for and against abstractionist and episodic/specific effects in visual word-form recognition may be explained in part through tapping different subsystems underlying abstract and specific word-form priming effects (Marsolek, 2001). Furthermore, by the theory above, priming of unfamiliar visual-form information may occur in neocortical subsystems, and such priming effects may occur in addition to new memories for the unfamiliar information in an unconsolidated memory subsystem. A recent study explores how these two sources of memory for unfamiliar objects can differ yet both contribute to memory expression (Burgund and Marsolek, 2001).

Conclusion

Why does long-term repetition priming occur? A theory with explanatory adequacy is needed to provide a satisfactory answer, one that explains why it occurs in one way and not in other plausible ways. Such a theory must rationally organize previous behavioral observations of priming well enough to account for them and well enough to generate interesting new questions and research. But, such a theory also must indicate how the phenomenon stems from independently motivated properties and principles from multiple domains and levels of explanation, all of which mutually constrain each other. A theory of long-term repetition priming with explanatory adequacy can be offered, stemming from hypotheses about the architecture, functions, and processing mechanisms of neural processing subsystems and their interactions. This theory does not fit very cleanly into only one or another of the typical topics in cognitive psychology textbooks. For example, a neocortical visual-form recognition subsystem plays at least some role in visual perception (shape recognition), some aspects of language (word recognition and reading), some aspects of memory (consolidated memory of visual shape, priming of familiar and unfamiliar visual shapes), some aspects of categorization (for shape information), and other areas of cognition. It may be interesting that a cost to pay for developing such a theory with explanatory adequacy is that it does not easily adhere to the traditional organization of cognitive research.

Acknowledgments

Writing of this chapter was supported by the National Institute of Mental Health, Grant MH60442. I sincerely thank Hedy Amiri, David Andresen, Jeff Bowers, Lisa Elo, and Carmen Westerberg for helpful comments on an earlier draft, and Chris Azorson for insightful discussion.

References

Artola, A. and Singer, W. (1987). Long-term potentiation and NMDA receptors in rat visual cortex. *Nature*, **330**, 649–52.

Artola, A., Bröcher, S., and Singer, W. (1990). Different voltage-dependent thresholds for inducing long-term depression and long-term potentiation in slices of rat visual cortex. *Nature*, **347**, 69–72.

Ballard, D. H. (1986). Cortical connections and parallel processing: Structure and function. *Behavioral and Brain Sciences*, **9**, 67–120.

Bartram, D. J. (1974). The role of visual and semantic codes in object naming. *Cognitive Psychology*, **6**, 325–56.

Baylis, G. C. and Rolls, E. T. (1987). Responses of neurons in inferotemporal cortex in short term and serial recognition memory tasks. *Experimental Brain Research*, **65**, 614–22.

Becker, S., Moscovitch, M., Behrmann, M., and Joordens, S. (1997). Long-term semantic priming: A computational account and empirical evidence. *Journal of Experimental Psychology: Learning, Memory, and Cognition*, **23**, 1059–82.

Biederman, I. and Cooper, E. E. (1992). Size invariance in visual object priming. *Journal of Experimental Psychology: Human Perception and Performance*, **18**, 121–33.

Biederman, I. and Gerhardstein, P. C. (1993). Recognizing depth-rotated objects: Evidence and conditions for three-dimensional viewpoint invariance. *Journal of Experimental Psychology: Human Perception and Performance*, **19**, 1162–82.

Blaxton, T. A., Bookheimer, S. Y., Zeffiro, T. A., Figlozzi, C. M., Gaillard, W. D., and Theodore, W. H. (1996). Functional mapping of human memory using PET: Comparisons of conceptual and perceptual tasks. *Canadian Journal of Experimental Psychology*, **50**, 42–56.

Bowers, J. S. (1999). Priming is not all bias: Commentary on Ratcliff and McKoon (1997). *Psychological Review*, **106**, 582–96.

Bowers, J. S. and Schacter, D. L. (1993). Priming of novel information in amnesic patients: Issues and data. In *Implicit memory: New directions in cognition, development, and neuropsychology* (ed. P. Graf and M. E. J. Masson), pp. 303–26. Hillsdale, NJ: Erlbaum.

Bowers, J. S., Damian, M. F., and Havelka, J. (2002). Can distributed orthographic knowledge support word-specific long-term priming? Apparently so. *Journal of Memory and Language*, **46**, 24–38.

Broadbent, D. (1985). A question of levels: Comment on McClelland and Rumelhart. *Journal of Experimental Psychology: General*, **114**, 189–92.

Brown, M. W., Wilson, F. A. W., and Riches, I. P. (1987). Neuronal evidence that inferomedial temporal cortex is more important than hippocampus in certain processes underlying recognition memory. *Brain Research*, **409**, 158–62.

Buckner, R. L., Goodman, J., Burock, M., Rotte, M., Koutstaal, W., Schacter, D. L. *et al.* (1998). Functional-anatomic correlates of object priming in humans revealed by rapid presentation event-related fMRI. *Neuron*, **20**, 285–96.

Buckner, R. L., Petersen, S. E., Ojemann, J. G., Miezin, F. M., Squire, L. R., and Raichle, M. E. (1995). Functional anatomical studies of explicit and implicit memory retrieval tasks. *Journal of Neuroscience*, **15**, 12–29.

Burgund, E. D. and Marsolek, C. J. (1997). Letter-case specific priming in the right cerebral hemisphere with a form-specific perceptual identification task. *Brain and Cognition*, **35**, 239–58.

Burgund, E. D. and Marsolek, C. J. (2000). Viewpoint-invariant and viewpoint-dependent object recognition in dissociable neural subsystems. *Psychonomic Bulletin and Review*, **7**, 480–9.

Burgund, E. D. and Marsolek, C. J. (2001). Separable processes for initial storage of unfamiliar three-dimensional objects. Manuscript submitted for publication. *Perception and Psychophysics*.

Chen, W. R., Lee, S., Kato, K., Spencer, D. D., Shepherd, G. M., and Williamson, A. (1996). Long-term modifications of synaptic efficacy in the human inferior and middle temporal cortex. *Proceedings of the National Academy of Sciences USA*, **93**, 8011–5.

Chomsky, N. (1965). *Aspects of a theory of syntax*. Cambridge, MA: MIT Press.

Clark, S. E. and Gronlund, S. D. (1996). Global matching models of recognition memory: How the models match the data. *Psychonomic Bulletin and Review*, **3**, 37–60.

Cofer, C. C. (1967). Conditions for the use of verbal associations. *Psychological Bulletin*, **68**, 1–12.

Cooper, L. A., Schacter, D. L., Ballesteros, S., and Moore, C. (1992). Priming and recognition of transformed three-dimensional objects: Effects of size and reflection. *Journal of Experimental Psychology: Learning, Memory, and Cognition*, **18**, 43–57.

Desimone, R. (1996). Neural mechanisms for visual memory and their role in attention. *Proceedings of the National Academy of Sciences USA*, **93**, 13494–9.

Desimone, R., Miller, E. K., Chelazzi, L., and Lueschow, A. (1995). Multiple memory systems in the visual cortex. In *The cognitive neurosciences* (ed. M. S. Gazzaniga), pp. 475–86. Cambridge, MA: MIT Press.

Felleman, D. J. and Van Essen, D. C. (1991). Distributed hierarchical processing in primate visual cortex. *Cerebral Cortex*, **1**, 1–47.

Földiák, P. and Young, M. P. (1995). Sparse coding in the primate cortex. In *The handbook of brain theory and neural networks* (ed. M. A. Arbib), pp. 895–8. Cambridge, MA: MIT Press.

Forster, K. I. and Davis, C. (1984). Repetition priming and frequency attenuation in lexical access. *Journal of Experimental Psychology: Learning, Memory, and Cognition*, **10**, 680–9.

Gabrieli, J. D. E., Fleischman, D. A., Keane, M. M., Reminger, S. L., and Morrell, F. (1995). A double dissociation between memory systems underlying explicit and implicit memory in the human brain. *Psychological Science*, **6**, 76–82.

Gabrieli, J. D. E., Desmond, J. E., Demb, J. B., Wagner, A. D., Stone, M. V., Vaidya, C. J. *et al.* (1996). Functional magnetic resonance imaging of semantic memory processes in the frontal lobes. *Psychological Science*, **7**, 278–83.

Graf, P. and Ryan, L. (1990). Transfer-appropriate processing for implicit and explicit memory. *Journal of Experimental Psychology: Learning, Memory, and Cognition*, **16**, 978–92.

Gross, C. G., Rocha-Miranda, C. E., and Bender, D. B. (1972). Visual properties of neurons in inferotemporal cortex of the macaque. *Journal of Neurophysiology*, **35**, 96–111.

Henson, R., Shallice, T., and Dolan, R. (2000). Neuroimaging evidence for dissociable forms of repetition priming. *Science*, **287**, 1269–72.

Hinton, G. E., McClelland, J. L., and Rumelhart, D. E. (1986). Distributed representations. In *Parallel distributed processing: Explorations in the microstructure of cognition* (ed. D. E. Rumelhart and J. L. McClelland), Vol. 1, Foundations, pp. 77–109. Cambridge, MA: MIT Press.

Hull, C. L. (1943). *Principles of behavior*. New York: Appleton-Century.

Hummel, J. E. and **Stankiewicz, B. J.** (1998). Two roles for attention in shape perception: A structural description model of visual scrutiny. *Visual Cognition*, 5, 49–79.

Jacoby, L. L. (1991). A process dissociation framework: Separating automatic from intentional uses of memory. *Journal of Memory and Language*, 30, 513–41.

James, T. W., **Humphrey, G. K., Gati, J. S., Menon, R. S.,** and **Goodale, M. A.** (2000). The effects of visual object priming on brain activation before and after recognition. *Current Biology*, 10, 1017–24.

Kirkwood, A. and **Bear, M. F.** (1994). Homosynaptic long-term depression in the visual cortex. *Journal of Neuroscience*, 14, 3404–12.

Knapp, A. and **Anderson, J. A.** (1984). A signal averaging model for concept formation. *Journal of Experimental Psychology: Learning, Memory, and Cognition*, 10, 616–37.

Komatsu, Y., **Fujii, K., Maeda, J., Sakaguchi, H.,** and **Toyama, K.** (1988). Long-term potentiation of synaptic transmission in kitten visual cortex. *Journal of Neurophysiology*, 59, 124–41.

Koutstaal, W., **Wagner, A. D., Rotte, M., Maril, A., Buckner, R. L.,** and **Schacter, D. L.** (2001). Perceptual specificity in visual object priming: Functional magnetic resonance imaging evidence for a laterality difference in fusiform cortex. *Neuropsychologia*, 39, 184–99.

Li, L., **Miller, E. K.,** and **Desimone, R.** (1993). The representation of stimulus familiarity in anterior inferior temporal cortex. *Journal of Neurophysiology*, 69, 1918–29.

Logan, G. D. (1990). Repetition priming and automaticity: Common underlying mechanisms? *Cognitive Psychology*, 22, 1–35.

Lueschow, A., **Miller, E. K.,** and **Desimone, R.** (1994). Inferior temporal mechanisms for invariant object recognition. *Cerebral Cortex*, 5, 523–31.

Marr, D. (1982). *Vision*. San Francisco, CA: W. H. Freeman.

Marsolek, C. J. (1992). *Visual form systems in the cerebral hemispheres*. Unpublished doctoral dissertation, Harvard University, Cambridge, MA.

Marsolek, C. J. (1994, March). *Computational incompatibility for processing specific- vs. abstract-visual-form information*. Presented at the Cognitive Neuroscience Society Annual Meeting, San Francisco, CA.

Marsolek, C. J. (1999). Dissociable neural subsystems underlie abstract and specific object recognition. *Psychological Science*, 10, 111–8.

Marsolek, C. J. (2001). Neural subsystems resolution to abstractionist versus episodic visual word recognition. Manuscript submitted for publication. *Quarterly Journal of Experimental Psychology*.

Marsolek, C. J. and **Burgund, E. D.** (1997). Computational analyses and hemispheric asymmetries in visual-form recognition. In *Cerebral asymmetries in sensory and perceptual processing* (ed. S. Christman), pp. 125–58. Amsterdam: Elsevier.

Marsolek, C. J. and **Hudson, T. E.** (1999). Task and stimulus demands influence letter-case specific priming in the right cerebral hemisphere. *Laterality*, 4, 127–47.

Marsolek, C. J., **Schacter, D. L.,** and **Nicholas, C. D.** (1996). Form-specific visual priming for new associations in the right cerebral hemisphere. *Memory and Cognition*, 24, 539–56.

Marsolek, C. J., **Jax, S. A., Andresen, D. R., Burgund, E. D., Westerberg, C. E.,** and **Henrickson, B. J.** (1999, November). *Contradictory neurocomputational properties for abstract-category and specific-exemplar object recognition*. Presented at the Psychonomic Society Annual Meeting, Los Angeles, CA.

Marsolek, C. J., **Andresen, D. R., Westerberg, C. E., Stevenson, W. E., Jax, S. A., Zhuang, J.** *et al.* (2001, July). *Integrating neurocomputational and neuroimaging evidence to explain repetition priming*. Presented at the International Conference on Memory III, Valencia, Spain.

Mazzoni, P., Andersen, R. A., and Jordan, M. I. (1991). A more biologically plausible learning rule for neural networks. *Proceedings of the National Academy of Sciences USA*, **88**, 4433–7.

McClelland, J. L. (1993). The GRAIN model: A framework for modeling the dynamics of information processing. In *Attention and performance XIV: Synergies in experimental psychology, artificial intelligence, and cognitive neuroscience* (ed. D. E. Meyer and S. Kornblum), pp. 655–88. Hillsdale, NJ: Erlbaum.

McClelland, J. L. and Rumelhart, D. E. (1985). Distributed memory and the representation of general and specific information. *Journal of Experimental Psychology: General*, **114**, 159–88.

McClelland, J. L., McNaughton, B. L., and O'Reilly, R. C. (1995). Why there are complementary learning systems in the hippocampus and neocortex: Insights from the successes and failures of connectionist models of learning and memory. *Psychological Review*, **102**, 419–57.

McCloskey, M. and Cohen, N. J. (1989). Catastrophic interference in connectionist networks: The sequential learning problem. In *The psychology of learning and motivation* (ed. G. H. Bower), Vol. 24, pp. 109–65. New York: Academic Press.

Meyer, D. E. and Schvaneveldt, R. W. (1976). Meaning, memory structure, and mental processes. *Science*, **192**, 27–33.

Miller, E. K. and Desimone, R. (1994). Parallel neuronal mechanisms for short-term memory. *Science*, **263**, 520–2.

Miller, E. K., Li, L., and Desimone, R. (1991). A neural mechanism for working and recognition memory in inferior temporal cortex. *Science*, **254**, 1377–9.

Miller, E. K., Li, L., and Desimone, R. (1993). Activity of neurons in anterior inferior temporal cortex during a short-term memory task. *Journal of Neuroscience*, **13**, 1460–78.

Milner, B., Corkin, S., and Teuber, H. L. (1968). Further analysis of the hippocampal amnesic syndrome: 14 year follow-up study of H. M. *Neuropsychologia*, **6**, 215–34.

Morris, C. D., Bransford, J. D., and Franks, J. J. (1977). Levels of processing versus transfer appropriate processing. *Journal of Verbal Learning and Verbal Behavior*, **16**, 519–33.

Morton, J. (1969). Interaction of information in word recognition. *Psychological Review*, **76**, 165–78.

Nosofsky, R. M. and Zaki, S. R. (1998). Dissociations between categorization and recognition in amnesic and normal individuals: An exemplar-based interpretation. *Psychological Science*, **9**, 247–55.

O'Reilly, R. C. (1996). Biologically plausible error-driven learning using local activation differences: The generalized recirculation algorithm. *Neural Computation*, **8**, 895–938.

O'Reilly, R. C. and Munakata, Y. (2000). *Computational explorations in cognitive neuroscience*. Cambridge, MA: MIT Press.

Palmeri, T. J. and Flanery, M. A. (1999). Learning about categories in the absence of training: Profound amnesia and the relationship between perceptual categorization and recognition memory. *Psychological Science*, **10**, 526–30.

Ratcliff, R. and McKoon, G. (1995). Bias in the priming of object decisions. *Journal of Experimental Psychology: Learning, Memory, and Cognition*, **21**, 754–67.

Ratcliff, R. and McKoon, G. (1996). Bias effects in implicit memory tasks. *Journal of Experimental Psychology: General*, **125**, 403–21.

Ratcliff, R. and McKoon, G. (1997). A counter model for implicit priming in perceptual word identification. *Psychological Review*, **104**, 319–43.

Rioult-Pedotti, M., Friedman, D., and Donoghue, J. P. (2000). Learning-induced LTP in neocortex. *Science*, **290**, 533–6.

Roediger, H. L. (1990). Implicit memory: Retention without remembering. *American Psychologist*, **45**, 1043–56.

Roediger, H. L. and McDermott, K. B. (1993). Implicit memory in normal human subjects. In *Handbook of neuropsychology* (ed. F. Boller and J. Grafman), Vol. 8, pp. 63–131. Amsterdam: Elsevier.

Rolls, E. T. and Milward, T. (2000). A model of invariant object recognition in the visual system: Learning rules, activation functions, lateral inhibition, and information-based performance measures. *Neural Computation*, **12**, 2547–72.

Rolls, E. T. and Tovee, M. J. (1995). Sparseness of the neuronal representation of stimuli in the primate temporal visual cortex. *Journal of Neurophysiology*, **73**, 713–26.

Rouder, J. N., Ratcliff, R., and McKoon, G. (2000). A neural network model of implicit memory for object recognition. *Psychological Science*, **11**, 13–9.

Rueckl, J. G. (1990). Similarity effects in word and pseudoword repetition priming. *Journal of Experimental Psychology: Learning, Memory, and Cognition*, **16**, 374–91.

Ruja, H. (1956). Productive psychologists. *American Psychologist*, **11**, 148–9.

Rumelhart, D. E. and McClelland, J. L. (1985). Levels indeed! A response to Broadbent. *Journal of Experimental Psychology: General*, **114**, 193–7.

Schacter, D. L. (1987). Implicit memory: History and current status. *Journal of Experimental Psychology: Learning, Memory, and Cognition*, **13**, 501–18.

Schacter, D. L. (1990). Perceptual representation systems and implicit memory: Toward a resolution of the multiple memory systems debate. *Annals of the New York Academy of Sciences*, **608**, 543–71.

Schacter, D. L. (1992). Understanding implicit memory: A cognitive neuroscience approach. *American Psychologist*, **47**, 559–69.

Schacter, D. L. and Badgaiyan, R. D. (2001). Neuroimaging of priming: New perspectives on implicit and explicit memory. *Current Directions in Psychological Science*, **10**, 1–4.

Schacter, D. L. and Buckner, R. L. (1998). Priming and the brain. *Neuron*, **20**, 185–95.

Schacter, D. L. and Tulving, E. (1994). What are the memory systems of 1994? In *Memory systems 1994* (ed. D. L. Schacter and E. Tulving), pp. 1–38. Cambridge, MA: MIT Press.

Schacter, D. L., Reiman, E., Uecker, A., Polster, M. R., Yun, L. S., and Cooper, L. A. (1995). Brain regions associated with retrieval of structurally coherent visual information. *Nature*, **376**, 587–90.

Schacter, D. L., Alpert, N., Savage, C., Rauch, S., and Alpert, M. S. (1996). Conscious recollection and the human hippocampal formation: Evidence from positron emission tomography. *Proceedings of the National Academy of Sciences USA*, **93**, 321–5.

Seidenberg, M. S. (1993). Connectionist models and cognitive theory. *Psychological Science*, **4**, 228–35.

Spence, K. W. (1952). Clark Leonard Hull: 1884–1952. *American Journal of Psychology*, **65**, 639–46.

Squire, L. R. (1994). Declarative and nondeclarative memory: Multiple brain systems supporting learning and memory. In *Memory systems 1994* (ed. D. L. Schacter and E. Tulving), pp. 203–31. Cambridge, MA: MIT Press.

Squire, L. R., Ojemann, J. G., Miezin, F. M., Petersen, S. E., Videen, T. O., and Raichle, M. E. (1992). Activation of the hippocampus in humans: A functional anatomical study of memory. *Proceedings of the National Academy of Sciences USA*, **89**, 1837–41.

Srinivas, K. (1996). Size and reflection effects in priming: A test of transfer appropriate processing. *Memory and Cognition*, **24**, 441–52.

Tanaka, K. (1993). Neuronal mechanisms of object recognition. *Science*, **262**, 685–8.

Tarr, M. J. (1995). Rotating objects to recognize them: A case study on the role of viewpoint dependency in the recognition of three-dimensional objects. *Psychonomic Bulletin and Review*, **2**, 55–82.

Tulving, E. and Schacter, D. L. (1990). Priming and human memory systems. *Science*, **247**, 301–5.

Ungerleider, L. G. (1995). Functional brain imaging studies of cortical mechanisms for memory. *Science*, **270**, 769–75.

Van Essen, D. C. and DeYoe, E. A. (1995). Concurrent processing in the primate visual cortex. In *The cognitive neurosciences* (ed. M. S. Gazzaniga), pp. 383–400. Cambridge, MA: MIT Press.

Vinje, W. E. and Gallant, J. L. (2000). Sparse coding and decorrelation in primary visual cortex during natural vision. *Science*, **287**, 1273–6.

Wagenmakers, E.-J. M., Zeelenberg, R., Schooler, L. J., and Raaijmakers, J. G. (2000a). A criterion-shift model for enhanced discriminability in perceptual identification: A note on the counter model. *Psychonomic Bulletin and Review*, **7**, 718–26.

Wagenmakers, E.-J. M., Zeelenberg, R., and Raaijmakers, J. G. W. (2000b). Testing the counter model for perceptual identification: Effects of repetition priming and word frequency. *Psychonomic Bulletin and Review*, **7**, 662–7.

Warrington, E. K. and Weiskrantz, L. (1974). The effect of prior learning on subsequent retention in amnesic patients. *Neuropsychologia*, **12**, 419–28.

Wiggs, C. L. and Martin, A. (1998). Properties and mechanisms of perceptual priming. *Current Opinion in Neurobiology*, **8**, 227–33.

Young, M. P. and Yamane, S. (1992). Sparse population coding of faces in the inferotemporal cortex. *Science*, **256**, 1327–31.

Zola-Morgan, S. and Squire, L. R. (1990). The primate hippocampal formation: Evidence for a time-limited role in memory storage. *Science*, **250**, 288–90.

PRIMING EMBEDDED IN WORD AND OBJECT RECOGNITION

CHAPTER 4

A CONNECTIONIST PERSPECTIVE ON REPETITION PRIMING

JAY G. RUECKL

The term *repetition priming* refers to a change in the processing of a stimulus as a consequence of a prior encounter with that stimulus. For example, in one of the earliest experimental demonstrations of a priming effect, Neisser (1954) found that studying a word such as PHRASE during a training task lowered the visual duration threshold for that word in a subsequent tachistoscopic identification task. In the half-century since Neisser's seminal study, the literature concerning repetition effects has been dominated by two contrasting theoretical traditions.

One view is that repetition priming is a kind of cognitive 'after-effect'—the manifestation of a temporary change in the process by which words (or other classes of stimuli) are identified. For example, in the classic logogen model (Morton, 1969, 1979), it is assumed that a logogen's threshold (the amount of evidence required to make it 'fire') is lowered each time it fires. Repetition priming is a consequence of this process: If a logogen fires once, it is more likely to fire again due to its lowered threshold. As the logogen model has evolved, it has become more common to speak of the 'flow of activation' rather than the 'accumulation of evidence', and to attribute priming to a persistence in activation rather than a lowering of the threshold. Nonetheless, modern activation theories continue to treat repetition priming as a kind of cognitive after-effect.

An important characteristic of this perspective is that it makes a strong distinction between the mechanism underlying priming and more general learning mechanisms. Thus, for activation theories priming is not a form of learning, and the process by which a representation is primed is unrelated to the process by which that representation came into existence in the first place. In contrast, the other primary approach to repetition priming assumes that it is a manifestation of the very same learning and retrieval processes that give rise to a wide variety of learning and memory phenomena. From this perspective, repetition priming is a form of implicit memory, and as such shares a kinship with phenomena such as classical and operant conditioning and the acquisition of motor skills (Roediger and McDermott, 1993; Schacter, 1987; Squire, 1992).

The activation and memory perspectives represent not only different theories about the processes underlying priming, but also different traditions with respect to theoretical orientation and assumptions about explanatory adequacy. The primary goal of research within the activation tradition has typically been to elucidate the nature of psychological processes within a specific cognitive domain (e.g., the perception of words, faces, or objects). In this tradition priming is as much a diagnostic tool as a phenomenon to be explained. Thus, for example, Morton designed priming experiments to determine whether logogens represent words or morphemes (the latter, according to Murrell and Morton, 1974), and to determine whether spoken and written words are recognized using the same set of logogens (no, according to Morton, 1979).

Research on priming within the memory tradition emphasizes a different set of concerns. From this tradition, the interesting thing about priming lies in its comparison with performance on explicit memory tasks such as recognition and recall. In light of this comparison, repetition priming is relevant to broad issues concerning the organization of memory (e.g., whether there is a single system or separate stores divided along episodic/semantic or declarative/procedural lines), the relationship between encoding and retrieval processes, and the neuropsychological underpinnings of memory functions.

Thus, these two traditions have contrasting strengths and weaknesses. By focusing on specific cognitive domains, activation accounts tend to provide relatively detailed explanations of the mechanisms underlying priming and couch these mechanisms in an explanatory framework that explicitly addresses other classes of phenomena (in the case of word perception, frequency and context effects, short-term priming, and effects of phonological regularity, to name just a few). On the other hand, activation models tend to have the flavor of special-purpose devices whose properties cannot be deduced from or even related to a set of general principles. For example, in the logogen model (Morton, 1969) the threshold-lowering mechanism involves two assumptions: A threshold is initially lowered by a relatively large amount, and over time it returns to a value slightly less than its original value. The first assumption is intended to account for the time course of repetition priming, the second for frequency effects. Neither is logically dependent on the other—the initial change could be small, or the threshold could return to its original value—and if readers turned out to exhibit repetition effects but not frequency effects, the ramifications for the logogen model would be minimal.

Work within the memory tradition has the opposite flavor. The tendency here is to seek explanations that capture the commonalities of priming effects across cognitive domains, and a premium is placed on relating these effects to general, domain-independent principles (e.g., the principle of transfer-appropriate processing, Roediger, 1990, or the consequences of computational incompatibility, Sherry and Schacter, 1987). While this attitude towards explanatory strategy is laudable in many ways, it also has its drawbacks. For example, memory accounts tend to divorce priming effects from other phenomena involving the same perceptual system—if not in principle, at least in practice. (For example, if you want an account of phonological regularity effects within the context of a memory theory, feel free to make one up, but you'll be hard-pressed to find one in the literature.) Moreover, with rare exception (e.g., Hintzman, 1986) theoretical accounts which emphasize broad principles typically have relatively little to say about the characteristics of the mechanisms which implement those principles.

In sum, two distinct traditions have evolved since Neisser's demonstration of repetition priming nearly a half-century ago. One tradition views priming as a form of learning, emphasizes the relation between priming and other memory phenomena, and values explanation in terms of general, domain-independent principles. The other tradition sees priming as a cognitive after-effect, places this effect in the context of other perceptual phenomena, and values explanation in terms of explicitly described, domain-specific mechanisms. To be sure, not every account of repetition priming developed in the last 50 years falls neatly into one or the other of these descriptions. Nonetheless, the contrast drawn above is a reasonable characterization of the literature concerning repetition priming as a whole.

This being said, it should also be noted that the clustering of characteristics which distinguish the two traditions is not a consequence of logical necessity. For example, nothing precludes a perceptual theory from being couched in terms of general principles, nor must theories concerned with memory phenomena eschew attention to processing mechanisms. Thus, while there are historical and pragmatic reasons for the evolution of the theoretical traditions described above, theoretical approaches that break from these traditions remain, in principle, viable options. Indeed, one of the primary motivations for the present volume is to bring together a variety of opinions concerning the benefits (and costs) of alternatives to these traditional perspectives.

One such alternative is offered by the connectionist framework. The purpose of this chapter is to describe the connectionist perspective on repetition priming. The first section provides an overview of the connectionist framework, and more specifically, connectionist models of word perception. The section that follows reviews empirical findings concerning several different issues related to repetition priming—the purpose of this section is both to show how the network approach has served to generate new hypotheses and to demonstrate how this approach allows for new conceptualizations of some old ideas. The chapter closes with a discussion of the relationship between the connectionist approach and accounts which have developed within the activation and memory traditions.

The connectionist approach

From a connectionist perspective, behavior is determined by the massively parallel interactions of many simple, neuron-like processing units. These units, called nodes, communicate by sending excitatory and inhibitory signals to one another, resulting in changes in the pattern of activation across the network. A learning algorithm is used to adjust the strengths of the connections among the weights such that the flow of activation is tailored to the structure and task demands of the environment in which the network is embedded. (For overviews, see Elman *et al.*, 1996; Rumelhart *et al.*, 1986, among many others.)

A fundamental tenet of the connectionist approach is the principle of *distributed representation*. In connectionist networks, meaning resides in the pattern of activation across a set of nodes, and not in the activation of individual nodes. Thus, representations are distributed across many nodes, and each node plays a role in many different representations. Moreover, because the causal relationships among these representations are encoded by the strengths of the connections, given that each node participates in many representations, each connection must encode information concerning many causal relationships. Hence, distributed representation necessitates *superimpositional storage,* another cornerstone of the connectionist approach.[1]

An important point about distributed representation is that patterns of activation can be more or less similar to one another. Thus, inherent in the notion of distributed representation is the notion of a similarity metric: Some patterns of activation are more similar than others. An upshot of this fact is that a network's behavior follows the *similarity principle:* Similar states tend to have similar consequences. Thus, for example, similar patterns of activation over one set of nodes tend to evoke similar responses over another. Mathematically, the similarity principle follows from the manner in which a node's activation is determined by the excitatory and inhibitory signals it receives from other nodes. Small changes in the pattern of these signals—corresponding to small changes in the pattern of activation of the nodes sending them—generally result in small differences (if any) in the activation of the nodes that receive them. Functionally, the similarity principle reflects the kinds of interference effects that arise as a consequence of superimpositional storage. Because the strength of each connection is determined by the superimposition of knowledge about many different causal relationships, the response to a given input tends to be pulled (for better or for worse) in the direction of the responses associated with other, similar inputs. As we will see, the similarity principle sits behind a wide variety of behavioral phenomena.

In the 'first wave' of connectionist models (e.g., Rumelhart and McClelland, 1986a; Seidenberg and McClelland, 1989), the psychological relevance of distributed representation, superimpositional storage, and the similarity principle was explored using relatively simple feedforward networks. In feedforward networks there is a unidirectional flow of activation from input nodes to output nodes (often with a set of 'hidden' nodes in between). Although feedforward networks have many interesting computational properties, it is now widely appreciated that interactive networks (i.e., networks that include recurrent connections) are much more powerful computationally and much more interesting psychologically. Interactivity allows the pattern of activation in a network to evolve over time, even if the external input to the network remains constant. As a consequence, interactive networks exhibit *self-organizing attractor dynamics*—over time a network's pattern of activation migrates towards a stable state called an 'attractor', and once the network reaches an attractor it remains there until the input to the network changes.

The self-organizing behavior of a connectionist network emerges from the excitatory and inhibitory interactions of its nodes. These interactions depend on the weights of the connections among the nodes, which in turn are determined by an incremental learning process that gradually attunes a network to its environment. Thus, the flow of activation at one time scale is shaped by a learning process that occurs at a slower time scale.

---

[1] It is worth noting that given the prominent role of distributed representation and superimpositional storage in the present account, the term *connectionism* as used here does not extend to models of the 'localist connectionism' variety (e.g., Grainger and Jacobs, 1998; McClelland and Rumelhart, 1981.) In terms of their theoretical assumptions and explanatory strategies, localist connectionist models are fully representative of the activation tradition described above. In many ways the connectionist approach described here should be understood as a rejection of these assumptions and strategies.

Learning influences both the layout of the attractors (i.e., which patterns of activation are stable) and the characteristics of their 'basins of attraction' (e.g., which non-stable patterns will result in movement towards a particular attractor, and the speed of this movement).

Network models of visual word identification

Many of the attempts to apply the connectionist framework to the understanding of cognitive processes have focused on the case of visual word identification (e.g., Grossberg and Stone, 1986; Harm and Seidenberg, 1999; Kawamoto *et al.*, 1994; Masson, 1995; Plaut *et al.*, 1996; Rueckl and Raveh, 1999; Seidenberg and McClelland, 1989; and Stone and Van Orden, 1994). These efforts have converged on a canonical 'triangle model', a network which includes separate layers of nodes responsible for representing the orthographic, phonological, and semantic properties of a word, with hidden units mediating the inter-actions among these layers. The representations of the triangle model are organized such that similarly spelled words have similar patterns of activation over the orthographic layer, semantically similar words have similar patterns of activation over the semantic layer, and so on. When a given word comes into view, the resulting input initiates a flow of activation within the network. The direction, speed, and outcome of this flow depend not only on the environmental input, but also on the knowledge of the network (as embedded in its weights) and its pattern of activation at the time when the word was first encountered.

Advocates of this position maintain not only that the characteristics of a network's behavior resemble those of human readers in important ways, but also that these charac-teristics are consequences of distributed representation, superimpositional storage, and the similarity principle. For example, both networks (Plaut *et al.*, 1996) and readers (Glushko, 1979; Jared *et al.*, 1990) exhibit phonological consistency effects: Regular words such as *mint* are read faster than irregular words such as *pint*.[2] For a network, and by theory, for readers, the phonological consistency effect occurs because the response to a given word is interfered with by the knowledge of other, orthographically similar words. In the case of *mint* and *pint*, *mint* benefits from experience with words such as *lint*, *tint*, and *hint*, whereas this knowledge is costly with respect to the identification of *pint*. Seen in this light, the phonological consistency effect has the same underlying basis as other ambiguity effects, such as the costs associated with the phonological ambiguity of words like *read* and *wind* (Seidenberg and McClelland, 1989) and the semantic ambiguity of words such as *watch* and *bat* (Kawamoto *et al.*, 1994; but see Joordens and Besner, 1994). All of these phenom-ena are manifestations of the similarity principle—the tendency for similar states to have similar consequences. This tendency works to a network's advantage in the case of consis-tent words, but it imposes a cost when it must be overcome, as is the case for inconsistent

---

[2] In Glushko's (1979) original formulation of the notion of consistency, a word like *mint* was classified as a (regu-lar) inconsistent word—only words with bodies always pronounced in the same way (e.g., *pill*) were classified as consistent. However, as the term consistency is now used, words that rhyme with the majority of other words sharing their bodies (including *mint*) are considered consistent words.

or ambiguous words, as well as, for example, the famous XOR problem (e.g., Minsky and Papert, 1969; Rumelhart *et al.*, 1986).[3]

Networks and repetition priming: a selective review

It is probably fair to say that if repetition effects were not an empirical fact connectionism would not be a viable theoretical option. This is not to say that the study of repetition priming played an important role in the development of the connectionist framework—it didn't. The point is instead that repetition priming so naturally falls out of the behavior of connectionist networks that it would be an embarrassment for the connectionist approach if repetition effects weren't as ubiquitous as they are.

From a connectionist perspective, repetition effects are a consequence of the incremental learning process that continually modifies the connection weights so as to attune the network to the structure of its environment (McClelland and Rumelhart, 1985; Rueckl, 1990; Stark and McClelland, 2000). From this perspective learning never ceases—even the networks underlying highly skilled behavior continue to change with experience (sometimes with rather dramatic results—see Plaut *et al.*, 1996). Repetition effects, like consistency and frequency effects, are a manifestation of this process—but whereas consistency and frequency effects reflect the collective influence of many learning events, repetition effects reveal the influence of individual events on behavior.

Although the link between priming and learning is intrinsic to the connectionist approach, accounts developed within the memory tradition discussed above also make a link between learning and priming. However, the connectionist approach differs from these other accounts in a number of ways: In its commitment to a particular understanding of the learning process (as changes in the patterns of connectivity within a network); In the endorsement of basic principles such as distributed representation, superimpositional memory, and self-organizing dynamics; And in the emphasis on instantiating these principles in computationally explicit, domain-specific processing models that address a variety of empirical phenomena, most of which fall outside the realm of learning and memory as traditionally defined.

These aspects of the connectionist perspective have both theoretical and strategic implications for the investigation of repetition priming. One implication concerns the classification of experimental phenomena: The understanding that priming is a form of learning results in a different partitioning of phenomena than has sometimes been assumed. Another implication is that we should expect the nuances of priming to reflect the operation of principles such as distributed representation and superimpositional memory. A third is that we should strive for an account of priming that links it to other classes of phenomena in deep and insightful ways. In the following sections I illustrate these points by reviewing several lines of investigation into the characteristics of repetition priming.

---

[3] It is worth noting that although these examples illustrate how behavior depends on the degree to which similar *inputs* are mapped onto similar *outputs*, the similarity principle derives from the characteristics of the local interactions between layers of nodes. Thus, although hidden units allow a network to solve the XOR problem (and thus overcome the constraints of the similarity principle), the hidden units are themselves constrained by the similarity principle. The implications of this point are considered below.

Short- versus long-term priming

'Priming' is typically defined as the effect of an encounter with a stimulus on the subsequent processing of another stimulus (typically, a stimulus that is either the same as or related to the prime). On this definition a variety of experimental procedures can be used to study priming. For example, in short-term priming paradigms (e.g., Forster, 1987; Humphreys et al., 1988) the prime precedes the target by a few tens or hundreds of milliseconds, and typically nothing intervenes between the presentation of the prime and target except perhaps a blank screen. On the other hand, in long-term priming paradigms (e.g., Jacoby and Dallas, 1981; Murrell and Morton, 1974) the lag between the prime and target is on the order of seconds, minutes, or even days, and any number of stimuli might occur between the presentation of the prime and target.

A question of theoretical interest is whether the priming effects observed using these two kinds of paradigms are brought about by the same underlying mechanism. According to some activation accounts, the answer is yes. On these accounts, both short- and long-term priming are a consequence of a change in the activation of one or more lexical nodes brought about by the presentation of the prime. However, although such an account is appealing in its parsimony, the empirical facts are that short- and long-term priming are quite different in their characteristics. Short- and long-term priming differ in their persistence (short-term priming is much more limited in duration), in their sensitivity to formal (i.e., orthographic and phonological) and semantic similarity, in the effects of frequency and lexicality, and in their susceptibility to disruption by intervening items (see Forster, 1987; Humphreys et al., 1988; Raveh and Rueckl, 2000, for reviews.) Together, these findings suggest that different mechanisms underlie short- and long-term priming.

In the connectionist framework, short- and long-term priming reflect the operation of two distinct but interrelated processes performed by connectionist networks. As explained above, long-term priming is linked to the learning process that adjusts the pattern of connectivity within the network. In contrast, short-term priming is tied to the flow of activation within the network, a faster process which occurs at a time scale commensurate with the processing of individual stimuli. When a stimulus is encountered, the network moves towards the pattern of activation which represents that stimulus (its 'attractor'). How long it takes to reach the attractor depends not only on its strength (which is determined by factors such as word frequency and phonological consistency), but also on the distance between the attractor and the initial state of the network (i.e., the pattern of activation at the time the stimulus was presented). Short-term priming paradigms involve the manipulation of this initial state: A prime that is similar or identical to the target will tend to put the network closer to the target's attractor than will an unrelated prime. This understanding of short-term priming as, in the vernacular of dynamical systems theory, an 'effect of initial conditions' has been used to account for a variety of findings (see Cree et al., 1999; Kawamoto, 1993; Masson, 1995, 1999; Plaut and Booth 2000; Plaut and Gonnerman, 2000).

The view that short- and long-term priming are the result of different underlying mechanisms is not unique to the connectionist approach (cf. Forster, 1987; Monsell, 1985). Even activation accounts can be formulated such that short- and long-term priming are attributed to different processes. For example, in McClelland and Rumelhart's (1981) interactive acti-vation model, short-term priming might be attributed to the effect of the prime on the target's activation value, whereas long-term priming might be tied to a change in a second parameter associated with each node—the baseline activation value towards which the actual activation eventually decays. This being said, it should also be noted that activation accounts typically treat short- and long-term priming as manifestations of the same underlying process.

Thus, the points to be made concerning the contrast between short- and long-term priming are twofold. First, the connectionist approach attributes these forms of priming to different mechanisms, a view shared by some but not all theoretical perspectives. Second, the connectionist perspective puts the horse before the cart: The existence of each form of priming follows from basic assumptions at the very core of the connectionist framework.

Word and pseudoword priming

Pseudowords are pronounceable nonwords such as *mave* and *zill*. Because pseudowords resemble real words in structure and yet differ from them in familiarity and meaningful-ness, the study of pseudoword priming affords an opportunity to disentangle the influence of these variables on repetition priming (and word recognition more broadly). Consequently, pseudoword priming has played an important and somewhat controversial role in the development of theories of repetition priming.

The results of several early studies suggested that, in contrast to the ubiquitous effects of priming on the identification of real words, priming has no effect on the identification of pseudowords. For example, Forbach *et al.* (1974) and Ratcliff *et al.* (1985) observed priming for words but not for pseudowords in the lexical decision task. Similarly, Cermak *et al.* (1985) concluded that, for amnesics, repetition priming facilitates word identification but not pseudoword identification. Diamond and Rozin (1984) reached the same conclu-sion about amensics' performance on a stem completion task. From the perspective of activation theories, this pattern of results is quite appealing. After all, if repetition priming is brought about by a persisting change in the activation of a lexical representation, then priming should only affect the processing of stimuli that have lexical representations. Pseudowords by definition have no lexical representations, and thus the identification of a pseudoword should not be influenced by repetition.

Upon further examination, however, these early results proved to be somewhat mislead-ing. In particular, pseudoword priming is regularly found in studies employing test tasks other than lexical decision (e.g., Feustel *et al.*, 1983; Rueckl, 1990; Rueckl and Olds, 1993; Bowers, 1996). It seems likely that the failures of Forbach *et al.* (1974) and Ratcliff *et al.* (1985) to observe pseudoword priming are due to the task demands of lexical decision: To the extent that lexical decisions are based on familiarity, any facilitative effects of repetition on the speed of identification may be offset by the tendency for familiarity to inhibit cor-rect 'no' responses (Feustel *et al.*, 1983; Richardson-Klahven and Bjork, 1988). Because repetition has been found to facilitate lexical decisions to pseudowords in some studies (e.g., Danenbring and Briand, 1982; Kirsner and Smith, 1974; Scarborough *et al.*, 1977) and inhibit it in others (e.g., Bowers, 1994), it seems likely that the trade-off between these factors may be modulated by methodological variables.

In contrast to the results of Diamond and Rozin (1984) and Cermak *et al.* (1985), amnesic readers have also been found to exhibit pseudoword repetition effects (Haist *et al.*, 1991; Keane *et al.*, 1991; Musen and Squire, 1991). In retrospect, the conclusions drawn from the earlier studies were based on rather unconvincing evidence. In the Diamond and Rozin (1984) study, priming was measured by performance on a stem completion task—a rather odd task ('Name a nonword beginning with zil___') that seems quite likely to invoke explicit memory strategies. In the Cermak *et al.* (1985) study, the pseudoword priming effect for amensics was not significant, but numerically it was nearly twice as large as the comparable (and significant) effect on word identification.

Thus, the empirical facts are clear: Repetition facilitates the identification of both words and pseudowords. The theoretical question raised by these facts is whether word and pseudoword priming have a common basis. For activation accounts, the answer must clearly be 'no'. If word priming is due to changes in the activation of pre-existing lexical representations, then a different mechanism must be responsible for pseudoword priming. Thus, for example, word and pseudoword priming have been attributed to processes involving 'activation' and 'elaboration' (Dorfman, 1994) or 'lexical' and 'episodic' memory (Feustel *et al.*, 1983). An appealing aspect of these accounts is that the process underlying pseudoword effects might open the door to a theory of how lexical representations come into existence, and thus positing such a process could be justified on a priori grounds. On the other hand, resort to a second process can also be seen as the application of a theoretical strategy employed all too often in cognitive psychology: For each effect posit a new cause.

The connectionist approach joins with certain other accounts (e.g., Marsolek *et al.*, 1992; Keane *et al.*, 2000; Schacter, 1992; Whittlesea, 1987) in rejecting the claim that word and pseudoword priming are brought about by different mechanisms. A general tenet of the connectionist approach is that both familiar and unfamiliar inputs are processed in the same way. Seeing a pseudoword, like seeing a real word, causes a flow of activation within the lexical processing network. Over time the network moves into an attractor state that allows the reader to behave in appropriate ways (e.g., pronouncing the word in a sensible way). Thus, pseudoword identification is an example of *automatic generalization*—unfamiliar inputs are processed in fundamentally the same way as familiar inputs. Due to the similarity principle (the tendency for similar states to have similar consequences), the response to an unfamiliar input resembles the responses associated with similar previously experienced inputs.

On this view, just as words and pseudowords are identified in the same way, so too are word and pseudoword priming the consequence of the same process—the learning algorithm that adjusts the network's pattern of connectivity. The goal of the learning process is to adapt the network to its environment by strengthening an input's attractor (and repositioning it if necessary) so that in future encounters with that input the network responds quickly and accurately. Because the environment may change over time, and because the network's ability to sample the environment is limited, the attunement of the network to its environment must be an ongoing process. Thus, each event provides an opportunity for learning, whether that event is the first or the millionth encounter with a stimulus, and each opportunity is taken. Word priming and pseudoword priming are manifestations of the same underlying process.

Several general points can be made about this perspective on pseudoword priming. First, whereas the connectionist account distinguishes between short- and long-term priming, attributing each class of phenomena to different underlying mechanisms, it treats word and pseudoword priming as fundamentally the same. In its stance on each of these contrasts, the connectionist approach differs from some accounts and resembles others.

Second, the connectionist account of pseudoword priming follows directly from the foundational principles of the connectionist framework. Because networks employ distributed representations, there is no need to draw a qualitative distinction between the representations of words and pseudowords: Both familiar and unfamiliar inputs are represented by distributed patterns of activation which are constructed 'on the fly' via self-organizing activation dynamics. Because distributed representation is coupled with superimpositional memory, knowledge acquired from past experiences with real words and distributed across the network's connections can be used to respond appropriately to pseudowords as well as real words. Finally, because learning is a process of attunement rather than a process designed to create lexical representations and store them in memory, it must be understood as an ongoing process that results in changes in the pattern of connectivity each time an input is processed, regardless of the lexical status or familiarity of the input.

A third general point to be made here is that the contrast between the connectionist and two-process accounts of priming parallels several prominent debates concerning other aspects of word perception and production. One of these debates concerns reading aloud. According to dual-route models (e.g., Coltheart, 1978; Coltheart et al., 2001), readers have two options: Words can be identified via a lexical look-up route or via the application of grapheme-phoneme conversion rules. Both routes are thought to be necessary because pseudowords cannot be read via the lexical route and rule-violating exception words (e.g., pint, have) cannot be read correctly using sublexical rules. (Regular [rule-following] words can be read via either route.) In contrast, connectionist accounts (Plaut et al., 1996; Seidenberg et al., 1994; Seidenberg and McClelland, 1989) reject the claim that different processes are needed to name exception words and pseudowords. According to these accounts, regular words, exception words, and pseudowords can all be named by a single mechanism—a network trained to map orthographic representations to phonological representations.[4]

A similar (and equally hotly contested) debate concerns the production of English past-tense forms (cf. Rumelhart and McClelland, 1986b; Pinker and Prince, 1988). Here too, dual-route accounts hold that skilled performance depends on two processes: a rule-based mechanism that can be used to generate the past-tense forms of regular words and pseudowords (e.g., wug–wugged), and a second process (lexical look-up) that is needed for rule-violating exception words (e.g., ran, spoke). Again, from a connectionist perspective a single mechanism suffices—a network capable of producing the past-tense form for regular words and pseudowords is also capable of generating the past-tense forms of exception words.

Although the phenomena involved are rather different (repetition priming, word naming, past-tense production), in all three cases the connectionist position is founded on

---

[4] Because phonological codes can be computed either directly or via semantics, there is a sense in which the triangle model is a dual-route model. However, in the triangle model the two routes are more redundant rather than complementary and both routes operate in accordance with the same principles. Moreover, although the relative contributions of the two routes may differ for different types of stimuli, in the triangle model the phonological route plays a fundamental role in the naming of regular words, pseudowords, AND exception words (Harm, 1998; Plaut, 1997; Plaut et al., 1996).

the same basic assumptions (distributed representation; superimpositional storage; incremental learning) and prejudices (that the same fundamental principles are at work across cognitive domains; that a theory of skilled behavior should not be divorced from a theory of learning; that often apparently distinct phenomena turn out to be different facets of the same underlying mechanism). It is also worth noting that in all three cases the two-process accounts are forced into their positions by the discrete nature of the underlying representations and processes. A stimulus either has a lexical representation or not; it either follows the rules or not. The use of distributed representation and superimpositional memory obviate the need for a language user (or a model thereof) to draw such distinctions. Effects of lexicality and regularity are quantitative, not qualitative.

Interference and similarity effects

According to the connectionist account, when a reader encounters a word, the resulting weight changes are distributed across the lexical network's entire connection matrix. Because these weight changes act to strengthen a word's attractor, the next time that word is seen it will be responded to faster and more accurately. The effects of a learning event are more far-reaching than this, however. In particular, because networks employ distributed representation and superimpositional storage, the response to every word is determined by the same set of connections. Thus, learning about one word has consequences for the identification of other words as well. These consequences are reflected in the similarity principle—the tendency for similar inputs to be mapped onto similar outputs. Depending on the circumstances, this tendency may be either beneficial or detrimental.

To further illustrate this point, consider a gravitational system such as a solar system comprised of numerous massive bodies. Each body exerts a gravitational force which attracts nearby objects, but in general the gravitational field controlling the movement of an object is determined jointly by all of the bodies within the system. Thus, changing the mass of one body, or introducing a new body such as a passing star, has consequences for the gravitational field everywhere within the system (although they may be negligible at great enough distances). Note too that the interaction of the gravitational forces generated by different bodies depends on their spatial relationships: When the moon is full, the earth and sun pull in the same direction; when the moon is new they tug in opposite directions.

Gravitational systems provide a useful metaphor for understanding the dynamics of connectionist networks (Tabor and Tanenhaus, 1999). The patterns of activation acting as attractors in the state space of a network are analogous to the bodies of mass acting as attractors in the physical space of a solar system, with similar words occupying nearby positions in space. Similarly, the trajectory of the network's movement through its state space (the changes in its pattern of activation over time) corresponds to the trajectory of an object through the solar system. When learning strengthens a word's attractor, the consequences are (due to superimpositional memory) global: The entire activation flow field changes, although the impact of the changes diminishes with the distance from that word's attractor. Finally, how learning about one word affects the apparent strength of the attractor of another word is situation-dependent: Aligned in one way, strengthening one word's attractor has the effect of moving the system more quickly towards a neighboring word's attractor as well;

aligned in a different way, the effect may be to slow down the rate with which the system moves towards the neighbor, or perhaps prevent the system from getting there at all. In either case, the degree to which learning about one input influences the response to another will vary with similarity—the greater the similarity, the more the interference.

The susceptibility of networks to interference is well-documented, and the factors that modulate its impact are well-understood (cf. Hetherington and Seidenberg, 1989; McClelland *et al.*, 1995; McCloskey and Cohen, 1989; Murre, 1992; Ratcliff, 1990; Rueckl, 1993). What is perhaps less well-appreciated is that from a connectionist perspective inter-ference—the effect of learning about one input on the response to other inputs—underlies a variety of seemingly disparate phenomena. For example, interference clearly underlies for-getting in the A–B A–C paired-associate task (McCloskey and Cohen, 1989). However, from the right vantage point interference also gives rise to the ability to pronounce a nonword aloud or generate its past-tense form. In all three cases, the response to one input is influ-enced by the weight changes made during learning events associated with other inputs. The fact that transfer is beneficial in some cases and detrimental is not uninteresting, but it should not obscure the fact that positive and negative transfer are both forms of interference.

Thus, although it may seem odd to think of nonword naming and forgetting in the paired-associate task as related, from the connectionist perspective they are both conse-quences of superimpositional storage. To take another example, consider the consistency effect in reading aloud described in a previous section: Words with many friends (words with bodies that are pronounced the same way in many words, such as the -*int* in *lint, hint, tint,* and *mint*) are named faster than words with many enemies (words with the same body but a different pronunciation; *hint, tint,* and *mint* are enemies of *pint*). Because friends are similar in both spelling and pronunciation, they require similar patterns of connectivity in the weights between these layers. Thus, the weight changes made to improve the response to one word will generally improve the response to its friends as well. In contrast, because enemies are similar orthographically but not phonologically, they require different patterns of connectivity. In this case, learning about one word weakens the response to its enemies. Consistency effects reflect the degree to which the response to a word benefits from know-ledge of its friends or suffers from the knowledge of its enemies.

To summarize, because networks employ superimpositional memory, strengthening the attractor for one word has consequences for the identification of other words as well. The consistency effect provides one demonstration of the effects of this cross-talk on word identification, but the account predicts that interference should show up in other guises as well. In particular, it predicts that because repetition priming is a manifestation of learn-ing, priming one word should influence not only the subsequent identification of that word, but also the identification of other words, especially words that are similar to the prime. The following sections review the evidence related to this prediction, beginning with evidence of positive transfer and then turning to the negative effects of interference.

Positive transfer effects

One of the first studies to look for evidence of transfer effects in repetition priming was the seminal experiment by Murrell and Morton (1974). Subjects in their experiment were asked to identify tachistoscopically presented words that differed in their relationships to the words on a previously studied list. Compared to words that were unrelated to any of the study items, words that had been presented on the study list were more accurately identified, as were words that had been primed by a morphological relative (e.g., *cars–car*). In contrast, priming had no effect on the identification of target words that were related to study items orthographically but not morphologically (e.g., *card–car*). Thus, Murrell and Morton found evidence for a transfer effect in long-term repetition priming, but in their study transfer extended only to morphologically related words.

The implications of morphological priming will be considered in a subsequent section. For now the question we will address is whether transfer effects occur on the basis of orthographic similarity. The Murrell and Morton (1974) results suggest not: The identification of a target word was neither facilitated nor impaired as a result of studying an orthographically related word. A variety of other studies have yielded similar patterns of results (e.g., Napps and Fowler, 1987; Ross *et al.*, 1956; Ratcliff and McKoon, 1996; Rueckl *et al.*, 1997). However, before the conclusion is drawn that repetition priming has *no* effect on orthographically similar words, it should be noted that the results of several other studies suggest exactly the opposite.

For example, evidence of a purely orthographic transfer effect in word identification was reported by Feustel *et al.* (1983), who found that the naming latency for a letter string emerging from a background noise mask was faster when it had been preceded by an orthographically similar item. For words, this effect was statistically significant only when the prime had already been presented three or four times: after one or two presentations of the prime, a non-significant trend was obtained. In contrast, with pseudoword targets a single presentation of the prime was enough to produce similarity priming, although again the amount of facilitation increased with the number of presentations of the prime.

Transfer effects based on orthographic similarity have also been found when target items were primed by clusters of orthographically similar items. In one line of experiments, this was accomplished by constructing all of the primes from a set of 13 letters. In experiments employing this *similarity priming* paradigm (Rueckl, 1990; Rueckl, submitted; Rueckl and Olds, 1993), the identification of new items that were similar in spelling to the study items (by virtue of being composed of letters from the same letter set) were more accurately identified than items that were composed only of letters not appearing during the study task. Similarity priming was observed for both words and pseudowords, and cross-experiment comparisons suggested that the transfer effect was due to facilitation in the identification of the similar items, rather than a decrement in the identification of the dissimilar items. An effect of positive transfer on pseudoword identification was also reported by Whittlesea (1987), who generated cohorts of orthographically similar pseudowords by adapting a technique commonly used in categorization studies: Several five-letter pseudowords were chosen as 'prototypes', and a set of 'category members' were generated by replacing one, two, three, or four letters in the prototype. Whittlesea found that the identification of a previously unseen pseudoword was facilitated by the prior presentation of pseudowords from the same category; the degree to which a new pseudoword benefited from transfer increased with its similarity to the primes (and hence, typically, with its similarity to the prototype).

Facilitative effects have also been found with regard to other dimensions of similarity. Consider, for example, the results of a series of experiments investigating the effects of rhyme priming on visual stem completion. During the study phase of these experiments, subjects read either a list of words (Mandler *et al.*, 1986; Mandler *et al.*, 1990) or a poem (Overson and Mandler, 1987) that contained words that rhymed with a target word, but not the target word itself. Relative to an unprimed baseline condition, rhyme priming both increased the likelihood that target words were generated during a subsequent stem completion task (Mandler *et al.*, 1986, 1990; Overson and Mandler, 1987) and reduced the time needed to generate these completions (Mandler *et al.*, 1990). Although the effect of rhyme priming appears to be fairly short-lived relative to full identity priming (Mandler *et al.*, 1986), the fact that it occurs at all provides evidence of similarity-based transfer effects in repetition priming.

Semantic similarity can also give rise to transfer effects. For example, although it is fairly widely believed that long-term priming does not occur on the basis of semantic related-ness, Becker *et al.* (1997) observed just such an effect using a variant of the similarity priming paradigm. In their experiment, lexical decisions were facilitated for target words that were semantically related to a number of words on a study list, even though the critical targets were not themselves presented during study. A similar result was obtained by McDermott (1997) using Deese's (1959) paradigm, which also involves priming a target word with a set of semantically associated words. Finally, Joordens and Becker (1997) demonstrated that under some conditions the presentation of even a single semantic associate can give rise to similarity priming.

In sum, a number of results suggest that the processing of a word or pseudoword can benefit from a recent experience with a similar item. However, it must also be noted that a number of studies looking for such effects have failed to find them. To some extent, methodological factors are probably responsible for this 'now you see it, now you don't' pattern. In most of the studies that failed to detect positive transfer, a target was primed by a single similar item (Murrell and Morton, 1974; Napps and Fowler, 1987; Ratcliff and McKoon, 1996; Rueckl and Mathew, 1999). In contrast, many of the studies where positive transfer was observed involved either multiple related primes (Becker *et al.*, 1997; McDermott, 1997; Rueckl, 1990; Rueckl, submitted; Rueckl and Olds, 1993) or multiple repetitions of a single related prime (Feustel *et al.*, 1983; also see Seidenberg and McClelland, 1989, Fig. 15). Moreover, positive transfer effects in priming appear to be stronger for pseudowords than for real words (Feustel *et al.*, 1983; Rueckl, 1990), and stronger for 3rd graders than for skilled adult readers (cf. Feldman *et al.*, in press; Rueckl *et al.*, 1997). Together, these results suggest that positive transfer effects are (not surpris-ingly) relatively weak, and hence are more likely to be detected with items that benefit from multiple learning events or have relatively weak attractors to begin with.

Negative transfer effects

Another likely reason for the somewhat elusive nature of positive transfer effects is that priming one word can also have detrimental consequences for the identification of other words. Thus, whether positive or negative transfer will be observed depends on the balance between these cooperative and competitive effects.

Investigations of negative transfer effects have taken two general approaches. One approach seeks to determine whether priming one word reduces the magnitude of repetition effects for other primed words. For example, Jacoby (1983) had subjects perform both a study task (naming words aloud) and a test task (tachistoscopic identification) on each of five successive days. As expected, previously presented words were more accurately identified than unstudied words. However, the magnitude of this effect did not diminish over the five days, thus providing no evidence for the build-up of proactive interference. Moreover, a final identification task at the end of the fifth day revealed approximately equivalent levels of priming for words studied on days 1–5, thus suggesting that priming had not been diminished by retroactive interference. Experiments by Graf and Schacter (1987) and Sloman *et al.* (1988) also failed to find any evidence that the priming of one word has retroactive or proactive effects on the priming of another word.

Although the results described above suggest that repetition priming is not susceptible to negative transfer, the findings of several other studies point towards the opposite conclusion. Mayes *et al.* (1987) had subjects study two lists of semantically related word pairs. The word pairs for the second list were constructed by pairing each cue from the first list with another related word (thus, if *bee–wasp* was on the first list, *bee–honey* was on the second). Mayes *et al.* found more priming on a free association task for words from the first list than for words from the second list, suggesting that proactive interference had reduced the priming effect in the second phase. Similarly, Nelson *et al.* (1989) found evidence of retroactive interference in an experiment investigating priming in the word fragment completion task. Nelson *et al.* found that subjects who saw two lists were less likely to complete a fragment with a word from the first list than were subjects that only saw that list, provided that the words on the two lists were orthographically related.

Although the Mayes *et al.* (1987) and Nelson *et al.* (1989) studies appear to provide evidence of both proactive and retroactive interference in implicit memory, both studies employed 'non-unique cues'—cues for which more than one primed word was an acceptable response. This raises the possibility that the reductions in priming observed in these studies were artifacts arising from the constraint that only one primed item could be generated on each trial. However, Booker (1992) reported a series of experiments in which statistical procedures were used to correct for this response constraint and still obtained evidence that priming was reduced by proactive interference. Rueckl (submitted) also found that priming was reduced by proactive interference in a variant of the similarity priming paradigm where the presentation of primes composed of letters from one 13-letter set was followed by the presentation of primes composed of letters from the complementary 13-letter set.

Thus, one line of evidence suggests that priming one word reduces the magnitude of repetition effects for other primed words. A second line of evidence indicates that negative transfer influences the processing of unprimed words as well. For example, in the same experiments that demonstrated proactive interference on identity priming, Rueckl (submitted) also showed that positive transfer effects were eliminated when a set of primes composed of one set of letters was followed by another set of primes composed of different letters. Thus, for the unprimed test words, what one set of primes giveth, another set of primes taketh way.

Negative transfer effects on unprimed words have been observed in other experimental paradigms as well. For example, Smith and Tindell (1997) found that subjects were less likely to find the target word completing a word fragment (e.g., *symphony* for *s_mp_o_y*) if they had been primed with an orthographically similar word (e.g., *sympathy*). (Also see Lustig and Hasher, 2001.) Bowers *et al.* (in press) reported an experiment where positive transfer was found for word pairs that rhymed (e.g., *boast–toast*), but negative transfer was found for word pairs that did not (e.g., *pint–mint*).

One paradigm that has played an especially prominent role in the study of negative transfer effects is the two-alternative forced-choice task (Ratcliff and McKoon, 1996, 1997). In this paradigm the presentation of a tachistoscopically presented target word is followed by the presentation of two response alternatives; the reader's task is to decide which of the alternatives had been presented as the target. Studies using this paradigm have consistently found that relative to an unprimed baseline, performance is better if the target had been presented during an earlier task, but worse if that non-target alternative had been primed (e.g., Bowers, 1999; Ratcliff and McKoon, 1996, 1997; and many others). Moreover, costs associated with a primed non-target alternative occur when the alternatives are orthographically similar (e.g., *lied–died*) but not when they are dissimilar (e.g., *sofa–died*). Although certain issues concerning the forced-choice paradigm remain rather controversial,[5] the resulting body of findings provides clear evidence of negative transfer: Under some conditions priming one word diminishes the likelihood that another word will be correctly identified.

Interference and similarity effects: redux

In summary, the evidence concerning similarity-based transfer effects in priming is mixed in two respects. First, transfer effects based on similarity in form or meaning are somewhat elusive—they've been found in some experiments, but not in others. Second, when they do occur, their effect is sometimes beneficial and sometimes detrimental.

The elusive nature of these effects suggests that transfer effects are relatively small, especially for skilled readers reading familiar words, and thus that various methodological factors can either bring them into view or submerge them into the background noise. A number of likely factors have been identified, including the number and variety of the primes that are similar to a given target, the familiarity of that target, and the amount of experience that a reader brings into the experimental setting.

The fact that transfer effects can take the form of either costs or benefits probably reflects several trade-offs among the consequences of the learning that takes place when a word is identified. First, at the microlevel modifying the weights to strengthen the attractor for one word will generally have both helpful and costly effects on the degree to which those weights are also appropriate for a similar word. For example, learning about *mint* increases the strength of the association between the word body *-int* and the word rime /-int/, thus benefiting processing of *hint* as well as *mint*. On the other hand, the association between *-int* and the phonological onset /m/ also get stronger, to the benefit of *mint* but at a cost to *hint*.

---

[5] Controversies concerning the forced-choice paradigm include whether the effects of priming reflect increased sensitivity as well as bias (cf. Bowers, 1999; Neaderhiser and Church, 2000; Ratcliff and McKoon, 1997), and the extent to which the costs and benefits observed in this paradigm reflect the effects of priming on the processing of the target or on the processing of the response alternatives (see Bowers, 1999, for discussion).

A second potential trade-off concerns the competitive interactions among attractors in determining the activation dynamics. Although priming may increase the strength of the attractor for a word that is similar to the prime, the attractor for the prime itself will be strengthened to an even greater extent. Thus, in situations where these attractors are put into competition, the effect of priming is to put the attractor for the similar word in a competitive disadvantage, even if the attractor for the similar word is stronger in an absolute sense (e.g., in terms of *energy*; Hopfield, 1982; Masson, 1995). The analogy with a gravitational system illustrates this point. Given one alignment (sun, earth, moon) increasing the mass of the sun pulls the moon towards the earth; given another alignment (sun, moon, earth), increasing the mass of the sun acts to pull the moon away from the earth. In this case, the border between the basins of attraction for the sun and the earth has shifted towards the earth.[6]

The gravitational analogy suggests that negative transfer effects should be most likely to occur in tasks that highlight the competition among similar words. Thus, perhaps it is not surprising that some of the strongest evidence for negative transfer has comes from experiments using the two-alternative forced-choice procedure. By specifying two response alternatives, there is a sense in which this task seems to pit their attractors in a direct competition, with priming tilting the outcome towards the repeated alternative. That negative transfer doesn't occur when the alternatives are dissimilar (e.g., *lied–sofa*) suggests that little competition occurs between distant attractors.[7]

Although this line of reasoning seems promising, much work remains before its promise can be fully evaluated. In particular, the methodological factors that determine whether similar words will cooperate or compete are not well understood. In this light, it is worth noting that a similar issue has cropped up with regard to neighborhood effects in word identification. Neighborhood effects (effects of the number of words that are similar to a target, as well as the frequency and distribution of these 'neighbors') have been a focus of intense scrutiny in the word identification literature, and for reasons not yet fully understood, they turn out to appear in both facilitative and inhibitory forms (see Andrews, 1997; Grainger and Jacobs, 1996, for reviews). Because both neighborhood effects and transfer effects in priming involve the mechanisms by which the identification of one word is influenced by experience with other words, it is not unreasonable to speculate that identifying the factors that determine the balance between competition and cooperation in one domain will help clarify the results of the other as well.

Morphological priming

As noted above, Murrell and Morton (1974) found that the identification of a target word (e.g., *car*) was facilitated by the prior presentation of a morphologically related word

---

[6] To make the analogy more complete, one could suppose that when the mass of the sun in increased, the mass of the earth is also increased, but to a lesser extent. The primary point about competition and cooperation holds in either case, however.

[7] These intuitions are incorporated into Ratcliff and McKoon's (1997) counter model, which was devised largely to account for results involving the forced-choice task. One might argue that to the degree that the counter model succeeds, it does so because the processes it proposes mirror the activation and learning dynamics of a connectionist network.

(e.g., *cars*). In the years since, this basic finding has been replicated and extended in a variety of ways (see Feldman, 1991; Henderson, 1985, for reviews). Morphological priming has been demonstrated in a variety of languages (including Hebrew, Bentin and Feldman, 1990, Serbo-Croatian, Feldman and Fowler, 1987, and Italian, Burani and Carramazza, 1987, to name just a few). Moreover, although morphologically related words are usually related in form (i.e., spelling and pronunciation) and meaning, morphological priming cannot be attributed solely to similarity along these dimensions (Bentin and Feldman, 1990; Napps, 1989; Napps and Fowler, 1987; Stolz and Feldman, 1995).

For the most part, explanations of morphological priming fall into one of three categories: *Decompositional* accounts (e.g., Taft and Forster, 1975), which assume that words are parsed into their morphological constituents in order to access the lexicon; *Whole-word* accounts (e.g., Feldman and Fowler, 1987; Lukatela *et al.*, 1980), which hold that although each word has its own lexical entry, the lexicon is organized so that morphological relationships are explicitly represented (for example, by direct connections among the entries for morphologically related words); and *Dual-process* accounts (e.g., Baayen *et al.*, 1997; Caramazza *et al.*, 1988; Stanners *et al.*, 1979), which assume that both decompositional and whole-word processes are at work. Although these accounts differ from one another in many respects, they all assume that long-term priming is a consequence of a change in the activation of a pre-existing representation, and that priming transfers between morphological relatives because the lexicon is organized around morphological principles. More generally, because they are formulated within the activation tradition described in the Introduction, all of these accounts are meant to explain not just morphological priming, but rather a variety of phenomena involving the effects of morphological structure on word identification.

The connectionist framework provides a different perspective on morphological priming—one that views morphological effects not as the consequence of the structural properties of the lexicon, but instead as the influence of statistical regularities on the dynamics of the network that is responsible for visual word identification. On this view, morphological effects stem from the fact that, with the exception of morphologically related words, similarity in word-form bears no relationship to similarity in word meaning. Hence, morphological relationships are virtually the only source of statistical regularities in the mappings between (orthographic and phonological) form and meaning. Through the covariant learning process, these regularities structure a network's weight matrices, and as a result are reflected in that network's behavior, not only in long-term morphological priming, but also in phenomena such as short-term priming (e.g., Gonnerman *et al.*, 1995), morpheme-frequency effects (e.g., Taft, 1979), and family-size effects (Schreuder and Baayen, 1997).

Put another way, from a connectionist perspective morphological effects are fundamentally interference effects: Because morphological relatives are similar in form and meaning, changing the weights to strengthen the attractor for one word also strengthens the attractors for morphologically related words. Thus, morphological effects are a manifestation of the same similarity principle that is at work in a variety of superficially unrelated phenomena. For example, just as morphological effects arise from the tendency to map similar orthographic patterns to similar semantic patterns, phonological consistency effects arise from the tendency to map similar orthographic patterns to similar phonological outputs.

Note, however, that whereas the mapping from orthography to phonology is highly structured, the mapping from form to meaning is largely arbitrary, and thus the structure imparted by morphological regularities is especially influential.

If morphological priming is a transfer effect, the degree to which priming one word facilitates a morphological relative should vary with their similarity. Thus, for example, root forms (e.g., *teach*) would be expected to be primed more strongly by regular inflections (e.g., *teaching*), which are highly similar to their root forms, than by irregular inflections (e.g., *taught*), which are usually formed by changing the orthographic and/or phonological properties of their base forms. This prediction is, in fact, consistent with experimental results (Feldman, 1994; Stanners *et al.*, 1979). However, this pattern of results can also be accounted for by models that assume that morphological relationships are explicitly represented in the lexicon, provided that different classes of morphological relationships are represented in different ways (i.e., dual-process models such as Stanners *et al.*, 1979). Thus, the contrast between priming effects involving regular and irregular inflections is not particularly diagnostic.

Thus, a more telling case involves variability in similarity when the morphological relationship between the prime and target is held constant. For example, some irregular past-tense forms are fairly similar to their root forms (e.g., *made–make, swam–swim*), whereas others are less similar (e.g., *took–take, bought–buy*). From a connectionist perspective, more morphological priming would be expected in the former case. In contrast, models that link morphological priming to the explicit representation of morphology in the lexicon would be hard-pressed to explain an effect of formal similarity within morphological class.

It turns out that formal similarity does modulate morphological priming, although the effect is sometimes rather small. Thus, experiments by Fowler *et al.* (1985), Napps (1989), Stanners *et al.* (1979), and Stolz and Feldman (1995), all failed to find an effect of orthographic similarity on morphological priming. However, in each case the numerical trend was towards less priming with less orthographic similarity, and a meta-analysis indicates that consistent trend is itself statistically reliable (Rueckl *et al.*, 1997). Moreover, all of these experiments investigated morphological priming using the lexical decision task, which may be relatively insensitive to orthographic factors. In two experiments using word fragment completion, Rueckl *et al.* (1997) found strong and statistically significant effects of orthographic similarity on the magnitude of morphological priming. Similar results have been reported by Gonnerman *et al.* (1995) concerning morphological effects in short-term priming. (Although the connectionist account assumes that different mechanisms underlie short- and long-term, the rationale for why priming should vary with similarity is essentially the same in both cases—see Gonnerman *et al.*, 1995; Plaut and Gonnerman, 2000; Raveh and Rueckl, 2000; Rueckl and Raveh, 1999.)

Another prediction of the connectionist account is that if morphological effects are due to the structure that morphological regularities impart on the mappings from form to meaning, other regularities that structure this mapping should give rise to similar sorts of effects. To test this prediction, Rueckl and Dror (1994) asked subjects to study a set of pseudoword-definition pairings over a five-week period. For some of the subjects, the pairings were constructed so that pseudowords with word bodies were systematically paired with semantic categories (e.g., *durch–dog, hurch–cat, murch–cow*). For other subjects, the same set of pseudowords and definitions comprised the training set, but the pairings of pseudowords and definitions were constructed so that no such regularities existed (e.g., *durch–dog, hurch–shirt, murch–table*). The results revealed that the structured pairings were easier to learn, and, more importantly, that the pseudowords in this condition were more accurately identified in a tachistoscopic identification task. The advantage of the systematic pairings reflects the manner in which these pairings structure the mapping between form and meaning. As the memory traces for learning events involving these pairings are superimposed on the network's connections, their shared structure (or lack thereof) shapes the pattern of connectivity, which in turn shapes the network's flow of activation and the behavior that manifests this flow.

Perceptual specificity effects

The previous sections were concerned with the degree to which priming one word influences the subsequent processing of other words on the basis of formal, semantic, or morphological similarity. In this section we consider transfer not from one word to another, but instead from one token of a word to perceptually distinct tokens of that same word. The question of interest is whether changing the perceptual characteristics of a word between study and test diminishes the magnitude of repetition priming. This question goes to the heart of a major theoretical divide concerning the nature of perception, memory, and cognition more generally.

On one side of the divide, developed largely within the activation tradition discussed in the Introduction, are abstractionist theories (e.g., Bowers, 1996; Grainger and Jacobs, 1996; McClelland and Rumelhart, 1981; Morton, 1979; Paap *et al.*, 1982). These theories assume that because the visual (or acoustic) details that distinguish different tokens of a word are irrelevant to that word's identity, information about these details can and should be discarded relatively early in the identification process. Thus, according to abstractionist theories, the processing of a written word results in a representation of its abstract orthographic structure in a form that is invariant over differences in case, font, and so on. Because these representations do not preserve information about visual detail, abstractionist theories predict that equivalent levels of priming should be found regardless of whether the prime and target are visually identical.

On the other side of the divide, developed largely within the memory tradition, are instance-based theories of perception and cognition (e.g., Goldinger, 1998; Jacoby and Brooks, 1984; Kolers, 1979; Whittlesea, 1987). In the case of visual word identification, these theories deny the involvement of abstract lexical representations, and hold instead that a word is identified through the retrieval of memory traces for previous processing episodes. Each trace contains a record of the processes conducted during the corresponding episode, and the contribution of each to the identification process depends on the extent to which the stimulus and other contextual cues match the information stored in that trace. Repetition priming reflects the relative accessibility of memory traces for recent events. Because these traces are thought to be highly detailed, instance theories predict that priming should be reduced by changes in perceptual detail between study and test.

A large body of experimental evidence can be marshaled in support of each view. On the one hand, the abstractionist position is supported by a number of studies which have found that a change in case (Feustel *et al.*, 1983; Scarborough *et al.*, 1977), typeface (Carr *et al.*, 1989; Rajaram and Roediger, 1993), or script (Bowers and Michita, 1998; Brown *et al.*, 1984; Feldman and Moskovljevic, 1987) has little or no effect on the size of the priming effect. The abstractionist position is also supported by an array of findings from other experimental paradigms (e.g., eye tracking, McConkie and Zola, 1979; Rayner *et al.*, 1980; masked priming, Evett and Humphreys, 1981; and CaSe MiXiNg, Besner and Johnston, 1989; Coltheart and Freeman, 1981) which suggest that word identification is driven primarily by preliminary letter identification, and not by the extraction of more holistic features that would not be invariant over differences in case or font.

Although the abstractionist position is supported by a variety of experimental results, it is not wholly consistent with the empirical data. For example, even though a number of studies have found that a change in the visual-form a word has no effect on repetition priming, a comparable number of studies have found that priming is reduced by a change in form (e.g., Brown and Carr, 1993; Jacoby and Hayman, 1987; Kolers, 1975; see Tenpenny, 1995, for a review). Similarly, although the abstractionist position is supported by the finding that the word superiority effect survives case mixing, the complex interaction of case mixing and variables such as lexicality, word frequency, and task (e.g., lexical decision, naming) has led some theorists to argue that word recognition depends, in part, on representations that preserve at least some information about visual-form, and thus are not fully invariant over differences in case and font (Allen *et al.*, 1995; Mayall *et al.*, 1997). More generally, from the perspective of a language user, information about visual detail obviously makes a difference. English, for instance, is not unusual in having a complex set of rules specifying when a word must be capitalized. In addition, writers often make use of a set of conventions that allow them to vary the look of a word in ways that carry shades of meaning—e.g., stressing a word by either italicizing it or typing it in uppercase (e.g., 'I've got a BIG problem'.). Such rules and conventions would be pointless if readers paid no attention to letter case or type font.

In sum, neither the abstractionist position nor the instance approach is wholly consistent with key experimental findings, yet each position enjoys a substantial amount of empirical (and theoretical) support. One way to resolve this apparent paradox is to adopt a two-process model that includes both abstractionist and non-abstractionist components. For example, in the memory literature, the mixed effect of perceptual format manipulations on repetition priming has been taken to indicate that two kinds of representations underlie priming, one of which is perceptually abstract and the other of which preserves information about perceptual detail (Bowers, 1996; Brown and Carr, 1993; Marsolek *et al.*, 1992). Similarly, in the word identification literature, recent accounts of the effects of case mixing have posited that preliminary letter identification is supplemented by another process that uses word-specific visual patterns to access the lexical code associated with a visual input (McClelland, 1977; Mayall *et al.*, 1997) or to assess the familiarity of that input (Besner *et al.*, 1984; Besner and Johnston, 1989).

The connectionist perspective offers a different resolution of this empirical paradox. In an important sense, the dynamics of a connectionist network gives rise to abstraction while simultaneously allowing for the preservation of visual detail (McClelland and Rumelhart, 1985). From this perspective, findings that suggest abstraction and findings that suggest preservation of detail do not reflect the operation of two complementary processes, but rather are different manifestations of the same underlying process—the activation dynamics of a network employing distributed representation, superimpositional memory, and incremental learning.

To flesh out this idea, it should first be noted that although the weight changes that result from an experience with a word are distributed throughout the lexical network, the connections of most relevance to the issue at hand are those that project to or from the so-called 'orthographic' layer. In most extant connectionist models, the representations schemes employed at this level (e.g., 'wickelgraphs', Seidenberg and McClelland, 1989; position-specific letter units, Plaut *et al.*, 1996) are abstractionist in the sense that they carry information about the identity and order of the letters that comprise a word, but not about the case, font, or other properties of those letters. Indeed, the very labeling of this layer as the 'orthographic' layer reflects the abstractionist bent of these representational schemes. Thus, for reasons that will become apparent, throughout the rest of this section I will refer to this layer as the *visual word-form*, or *VWF*, layer.

For the most part, the use of abstractionist schemes has been pragmatically motivated. Because the VWF layer typically serves as the 'input' layer, the primary constraint on the representations at this level has been that they must be appropriate for capturing the sorts of statistical regularities that characterize, for example, the mapping from orthography to phonology. This is not an unreasonable strategy, particularly given that the debate over abstraction is largely tied to findings that are outside of the scope of phenomena extant models have been intended to address. Nonetheless, the sort of representational schemes typically used fail to take advantage of one of the most interesting properties of connectionist networks—the ability of a network to develop its own representational schemes as it learns about the structure of its environment. As many modelers can attest, a network left to its own devices will usually develop a representational scheme that is an appropriate (and often surprisingly elegant) solution for the computational problem that confronts it.

Thus, to address the abstraction issue from a connectionist perspective, one should apply the maxim 'They're all hidden units'. This means that rather than treating the VWF layer as the lexical network's input layer, the VWF layer is better thought of as a hidden layer that receives connections from an input layer representing the visual properties of a stimulus (say, in terms of coarsely coded retinotopic features) and sends connections to output layers responsible for representing a word's phonological and semantic properties. If the VWF layer is treated in this way, the goal of the modeler is not to specify the VWF representations a priori, but instead to determine what sort of organization will arise given the statistical structure of the tasks that the lexical network must perform.

One important constraint on the organization of a hidden layer's representations is the similarity principle—the tendency for similar states to have similar consequences. The similarity principle implies that the organization of a hidden layer's representations will tend to reflect both the organization of the patterns of activation that evoke them (such that if two input patterns are similar, they tend to evoke similar hidden patterns) and the organization of the patterns of activation that they in turn evoke (hence, similar output patterns also tend to be associated with similar hidden patterns). (See Plaut *et al.*, 1996; Rueckl and Raveh, 1999, for analyses illustrating this point.) In the case of the VWF layer, this implies that the organization of the VWF patterns will reflect a balance of both visual (bottom-up) and phonological and semantic (top-down) influences. The bottom-up constraints pressure the network to map similar visual inputs to similar VWF patterns. Conversely, the top-down constraints pressure the network to assign similar hidden patterns to input patterns that are similar in *function* (i.e., are mapped to similar phonological and semantic output representations). In some cases the bottom-up and top-down forces act in concert—that is, some visually similar forms (e.g., R/R, C/c) are generally mapped to the same phonological and semantic outputs. However, in many cases the bottom-up and top-down constraints are at odds: Visually similar forms (e.g., r/n) may be functionally dissimilar, and functionally similar forms (e.g., R/r) may be visually dissimilar.

Note that in some ways these constraints tend to that favor the adoption of an abstractionist representational scheme, but that in other ways they exert pressure in favor of the preservation of perceptual detail. With the exception of the relatively rare cases where differences in visual-form carry information about meaning (e.g., *Mark* versus *mark*, *Penny* versus *penny*), top-down constraints generally favor abstraction in the VWF layer. That is, these constraints pressure the system to assign similar VWF patterns to visual inputs that have similar phonological and semantic properties, even if they are visually dissimilar. In contrast, because bottom-up constraints pressure the system to map visually similar inputs to similar VWF patterns, these constraints often work against the tendency for abstraction by bringing together the hidden representation for functionally distinct inputs (e.g., *r* versus *n*) and pulling apart the hidden representations for functionally equivalent inputs (e.g., *R* versus *r*). Thus, the similarity principle implies that the organization of the VWF representations will be influenced by both constraints that pressure the system towards abstraction and constraints that pressure it towards an organization that preserves perceptual detail, and thus that the degree to which a network's VWF representations are perceptually abstract or perceptually detailed depends on the balance between these constraints.

A related principle provides further clarification of this issue. According to the principle of *quasi-equivalent states*, distinct patterns of activation can have the same behavioral consequences. In fact, due to both the linear transformations that occur when a pattern of activation is projected over a set of weights and the non-linear transformations that occur when the resulting excitatory and inhibitory signals are passed through an activation function, in some cases distinct patterns of activation at one layer result in responses that are literally indistinguishable at the next. More generally, however, if two patterns of activation at one level evoke highly similar responses, these patterns may be for all intents and purposes indistinguishable to an outside observer (hence the term '*quasi-equivalent*').

The principle of quasi-equivalent states implies that although the top-down constraints favoring abstraction must be honored, they need not completely override the bottom-up constraints favoring an organization based on visual, rather than functional, similarity. Consequently, although it is appropriate to think about the representation of a particular *token* of a word as a pattern of activation, or point in the network's state space, the representation of a word *type* is better thought of as a region of such points—a 'region of functional equivalence' (see Elman, 1995). Visually distinct tokens of the same word (e.g., BAR, bar) can be represented by different points within this region, and yet the network can respond appropriately to each. If the two patterns are similar enough, the behaviors they drive will be virtually identical. As their differences grow, however, they may well have different behavioral consequences. Such consequences might occur, for example, if they differ in the efficiency with which they produce their associated phonological and semantic output patterns, even though, by assumption, they ultimately produce identical output patterns.[8] On this view, abstraction is not all-or-none but a matter of degree. Whether the representations involved in word identification appear to be abstract or perceptually detailed depends on both the similarity of the VWF patterns activated by different visual-forms and the measure of performance used to assess a reader's internal state.

This perspective on the representation of visual word-form suggests a way to reconcile the conflicting patterns of results described above. Advocates of the abstractionist and instance approaches have often attempted to reconcile these patterns by downplaying the implications of one set of results or the other. For example, proponents of abstractionist accounts (e.g., Bowers, 1996; Carr *et al.*, 1989; Ratcliff and McKoon, 1997) have sometimes argued that specificity effects usually occur under relatively atypical circumstances (e.g., when stimuli are presented in highly unusual fonts), and that these effects therefore reflect the operation of a supplementary process that plays little role in 'normal' reading. Conversely, proponents of episodic theories of priming (e.g., Jacoby and Hayman, 1987; Tenpenny, 1995) have downplayed evidence favoring the abstractionist position by pointing out that this evidence rests on the acceptance of a null effect and that, in most cases where the specificity effect is not statistically significant, the trend is in the right direction.

From the connectionist perspective, the claim that specificity effects have little to do with 'normal' reading, like the claim that pseudoword identification has little to do with word identification, rings hollow. At the same time, although it is certainly true that null effects must be treated cautiously, the fact that specificity effects often fail to occur must be given some weight. Thus, it seems likely that both patterns of results hold important clues about the nature of the processes that underlie word perception. Indeed, it is no accident that the word identification system seems to operate in an abstractionist mode in some circumstances and a non-abstractionist mode in others—these patterns of behavior reflect the fact that the dynamics of visual word identification are under the influence of a multiplicity of factors.

Consider, for example, the effect of script familiarity on specificity effects in priming. As several authors have pointed out (Bowers, 1996; Brown and Carr, 1993; Tenpenny, 1995), specificity effects seem to occur more reliably when the target stimuli have relatively novel surface forms. Specificity effects are often found when the target words are handwritten (Brown and Carr, 1993), printed in an unusual font (e.g., Graf and Ryan, 1990; Jacoby and Hayman, 1987), or presented in alternating case (Brooks, 1978). In contrast, when the target words are printed in a standard type font, specificity effects often fail to occur (e.g., Brown and Carr, 1993; Levy and Kirsner, 1989; Scarborough *et al.*, 1977), even if the primes are presented in relatively novel forms. Thus, there is an asymmetry in the transfer of

---

[8] With a sufficiently large distance between the patterns, of course, the patterns will fall into different regions of equivalence, and hence will be mapped onto different output patterns.

priming between typical and atypical visual-forms: Relative to the same-form condition, atypical forms prime typical forms more fully than the reverse.

This asymmetry in the transfer of priming between typical and atypical visual-forms can be understood in terms of the effect of learning on the dynamics of a system that is better-attuned for the processing of typical forms. Because a stimulus printed in a standard type font is more representative of the experiences that have structured the network's weights, a word written in a typical script will be represented by an attractor near the center of that word's region of functional equivalence, and consequently, because it benefits from a relatively large number of past experiences, the activation dynamics stabilize relatively quickly. In contrast, a word written in an unusual form will be represented by an attractor on the periphery of its region of functional equivalence, and because it benefits less from past experiences, the activation dynamics take longer to settle. As a result of these differences in the 'baseline' dynamics, the effect of a single additional learning event will have a greater impact on the processing of atypical forms than on the processing of typical forms, and as well, the effect of differences in the visual-form of the prime and target will be magnified. Thus, specificity effects should be more readily observed when the target is presented in an unusual form, even though (in an absolute sense) a change in the form between study and test must always result in a reduction in priming.

It is worth noting that each facet of this account is consistent with extant data. Words printed in unusual forms are generally more difficult to process (Adams, 1979; Allen *et al.*, 1995; Besner *et al.*, 1984; Brown and Carr, 1993; McClelland, 1976). As well, in experiments where a specificity effect is obtained in one condition but not another, the magnitude of same-form priming is usually greater in the condition where the specificity effect was found (e.g., Bowers, 1996; Brown and Carr, 1993; Marsolek *et al.*, 1992). Finally, specificity effects are sometimes found with stimuli presented in standard fonts (Blaxton, 1989; Jacoby and Hayman, 1987), and as noted above, when the specificity effect does not reach statistical significance, the numerical difference between the same- and different-form conditions is consistently in the expected direction (Tenpenny, 1995). This pattern is consistent with the position that the effect of script familiarity on the specificity effect is quantitative rather than qualitative.

Although script typicality appears to play an especially critical role in determining the magnitude of specificity effects, other factors may also be relevant. For example, specificity effects appear to be larger for low-frequency words than for high-frequency words (Jacoby and Hayman, 1987), and for pseudoword targets than for word targets (Bowers, 1996; Brown and Carr, 1993).[9] Because more encounters with an input tend to increase the 'center of mass' of a word's region of functional equivalence, attractors for tokens of a high-frequency words will tend to gravitate toward the center of that word's region more so than will the attractors for low-frequency words or pseudowords. Thus, high-frequency

---

[9] Brown and Carr (1993) concluded that specificity effects were equivalent for words and pseudowords. However, their conclusion was based on analyses combining lexical decision and speeded naming data, and as noted in an earlier section, the lexical decision task may be an inappropriate task for studying pseudoword priming. In fact, in the lexical decision task, Brown and Carr did not obtain a significant pseudoword priming effect. When only the naming results are considered, the specificity effect was about 11 ms for pseudowords and about 2 ms for words.

words will tend to be represented by relatively 'abstract' representations, whereas the representations of pseudowords will tend to preserve perceptual detail. Moreover, because lexicality and word frequency influence an item's baseline settling time, they modulate the sensitivity to specificity manipulations in the same manner as does script typicality.

Manipulations of task demands have also been associated with differences in specificity effects in repetition priming. For example, with other factors held constant, a change in visual format reduced priming when the study task emphasized perceptual processing, but not when the study task focused on semantic properties (Blaxton, 1989; Curran et al., 1996; Graf and Ryan, 1990). It is not hard to see how task demands might affect the dynamics of word identification to give rise to this pattern of results. Network models often include 'gain' parameters that specify the slope of the activation function computed by nodes within a layer or the rate with which this activation is transmitted to other layers (Farrar and Van Orden, submitted; Hinton and Sejnowski, 1986; Plaut et al., 1996). These parameters could easily be tuned in accordance with task demands. For example, when the task draws attention to the perceptual characteristics of the stimulus, the control parameters might be set so that the bottom-up influence on the dynamics is relatively strong. Conversely, if the task emphasizes higher-level processes, the gain parameters at these levels might be increased, shifting the balance towards more top-down influence on the activation dynamics. As the balance between the bottom-up and top-down influences on the activation dynamics shifts with task demands, so too would the likelihood that priming would be affected by a change in visual-form.

A final factor that should be considered with regard to specificity effects is hemispheric specialization. In a series of studies, Marsolek and others (Marsolek et al., 1992, 1994; Marsolek and Burgund, 1997; Marsolek and Hudson, 1999) have found that specificity effects are larger when the right hemisphere plays a relatively large role in visual processing (as a consequence of lateralized presentation, for example). Because network models of letter and word processing have rarely taken cerebral lateralization into account (see Shevtsova and Reggia, 1999, for an exception), these findings pose a challenge for the connectionist approach. One possibility is to modify the structure of the triangle model so that the phonological and semantic pathways receive input from two layers of nodes corresponding to visual word-form areas in the left and right hemisphere. If, as the data suggest, the VWF area in the left hemisphere tends to adopt a more abstractionist organization than the corresponding right hemisphere structure, one could ask whether this difference should be attributed to an intrinsic hemispheric difference in, say, activation functions or initial patterns of connectivity, or whether instead it is a consequence of hemispheric differences in the nature of the bottom-up input or top-down feedback received by these areas.

It is worth noting that if a network model posits two distinct visual word-form areas to account for the hemispheric differences in perceptual specificity effects, it would in some sense be a 'two-process' model, but not of the sort favored by proponents of the abstractionist position (e.g., Bowers, 1996; Brown and Carr, 1993). In particular, in the network model it would not be the case that, strictly speaking, the left hemisphere uses abstract representations and the right maintains perceptual detail. Instead, given the constraints that determine a network's activation dynamics, in both hemispheres abstraction would necessarily be a matter of degree. Thus, even the left hemisphere could give rise to specificity effects under some circumstances, as suggested by the results of Marsolek and Hudson (1999).

In summary, from the connectionist perspective it is no accident that experimental results sometimes suggest that readers make use of abstract representations and sometimes suggest that perceptual detail matters. To a certain extent, these contrasting patterns of results reflect the limitations of our methodologies—how much detail we can see in the representations underlying visual word identification depends in part on the resolving power of the instruments we use to observe them. More importantly, however, because of the conflicting constraints imposed by the similarity principle, these representations are organized such that different tokens of a word are mapped onto similar, but generally not identical, patterns of activation. Thus, abstraction is neither all nor none, but instead is a matter of degree.

Summary: network models and other accounts

The purpose of this chapter is to provide an overview of the connectionist perspective on repetition priming in visual word identification. From this perspective word identification, like other cognitive tasks, is accomplished by a network of simple processing units that interact by sending each other inhibitory and excitatory signals. A learning process shapes these interactions by adjusting the strengths of the connections among the nodes, thus attuning the behavior of the network to the regularities and task demands of its environment. Repetition priming is a manifestation of this learning process, revealing how the dynamical behavior of the network changes as a consequence of a single learning event.

The connectionist framework incorporates several major assumptions about the structure and operation of the networks underlying cognitive tasks. One of these is that representations are distributed across many nodes, and thus that each node plays a role in many different representations. Inherent in the notion of distributed representation is the fact that some patterns are more similar than others. Thus, for example, orthographically similar words are represented by relatively similar patterns of activation at the visual word-form level; the representations at this level are even more similar for morphologically related words, and more similar still for different tokens of the same word.

One of the major themes running throughout this chapter is that the core assumptions of the connectionist framework leave their fingerprints on the characteristics of repetition priming. For example, because distributed representation is coupled with superimpositional storage, repetition priming gives rise to transfer effects—modifying the weights to improve the response to one word changes the manner in which the network responds to other words as well. Similarly, because the similarity principle and the principle of quasi-equivalent states imply that different tokens of a word are represented by different but highly similar patterns of activation, perceptual abstraction is a matter of degree. As a result, perceptual specificity effects come and go depending on various aspects of the experimental circumstance.

Another major theme running throughout this chapter is that there is a deep and intimate relationship between repetition priming and other classes of behavioral phenomena. Repetition priming takes its form due to the same mechanisms and principles that shape other aspects of behavior. Thus, both transfer effects in priming and consistency effects in naming can be understood as manifestations of the similarity principle; morphological effects in long-term priming and morphological effects in short-term priming both reflect the manner in which statistical regularities in the environment structure a network's weights, and hence its activation dynamics; neither the processes responsible for identification nor the processes responsible for priming distinguish between words and pseudowords.

In this light, it is worth considering the relationships between the connectionist approach and the two theoretical traditions discussed at the beginning of the chapter. Like the memory tradition, the connectionist approach views repetition priming as a form of learning, and explains priming in terms of principles that apply to a wide variety of phenomena. Like the activation tradition, the connectionist approach provides a mechanistic account of repetition priming, and places this account in the context of an explanatory framework that explicitly addresses other classes of phenomena related to specific perceptual tasks. Thus, to a certain extent the connectionist approach represents a blend of the activation and memory traditions.

However, it is also the case that the connectionist approach makes some assertions that either conflict with other kinds of accounts or concern issues about which these accounts are relative mute. Yet, even on these issues it is possible to see potential avenues of convergence. For example, instance theories (e.g., Goldinger, 1998; Hintzman, 1986; Jacoby and Brooks, 1984; Kolers, 1979; Whittlesea, 1987) have emerged as one important class of models within the memory tradition. To the extent that these models are described in terms of explicit encoding and retrieval processes, they generally posit mechanisms that are rather unlike the activation and learning processes assumed by connectionist models. Yet, instance models and connectionist models share some common ground—both deny the psychological reality of abstract representations (at least as they are commonly understood), both emphasize the notion of 'representations' as emergent states, and both assume that every experience can potentially play a role in the emergence of these states. An exploration of these points of agreement may reveal that the primary insights of the instance approach can be understood in terms of the dynamics of a connectionist network, and conversely, these insights may provide the basis for a deeper understanding of these dynamics.

A similar point can be made with regard to some of the structural models that have emerged from the memory tradition. In particular, multiple-memory-systems accounts (e.g., Marsolek *et al.*, 1992; Schacter, 1992; Squire, 1992) hold that the dissociations between priming and other forms of memory (as well as dissociations among forms of priming) occur because different neural subsystems are responsible for different kinds of processes. Typically, systems accounts focus on the macrolevel: They are more concerned with determining the functional partitioning of the brain and identifying the role of each subsystem than with providing an explicit account of how each subsystem accomplishes its task. Connectionist models can complement the systems approach by offering insights about how each subsystem operates, thus clarifying, for example, why certain functions appear to be 'computationally incompatible' (Rueckl *et al.*, 1989; Marsolek *et al.*, 1992; Marsolek and Burgund, 1997). Conversely, to a certain extent there is little justification for the architectural assumptions of current connectionist models. For example, the architecture of the triangle model (Harm, 1998; Plaut *et al.*, 1996; Seidenberg and McCelland, 1989) seems to be based more on intuition than on solid theoretical or empirical grounds, and in fact other kinds of architectures have been explored with some success (Kello and Plaut, submitted; Zorzi *et al.*, 1998). Thus, theorists working within the systems approach may be able to provide connectionist modelers with useful theoretical insights and empirical constraints. (For an example, see the discussion of hemispheric specialization in the section titled *Perceptual specificity effects.*)

Finally, while the connectionist approach is clearly more at odds with activation theories than with theories developed within the memory tradition, there are ways in which the gap between the two kinds of approaches might be bridged. One of the main conflicts between these approaches lies in their conceptions of mental representations—as either localist, abstract entities or distributed patterns of activation. Perhaps it would be possible to think about the representations in an activation model as shorthand descriptions for the attractors in a connectionist network. One benefit of this approach is that the flow of activation within a localist network is relatively easy to track and interpret. Thus, the connectionist approach might gain in its understanding of the cooperative and competitive forces that underlie cognition by relating the dynamics of a distributed system to, say, the excitatory and inhibitory interactions among word nodes (Grainger and Jacobs, 1996; McClelland and Rumelhart, 1981).

Another major conflict between the connectionist and activation approaches is more meta-theoretical in nature. From the connectionist perspective, one of the least appealing aspects of the activation approach is its tendency to mirror the complexity of the behavior it intends to explain in the complexity of the models that it offers as explanations. It is an exaggeration to claim that abstractionist theories are constructed in accordance with the maxim 'For each effect posit a new cause', but it is less of an exaggeration than one might like. According to models developed within the abstractionist position: Different processes underlie word and pseudoword priming; different processes are needed to read *pint* and *mave* aloud; morphologically complex words can be read in either of two ways; morphologically complex words can be produced in either of two ways; priming is sometimes due to representations that are perceptually abstract, and other times due to representations that preserve perceptual detail. And so on.

The point here is not so much about the sheer complexity of the organization of the cognitive processes posited by activation accounts, although arguably the reliance on symbolic representations and symbol manipulating processes introduces more complexity than is actually needed. The point instead is that activation accounts rarely attempt to explain where this organization comes from. If each word in a reader's vocabulary is represented by a logogen, how did these logogens get into the reader's head in the first place? If the architecture of the reading system includes two different routes that make use of fundamentally different kinds of processes, how did this architecture get put into place? In the words of the philosopher Dan Dennett, a theory 'takes out a loan on intelligence' when it takes the organization of a cognitive processes as a given. A loan on intelligence is fine if it is paid back with an explanation of how that organization came about. The worry about the activation tradition is that generally it has exhibited little if any concern with paying back its loans. It has the flavor of a Reaganomics approach to cognitive theories.

In contrast, connectionism's emphasis on learning and self-organization is an acknowledgement that the need to explain the organization of psychological processes is as important as the need to explain the organization of the behaviors that those processes generate. In the connectionist approach richly organized activation dynamics are a consequence of both the interactions of processing units that follow a simple algebraic rule and the pattern of connectivity that constrains these interactions. The pattern of connectivity is itself the product of a dynamic process (at a slower time scale) involving a simple algebraic rule and the constraints provided by the environment inhabited by the network. A major theme of this chapter (and of the relevant studies cited within) has been to demonstrate how these self-organizing dynamics give rise to the effects of repetition priming, phonological consistency, morphological complexity, lexicality, word frequency, and so forth.

To be clear: The claim is not that connectionist models fully explain the organization of cognitive processes and thus don't take out loans on intelligence. Rather, the claim is that a major emphasis of the connectionist approach is to minimize the need for such loans and to pay back the ones that are taken out. For example, simulations of the triangle model of word identification (Plaut *et al.*, 1996; Seidenberg and McClelland, 1989) make assumptions about the input and output representations, the teacher (i.e., the source of the target patterns that drive error-correction learning), and the structure of the architecture. Paying back these loans forms part of the connectionist research agenda, and it is worth noting that possible means of payback for each assumption can be identified:

(a)   In the long run, the input and output units of the triangle model can (and must) be treated as hidden units, and thus the principles that apply to the organization of hidden unit representations will apply here as well (see the section on *Perceptual specificity effects*).

(b)   In some cases a network can use its own behavior as the basis for an error signal (O'Reilly, 1996); alternatively, some algorithms do not require an error signal to drive learning (Grossberg, 1987; Stark and McClelland, 2000).

(c)   In some learning algorithms regions of an initially undifferentiated network become specialized for specific computational tasks, such that a more-or-less modular architecture emerges with experience (e.g., Jacobs and Jordan, 1992; see Elman *et al.*, 1996, for a broad discussion).

Of course, there is no guarantee that any of these possibilities will ultimately prove fruitful. Only time and hard work will tell. Even so, these issues and avenues of research illustrate two of the central—and to me, most attractive—aspects of the connectionist approach: The desire for theories that explain, rather than assume, the organization of mental processes, and a rich set of theoretical constructs that are conducive to the development of explanations of this sort.

Acknowledgments

The preparation of this chapter, and some of the research described herein, were supported by National Institute for Child Health and Development grant HD-01994 to Haskins Laboratories.

References

Adams, M. J. (1979). Models of word recognition. *Cognitive Psychology*, **11**, 133–76.

Allen, P. A., Wallace, B., and Weber, T. A. (1995). Influence of case type, word frequency, and exposure duration on visual word recognition. *Journal of Experimental Psychology: Human Perception and Performance*, **21**, 914–34.

Andrews, S. (1997). The effect of orthographic similarity on lexical retrieval: Resolving neighborhood conflicts. *Psychonomic Bulletin and Review*, **4**, 439–61.

Baayen, R. H., Dijkstra, T., and Schreuder, R., (1997). Singulars and plurals in Dutch: Evidence for a parallel dual route model. *Journal of Memory and Language*, **37**, 94–117.

Becker, S., Moscovitch, M., Behrmann, M., and Joordens, S. (1997). Long-term semantic priming: A computational account and empirical evidence. *Journal of Experimental Psychology: Learning, Memory, and Cognition*, **23**, 1059–82.

Bentin, S. and Feldman, L. B. (1990). The contribution of morphological and semantic relatedness to repetition priming at short and long lags: Evidence from Hebrew. *Quarterly Journal of Experimental Psychology*, **42A** (4), 693–711.

Besner, D. and Johnston, J. C. (1989). Reading and the mental lexicon: On the uptake of visual information. In *Lexical processes and representation* (ed. W. Marslen-Wilson), pp. 291–316. Cambridge, MA: MIT Press.

Besner, D., Davelaar, E., Alcott, D., and Perry, P. (1984). Wholistic reading of alphabetic print: Evidence from the FBM and the FBI. In *Orthographies and reading* (ed. L. Henderson), pp. 121–35. Hillsdale, NJ: Erlbaum.

Blaxton, T. A. (1989). Investigating dissociations among memory measures: Support for a transfer-appropriate processing framework. *Journal of Experimental Psychology: Learning, Memory, and Cognition*, **15**, 657–88.

Booker, J. (1992). *Interference effects in implicit and explicit memory*. Unpublished doctoral dissertation. University of Arizona.

Bowers, J. S. (1994). Does implicit memory extend to legal and illegal nonwords? *Journal of Experimental Psychology: Learning, Memory, and Cognition*, **20**, 534–49.

Bowers, J. S. (1996). Different perceptual codes support priming for words and pseudowords: Was Morton right all along? *Journal of Experimental Psychology: Learning, Memory, and Cognition*, **22**, 1336–53.

Bowers, J. S. (1999). Priming is not all bias: Commentary on Ratcliff and McKoon (1997). *Psychological Review*, **106**, 582–96.

Bowers, J. S. and Michita, Y. (1998). An investigation into the structure and acquisition of orthographic knowledge: Evidence from cross-script Kanji-Hiragana priming. *Psychonomic Bulletin and Review*, **5**, 259–64.

Bowers, J. S., Damian, M., and Havelka, J. (in press). Can distributed orthographic knowledge support word specific long-term priming? Apparently so. *Journal of Memory and Language*.

Brooks, L. (1978). Nonanalytic concept formation and memory for instances. In *Cognition and categorization* (ed. E. Rosch and B. B. Lloyd), pp. 169–211. New York: Wiley.

Brown, H. L., Sharma, N. K., and Kirsner, K. (1984). The role of script and phonology in lexical representation. *Quarterly Journal of Experimental Psychology: Human Experimental Psychology*, **36A**, 491–505.

Brown, J. S. and Carr, T. H. (1993). Limits on perceptual abstraction in reading: Asymmetric transfer between surface forms differing in typicality. *Journal of Experimental Psychology: Learning, Memory, and Cognition*, **19**, 1277–96.

Burani, C. and Caramazza, A. (1987). Representation and processing of derived words. *Language and Cognitive Processes*, **2**, 217–27.

Caramazza, A., Laudanna, A., and Romani, C. (1988). Lexical access and inflectional morphology. *Cognition*, **28**, 297–332.

Carr, T. H., Brown, J. S., and Charalambous, A. (1989). Repetition and reading: Perceptual encoding mechanisms are very abstract but not very interactive. *Journal of Experimental Psychology: Learning, Memory, and Cognition*, **15**, 763–78.

Cermak, L. S., Talbot, N., Chandler, K., and Wolbarst, L. (1985). The perceptual priming phenomenon in amnesia. *Neuropsychologia*, **23**, 615–22.

Coltheart, M. (1978). Lexical access in simple reading tasks. In *Strategies of information processing* (ed. G. Underwood), pp. 151–216. London: Academic Press.

Coltheart, M. and Freeman, N. (1974). Case alternation impairs word identification. *Bulletin of the Psychonomic Society*, **3**, 102–4.

Coltheart, M., Rastle, K., Perry, C., Langdon, R., and Ziegler, J. (2001). DRC: A dual route cascaded model of visual word recognition and reading aloud. *Psychological Review*, **108**, 204–56.

Cree, G. S., McRae, K., and McNorgan, C. (1999). An attractor model of lexical conceptual processing: Simulating semantic priming. *Cognitive Science*, **23**, 371–414.

Curran, T., Schacter, D. L., and Bessenoff, G. (1996). Visual specificity effects on word stem completion: Beyond transfer appropriate processing? *Canadian Journal of Psychology*, **50**, 22–33.

Danenbring, G. L. and Briand, K. (1982). Semantic priming and the word repetition effect in a lexical decision task. *Canadian Journal of Psychology*, **36**, 435–44.

Deese, J. (1959). On the prediction of occurrence of particular verbal intrusions in immediate recall. *Journal of Experimental Psychology*, **58**, 17–22.

Diamond, R. and Rozin, P. (1984). Activation of existing memories in the amnesic syndrome. *Journal of Abnormal Psychology*, **93**, 98–105.

Dorfman, J. (1994). Sublexical components in implicit memory for novel words. *Journal of Experimental Psychology: Learning, Memory, and Cognition*, **20**, 1108–25.

Elman, J. L. (1995). Language as a dynamical system. In *Mind as motion: Explorations in the dynamics of cognition* (ed. R. F. Port and T. van Gelder), pp. 195–226. Cambridge, MA: MIT Press.

Elman, J. L., Bates, E. A., Johnson, M. H., Karmiloff-Smith, A., Parisi, D., and Plunkett, K. (1996). *Rethinking innateness: A connectionist perspective on development*. Cambridge, MA: MIT Press.

Evett, L. J. and Humphreys, G. W. (1981). The use of abstract graphemic information in lexical access. *Quarterly Journal of Experimental Psychology*, **33A**, 325–50.

Farrar, W. T. and Van Orden, G. C. (submitted). Nonlinear dynamics of naming errors. Manuscript submitted for publication.

Feldman, L. B. (1991). The contribution of morphology to word recognition. *Psychological Research*, **53**, 33–41.

Feldman, L. B. (1994). Beyond orthography and phonology: Differences between inflections and derivations. *Journal of Memory and Language*, **33**, 442–70.

Feldman, L. B. and Fowler, C. A. (1987). The inflected noun system in Serbo-Croatian: Lexical representation of morphological structure. *Memory and Cognition*, **15** (1), 1–12.

Feldman, L. B. and Moskovljevic, J. (1987). Repetition priming is not purely episodic in origin. *Journal of Experimental Psychology: Learning, Memory, and Cognition*, **13**, 573–81.

Feldman, L. B., Rueckl, J. R., DiLiberto, L., Pastizzo, M., and Vellutino, F. R. (in press). Morphological analysis by child readers as revealed by the fragment completion task. *Psychonomic Bulletin and Review*.

Feustel, T. C., Shiffrin, R. M., and Salasoo, A. (1983). Episodic and lexical contributions to the repetition effect in word identification. *Journal of Experimental Psychology: General*, **112**, 309–46.

Forbach, G., Stanners, R., and Hochaus, L. (1974). Repetition and practice effects in a lexical decision task. *Memory and Cognition*, **2**, 337–9.

Forster, K. (1987). Form-priming with masked primes: The best match hypothesis. *Attention and Performance XII*, 127–45.

Fowler, C. A., Napps, S. E., and Feldman, L. B. (1985). Relations among regular and irregular morphologically related words in the lexicon as revealed by repetition priming. *Memory and Cognition*, **13**, 241–55.

Glushko, R. J. (1979). The organization and activation of orthographic knowledge in reading aloud. *Journal of Experimental Psychology: Human Perception and Performance*, **5**, 674–91.

Goldinger, S. D. (1998). Echoes of echoes? An episodic theory of lexical access. *Psychological Review*, **105**, 251–79.

Gonnerman, L., Devlin, J., Andersen, E. S., and Seidenberg, M. S. (1995). 'Morphological' priming without a morphological level of representation. *Journal of the International Neuropsychological Society*, **1**, 142.

Graf, P. and Ryan, L. (1990). Transfer-appropriate processing for implicit and explicit memory. *Journal of Experimental Psychology: Learning, Memory, and Cognition*, **16**, 978–92.

Graf, P. and Schacter, D. L. (1987). Selective effects of interference on implicit and explicit memory for new associations. *Journal of Experimental Psychology: Learning, Memory, and Cognition*, **13**, 45–53.

Grainger, J. and Jacobs, A. M. (1996). Orthographic processing in visual word recognition: A multiple read-out model. *Psychological Review*, **103**, 518–65.

Grainger, J. and Jacobs, A. M. (1998). On localist connectionism and psychological science. In *Localist connectionist approaches to human cognition* (ed. J. Grainger and A. M. Jacobs), pp. 1–38. Mahwan, NJ: Lawrence Erlbaum Associates.

Grossberg, S. (1987). Competitive learning: From interactive activation to adaptive resonance. *Cognitive Science*, **11**, 23–63.

Grossberg, S. and Stone, G. (1986). Neural dynamics of word recognition and recall: Attentional priming, learning, and resonance. *Psychological Review*, **93**, 46–74.

Harm, M. W. (1998). Division of labor in a computational model of visual word recognition. Unpublished dissertation: Southern California University.

Harm, M. W. and Seidenberg, M. S. (1999). Phonology, reading acquisition, and dyslexia: Insights from connectionist models. *Psychological Review*, **106**, 491–528.

Henderson, L. (1985). Towards a psychology of morphemes. In *Progress in the psychology of language* (ed. A. W. Ellis), Vol. 1, pp. 15–72. London: Erlbaum.

Hetherington, P. A. and Seidenberg, M. S. (1989). Is there 'catastrophic interference' in connectionist networks? In *Proceedings of the 11th Annual Meeting of the Cognitive Science Society*. pp. 26–33. Hillsdale, NJ: Erlbaum.

Hinton, G. E. and Sejnowski, T. J. (1986). Learning and relearning in Boltzmann machines. In *Parallel distributed processing: Explorations in the microstructure of cognition* (ed. D. E. Rumelhart and J. L. McClelland), Vol. 1, Foundations. Cambridge, MA: MIT Press.

Hintzman, D. L. (1986). 'Schema abstraction' in a multiple-trace memory model. *Psychological Review*, **93**, 411–28.

Hopfield, J. J. (1982). Neural networks and physical systems with emergent collective computational properties. *Proceedings of the National Academy of Sciences USA*, **79**, 2554–8.

Humphreys, G. W., Besner, D., and Quinlan, P. T. (1988). Event perception and the word repetition effect. *Journal of Experimental Psychology: General*, **117**, 51–67.

Jacobs, R. A. and Jordan, M. I. (1992). Computational consequences of a bias towards short connections. *Journal of Cognitive Neuroscience*, **4**, 323–6.

Jacoby, L. (1983). Perceptual enhancement: Persistent effects of an experience. *Journal of Experimental Psychology: Learning, Memory, and Cognition*, **9**, 21–38.

Jacoby, L. L. and Brooks, L. R. (1984). Nonanalytic cognition: Memory, perception, and concept learning. In *The psychology of learning and motivation: Advances in research and theory* (ed. G. H. Bower), Vol. 18, pp. 1–47. New York: Academic Press.

Jacoby, L. L. and Dallas, M. (1981). On the relationship between autobiographical memory and perceptual learning. *Journal of Experimental Psychology: General*, **110**, 306–40.

Jacoby, L. L. and Hayman, C. A. G. (1987). Specific visual transfer in word identification. *Journal of Experimental Psychology: Learning, Memory, and Cognition*, **13**, 456–63.

Jared, D., McRae, K., and Seidenberg, M. S. (1990). The basis of consistency effects in word naming. *Journal of Memory and Language*, **29**, 687–715.

Joordens, S. and Becker, S. (1997). The long and short of semantic priming effects in lexical decision. *Journal of Experimental Psychology: Learning, Memory, and Cognition*, **23**, 1083–105.

Joordens, S. and Besner, D. (1994). When banking on meaning is not (yet) money in the bank: Explorations in connectionist modeling. *Journal of Experimental Psychology: Learning, Memory, and Cognition*, **20**, 1051–62.

Kawamoto, A. H. (1993). Nonlinear dynamics in the resolution of lexical ambiguity: A parallel distributed processing account. *Journal of Memory and Language*, **32**, 474–516.

Kawamoto, A. H., Farrar, W. T., and Kello, C. (1994). When two meanings are better than one: Modeling the ambiguity advantage using a recurrent distributed network. *Journal of Experimental Psychology: Human Perception and Performance*, **20**, 1233–48.

Keane, M. M., Gabrieli, J. D., Growdon, J. H., and Corkin, S. (1994). Priming in perceptual identification of pseudowords is normal in Alzheimer's disease. *Neuropsychologia*, **3**, 343–56.

Keane, M. M., Verfaellie, M., Gabrieli, J. D. E., and Wong, B. M. (2000). Bias effects in perceptual identification: A neuropsychological investigation of the role of explicit memory. *Journal of Memory and Language*, **43**, 316–44.

Kello, C. T. and Plaut, D. C. (submitted). Strategic control by gain manipulation in a computational model of word reading in the tempo naming task.

Kirsner, K. and Smith, M. (1974). Modality effects in word identification. *Memory and Cognition*, **2**, 637–40.

Kolers, P. A. (1975). Specificity of operations in sentence recognition. *Cognitive Psychology*, **1**, 289–306.

Kolers, P. A. (1979). A pattern-analyzing basis for recognition memory. In *Levels of processing and human memory* (ed. L. S. Cermak and F. I. M. Craik). Hillsdale, NJ: Erlbaum.

Levy, B. A. and Kirsner, K. (1989). Reprocessing text: Indirect measures of word and message level processing. *Journal of Experimental Psychology: Learning, Memory, and Cognition*, **15**, 407–17.

Lukatela, G., Gligorijevic, B., Kostic, A., and Turvey, M. T. (1980). Representation of inflected nouns in the internal lexicon. *Memory and Cognition*, **8**, 415–23.

Lustig, C. and Hasher, L. (2001). Implicit memory is vulnerable to proactive interference. *Psychological Science*, **12**, 408–12.

Mandler, G., Graf, P., and Kraft, D. (1986). Activation and elaboration effects in recognition and word priming. *Quarterly Journal of Experimental Psychology*, **38A**, 645–62.

Mandler, G., Hamson, C. O., and Dorfman, J. (1990). Tests of dual process theory: Word priming and recognition. *Quarterly Journal of Experimental Psychology*, **42A**, 713–39.

Marsolek, C. J. and Burgund E. D. (1997). Computational analyses and hemispheric asymmetries in visual-form processing. In *Cerebral asymmetries in sensory and perceptual processing* (ed. S. Christman), pp. 125–58. Amsterdam: Elsevier.

Marsolek, C. J. and Hudson, T. E. (1999). Task and stimulus demands influence letter-case specific priming in the right cerebral hemisphere. *Laterality*, **4**, 127–47.

Marsolek, C. J., Kosslyn, S. M., and Squire, L. R. (1992). Form-specific visual priming in the right cerebral hemisphere. *Journal of Experimental Psychology: Learning, Memory, and Cognition*, **18**, 492–508.

Marsolek, C. J., Squire, L. R., Kosslyn, S. M., and Lulenski, M. (1994). Form-specific explicit and implicit memory in the right cerebral hemisphere. *Neuropsychology*, **8**, 588–97.

Masson, M. J. (1995). A distributed memory model of semantic priming. *Journal of Experimental Psychology: Learning, Memory, and Cognition*, **21** (1), 3–23.

Masson, M. E. J. (1999). Semantic priming in a recurrent network: Comment on Dalrymple-Alford and Marmurek (1999). *Journal of Experimental Psychology: Learning, Memory, and Cognition*, **25**, 776–94.

Mayall, K. A., Humphreys, G. W., and Olson, A. (1997). Disruption to word or letter processing? The origins of case-mixing effects. *Journal of Experimental Psychology: Learning, Memory, and Cognition*, **23**, 1275–86.

Mayes, A., Pickering, A., and Fairbairn, A. (1987). Amnesic sensitivity to proactive interference: its relationship to priming and the causes of amnesia. *Neuropsychologia*, **25**, 211–20.

McClelland, J. L. (1976). Preliminary letter identification in the perception of words and nonwords. *Journal of Experimental Psychology: Human Perception and Performance*, **4**, 80–91.

McClelland, J. L. (1977). Letter and configurational information in word identification. *Journal of Verbal Learning and Verbal Behavior*, **16**, 147–50.

McClelland, J. L. and Rumelhart, D. E. (1981). An interactive activation model of context effects in letter perception: Part 1. *Psychological Review*, **88**, 375–407.

McClelland, J. L. and Rumelhart, D. E. (1985). Distributed memory and the representation of general and specific knowledge. *Journal of Experimental Psychology: General*, **114**, 159–88.

McClelland, J. L., McNaughton, B. L., and O'Reilly, R. C. (1995). Why there are complimentary learning systems in the hippocampus and neocortex: Insights from the successes and failures of connectionist models of learning and memory. *Psychological Review*, **102**, 419–57.

McCloskey, M. and Cohen, N. (1989). Catastrophic interference in connectionist networks: The sequential learning problem. *The Psychology of Learning and Motivation*, **24**, 109–65.

McConkie, G. and Zola, D. (1979). Is visual information integrated across successive fixations in reading? *Perception and Psychophysics*, **25**, 221–4.

McDermott, K. (1997). Priming on perceptual implicit memory tests can be achieved through presentation of associates. *Psychonomic Bulletin and Review*, **4**, 582–6.

Minsky, M. and Papert, S. (1969). *Perceptrons.* Cambridge, MA: MIT Press.

Monsell, S. (1985). Repetition and the lexicon. In *Progress in the psychology of language* (ed. A. W. Ellis), Vol. 2. London: Erlbaum.

Morton, J. (1969). Interaction of information in word identification. *Psychological Review*, **76**, 165–78.

Morton, J. (1979). Facilitation in word recognition: Experiments causing a change in the logogen model. In *Processing visible language I* (ed. P. A. Kolers, M. E. Wrostal, and H. Bouma), pp. 259–68. New York: Plenum Press.

Murre, J. (1992). The effects of pattern presentation on interference in backpropagation networks. In *Proceedings of the 14th Annual Meeting of the Cognitive Science Society,* pp. 54–9. Hillsdale, NJ: Erlbaum.

Murrell, G. A. and Morton, J. (1974). Word recognition and morphemic structure. *Journal of Experimental Psychology,* **102**, 963–8.

Napps, S. E. (1989). Morphemic relationships in the lexicon: Are they distinct from semantic and formal relationships? *Memory and Cognition,* **17**, 729–39.

Napps, S. E. and Fowler, C. A. (1987). Formal relationships among words and the organization of the mental lexicon. *Journal of Psycholinguistic Research,* **16**, 257–72.

Neaderhiser, B. J. and Church, B. A. (2000, April). Priming in forced choice identification: Memory or bias? Paper presented at the 92nd Meeting of the Southern Society for Philosophy and Psychology, Atlanta.

Neisser, U. (1954). An experimental distinction between perceptual processes and verbal response. *Journal of Experimental Psychology,* **47**, 399–402.

Nelson, D., Keelean, P., and Negrao, M. (1989). Word-fragment cueing: The lexical search hypothesis. *Journal of Experimental Psychology: Learning, Memory, and Cognition,* **15**, 333–97.

O'Reilly, R. C. (1996). Biologically plausible error-driven learning using local activation differences: The generalized recirculation algorithm. *Neural Computation,* **8** (5), 895–938.

Overson, C. and Mandler, G. (1987). Indirect word priming in connected and phonological contexts. *Bulletin of the Psychonomic Society,* **25**, 229–32.

Paap, K. R., Newsome, S. L., McDonald, J. E., and Schvaneveldt, R. W. (1982). An activation-verification model for letter and word recognition: The word superiority effect. *Psychological Review,* **89**, 573–94.

Pinker, S. and Prince, A. (1988). On language and connectionism: Analysis of a parallel distributed processing model off language acquisition. *Cognition,* **28**, 73–193.

Plaut, D. C. (1997). Structure and function in the lexical system: Insights from distributed models of word reading and lexical decision. *Language and Cognitive Processes,* **12**, 767–808.

Plaut, D. C. and Booth, J. R. (2000). Individual and developmental differences in semantic priming: Empirical and computational support for a single-mechanism account of lexical processing. *Psychological Review,* **107**, 786–823.

Plaut, D. C. and Gonnerman, L. M. (2000). Are non-semantic morphological effects incompatible with a distributed connectionist approach to lexical processing? *Language and Cognitive Processes,* **15**, 445–85.

Plaut, D. C., McClelland, J. L., Seidenberg, M. S., and Patterson, K. (1996). Understanding normal and impaired word reading: Computational principles in quasi-regular domains. *Psychological Review,* **103**, 56–115.

Rajaram, S. and Roediger, H. L. (1993). Direct comparison of four implicit memory tests. *Journal of Experimental Psychology: Learning, Memory, and Cognition,* **19** (4), 765–76.

Ratcliff, R. (1990). Connectionist models of recognition memory: Constraints imposed by learning and forgetting functions. *Psychological Review,* **97**, 285–308.

Ratcliff, R. and McKoon, G. (1996). Bias effects in implicit memory tasks. *Journal of Experimental Psychology: Learning, Memory, and Cognition,* **21**, 754–67.

Ratcliff, R. and McKoon, G. (1997). A counter model for implicit priming in perceptual word identification. *Psychological Review,* **104**, 319–43.

Ratcliff, R., Hockley, W., and McKoon, G. (1985). Components of activation: Repetition and priming effects in lexical decision and recognition. *Journal of Experimental Psychology: General*, 114, 435–50.

Raveh, M. and Rueckl, J. (2000). Equivalent effects of inflected and derived primes: Long-term morphological priming in fragment completion and lexical decision. *Journal of Memory and Language*, 42, 103–19.

Rayner, K., McConkie, G., and Zola, D. (1980). Integrating information across eye movements. *Cognitive Psychology*, 12, 206–26.

Richardson-Klavehn, A. and Bjork, R. A. (1988). Measures of memory. *Annual Review of Psychology*, 39, 475–543.

Roediger, H. L. (1990). Implicit memory: Retention without awareness. *American Psychologist*, 45, 1043–56.

Roediger, H. L. and McDermott, K. B. (1993). Implicit memory in normal human subject. In *Handbook of neuropsychology* (ed. H. Spinnler and F. Boller), Vol. 8, pp. 63–130. Amsterdam: Elsevier.

Ross, S., Yarcowzer, M., and Williams, G. M. (1956). Recognitive thresholds for words as a function of set and similarity. *American Journal of Psychology*, 69, 82–6.

Rueckl, J. G. (1990). Similarity effects in word and pseudoword repetition priming. *Journal of Experimental Psychology: Learning, Memory, and Cognition*, 16, 374–91.

Rueckl, J. G. (1993). Jumpnet: A multiple-memory systems connectionist architecture. *Proceedings of the 15th Annual Meeting of the Cognitive Science Society*, pp. 866–71. Hillsdale, NJ: Erlbaum Publishers.

Rueckl, J. G. (submitted). Interference effects in implicit memory. Manuscript submitted for publication.

Rueckl, J. G. and Dror, I. (1994). The effect of orthographic-semantic systematicity on the acquisition of new words. In *Attention and performance XV* (ed. C. Umilta and M. Moscovitch), pp. 571–88. Hillsdale, NJ: Erlbaum.

Rueckl, J. G. and Mathew, S. (1999). Implicit memory for phonological processes in visual stem completion. *Memory and Cognition*, 27, 1–11.

Rueckl, J. G. and Olds, E. M. (1993). When pseudowords acquire meaning: The effect of semantic associations on pseudoword repetition priming. *Journal of Experimental Psychology: Learning, Memory, and Cognition*, 3, 515–27.

Rueckl, J. G. and Raveh, M. (1999). The influence of morphological regularities on the dynamics of a connectionist network. *Brain and Language*, 68, 110–7.

Rueckl, J. G., Cave, K. R., and Kosslyn, S. M. (1989). Why are 'what' and 'where' processed by separate cortical visual systems? A computational investigation. *Journal of Cognitive Neuroscience*, 1, 171–86.

Rueckl, J. G., Mikolinski, M., Raveh, M., Miner, C., and Mars, F. (1997). Morphological priming, fragment completion, and connectionist networks. *Journal of Memory and Language*, 36, 382–405.

Rumelhart, D. E. and McClelland, J. (ed.) (1986a). *Parallel distributed processing: Explorations in the microstructure of cognition*. Vol. 1, Foundations. Cambridge, MA: MIT Press.

Rumelhart, D. E. and McClelland, J. L. (1986b). On learning the past tense of English verbs. In *Parallel distributed processing* (ed. D. E. Rumelhart and J. L. McClelland), Vol. 1, Foundations. Cambridge, MA: MIT Press.

Rumelhart, D., Hinton, G., and Williams, R. (1986). Learning internal representations by error propagation. In *Parallel distributed processing: Explorations in the microstructure of cognition* (ed. D. Rumelhart and J. McClelland), Vol. 1, Foundations. Cambridge, MA: MIT Press.

Scarborough, D. L., Cortese, C., and Scarborough, H. S. (1977). Frequency and repetition effects in lexical memory. *Journal of Experimental Psychology: Human Perception and Performance*, 3, 1–17.

Schacter, D. L. (1987). Implicit memory: History and current status. *Journal of Experimental Psychology: Learning, Memory, and Cognition*, 13, 501–18.

Schacter, D. L. (1992). Priming and multiple memory systems: Perceptual mechanisms of implicit memory. *Journal of Cognitive Neuroscience*, **4**, 244–56.

Schreuder, R. and Baayen, R. H. (1997). How complex simplex words can be? *Journal of Memory and Language*, **37**, 118–39.

Seidenberg, M. S. and McClelland, J. L. (1989). A distributed, developmental model of visual word recognition. *Psychological Review*, **96**, 523–68.

Seidenberg, M. S., Plaut, D. C., Petersen, A. S., McClelland, J. L., and McRae, K. (1994). Nonword pronunciation and models of word recognition. *Journal of Experimental Psychology: Human Perception and Performance*, **20**, 1177–96.

Sherry, D. and Schacter, D. (1987). The evolution of multiple memory systems. *Psychological Review*, **94**, 439–54.

Shevtsova, N. and Reggia, J. A. (1999). A neural network model of lateralization during letter identification. *Journal of Cognitive Neuroscience*, **11**, 167–81.

Sloman, S., Hayman, C., Ohta, N., Law, J., and Tulving, E. (1988). Forgetting in primed fragment completion. *Journal of Experimental Psychology: Learning, Memory, and Cognition*, **14**, 223–39.

Smith, S. M. and Tindell, D. R. (1997). Memory blocks in word fragment completion caused by involuntary retrieval of orthographically related primes. *Journal of Experimental Psychology: Learning, Memory, and Cognition*, **23**, 355–70.

Squire, L. R. (1992). Memory and the hippocampus: A synthesis from findings with rats, monkeys, and humans. *Psychological Review*, **99**, 195–231.

Stanners, R. F., Neiser, J. J., Hernon, W. P., and Hall, R. (1979). Memory representation for morphologically related words. *Journal of Verbal learning and Verbal Behavior*, **18**, 399–412.

Stark, C. E. L. and McClelland, J. L. (2000). Repetition priming of words, pseudowords, and nonwords. *Journal of Experimental Psychology: Learning, Memory, and Cognition*, **26**, 945–72.

Stolz, J. A. and Feldman, L. B. (1995). The role of orthographic and semantic transparency of the base morpheme in morphological processing. In *Morphological aspects of language processing* (ed. L. B. Feldman), pp. 109–30. Hillsdale, NJ: Erlbaum.

Stone, G. O. and Van Orden, G. C. (1994). Building a resonance framework for recognition using design and system principles. *Journal of Experimental Psychology: Human Perception and Performance*, **20**, 1248–68.

Tabor, W. and Tanenhaus, M. K. (1999). Dynamical models of sentence processing. *Cognitive Science*, **23**, 491–515.

Taft, M. (1979). Recognition of affixed words and the word frequency effect. *Memory and Cognition*, **7**, 263–72.

Taft, M. and Forster, K. I. (1976). Lexical storage and retrieval of polymorphemic and polysyllabic words. *Journal of Verbal Learning and Verbal Behavior*, **15**, 607–20.

Tenpenny, P. L. (1995). Abstractionist vs. episodic theories of repetition priming and word identification. *Psychonomic Bulletin and Review*, **2**, 339–63.

Whittlesea, B. W. A. (1987). Preservation of specific experiences in the representation of general knowledge. *Journal of Experimental Psychology: Learning, Memory, and Cognition*, **13**, 3–17.

Zorzi, M., Houghton, G., and Butterworth, B. (1998). Two routes or one in reading aloud? A connectionist dual-process model. *Journal of Experimental Psychology: Human Perception and Performance*, **24**, 1131–61.

CHAPTER 5

REMI AND ROUSE: QUANTITATIVE MODELS FOR LONG-TERM AND SHORT-TERM PRIMING IN PERCEPTUAL IDENTIFICATION

ERIC-JAN M. WAGENMAKERS, RENÉ ZEELENBERG, DAVE HUBER, JEROEN G. W. RAAIJMAKERS, RICHARD M. SHIFFRIN, AND LAEL J. SCHOOLER

Abstract

The REM model originally developed for recognition memory (Shiffrin and Steyvers, 1997) has recently been extended to implicit memory phenomena observed during threshold identification of words. We discuss two REM models based on Bayesian principles: a model for long-term priming (REMI; Schooler *et al.*, 2001), and a model for short-term priming (ROUSE; Huber *et al.*, 2001). Although the identification tasks are the same, the basis for priming differs in the two models. In both paradigms we ask whether prior study merely reflects a *bias* to interpret ambiguous information in a certain manner, or instead leads to *more efficient encoding*. The observation of a 'both-primed benefit' in two-alternative forced-choice paradigms appears to show that *both* processes are present. However, the REMI model illustrates that the both-primed benefit is not necessarily indicative of an increase in perceptual sensitivity but might be generated by a criterion bias. The ROUSE model demonstrates how the amount of attention paid to the prime, and the consequent effect upon decision making, may lead to the *reversal* of the normal short-term priming effect that is observed in certain conditions.

Introduction

A stimulus in a current task is said to be *primed* when it has been encountered previously, but the memory for that prior occurrence is not required for performance of the current task. Primed stimuli are generally responded to faster and more accurately than unprimed stimuli. For instance, the earlier presentation of a word enhances probability of correctly identifying that word in a later identification task (Church and Schacter, 1994). It is important to note that this priming effect can come about without subjects being aware of any relation between the task used at test and the earlier study episode. Moreover, repetition priming effects can even be observed in amnesic patients who are unable to remember the study episode (Shimamura and Squire, 1984). Such an effect upon performance is termed an *implicit* memory effect. A large variety of tasks have been used to study implicit memory processes. Among these tasks are auditory and visual word identification (Bowers, 1999; Jacoby and Dallas, 1981; Masson and Freedman, 1990; Salasoo *et al.*, 1985), picture identification, word stem completion (Graf *et al.*, 1984), word fragment completion (Roediger *et al.*, 1992), and free association (Zeelenberg *et al.*, 1999).

In this chapter, we will present two models of priming. The primary task under consideration is the identification of words presented visually at threshold. The first model, REMI (for Retrieving Effectively from Memory, the 'I' stands for implicit) developed by Schooler *et al.* (2001), is a model for *long-term priming* in implicit memory. It explains repetition priming effects by assuming that during study of a word some contextual information is added to the corresponding lexical trace. This contextual information stored during the study task will tend to match the contextual information present during the test task, leading subjects to prefer studied words over non-studied words. The second model, ROUSE (Huber *et al.*, 2001), is a model of *short-term* priming. ROUSE stands for Responding Optimally with Unknown Sources of Evidence, and it is able to explain an intricate pattern of results. ROUSE assumes that:

(a) Information arriving due to presentation of the primes can be mistaken for valid target information (i.e., *source confusion*).
(b) Subjects *discount* evidence from such features to a degree determined by their estimate of this source confusion.

ROUSE accounts for the finding that short-term repetition priming results in a bias to choose *repeated* words following the *passive* viewing of primes whereas the *active* processing of primes results in a bias to choose *non-repeated* words. Both REMI and ROUSE can be thought of as natural extensions of the REM model (for details of the REM model applied to episodic recognition memory see Shiffrin and Steyvers, 1997). The REM model is a general memory model based upon the idea that subjects make decisions in an optimal (i.e., Bayesian) fashion on the basis of noisy information. Although derived on a quite different basis, REM shares many similarities with the well-known SAM model for episodic memory tasks such as recognition and recall (e.g., Gillund and Shiffrin, 1984; Raaijmakers and Shiffrin, 1981). REMI and ROUSE demonstrate how priming effects in implicit memory can be explained in the framework of traditional information processing models (cf. Ratcliff and McKoon, 1997).

The priming models we will discuss here are *quantitative* models. They are based on mathematical expressions and provide detailed fits to a wide variety of empirical results. Until recently, most theory development in implicit memory has been *qualitative* in nature, that is, based on verbal descriptions. Although verbal labels are readily accessible to researchers, they are by their very nature imprecise and notoriously susceptible to alternative interpretation.

The outline of this chapter is as follows. We first describe briefly the two-alternative forced-choice perceptual identification task that is used to explore short- and long-term priming, and sketch in broad terms the way we model performance in such tasks. We then discuss the nature of long-term priming in implicit memory tasks, present data from our basic task, and describe the REMI model and its fit to the data. We end by discussing short-term priming, data from our basic task, and finally the ROUSE model and its fit to the findings.

Two-alternative forced-choice perceptual identification

The task used to explore both short- and long-term priming is quite simple: A word (termed a target) is presented visually for a brief period of time, and then followed by a mask, conditions that make perception difficult. This display is followed almost immediately by two choice words: the flashed *target* word and an incorrect *foil* word. The subject attempts to decide which choice word had been flashed. The use of a two-alternative procedure allows the set of alternatives and their similarity to be controlled, and allows the relation to prior primes to be precisely manipulated.

The REM-inspired modeling for such a task assumes that the result of perception of the initial display is a noisy vector of features. Each alternative is represented as a vector of features, albeit without noise. A comparison of the perceived vector to the choice vectors is carried out and an optimal, Bayesian-based, decision is made (e.g., in some, but not all, cases, the better matching alternative is chosen). Long- and short-term priming are assumed to have an effect by altering the degree of matching, as we describe in the sections below. One way to affect matching is to improve the accuracy of the perceived vector, which could be thought of as 'more efficient encoding'. A second way to affect matching is by incorporating features from the prime in the perceived vector, independent of the actual flash. This may be thought of as 'bias'. The REMI and ROUSE models account for the data in terms of bias, proposing different bias-mechanisms for long- and short-term priming.

Long-term priming in implicit memory tasks: perceptual improvement or bias?

In long-term priming, the prime occurs a considerable time before the primary task. Generally, effects of long-term priming are only observed when the target is a repetition of a studied item (but see Becker *et al.*, 1997). The effect of long-term repetition priming in implicit memory tasks is usually interpreted as *perceptual facilitation* due to prior exposure (e.g., Salasoo *et al.*, 1985; Squire, 1992). Schacter (1990) has argued that 'visual priming may make it easier...to extract visual information from the test cue' (p. 237). The general notion is that the perceptual analysis of a primed stimulus in the test task involves the same encoding processes employed when the stimulus was first seen in the study task. The encoding processes supposedly learn from the earlier encounter with the stimulus, resulting in a faster rate of feature extraction the second time the stimulus is presented. In this account, the priming effect is due to low level perceptual learning. This perceptual learning is supposedly dissociated from conscious awareness and its existence has been taken to suggest the presence of several separate memory systems, such as for example the visual word-form system (e.g., Schacter, 1990). Generally, however, the mechanisms underlying enhanced feature extraction are not clearly specified. Thus it remains somewhat unclear *why* or *how* prior study results in better performance. This makes it hard to derive testable predictions.

Ratcliff and McKoon (1997; Ratcliff *et al.*, 1989) have proposed a different account of repetition priming. According to Ratcliff and McKoon, prior study does not result in a more accurate perception of the repeated stimulus, but rather biases subjects to identify the stimulus as one they studied before. The most convincing evidence supporting their claim came from several experiments using the *two-alternative forced-choice (2-AFC) paradigm* for perceptual identification of visually presented stimuli. In a typical 2-AFC experiment, a word, say LIED, is briefly flashed and subsequently masked. Next, two alternatives appear: the target word LIED and an orthographically similar foil word, say DIED. Subjects have to choose which of the two alternatives was flashed. Suppose the target word LIED has been studied some time prior to the 2-AFC test (the typical study instruction is 'study these words for a later memory test'). Consistent with the traditional 'encoding advantage' view of priming, prior study of the target word *enhances* performance compared to the condition in which neither alternative was studied. Several studies, however, have shown that when the orthographically similar foil DIED has been studied, performance *decreases* (Ratcliff and McKoon, 1996, 1997; Ratcliff *et al.*, 1997). Moreover, the costs in performance of studying the foil alternative about *equals* the gain or benefit due to studying the target alternative, leading Ratcliff and McKoon to characterize priming as *bias*. Two additional findings further supported the notion of bias. First, when flash time is so short that performance is at chance, or even when instead of a word some noise characters are flashed, the priming pattern of costs and benefits is left largely unaffected. Second, when the two alternatives are not orthographically similar to each other (e.g., LIED–SOFA) Ratcliff and McKoon (1997) found little or no effect of prior study, contradicting the claim that prior study results in enhanced processing (alternative findings by Bowers, 1999, will be discussed later).

Ratcliff and McKoon (1997) presented an elegant model to account for these data, the so-called *counter-model*. The counter-model assumes that perceptual information extracted from the flash can be of two kinds. Information that is helpful in making a correct decision (i.e., the first letter of a choice between LIED and DIED) is termed diagnostic and will always provide evidence in favor of the target alternative. Information that is non-diagnostic (whether it be the last three letters of the LIED–DIED pair or perceptual noise), will sometimes be taken to support the target alternative, and sometimes be taken to support the foil alternative. When neither alternative has been studied previously, non-diagnostic information is equally likely to support either the target alternative or the foil alternative. If one alternative has been studied however, this results in the studied alternative having a greater probability of acquiring the support of the non-diagnostic information than the non-studied alternative. Thus, the counter-model assumes ambiguous information is processed to be consistent with previous experience. Ratcliff and McKoon term this 'stealing' of information (i.e., the studied alternative steals non-diagnostic information from the non-studied alternative). When it is additionally assumed that such stealing of information is assumed to occur only between similar alternatives (e.g., LIED–DIED) the model predicts the observed pattern of costs and benefits resulting from prior study. Since stealing also applies to perceptual noise, the counter-model correctly predicts that the bias effect due to prior study should be present even when noise characters are flashed instead of a regular target word. In sum, the counter-model explains repetition priming effects not through a higher rate of feature extraction, but through a biased allocation of available features.

As illustrated by the work of Ratcliff and McKoon outlined above, the 2-AFC paradigm can be used to distinguish between a target selective improvement in performance on the one hand and a simple processing bias on the other. Now consider what the different hypotheses of priming (i.e., the 'encoding-advantage' versus 'processing bias' view) predict for performance in the 2-AFC task when both alternatives are studied. The encoding-advantage view of priming predicts a target selective advantage such that performance will be better whenever the target has been studied. As compared to the condition where neither alternative was studied this will result in performance improvements when *both* alternatives were studied as well as when only the target was studied. In contrast, the counter-model predicts no 'both-primed benefit',[1] since it assumes that the biases for the target and foil alternative cancel. Recent work has specifically addressed this issue and has consistently found a both-primed benefit with low-frequency words (as well as the usual bias effects). Figure 5.1 shows typical data from an auditory word identification experiment (Zeelenberg *et al.*, 2002, Experiment 2). The size of the both-primed benefit is reflected by the difference between the middle two bars in Figure 5.1. Although the bias effect appears to be larger than the both-primed benefit, the latter has been consistently found across a range of tasks such as visual word recognition (Bowers, 1999; McKoon and Ratcliff, 2001; Wagenmakers *et al.*, 2000), auditory word recognition, and fragment completion and picture identification (Zeelenberg *et al.*, 2002). These data illustrate that there is more to priming than just a simple bias to prefer the studied word.

It is tempting to view the both-primed benefit as an existence proof for the encoding-advantage view of priming. Indeed, Ratcliff and McKoon (McKoon and Ratcliff, 2001; Ratcliff and McKoon, 2000) have recently modified their counter-model to account for the both-primed benefit. The counter-model now explains this effect by increasing the rate of feature extraction for studied low-frequency words compared to non-studied low-frequency words. It is important to note that although enhanced discriminability as demonstrated by the both-primed benefit is a necessary condition in order to conclude priming affects low level perceptual encoding, it is not a sufficient condition (cf. Masson and McLeod, 1996). Wagenmakers *et al.* (2000) have shown that an alternative version of the counter-model can handle the both-primed benefit *without* altering the rate of feature extraction for studied words. We turn next to the REMI account of this same set of data, and show that there exists a version of this model in which a both-primed benefit can be predicted without assuming perceptual enhancement due to priming. Of course there are other versions in which the both-primed benefit is due to factors better termed perceptual enhancement.

---

[1] In earlier work, we used the more general term 'enhanced discriminability', denoting that the system is better in distinguishing the target from the foil. In the following, we use the term 'both-primed benefit' as a shorthand for 'enhanced discriminability due to priming of both alternatives'.

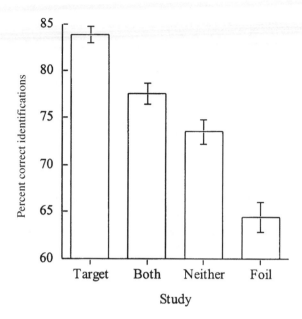

Figure 5.1 Percentage correct identifications in forced-choice auditory word identification as a function of study condition (Zeelenberg *et al.*, 2002, Experiment 2).

REMI: a model for long-term priming

Ratcliff and McKoon (1997) argued that in order to explain the interaction of the priming effect with similarity of the alternatives one has to assume that priming changes subsequent *processing* of ambiguous information. This way, one can state that for similar alternatives, processing is of type A (i.e., 'stealing') and for dissimilar alternatives processing is of type B (i.e., 'no stealing'). However, most models of priming, such as Morton's (1969) logogen model, assume that priming affects the representation of the stimulus (e.g., by raising its level of activation). These models would seem to predict that priming effects are ubiquitous and independent of orthographic similarity of the two alternatives:

> The main reason that other existing models cannot explain priming effects is their assumption that prior exposure to a word changes some property of the representation of the word itself. (...) When a property of the word itself changes, then processing of the word should always show facilitation relative to processing of other words. (Ratcliff and McKoon, 1997, p. 339.)

The REMI model demonstrates that this claim is too strong. In the REMI model, repetition priming alters the lexical/semantic representation of the studied item by adding general contextual information to that trace. As we will explain below, REMI predicts that the impact that this stored contextual information has on the decision process varies with similarity of the alternatives: Prior study affects similar alternatives more than dissimilar alternatives.

In the REMI model, words are represented as vectors of feature values (e.g., $< 2, 3, 1, 4, 4, \ldots, 4, 8 >$). These features can be of two kinds. First, they can contain *content*-information such as orthographic, phonological, and semantic information of the particular word. Second, the features can contain *context*-information defining the setting in which the word has been encountered. Crucially, the context information is common to foils and targets in the 2-AFC task. The value of a feature defines its base rate: Common features have low values, whereas rare features have high values (sampled according to a geometric distribution). The REMI model for forced-choice perceptual identification assumes that when the alternatives are presented, their corresponding lexical memory traces are activated and matched simultaneously to the error-prone and noisy perceived features from the flash. The trace that has the greater number of matching features is chosen (guessing occurs if there is a tie). In addition, the perceived vector is influenced by the context in which the target word is flashed.

REMI models repetition priming by storing context features in the lexical representation for a word during study. The general assumption of the REM model on which REMI is based is that information is not added to existing traces if that information is already present in the trace. For well known words, content features that discriminate targets from foils are already stored in the lexical trace, and are not added. At the time of test, it is assumed that the perceived vector contains features that are unique to the current test context. Thus when the two lexical memory traces corresponding to the two alternatives are matched to the perceived vector, the studied alternative will have an advantage over a non-studied alternative. This advantage occurs because the stored study context of the presentation will tend to match the current test context and test features, creating additional matches for the studied alternative, regardless of whether the studied alternative is the target or foil. Thus the addition of matching context features from the study episode to the lexical trace results in *bias*. The amount of bias will depend on the ratio of the number of extra matching features in comparison to the total number of features that differ between the two alternatives (i.e., the number of diagnostic features). Bias is higher when there are fewer diagnostic features, predicting the smaller bias for dissimilar alternatives. An illustration of the REMI model's predictions is given in Figures 5.2 and 5.3 (see Schooler *et al.*, 2001, for details).

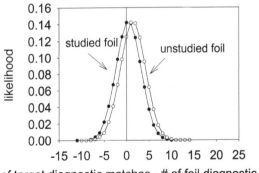

Figure 5.2 The distributions for the difference between the number of matches for the target and a *similar* foil (e.g., LIED–DIED), both for a studied foil and for an unstudied foil.

Figure 5.2 shows the effect of studying the *foil* alternative on a choice between similar words. An optimal decision strategy only considers diagnostic matches (i.e., matches that differentiate between the target and the foil). More specifically, the number of diagnostic matches for the target alternative is compared to the number of diagnostic matches for the foil alternative. Whichever alternative has more diagnostic matches is chosen. Therefore performance can be determined in Figure 5.2 by considering the area under the curve to the right of the normative criterion of zero. In Figure 5.2 we see that the effect of studying the foil is to provide an additional context match to the foil alternative, causing the distribution to shift to the left. This leftward shift indicates decreased performance. Figure 5.3 shows the same distributions for a choice between dissimilar alternatives. When the alternatives are dissimilar there are many more diagnostic features. Since these diagnostic features are stochastically provided through perception, the potential for more diagnostic features results in greater variability in the number of diagnostic matches. As compared to Figure 5.2 the distributions in Figure 5.3 have greater variance, yet the downward shift in the distribution due to study of the foil alternative is the same. The net result is that the change in the area to the right of zero due to studying the foil is much less for dissimilar alternatives than for similar alternatives. The important point, clarified by Figures 5.2 and 5.3, is that an identical shift in the difference distributions due to prior study has more impact for similar alternatives than for dissimilar alternatives, because the variance of the difference distribution for similar alternatives is smaller than for dissimilar alternatives. Note that this model predicts bias at low flash times, because an extra match due to context occurs independent of the flash.

Thus, REMI demonstrates that priming can be explained by assuming a change in the representation of the repeated stimulus. This is a conceptually different approach than the one taken by Ratcliff and McKoon (1997). On the other hand, both models agree that priming causes bias, not an improvement in perception of the repeated stimulus.

We now turn to ways in which this simple version of the REMI model might be modified to predict the both-primed benefit that has been found in recent studies (as discussed

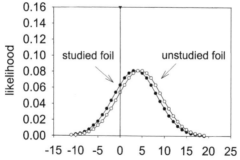

Figure 5.3 The distributions for the difference between the number of matches for the target and a *dissimilar* foil (e.g., LIED–SOFA), both for a studied foil and for an unstudied foil.

earlier). The simple version of REMI predicts (as did the 1997 version of the counter-model) that prior study of both alternatives has no effect, since the context benefits are obtained by both alternatives alike, canceling each other. In one modification, the REMI model could use the approach adopted by Ratcliff and McKoon (2000), by assuming a higher rate of feature extraction for studied low-frequency words: It could be assumed that study of a low-frequency word has an additional effect (beyond context storage) of increasing the accuracy of the perceived vector. For example, lexical traces for low-frequency words might not be complete, so that prior study could add some content features that are useful for discriminating targets from foils.

However, it is important to note that there are other approaches that can explain both-primed benefits; approaches that do not posit improved perception of the flash. REMI can account for the both-primed benefit by assuming that the number of matching features needs to reach a minimum value to avoid guessing (i.e., a criterion number of matches must be exceeded). If both alternatives have too few matches the subject guesses randomly between the two alternatives (for similar discrete models using pure guessing, see for instance Anderson and Lebiere, 1998, p. 161; De Jong, 1991; Wagenmakers *et al.*, 2000). Additional matches due to prior study serve to reduce the proportion of trials on which the subject has to guess, improving performance. To see how the model can handle frequency effects, it could be assumed that high-frequency words have more common features, increasing the number of matches that occur by chance. The criterion can therefore be chosen so that high-frequency words usually have enough matches to pass the criterion even without prior study, but low-frequency words do not. This approach is theoretically interesting because it predicts the both-primed benefit, as well as its dependency upon word frequency, through a criterion amount of evidence required to avert guessing.

In this modification of REMI the both-primed benefit could be viewed as a bias effect, since it is not necessary to assume an improvement in encoding of the flash. However, the assumption of a criterion and guessing when the criterion is not exceeded means that studied words are dealt with more efficiently than non-studied words. Thus the issue of whether to label the criterion mechanism used by REMI either *bias* or enhanced *perception* is somewhat arbitrary, and might depend on that point in processing where one believes perception to cease and decision to start. This is one of those cases where the model is explicit, but it is hard to find labels that are not ambiguous.

In summary, REMI is capable of explaining various implicit priming phenomena in the 2-AFC paradigm (for detailed fits to data see Schooler *et al.*, 2001), including the bias effect due to prior study, the interaction of prior study with similarity of alternatives, the effects of flash time, and the both-primed benefit. Both REMI and the counter-model can also handle results from free response perceptual identification (in which subjects have to name the flashed word without the explicit presence of alternatives) and from the 'yes–no' task (see Schooler *et al.*, 2001; Ratcliff and McKoon, 1997, for details).

The critical role played by biased decision making in these priming tasks seems incontrovertible. Recent demonstrations of both-primed benefits have raised the possibility of an additional factor of perceptual enhancement. The version of the REMI model in Schooler *et al.* (2001) and the version of the counter-model presented by Wagenmakers *et al.* (2000) demonstrate that such benefits could be explained by what might be considered a form of bias, although not ruling out the possibility of perceptual enhancement. Whether or not future research should demonstrate that priming sometimes produces a true perceptual benefit, as opposed to various forms of biased responding and decision making, it is worth noting that present research on word priming shows the size of priming effects due to bias are much larger than those that might be due to perceptual change.

The present state of long-term priming

Both empirically and theoretically there are at present a number of open issues in the field, in addition to the question of perceptual facilitation. One issue is raised by results of Bowers (1999). He used a paradigm almost identical to that used by Ratcliff and McKoon (1997) and found long-term repetition priming effects to be as large for dissimilar as for similar alternatives. McKoon and Ratcliff (2001) have identified one critical difference, the nature of the instructions. Differing instructions might cause differential search for memory for priming instances, and differential decision making based on the results of such memories. We hope that the near future will see quantitative models capable of handling both sets of findings in a conceptually consistent fashion.

A second issue has been raised by Masson and Bodner (2000), who suggest that implicit long-term priming effects in 2-AFC might originate through 'perceptual fluency' of the alternatives. For a choice between similar alternatives (e.g., LIED–DIED), there exists a common (in this case orthographic) ground on which the alternatives can be compared. The repeated stimulus (e.g., LIED) is perceived more fluently than its unstudied counterpart DIED, and hence it will be preferred. It is assumed that for dissimilar alternatives (e.g., LIED–SOFA) there is no common ground for comparing the two alternatives, and hence no priming effect. According to Masson and Bodner, priming effects should be observed whenever the two alternatives share some properties on which they can be compared. Indeed, for orthographically dissimilar pairs that are semantically associated (e.g., a choice between KIWI and PEAR), Masson and Bodner *did* observe a reliable priming effect. (Of course, from the REMI perspective, such a manipulation could be viewed as producing an intermediate degree of similarity, and hence an intermediate effect size.) It should be noted that Masson and Bodner did *not* find bias effects for alternatives that were both orthographically and semantically unrelated (e.g., MOUSE–PIANO), making an explanation of their results in terms of episodic retrieval attempts induced by instructions less plausible.

ROUSE: a model for short-term priming

ROUSE (Responding Optimally with Unknown Sources of Evidence) is a model for short-term priming in the same primary task we have been considering: two-alternative perceptual word identification. In contrast with long-term priming, the prime or primes are presented a few seconds before the primary test phase. Before introducing the model, we explain the short-term priming paradigm, and present relevant data.

Figure 5.4 shows a typical presentation sequence (Huber *et al.*, 2001, Experiment 1). A target is briefly flashed, subsequently masked, and then followed by two alternatives,

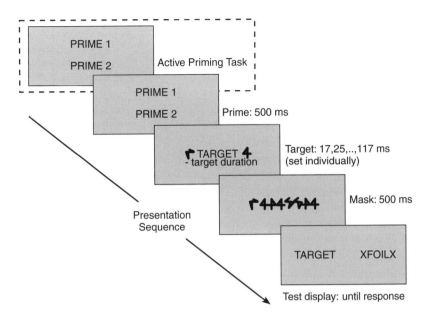

Figure 5.4 A typical sequence of displays in a 2-AFC short-term priming experiment. The display contained within the dashed box only appears in the active priming condition.

from which the subject attempts to choose the alternative that was flashed. The primes are presented immediately preceding the flashed target (instead of in a list of words studied several minutes earlier). In Huber *et al.*'s (2001) Experiment 1, one group of participants were told that the primes were a warning signal for the onset of the flash (the *passive* priming condition), and the primes appeared for 500 ms. Another group were instructed to make an animacy (i.e., alive or dead) decision on the primes (the *active* priming condition). The animacy decision task is indicated in Figure 5.4 by the dashed box, and took about three seconds to complete. (As we will see, the way subjects study the prime, actively or passively, has a profound impact on the results.) The use of two primes made it possible to repetition-prime both alternatives. The alternatives used in Experiment 1 from Huber *et al.* (2001) were dissimilar. (Later studies in Huber *et al.*, 2001, demonstrated that similarity of alternatives does affect the results, in complex ways that are predicted by ROUSE, and the reader is referred to that article for details.)

Although Huber *et al.* (2001) used many types of priming relations, we will discuss here only the results for repetition priming. There were four conditions:

(1) Neither the target nor the foil were primed.
(2) Both the target and the foil were primed.
(3) The target was primed.
(4) The foil was primed.

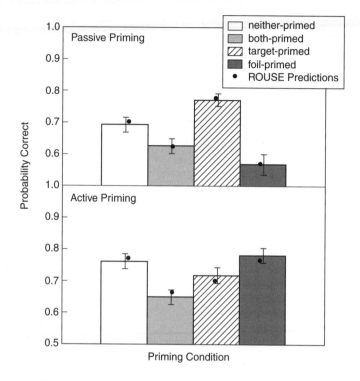

Figure 5.5 Results and ROUSE-predictions for data from Huber *et al.*, 2001 (Experiment 1). Error bars are two standard errors of the mean.

The results can be seen in Figure 5.5. Remarkably, when both alternatives were primed by presenting them immediately before the target flash, performance is decreased compared to when neither alternative was primed, a result obtained for both passive priming and active priming (see the first two columns of Figure 5.5). Thus, whereas in long-term priming a both-primed benefit is observed, short-term priming is characterized by a 'both-primed *deficit*'. The second surprising result is that subjects prefer the primed alternative in the passive condition (similar to the bias findings in long-term priming), but this preference is *reversed* in the active priming condition (see the last two columns in Figure 5.5). In other words, after thorough processing of the primes, subjects have a tendency *not* to choose the primed alternative but rather to choose the unprimed alternative. Next, we will introduce the ROUSE model capable of handling these results (as well as many others results that space considerations prevent us from discussing).

ROUSE models the primary task in essentially the same fashion as REMI: The perceived information is matched to the two alternatives, producing vectors of matches and mismatches. More precisely the results of matching a given feature are represented by one of two states: 'match' or 'mismatch', termed 'ON' and 'OFF' for short. Prior to the flash, all features are 'OFF'. However, three sources of activation, operative during task execution, can change

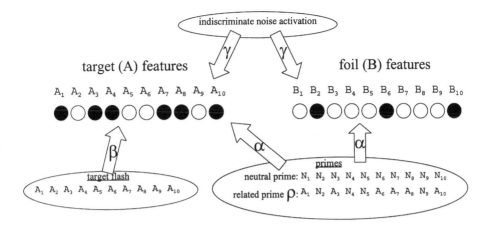

Figure 5.6 The ROUSE model for short-term priming.

the state of any feature to 'ON'. Figure 5.6 illustrates these three sources of activation: First, features from the target alternative (e.g., LIED) can be activated by perceived features extracted from the flash (e.g., LI) with probability β. This probability β indicates perceptual encoding and increases with flash time. Second, noise, either due to perturbation from the mask or from random fluctuations in the perceptual system itself, turns features 'ON' randomly in the target vector and the foil vector with probability γ. Finally, features that are part of the *primes* can activate corresponding features in either alternative with probability α. This source confusion results in a bias for alternatives similar (or identical) to prime words. After the three sources of activation have turned features 'ON' and left other features 'OFF', a near-optimal decision is made between the two alternatives: Likelihoods are calculated for each alternative, and the higher likelihood determines the choice. The critical feature of ROUSE occurs during the likelihood calculations: These take into account the possibility that features may be turned on by primes. In particular, the evidence provided by a feature that might have arisen from a prime is discounted. This discounting of features known to be in a prime word can result in a reversal of the bias effect.

Consider a diagnostic feature that has been turned 'ON' in alternative A (e.g., the letter L in LIED when the choice is between LIED and DIED). This feature provides strong evidence in favor of LIED because it could have been turned on only by correct perception or by noise (and γ in ROUSE is actually a very small probability). However, suppose that LIED had been presented as a prime. Now the L feature being 'ON' provides less evidence because it could have been turned 'ON' by the prime, rather than correct perception or noise.

In an optimal system, the likelihood calculations would use an accurate estimate for the probability of source confusion due to the primes (i.e., the estimate of α denoted α'). However, it is assumed that passive priming leads the estimate to be slightly too low, producing too little discounting, and hence a preference for the alternative that has been primed (since the 'ON' features will produce too much evidence for the primed alternative). It is assumed that active priming leads the estimate to be slightly too high, producing the opposite outcome—a preference for the alternative that was not primed. These mechanisms illustrate how ROUSE predicts the bias effects when one alternative is primed.

Consider next what happens when both alternatives are primed. By symmetry, neither alternative gains an advantage. However, the primes tend to turn 'ON' extra features in both alternatives. These extra 'ON' features produce extra noise, tending to drown out the signal from the features turned on by the flash. This extra noise is what produces the both-primed deficit that is observed in both priming conditions.

At this point it is worth noting that ROUSE models short-term priming as a bias or preference effect.[2] ROUSE does not assume priming to result in a higher rate of feature extraction for the repeated stimulus (i.e., a perceptual effect). However, Huber *et al.* (2001) did find a small but reliable benefit of associative priming when a prime word (e.g., MISTAKE) was associatively related to both choice words (e.g., ERROR and WRONG) compared to when the prime was not related to the choice words (see also Masson and Borowsky, 1998). Since the semantic overlap between prime and target is 100% for repetition priming, it is feasible that there might in fact be a semantic both-primed *benefit* in short-term repetition priming, albeit overshadowed by a much larger orthographic both-primed *deficit*. At present, ROUSE does not provide an explanation for the small both-primed benefit occasionally observed when the prime is associatively related to the choice words. Extensions of the model to handle such findings await further research, as does any final judgment whether such findings demonstrate perceptual enhancement rather than some more subtle form of bias.

Space does not permit discussion of the way in which ROUSE predicts results for other sorts of prime relations. In particular, we cannot discuss the many non-intuitive predictions that ROUSE makes as one manipulates the similarity of primes to choices, and choices to each other. Nevertheless, the fact that these predictions are borne out in the results is a major source of evidence in favor of the model (see Huber *et al.*, 2001, for details).

Discussion of ROUSE

The general notion that people sometimes mistrust salient information is not new. For instance, social psychologists have found a reversal of the priming effect for evaluative judgments (Lombardi *et al.*, 1987): Participants able to recall the priming event gave evaluative judgments *opposite* to the prime, whereas participants unable to recall the priming event tended to give evaluative judgments *consistent* with the prime. However, this general notion of discounting had not been applied to visual word recognition or formulated in a process model prior to the development of ROUSE. In addition, several priming phenomena can be re-interpreted when one considers how ROUSE can be applied to those phenomena. First, consider sub-threshold ('subliminal') priming: When a prime is presented so briefly that the subject is unable to identify it, effects of priming are still observed

---

[2] Huber *et al.* (2001) use the label 'preference' instead of 'bias', because 'bias' is, according to their view, a theory-laden concept that might suggest, wrongly, signal-detection theory to be applicable.

and can be larger than for supra-threshold priming. For example, Murphy and Zajonc (1993) had subjects give liking ratings to Chinese ideographs. These ideographs were preceded by positive or negative affective primes, shown either for a very brief duration or for a longer duration. For very brief durations, the priming effect was congruent (i.e., a positive prime led to a positive evaluation for the ideograph and vice versa). However, this effect disappeared and even tended to reverse when the affective primes were presented for longer durations. Murphy and Zajonc appeal to a theoretical relation between consciousness, emotion, and cognition to account for these interesting results. We believe ROUSE can give a more parsimonious explanation of their data: When subjects cannot identify the prime, they may not discount prime information appropriately. In fact, subjects might not be discounting information at all (i.e., their estimate of a may equal zero) causing a preference for a prime-related response. In contrast, when subjects can clearly see the prime, they may engage in a discounting process that suppresses prime-related responding. If subjects discount prime information too much (i.e., their estimate of α is greater than α), this might even lead to a preference for prime-unrelated responding.

ROUSE can provide an alternative explanation concerning the effects of orthographic priming in visual word recognition in a similar fashion.[3] When an orthographically related prime (e.g., HEAT) is presented immediately before presentation of the target (e.g., MEAT), this sometimes leads to inhibition and sometimes to facilitation of the response to the target relative to when an orthographically unrelated prime (e.g., TOSS) is presented. More specifically, in what is known as 'form-priming', the rapid successive presentation of a masked orthographically related prime and the target increases performance (e.g., Evett and Humphreys, 1981). In form-priming, subjects are usually unable to identify the prime and perceive prime and target as a single perceptual event. On the other hand, when the prime is clearly presented for a relatively long duration preceding the onset of the target, inhibitory effects due to priming the target with an orthographically similar word (i.e., a so-called 'neighbor') are sometimes observed (e.g., Colombo, 1986). The form-priming results are commonly interpreted as being due to *perceptual facilitation*, whereas the inhibitory neighbor priming results are often attributed to some kind of lexical suppression through inhibitory connections between simultaneously activated words. In ROUSE, facilitatory form-priming can arise once subjects do not discount prime-related information enough, and this is best characterized as a *preference* or bias effect. Further, ROUSE can account for the phenomenon of inhibitory neighbor priming by assuming subjects sometimes discount prime-related information too much. Rather than being due to lexical suppression, inhibitory neighbor priming can thus be due to a source monitoring problem (see O'Seaghdha and Marin, 2000, for a related account).

In general, ROUSE shows that the way subjects study the primes (i.e., passively or actively) can have a profound influence on the magnitude and even the direction of the priming effect. When one considers the amount of attention paid to the primes is sometimes

---

[3] A number of variations in orthographic priming were explored by Huber *et al.* (2001) within a forced choice paradigm, and were fit quite successfully by ROUSE. Prior research using other paradigms is the subject of this section.

not constrained or manipulated, it comes as no surprise that, for example in semantic priming, results are occasionally contradictory and ambiguous (e.g., Neely, 1991).

General discussion

In this chapter we have presented a common model framework for the task of threshold word identification assessed by two-alternative forced-choice testing. The models are based on an optimal approach to decision making utilizing Bayesian principles. Using this model framework we have shown how it is possible to model both long-term and short-term priming effects, thereby demonstrating how a variety of phenomena of implicit memory can be placed in a common conceptual framework in a rigorous, quantitative manner. Of course, the mechanisms of priming are somewhat different in the two cases, as one might expect.

First, REMI is a model for long-term priming that gives an explanation of priming based upon the storage of context information in the lexical trace during study of the prime. Because the context during the study phase will tend to match the context present in the test phase, a system using optimal decision principles will tend to choose the studied alternative to the non-studied alternative. The greater number of diagnostic features for dissimilar choices produces a great deal of variability due to chance, reducing the impact of extra matching features due to priming (see Figures 5.2 and 5.3). REMI is also able to account for the both-primed benefit that is found for low-frequency words by setting a criterion that has to be exceeded in order to avoid guessing. This demonstrates that the both-primed benefit does not need to imply a higher rate of feature extraction for repeated words.

Second, ROUSE is a model for short-term priming that gives an explanation of priming based upon source confusion for prime activated features. In producing an optimal decision, features that might have been activated by the prime provide a discounted level of evidence. The discounting mechanism gives a parsimonious account of many seemingly contradictory data (e.g., the reversal of the priming effect with increased processing of the prime). In addition, priming itself produces chance variability, accounting for the both-primed deficits that are observed with short-term repetition priming (see the first two columns of Figure 5.5).

REMI and ROUSE both account for priming through what might be considered *bias*, both models in their simplest form assuming the effect of prior study does not act to change the quality of information that is entering the system, but rather to change the *impact* that the incoming information has on the decision process. Generally speaking, the effect of priming is to tune the decisional mechanisms toward likely events, that is, events that recently occurred in the same environment. REMI and ROUSE are based on Bayesian principles and the idea that decisions are made to optimize performance in the face of noisy data. Although the brain is probably not calculating log odds or likelihood ratios, it might have learned to approximate such a calculation over developmental time in order to behave in a near-optimal fashion when confronted with a noisy and uncertain environment. One of the advantages of using a Bayesian approach is that it provides a rational framework for modeling that is not *ad hoc*.

We believe that priming phenomena, and implicit memory phenomena in general, can be better understood when they are modeled in a consistent way. We have demonstrated that both REMI and ROUSE, using a common theoretical framework, are capable of handling some of the most important extant findings in the field of priming as well as recent new data (e.g., the findings of the both-primed benefit in long-term memory, the both-primed deficit in short-term memory, and the reversal of preference when the nature of prime processing is changed). Much of this research is still at an early stage, but the successes we have presented in this chapter hold out hope for rapid theoretical progress in the near future.

Acknowledgments

René Zeelenberg was supported by a grant from the Foundation for Behavioral and Social Sciences of the Netherlands Organization for Scientific Research.

References

Anderson, J. R. and Lebiere, C. (1998). *The atomic components of thought.* Lawrence-Erlbaum Associates.

Becker, S., Moscovitch, M., Behrmann, M., and Joordens, S. (1997). Long-term semantic priming: A computational account and empirical evidence. *Journal of Experimental Psychology: Learning, Memory, and Cognition,* **23**, 1059–82.

Bowers, J. S. (1999). Priming is not all bias: Commentary on Ratcliff and McKoon (1997). *Psychological Review,* **106**, 582–96.

Church, B. A. and Schacter, D. L. (1994). Perceptual specificity of auditory priming: Implicit memory for voice intonation and fundamental frequency. *Journal of Experimental Psychology: Learning, Memory, and Cognition,* **20**, 521–33.

Colombo, L. (1986). Activation and inhibition with orthographically similar words. *Journal of Experimental Psychology: Human Perception and Performance,* **12**, 226–34.

De Jong, R. (1991). Partial information or facilitation? Different interpretations of results from speed-accuracy decomposition. *Perception and Psychophysics,* **50**, 333–50.

Evett, L. J. and Humphreys, G. W. (1981). The use of abstract graphemic information in lexical access. *Quarterly Journal of Experimental Psychology,* **33**, 325–50.

Gillund, G. and Shiffrin, R. M. (1984). A retrieval model for both recognition and recall. *Psychological Review,* **91**, 1–67.

Graf, P., Squire, L. R., and Mandler, G. (1984). The information that amnesic patients do not forget. *Journal of Experimental Psychology: Learning, Memory, and Cognition,* **10**, 164–78.

Huber, D. E., Shiffrin, R. M., Lyle, K. B., and Ruys, K. I. (2001). Perception and preference in short-term word priming. *Psychological Review,* **108**, 149–82.

Jacoby, L. L. and Dallas, M. (1981). On the relationship between autobiographical memory and perceptual learning. *Journal of Experimental Psychology: General,* **110**, 306–40.

Lombardi, W. J., Higgins, E. T., and Bargh, J. A. (1987). The role of consciousness in priming effects on categorization: Assimilation versus contrast as a function of awareness of the priming task. *Personality and Social Psychology Bulletin,* **13**, 411–29.

Masson, M. E. J. and Bodner, G. E. (2000, January). *Fluent encoding of probes guides masked word identification*. Paper presented at the 25th Annual Interdisciplinary Conference, Teton Village, Wyoming.

Masson, M. E. J. and Borowsky, R. (1998). More than meets the eye: Context effects in word identification. *Memory and Cognition*, **26**, 1245–69.

Masson, M. E. J. and Freedman, L. (1990). Fluent identification of repeated words. *Journal of Experimental Psychology: Learning, Memory, and Cognition*, **16**, 355–73.

Masson, M. E. J. and MacLeod, C. M. (1996). Contributions of processing fluency to repetition effects in masked word identification. *Canadian Journal of Experimental Psychology*, **50**, 9–21.

McKoon, G. and Ratcliff, R. (2001). Counter model for word identification: Reply to Bowers (1999). *Psychological Review*, **108**, 674–81.

Morton, J. (1969). Interaction of information in word recognition. *Psychological Review*, **76**, 165–78.

Murphy, S. T. and Zajonc, R. B. (1993). Affect, cognition, and awareness: Affective priming with optimal and suboptimal stimulus exposures. *Journal of Personality and Social Psychology*, **64**, 723–39.

Neely, J. H. (1991). Semantic priming effects in visual word recognition: A selective review of current findings and theories. In *Basic processes in reading: Visual word recognition* (ed. D. Besner and G. W. Humphreys), pp. 264–336. Hillsdale, NJ: Erlbaum.

O'Seaghdha, P. and Marin, J. W. (2000). Phonological competition and cooperation in form-related priming: Sequential and nonsequential processes in word production. *Journal of Experimental Psychology: Human Perception and Performance*, **26**, 57–73.

Raaijmakers, J. G. W. and Shiffrin, R. M. (1981). Search of associative memory. *Psychological Review*, **88**, 93–134.

Ratcliff, R. and McKoon, G. (1996). Bias effects in implicit memory tasks. *Journal of Experimental Psychology: General*, **125**, 403–21.

Ratcliff, R. and McKoon, G. (1997). A counter model for implicit priming in perceptual word identification. *Psychological Review*, **104**, 319–43.

Ratcliff, R. and McKoon, G. (2000). Modeling the effects of repetition and word frequency in perceptual identification. *Psychonomic Bulletin and Review*, **7**, 713–17.

Ratcliff, R., McKoon, G., and Verwoerd, M. (1989). A bias interpretation of facilitation in perceptual identification. *Journal of Experimental Psychology: Learning, Memory, and Cognition*, **15**, 378–87.

Ratcliff, R., Allbritton, D., and McKoon, G. (1997). Bias in auditory priming. *Journal of Experimental Psychology: Learning, Memory, and Cognition*, **23**, 143–52.

Roediger, H. L., III, Weldon, M. S., Stadler, M. L., and Riegler, G. L. (1992). Direct comparison of two implicit memory tests: Word fragment and word stem completion. *Journal of Experimental Psychology: Learning, Memory, and Cognition*, **18**, 1251–69.

Salasoo, A., Shiffrin, R. M., and Feustel, T. C. (1985). Building permanent codes: Codification and repetition effects in word identification. *Journal of Experimental Psychology: General*, **114**, 50–77.

Schacter, D. L. (1990). Priming and multiple memory systems: Perceptual mechanisms of implicit memory. In *Memory systems 1994* (ed. D. L. Schacter and E. Tulving), pp. 233–68. Cambridge, MA: MIT Press.

Schooler, L. J., Shiffrin, R. M., and Raaijmakers, J. G. W. (2001). Theoretical note: A Bayesian model for implicit effects in perceptual identification. *Psychological Review*, **108**, 257–72.

Shiffrin, R. M. and Steyvers, M. (1997). A model for recognition memory: REM—retrieving effectively from memory. *Psychonomic Bulletin and Review*, **4**, 145–66.

Shimamura, A. P. and Squire, L. R. (1984). Paired-associate learning and priming effects in amnesia: A neuropsychological study. *Journal of Experimental Psychology: General*, **113**, 556–70.

Squire, L. R. (1992). Memory and the hippocampus: A synthesis from findings with rats, monkeys, and humans. *Psychological Review*, **99**, 195–231.

Wagenmakers, E. M., Zeelenberg, R., Schooler, L. J., and Raaijmakers, J. G. W. (2000). A criterion-shift model for enhanced discriminability in perceptual identification: A note on the counter model. *Psychonomic Bulletin and Review*, **7**, 718–26.

Wagenmakers, E. M., Zeelenberg, R., and Raaijmakers, J. G. W. (2000). Testing the counter model for perceptual identification: Effects of repetition priming and word frequency. *Psychonomic Bulletin and Review*, **7**, 662–7.

Zeelenberg, R., Shiffrin, R. M., and Raaijmakers, J. G. W. (1999). Priming in a free association task as a function of association directionality. *Memory and Cognition*, **27**, 956–61.

Zeelenberg, R., Wagenmakers, E. M., and Raaijmakers, J. G. W. (2002). Repetition priming in implicit memory tasks: Prior study causes enhanced discriminability, not only bias. *Journal of Experimental Psychology: General*, **131**, 38–47.

CHAPTER 6

WHAT THE REPETITION PRIMING METHODOLOGY REVEALS ABOUT MORPHOLOGICAL ASPECTS OF WORD RECOGNITION

LAURIE BETH FELDMAN

One of the most popular methodologies for studying morphology is the long-term repetition priming task. Although various priming tasks have been developed, one very common procedure to study morphology requires participants to make a lexical decision to each visually presented letter string, primes, as well as targets. The primary variable of interest is decision latency to a target and how it is influenced by the presentation of a related word displayed earlier in the experimental list. Typically, prior presentation of a word formed from the same base morpheme as the target (morphologically related) but differing with respect to affixes (prefixes or suffixes) produces facilitation. Similar effects have been documented in a variety of languages including Serbian (e.g., Feldman, 1994a), Hebrew (e.g., Bentin and Feldman, 1990), and American Sign Language (e.g., Hanson and Feldman, 1989) as well as English (e.g., Feldman, 1992; Fowler, Napps, and Feldman, 1985; Neiser, Hernon, and Hall, 1979). When multiple items or more than a few seconds separate the second presentation from the first, the pattern of facilitation for word targets is distinct from the pattern in an immediate priming task in which the prime and target are presented in succession. Because regular formations are, by definition, formed from the same unit as their relatives (ADDS, ADDING, ADDED entail the base ADD plus an affix, either S, ING, or ED), morphologically related prime target pairs necessarily possess some degree of similarity with respect to form and to meaning. Nevertheless, neither similarity of form nor semantic association alone can account for facilitation to lexical decision latencies in the long-term repetition priming task although they do influence immediate priming. In the present chapter, I will summarize what the long-term repetition priming methodology with lexical decision has revealed about morphological processing. I will selectively sample over studies conducted in a variety of languages, but will focus on my work in English.

Morphological facilitation in the long-term repetition priming task is assessed by comparing lexical decision latency or accuracy to the target preceded by a morphological relative to:

(a) A first presentation of the target word (i.e., no prime).
(b) An identical repetition of the target word.

Sometimes facilitation with morphological relatives as a prime is equivalent to the effect of an identical repetition of the target. More typically, it is reduced relative to an identical repetition but is still significant (e.g., Fowler *et al.*, 1985). Accordingly, sometimes researchers use the *percent of identity facilitation* (viz., first presentation minus related/first presentation minus identity) rather than the magnitude of facilitation (first presentation minus related) as a measure of morphological facilitation. Researchers interpret the patterns of facilitation among morphological relatives as revealing about the character of lexical representations and the manner in which they are organized within the mental lexicon although emphases vary. For example, greater facilitation for identical repetitions than for successive presentations of morphological relatives has been interpreted as evidence of separate lexical entries for each morphological relative (e.g., Stanners *et al.*, 1979) and as evidence of interrelated entries (e.g., Fowler *et al.*, 1985).

For identity pairs in long-term priming, lexicality cannot change between prime and target. However, for non-identical but morphologically related prime target pairs, it can. For example, the target FEVER could follow either FEVERISH which is a real word or FEVERY which is not. Lexicality of the prime can influence acceptance latencies for word targets; at least those that are irregular morphological formations. More specifically, target latencies for ATE were significantly reduced following EATEN (53 ms) but not following EATED (2 ms). However, target latencies for FEVER were not significantly reduced following derived complex word forms such as the word FEVERISH (7 ms) or nonwords such as FEVERY (9 ms). The absence of facilitation for FEVER targets is ambiguous. The crucial interaction with lexicality of the prime could require reduced orthographic similarity due to irregularity of the base or inflectional as contrasted with derivational relatedness. By comparison with derivational affixes (e.g., Y, ISH, TION, OR), the addition of an inflectional affix (e.g., S, ED, ING) tends to introduce only minimal changes to the complex word form. However, irregular inflectional relatives such as EAT–ATE, tend to be less similar with respect to form than are derivational relatives. Similarly, in Hebrew (Feldman and Bentin, 1994; Experiment 3), when primes consisted of an illegal combination of real root and real derivational word pattern, reaction times to regular word targets composed from the same root as the prime were not significantly faster (6 ms) than to targets preceded by an unrelated prime.

In sum, for real word targets, repetition of the root does not produce morphological facilitation unless primes as well as targets are real words in which case, the decision is 'word' for prime as well as target. Effects of lexicality for word targets may indicate that response repetition contributes to facilitation. Nevertheless, the outcome of many studies suggests that morphological effects in the long-term priming variant of the lexical decision task are fundamentally linguistic in locus. I review those data in the present chapter. I focus first on semantic and orthographic dimensions of relatedness and then present some new data on asymmetries in the magnitude of facilitation that depend on the recursion of morphemes from the target in the prime.

Morphological facilitation when effects of semantic similarity are absent

Because regular morphological relatives are, by definition, formed from the same unit, they necessarily possess some degree of similarity with respect to meaning and to form. It is important, however, to differentiate the contribution of a shared morpheme from that of semantic relatedness. The semantic relationship typically shared by prime target pairs in a semantic priming study is an associative relationship, defined on whole word forms that co-occur (e.g., Lupker, 1984) but it may capture other dimensions of relatedness as well (e.g., Moss, Ostin, Tyler, and Marslen-Wilson, 1995). By contrast, semantic similarity among morphological relatives tends to reflect the degree to which they overlap in meaning because they share a meaningful component, the base morpheme. For derivationally related forms in particular, there are multiple dimensions of potential overlap. For example, LOGICAL and ILLOGICAL are antonyms. They share word class. The way in which their meanings are similar contrasts greatly with the verb SANCTIFY and the noun SANCTION. Nevertheless, both pairs are morphologically related and rarely co-occur.

It is difficult to produce effects of semantic association among morphologically unrelated items presented in the long-term repetition priming task unless the experimental context enhances the focus on semantics as might the inclusion of pseudohomophones (Becker, Moscovitch, Behrmann, and Joordens, 1997). Long-term facilitation in the lexical decision task in English is absent between antonyms such as COLD–HOT (Fowler cited in Feldman, 1992) and between other dimensions of semantic relatedness (Henderson, Wallace, and Knight, 1984). In a comprehensive study, Feldman (2000) compared patterns of long-term facilitation for prime target pairs that are related to targets along one of three dimensions. Critical primes and targets were either morphologically related (e.g., VOWED–VOW), orthographically related (e.g., VOWEL–VOW), or semantically related (e.g., PLEDGE–VOW), and each critical prime was paired with an unrelated prime matched for frequency, length, and morphological structure.

Across multiple test orders, each target was preceded by all six (type of prime × relatedness) prime conditions. Primes and targets were separated by an average of ten intervening items (the range was 7 to 13). Participants responded to each trial, primes as well as targets. Each experimental trial consisted of a fixation signal ' + ' for 450 ms, followed by a blank field for 50 ms, and then by the letter string. Items remained visible until the subject responded or until 1500 ms had elapsed. The inter-trial interval was 1500 ms.

In one experiment (Feldman, 2000; Experiment 2), morphological primes reduced response latencies to targets relative to their controls by 28 ms but semantic and orthographic primes had no significant effect (9 ms and −1 ms respectively) when primes and targets were separated by 7–13 items. In an immediate priming task with a stimulus onset asynchrony (SOA) of 66 ms (Feldman, 2000; Experiment 1), however, the same semantic and orthographic primes significantly reduced decision latencies to the same targets. These results are noteworthy because long-term morphological facilitation was evident in lexical decision under conditions in which neither significant semantic nor orthographic effects were present.

A similar study conducted with Hebrew materials contrasted facilitation from semantically related words with and without a common base morpheme at long lags and at zero lags (Bentin and Feldman, 1990). Visual primes preceded visual targets that were related morphologically, semantically, or both morphologically and semantically. For example, in Hebrew, the words for LIBRARY and LIBRARIAN share both a semantic and a morphological relationship (viz., the root morpheme SPR) whereas the words for LIBRARY and

NUMBER share a morpheme but have little semantic overlap. In that study, semantically related primes produced facilitation only in the 0 lag condition (i.e., +48 ms for lag 0 versus −5 ms for lag 15). At lag 15 (statistically) equivalent facilitation arose for the morphological plus semantic condition (+28 ms) and the morphological condition (+24 ms). Stated generally, the effects of morphological and semantic plus morphological relatedness did not differ in long-term repetition priming. These results suggest that semantic relatedness contributes little over and above morphological relatedness when relatives are presented with a lag of 15 items. However, in that study, the degree of semantic relatedness did influence the magnitude of facilitation among prime target pairs that were morphologically related when they appeared in immediate temporal succession.

Results with English materials are also consistent with the claim that semantic relatedness contributes little to long-term visual word recognition when primes and targets share morphology. Feldman and Stotko (unpublished, cited in Feldman, 1992) contrasted the effects of an identity repetition (e.g., CREATE) with the effects of both a 'semantically close' prime (e.g., CREATION), and a 'semantically far' morphological prime (e.g., CREATURE). Semantic distance was based on the ratings of 40 subjects. Whereas identity repetitions produced robust facilitation (93 ms) to target decision latencies, all morphologically related items produced smaller effects (33 ms). When 7–13 items intervened between prime and target, the degree of facilitation did not vary significantly depending on whether the morphologically related prime was a semantically close (36 ms) or a distant relative (30 ms) of the target. Once again, this time in English, the degree of semantic similarity between a morphologically related prime and target did not affect the magnitude of facilitation when primes and targets were separated by long lags.

The results from English summarized above indicate that facilitation in the long-term repetition priming task is not sensitive to semantic relatedness in the absence of shared morphology nor to the degree of semantic similarity between primes and targets that are formed from a common base morpheme. Similarly, Bentin and Feldman (1990) observed equivalent morphological facilitation for more and less semantically transparent morphological relatives at long lags in Hebrew. Effects of semantic transparency as well as semantic association were evident in immediate priming, however (Feldman and Soltano, 1999; Feldman, in press). Accordingly, Bentin and Feldman (1990) concluded that different mechanisms underlie facilitation in the long-term and in the immediate priming task. To elaborate, semantic transparency of the base morpheme, like the effects of associative relatedness, influence the immediate priming mechanism but not the mechanism that underlies long-term repetition priming (see also, Rueckl, Mikolinski, Raveh, Miner, and Mars, 1997; Raveh and Rueckl, 2000).

Morphological facilitation when effects of orthographic/ phonological similarity are attenuated

Regular morphological relatives are, by definition, formed from the same unit, therefore they necessarily possess some degree of similarity with respect to form as well as meaning. Nevertheless, long-term facilitation between morphologically related primes and targets differs distinctly from the effect of phonological or orthographic similarity in the absence of morphological relatedness. Moreover, it is difficult to demonstrate statistically that in the lexical decision task, long-term facilitation among morphologically related primes and targets is sensitive to the degree of phonological or orthographic similarity of prime and target (but see Rueckl et al., 1997).

Morphological and orthographic similarity were elegantly contrasted in German and Dutch (Drews and Zwitserlood, 1995). Orthographic primes (morphologically simple) as well as morphological primes (morphologically complex) had final letter sequences that could function as morphemes (e.g., EN, T, S, TE). Moreover, the letter sequence for both orthographic (KERST) and morphological (KERSEN) primes included the full target (KERS). Finally, orthographic and morphological primes were matched for frequency. At long lags, orthographically similar primes had no effect on target decision latencies. In immediate priming, by contrast, morphological primes produced facilitation and ortho-graphic primes produced inhibition. These results are quite similar to those reported by Feldman (2000) for English prime target such as VOWEL–VOW as contrasted with VOWED–VOW.

Throughout the former Yugoslavia, until recently, two alphabets were in use concur-rently so it was possible to present to readers primes and targets in different alphabets so as to render minimal their orthographic similarity. Further evidence against an ortho-graphic (or perhaps visual)[1] interpretation of morphological facilitation at long lags comes from the finding in Serbian that equivalent facilitation was obtained for targets preceded by morphologically related primes, whether the prime was printed in an alphabet different from or the same as the target. That is НОГОМ facilitated the target NOGA as strongly (90 ms) as did its Cyrillic transcription НОГОМ (Feldman and Moskovljevič, 1987; Feldman, 1992). However, because the transcriptions are of the same phonological entity, this finding does not rule out a phonological interpretation of facilitation.

There are, however, no definitive data to suggest that morphological facilitation at long lags is sensitive to gradations in phonological (or orthographic and phonological) similar-ity either. Similar patterns of long-term facilitation have been reported for (phonologically and orthographically) transparent and for (phonologically and orthographically) opaque base morphemes although the magnitudes of facilitation tend to be greater as form over-lap increases. That is, facilitation of MARK following MARKED was statistically equivalent to facilitation of SPEAK following SPOKE (Stolz and Feldman, 1995). Magnitudes were 32 ms and 24 ms respectively. In addition, analogous results were reported for inflected noun forms (viz., instrumental and dative case respectively) such as NOGOM–NOGA as con-trasted with NOZI–NOGA in Serbian (Feldman and Fowler, 1987). Most important, statistically equivalent facilitation (48 versus 39 ms) was observed for morphological rela-tives in which both prime and target are pronounced similarly (e.g., HEALER–HEAL) and in which the prime and target are pronounced differently (e.g., HEALTH–HEAL) (Fowler

---

[1] By some accounts, words printed in different alphabets are not orthographically unrelated and are more analo-gous to variations of case. For example, in Japanese complete repetition priming arises between kanji and hiragana items (Bowers and Michita, 1998) is interpreted as evidence of abstract lexical-orthographic codes. Whether or not alternations across alphabet represent orthographically unrelated forms may depend on the principle by which alphabets combine.

et al., 1985; Experiment 3A). These outcomes are consistent with the claim that those knowledge structures that underlie long-term morphological facilitation are tolerant of variation in form, both orthographic and phonological.

In concatenative languages such as English, Dutch, and German, morphological formation entails the addition of affixes either before or after a base morpheme so that the base morpheme is typically preserved as a unit. By contrast, morphological relatives do not necessarily preserve the base (or root) morpheme as an orthographic and phonological unit in Hebrew whose structure is not concatenative. Because the word pattern morpheme is infixed inside of the root morpheme, it is possible to disrupt the integrity of the root morpheme as an orthographic or as a phonological unit (see Feldman and Bentin, 1994). This occurs when the word pattern includes letters as well as the diacritics that are placed below (or inside of) the root.

Further evidence that the underlying knowledge structures must be relatively abstract derives from the pattern of long-term facilitation for Hebrew. Facilitation did not differ significantly depending on whether the word pattern of the prime did or did not disrupt the letter sequence that formed the root (Feldman and Bentin, 1994). For example, /nofal/ whose root is נפל (NFL) is disrupted by the letter for /o/. The strings pronounced as /nafal/ and as /nofel/ have the identical root although a letter does not disrupt the orthographic sequence that constitutes the root in the former. By contrast, the target pronounced /avadim/ has the root עבד (AVD). An additional letter does not disrupt the target or either of its morphologically related primes /eved/ or /avad/. If the orthographic integrity of the root form influenced the magnitude of facilitation in the long-term visual repetition priming task, disrupted and non-disrupted primes varying in form transparency should differentially influence target recognition latencies. Once again, however, the magnitude of facilitation was numerically but not statistically larger for prime target pairs whose structure preserved the orthographic continuity of the root (70 ms) than for those where infixation of an additional letter in the target disrupted continuity of its root (55 ms). One potential complication, however, is that the magnitudes of identity facilitation also differed numerically although not statistically. The magnitudes were 81 ms and 60 ms respectively.

Statistically comparable findings in concatenative languages such as English and Serbian and in the non-concatenative language of Hebrew suggest that long-term morphological facilitation is similar regardless of the manner in which morphemes combine to form morphologically complex forms. Linear concatenations of morphemes form morphologically complex words in English. In Hebrew, disrupted as well as more faithful preservation of root form across primes and targets both produce morphological facilitation. In summary, neither full phonological nor orthographic similarity of the base morpheme is necessary to produce facilitation when morphological relatives are separated by long lags. This outcome is conventionally interpreted as evidence that the basis of facilitation must be sufficiently abstract to tolerate allomorphic variation to the base morpheme. Nevertheless, across long-term priming experiments, the magnitude of facilitation does tend to vary with the degree of orthographic and phonological overlap (see Rueckl *et al.*, 1997).

In conclusion, words that have similar orthographic and phonological forms but do not share a base morpheme do not significantly influence lexical decision latencies to the target at long lags between target and prime. Moreover, preservation of the base morpheme in prime and in target is not necessary in order to observe effects of morphological relatedness at long lags although gradations in the degree of similarity produce small but systematic differences in the magnitude of long-term morphological facilitation. Evidently, the structures that underlie long-term facilitation must entail representations of morphology that can tolerate but are not totally insensitive to orthographic and phonological alterations to the base morpheme.

Factors that do influence the magnitude of morphological facilitation

In the remainder of the chapter, I will summarize the results of a new series of experiments that compare long-term facilitation after prefixed and suffixed morphological relatives when primes and targets are presented visually. The experiments differ with respect to the morphological composition of the target (i.e., base alone, prefix + base + suffix, base + suffix) as well as the morphological structure of the prime. The results are relevant to our understanding of long-term morphological facilitation and, in particular, of how repetition of components from the prime in the target, and from the target in the prime, influences patterns of facilitation.

Affix position

Adding a prefix or a suffix, or both a prefix and a suffix, to the base morpheme is the most typical way to form morphologically complex forms in English. Prefixes and suffixes differ along a variety of linguistic dimensions, however. Prefixes in English are always derivational in function. Sometimes their effect on the meaning of a stem can vary with stress (REVIEW—RE-VIEW). Moreover, prefixes are restricted to particular syntactic categories. Suffixes in English can be either inflectional or derivational in function and choice of suffix is typically governed by the syntactic structure of the context. Importantly, inflected formations tend to be of the same syntactic category as the base morpheme while derivational suffixes (but not prefixes) can change the syntactic category of the base.

There is evidence from a variety of sources that the beginnings and ends of words do not always inform word recognition processes in an identical manner and this may have implications for long-term morphological facilitation. Different magnitudes of facilitation among affix + base combinations and base + affix combinations would suggest that the linear organization of morphological components within a word is important. For words presented in isolation, prefixed forms and suffixed forms should differ if processing proceeds in a left to right direction throughout the word and if the base morpheme has a special role in processing (Hudson, 1990; Hudson and Buijs, 1995; Taft and Forster, 1975). Accordingly, in suffixed words, the base is available as a unit relatively early in the recognition process because it is at the beginning of the word. In contrast, in prefixed words, recognition processes for the base would operate at the same time as do those for the full word (Cole, Beauvillain, and Segui, 1989). Whether potential effects of left to right processing would carry over into the domain of long-term facilitation is unclear, however. The design of each experiment in the present study permitted an exploration of morphological facilitation following prefixed and suffixed forms, both of which are real words in English. Across experiments, targets varied in their morphological structure. They were either morphologically simple or complex (viz., prefix + base + suffix or base + suffix).

Target versus prime complexity

Facilitation between morphological relatives has been observed when primes are morphologically complex and targets are morphologically simple and when primes are simple and targets are complex (Feldman and Fowler, 1987; Schriefers, Friederici, and Graetz, 1992). However, with German materials, there is evidence that the magnitude of long-term morphological facilitation for targets (bases of adjectives) that followed inflected primes was greater than that of inflected adjective targets that followed base primes (Schriefers *et al.*, 1992). This finding suggests that patterns of facilitation among morphologically related pairs are asymmetric depending on whether the morphologically simple base form appears in the prime or in the target.

There are multiple ways to characterize asymmetries in the magnitude of facilitation depending on whether the prime or the target (or both) include affixes. The components of regular simple forms recur, by definition, in complex forms. It is also possible for both prime and target to be complex. Perhaps long-term morphological facilitation is sensitive to the number of target components that were also present in the prime or, alternatively, to the number of components in the target that were *not* also present in the prime. Asymmetries in the magnitude of facilitation depending on whether prime or target is morphologically simple could arise because of other differences as well. Morphologically simple words tend to be higher in frequency than morphologically complex words formed from the same base. Typically, higher frequency targets produce less facilitation. Attenuation to the magnitude of facilitation because of target frequency applies to identical repetitions (Bowers, 2000; Forster and Davis, 1984) as well as semantic dimensions of relatedness between prime and target. It may influence measures of morphological relatedness as well (Raveh, 1999). One way to minimize the effect of differences related to target frequency and magnitudes of identity priming is to express morphological facilitation as a proportion of identity priming. This measure is particularly useful when comparing the degree of facilitation across different experiments.

Simple targets with complex primes

One experiment in the series compared the magnitude of facilitation for simple targets preceded by morphologically related primes that included either a prefix or a suffix that was absent in the target. The primary experimental question was whether the position of the base within the letter string influenced the magnitude of facilitation.

Critical materials consisted of a morphologically simple word target (CALCULATE) and three types of morphologically related primes. The identity prime was identical to the target (CALCULATE). To form the target from either of the two affixed primes (MISCALCULATE, CALCULATION) an affix (MIS, TION) had to be deleted. That is, the prefixed prime (MISCALCULATE) was composed of a prefix in addition to the base morpheme that formed the target. Similarly, the suffixed prime (CALCULATION) was composed of the target plus a suffix. Prefixed and suffixed forms were selected so that changes to the meaning, pronunciation, and length of the base morpheme were minimal and they were matched across prime types. Because of the properties of prefixation in English, prefixed but not suffixed primes had the same word class as did the target. The average surface frequency per million was 5.6 (SD = 6.8) for prefixed primes and 8.3 (SD = 8.1) for suffixed primes. All primes had lower frequencies than their targets (mean = 116.1, SD = 155.5). All complex forms were derivations. In this and in subsequent experiments, subjects saw a target with only one of its primes. Across trials, each subject saw all types of relatedness between prime and target. Across experimental lists, each target appeared with each prime type. Nonword triples were constructed to resemble the word items with respect to affixation and were created around the base (CRUIT) of a pseudoaffixed word (rather than by altering one or two letters in a real base morpheme).

As summarized in Table 6.1, facilitation for simple targets following prefixed primes (32 ms) and suffixed primes (33 ms) did not differ. Both produced significant facilitation relative to the no prime condition. Identity primes produced facilitation (45 ms) that was numerically but not statistically greater than morphological primes. Expressed as a proportion of the magnitude of facilitation in the identity condition, prefixed morphological relatives and suffixed relatives reduced target decision latencies by (32/45 or) 71% and (33/45 or) 73% respectively.

Complex target with complex primes (recurring prime affixes)

In another experiment within the same study, I examined the magnitude of facilitation for morphologically complex targets preceded by complex morphologically related primes. Here, the entire prime recurred in the target although the target also included either a prefix or a suffix that was not present in the prime. Each set of experimental materials included a morphologically complex word target (e.g., MISCALCULATION) and three types of morphologically related primes. The identity prime was identical to the target (e.g., MIS-CALCULATION). To form the target from either of the two affixed primes, an affix had to

Table 6.1 Mean lexical decision latencies and percent correct for simple targets on their first presentation, or when preceded by identity, prefixed, and suffixed primes

		Type of prime		
	None	Identity	Prefix omitted	Suffix omitted
Prime		calculate	miscalculate	calculation
Target	calculate	calculate	calculate	calculate
	RT % COR	RT % COR	RT % COR	RT % COR
Words				
	581 (92)	536 (94)	549 (92)	548 (93)
Facilitation		45 (−2)	32 (0)	33 (−1)
% Identity			71	73

be added. That is, the omitted prefix prime (e.g., CALCULATION) excluded the prefix (viz., MIS) but retained the suffix (viz., TION) of the target. Similarly, the omitted suffix prime (e.g., MISCALCULATE) excluded the suffix (viz., TION) but retained the prefix (viz., MIS) of the target. Word class was preserved for CALCULATION–MISCALCULATION but not for MISCALCULATE–MISCALCULATION pairs. The average surface frequency was 14.7 (SD = 16.0) for prefixed primes and 11.9 (SD = 17.3) for suffixed primes. All primes had higher frequencies than their morphologically complex target (mean = 4.35, SD = 7.8). Again, nonword triples were constructed to resemble the word items in terms of affixation. Complex targets were necessarily longer than were the simple targets in the previous experiment.

Target facilitation following omitted prefix primes (48 ms) and omitted suffix primes (55 ms) did not differ significantly and each differed significantly from the no prime condition and from the identity condition (73 ms). These differences correspond to reductions of (48/73 or) 66% and (55/73 or) 75% relative to identity facilitation. Results are summarized in Table 6.2.

MISCALCULATE and MISCALCULATION have the first two components (viz., MIS + CALCULATE) in common whereas CALCULATION and MISCALCULATION do not. Conversely, CALCULATION and MISCALCULATION are similar because they share the base morpheme and the suffix (viz., TION). As noted above, affixation with a prefix does not change word class whereas affixation with a derivational suffix typically does. Consequently, CALCULATION and MISCALCULATION type items share word class as well as word final similarity. It is interesting that when targets were composed of a prefix, a base, and a suffix (such as MISCALCULATION), there was a non-significant tendency for word initial similarity to produce greater facilitation than did word final even though it was the latter pairs that preserved word class.

Complex targets with non-recurring target affixes

A third experiment in the series compared the magnitude of facilitation for complex targets preceded by morphologically related primes that included a prefix or a suffix that was

Table 6.2 Mean lexical decision latencies and percent correct for complex targets on their first presentation, or when preceded by identity, prefixed, and suffixed primes whose affixes recur in the target

		Type of prime		
	None	Identity	Prefix omitted	Suffix omitted
Prime		miscalculation	calculation	miscalculate
Target	miscalculation	miscalculation	miscalculation	miscalculation
	RT % COR	RT % COR	RT % COR	RT % COR
Words				
	694 (86)	621 (91)	646 (89)	639 (89)
Facilitation		73 (5)	48 (3)	55 (3)
% Identity			66	75

absent in the target. In addition, however, targets always included a suffix that was not present in any of the primes.

More specifically, critical materials included a morphologically complex word target (CALCULATION) and three types of morphologically related primes. The identity prime was identical to the target (CALCULATION). The prefixed prime (MISCALCULATE) was composed of a prefix and the base of the target. The suffixed prime was composed of a different derivational suffix and the base of the target (CALCULATOR). The simple prime (CALCULATE) consisted of the base form from which the target was derived. Following the convention adopted in previous experiments, prefixed and suffixed word forms were selected so that changes to the stem were minimal and, over items, the length of the affix in letters was matched. Finally, changes to the pronunciation of the stem were matched over prefixed and suffixed word forms. The average surface frequency was 8.2 (SD = 12.3) for prefixed primes, 10.1 (SD = 12.2) for suffixed primes, and 99.8 (SD = 73.3) for simple primes. All complex primes had lower frequencies than their targets (mean = 59.9, SD = 76.1). Nonword materials were constructed to resemble the morphological structure of word items.

Decision latencies are summarized in Table 6.3. They indicate that facilitation from prefixed primes and from suffixed primes did not differ. Simple primes (29 ms), prefixed primes (25 ms), and suffixed primes (30 ms) reduced target decision latencies comparably. These correspond to 60%, 52%, and 60% of the magnitude of identity facilitation respectively. Identity primes reduced target decision latencies by 48 ms.

Overview of long-term morphological facilitation

The present study examined long-term target facilitation in lexical decision following prefixed and suffixed primes. Position of affix was compared within each of three experiments and locus of affixation (on the prime and/or on the target) was manipulated across experiments. In all three experiments, target latencies were reduced following a morphologically related prime. While facilitation following a prefixed and a suffixed prime did not differ, there was a tendency across experiments for pairs with word initial similarity to show

Table 6.3 Mean lexical decision latencies and percent correct for complex targets on their first presentation, or when preceded by identity, prefixed, and simple primes

		Type of prime			
	None	Identity	Prefix omitted plus	Suffix omitted plus	Simple plus
Prime Target	calculation	calculation calculation	miscalculate calculation	calculator calculation	calculate calculation
	RT % COR	RT % COR	RT % COR	RT % COR	RT % COR
Words					
	590 (92)	542 (95)	565 (95)	560 (95)	561 (98)
Facilitation		48 (3)	25 (3)	30 (3)	29 (6)
% Identity			52	63	60

greater facilitation than did those with word final similarity. It was also the case, however, that within each experiment, the proportion of primes that shared word initial similarity with a target that occurred some number of items later in the list was greater than the proportion that shared word final similarity. If position of the base morpheme relative to the full form can be considered a manipulation of form, it is still the case that the evidence for effects of form similarity in long-term repetition priming are only suggestive. Systematic manipulations of morphological structure across experiments permitted the exploration of several other factors that do influence morphological facilitation. These include target frequency and the magnitude of identity priming, differential effectiveness of a prime for its various morphological relatives, and asymmetries in morphological priming as a function of whether prime or target is morphologically complex.

Frequency

A comparison of the magnitudes of facilitation for CALCULATE and CALCULATION type targets might suggest that frequency of the target relative to its prime does not govern magnitude of facilitation among morphological relatives. Target frequency for CALCULATION type targets was less (mean 59.9, SD 76.1) than for CALCULATE type targets (mean 116.1, SD 155.5). Nevertheless, the magnitude of facilitation in the identity condition was essentially unchanged (48 ms and 45 ms respectively). However, CALCULATE and CALCULATION type targets both have higher frequencies and reduced identity facilitation relative to MISCALCULATION type targets (mean 4.35, SD 7.8). Here, identity facilitation was 73 ms. The difference between CALCULATE and CALCULATION, on the one hand, and MISCALCULATION on the other is more consistent with the claim that target frequency does influence the magnitude of facilitation (e.g., Bowers, 2000).

In the identity conditions, the magnitude of morphological facilitation varied across experiments and ranged from 45 to 73 ms. In addition to the magnitudes of facilitation, target frequency, unprimed target decision latencies, and target length also differed. Therefore, in order to circumvent differences associated with these factors, I used facilitation in the identity condition as a baseline against which to gauge two aspects of morphological facilitation. First, I examined the effectiveness of one type of prime with respect to three targets that are morphologically related but differ in their composition (viz., simple, affix added, affix dropped, plus substitution). Then I examined asymmetries within morphological facilitation as a function of whether prime or target is morphologically complex.

All relatives are not the same

Expressed as a percent of identity facilitation, facilitation after the prime MISCALCULATE did not differ when an affix was omitted to form the target as in CALCULATE and when an affixed was added to form the target as in MISCALCULATION. Percent facilitation was (32/45 or) 71% and (55/73 or) 75% respectively. Apparently here there is no reliable differential advantage for word initial as compared with word final similarity. It is noteworthy, however, that MISCALCULATE was less effective as a prime for CALCULATION than for either of the other two targets. The percent reduction was only (25/48 or) 52%. One accounting of these findings is that some version of number of mismatching affixes between prime and target detracted from the facilitation due to a shared base morpheme. The overall similarity varied because relative to MISCALCULATE, MISCALCULATION and CALCULATE each differed by one affix (viz., TION and MIS) but CALCULATION differed by two (viz., MIS and TION)

Asymmetries in morphological facilitation

Evidently, among words that share a base morpheme, the magnitude of facilitation can vary in ways that do not reflect frequency or magnitude of identity facilitation. A second pattern derives from asymmetries in morphological priming as a function of whether prime or target was morphologically complex. Consistent with previous findings (Schreifers *et al.*, 1992), CALCULATION was a better prime for CALCULATE than CALCULATE was for CALCULATION. Expressed as a proportion of identity priming so as to avoid baseline issues, the prime CALCULATION yielded 33/45 or 73% of identity facilitation for CALCULATE. By contrast, CALCULATE produced significantly less (29/48 or only 60% of identity) facilitation for the target CALCULATION.

In conclusion, with complex targets, as with simple targets, long-term morphological facilitation following prefixed and suffixed primes did not differ. When targets were simple (e.g., CALCULATE), the prime included affixes that were not present in the target. When targets were complex (e.g., MISCALCULATION), the target included affixes that were not present in the prime. By either definition of affixation, prefixed forms and suffixed forms produced statistically equivalent facilitation. It appears that the position of the base form within the full form is not relevant and that the mechanism of long-term facilitation operates on all components of the prime at once. The failure to find effects of affix position in patterns of long-term facilitation is not surprising in light of earlier findings that fail to show compelling effects of form or of semantic similarity between prime and target. However, the consistent tendency for prime target pairs with word initial similarity to produce facilitation whose magnitude is numerically greater than that of word final pairs is also consistent with Rueckl *et al.*'s (1997) observation that across long-term priming experiments, the degree of form similarity is important.

Finally, the magnitude of long-term morphological facilitation varied as a function of the number of morphemes that mismatch but not the number of components that are recurred in prime and in target. Across experiments, percent of identity facilitation was greater when the prime (e.g., MISCALCULATE) mismatched with the target (e.g., CALCULATE) by only one component (viz., MIS) than when the same prime mismatched the target (CALCULATION) by two (viz., MIS, (T)ION). With respect to repeated components, MISCALCULATE type primes facilitated targets that shared only the base (e.g., CALCULATE) and targets that share the base plus an affix (e.g., MISCALCULATION) comparably. However, asymmetries in facilitation for CALCULATION–CALCULATE relative to CALCULATE–CALCULATION pairs suggests that the knowledge structures that support morphological facilitation may favor morphologically simple targets because they recur completely in the prime.

In conclusion, effects of word internal morphological structure in the lexical decision task are evident in long-term repetition priming, an experimental task that fails to reveal effects of form or semantic association among morphologically unrelated forms. At the same time, however, the magnitude of morphological facilitation is relatively insensitive to gradations in the degree of overlapping form or meaning among morphological relatives. Nevertheless, across types of morphological relatives, the percent of identity priming varies in systematic ways. In essence, counter to the claim that contamination from strategic or episodic factors (Forster and Davis, 1984; Marslen-Wilson *et al.*, 1994) invalidates it, the long-term repetition priming task is revealing about differential facilitation among various morphological relatives and about asymmetric morphological facilitation. These factors are relevant to our understanding of morphological processing and of long-term repetition priming in general.

Acknowledgments

The research reported here was conducted at the University at Albany, SUNY and was supported by funds from National Institute of Child Health and Development Grant HD-01994 to Haskins Laboratories.

References

Becker, S., Moscovitch, M., Behrmann, M., and Joordens, S. (1997). Long-term semantic priming: A computational account and empirical evidence. *Journal of Experimental Psychology: Learning, Memory, and Cognition*, **23**, 1059–82.

Bentin, S. and Feldman, L. B. (1990). The contribution of morphological and semantic relatedness to repetition priming at short and long lags: Evidence from Hebrew. *Quarterly Journal of Experimental Psychology*, **42A**, 693–711.

Bergman, B., Hudson, P., and Eling, P. (1988). How simple complex words can be: Morphological processing and word representations. *Quarterly Journal of Experimental Psychology*, **40A**, 41–72.

Bowers, J. S. (2000). The modality specific and non-specific components of long-term priming are frequency sensitive. *Memory and Cognition*, **28**, 406–14.

Bowers, J. S. and Michita, Y. (1998). An investigation into the structure and acquisition of orthographic knowledge: Evidence from cross-script Kanji-Hiragana priming. *Psychonomic Bulletin and Review*, **5**, 259–64.

Colé, P., Beauvillain, C., and Segui, J. (1989). On the representation and processing of prefixed and suffixed derived words: A differential frequency effect. *Journal of Memory and Language*, **28**, 1–13.

Drews, E. and Zwitserlood, P. (1995). Morphological and orthographic similarity in visual word recognition. *Journal of Experimental Psychology: Human Perception and Performance*, **21**, 1098–116.

Feldman, L. B. (1992). Morphological relationships revealed through the repetition priming task. In *Linguistics and literacy* (ed. M. Noonan, P. Downing, and S. Lima), pp. 239–54. Amsterdam/Philadelphia: John Benjamins.

Feldman, L. B. (1994a). Beyond orthography and phonology: Differences between inflections and derivations. *Journal of Memory and Language*, **33**, 442–70.

Feldman, L. B. (1994b, February). The role of orthography in morphological analysis. University of Arizona.

Feldman, L. B. (2000). Are morphological effects distinguishable form the effects of shared meaning and shared form? *Journal of Experimental Psychology: Learning, Memory, and Cognition*, **26**, 1431–44.

Feldman, L. B. and Bentin, S. (1994). Morphological analysis of disrupted morphemes: Evidence from Hebrew. *Quarterly Journal of Experimental Psychology*, **47A**, 407–35.

Feldman, L. B. and Fowler, C. A. (1987). The inflected noun system in Serbo-Croatian: Lexical representation of morphological structure. *Memory and Cognition*, **15**, 1–12.

Feldman, L. B. and Moskovljevič, J. (1987). Repetition priming is not purely episodic in origin. *Journal of Experimental Psychology: Learning, Memory, and Cognition*, **13**, 573–81.

Feldman, L. B. and Soltano, E. G. (1999). What morphological priming reveals about morphological processing. *Brain and Language*, **68**, 33–9.

Forster, K. I. and Davis, C. (1984). Repetition priming and frequency attenuation in lexical access. *Journal of Experimental Psychology: Learning, Memory, and Cognition*, **10** (4), 680–98.

Fowler, C. A., Napps, S. E., and Feldman, L. B. (1985). Relations among regular and irregular morphologically related words in the lexicon as revealed by repetition priming. *Memory and Cognition*, **13**, 241–55.

Hanson, V. L. and Feldman, L. B. (1989). Language specificity in lexical organization: Evidence from deaf signers' lexical organization of ASL and English. *Memory and Cognition*, **17**, 292–301.

Hudson, P. T. W. (1990). What's in a word? Levels of representation and word recognition. In *Comprehension processes in reading* (ed. D. A. Balota, G. B. Flores d'Arcais, and K. Rayner). Hillsdale: Erlbaum.

Hudson, P. T. W. and Buijs, D. (1990). Left to right processing of derivational morphology. In *Morphological aspects of language processing* (ed. L. B. Feldman), pp. 383–95. Hillsdale, NJ: Lawrence Erlbaum Associates.

Lupker, S. J. (1984). Semantic priming without association: A second look. *Journal of Verbal Learning and Verbal Behavior*, **23**, 709–33.

Moss, H. E., Ostin, R. K., Tyler, L. K., and Marslen-Wilson, W. (1995). Accessing different types of lexical semantic information: Evidence from priming. *Journal of Experimental Psychology: Learning, Memory, and Cognition*, **21**, 863–83.

Raveh, M. (1999). The contribution of frequency and semantic similarity to morphological processing. Dissertation submitted to The University of Connecticut.

Raveh, M. and Rueckl, J. G. (2000). Equivalent effects of inflected and derived primes: Long-term morphological priming in fragment completion and lexical decision. *Journal of Memory and Language*, **42**, 103–19.

Rueckl, J. G., Mikolinski, M., Raveh, M., Miner, C. S., and Mars, F. (1997). Morphological priming, connectionist networks, and masked fragment completion. *Journal of Memory and Language*, **36**, 382–405.

Schriefers, H., Friederici, A., and Graetz, P. (1992). Inflectional and derivational morphology in the mental lexicon: Symmetries and asymmetries in repetition priming. *Quarterly Journal of Experimental Psychology*, **44A**, 373–90.

Stanners, R. F., Neiser, J. J., Hernon, W. P., and Hall, R. (1979). Memory representation for morphologically related words. *Journal of Verbal Learning and Verbal Behavior*, **18**, 399–412.

Stolz, J. A. and Feldman, L. B. (1995). The role of orthographic and semantic transparency of the base morpheme in morphological processing. In *Morphological aspects of language processing* (ed. L. B. Feldman), pp. 109–29. Hillsdale, NJ: Lawrence Erlbaum Associates.

Taft, M. and Forster, K. I. (1975). Lexical storage and retrieval of prefixed words. *Journal of Verbal Learning and Verbal Behavior*, **14**, 638–47.

CHAPTER 7

VISUAL RECOGNITION AND PRIMING OF INCOMPLETE OBJECTS: THE INFLUENCE OF STIMULUS AND TASK DEMANDS

CHAD J. MARSOLEK AND E. DARCY BURGUND

Integrative evidence from computational, functional, and implementational levels of explanation of memory has led to a new understanding of what repetition priming is and why it is that way (see Marsolek, this volume). For example, recognizing visual objects in everyday life may not only provide us with information about our visual environment. It may also provide us with opportunities for the relevant long-term-memory representations in visual neocortex to be altered slightly in order to sculpt and maintain consolidated knowledge of object shapes. Feedback from post-visual subsystems can be used to guide small changes in the pre-existing representations of visual-form recognition subsystems. Such changes may help to overcome the potentially detrimental interference from learning of new object shapes on retention of familiar shape knowledge, and these changes may be responsible for what is measured as repetition priming effects for familiar objects. According to this theory, consolidated memory subsystems in neocortex underlie repetition priming, and they do so to serve an important purpose for memory and perception in everyday life.

By this theory, the consolidated memory subsystems that support perception and priming should not all be of the same type (Marsolek, this volume). Additional integrative evidence from computational, functional, and implementational levels of explanation has led to the hypothesis that dissociable visual subsystems operate in parallel to underlie recognition and priming of abstract categories of objects (e.g., cups versus pens) versus recognition and priming of specific exemplars of objects (e.g., individual pens; Marsolek, 1999; Marsolek *et al.*, 2001; Marsolek and Burgund, 1997). This hypothesis generates several important new questions. For example, with a parallel dual-subsystems architecture, what factors determine whether one or the other subsystem will recognize an input object and subsequently produce priming for it in a particular circumstance? In this chapter, we suggest that the demands on processing that are placed by the particular stimuli that are processed and by the particular tasks that are performed play crucial roles in determining which subsystem recognizes objects and supports repetition priming effects. Recognition and priming of incomplete objects in particular should be informative for testing this possibility. Thus, we summarize evidence from studies of priming for incomplete objects that support the hypothesized influence of stimulus and task demands.

Abstract and specific visual-form subsystems

Recent evidence suggests that priming of abstract categories of objects and priming of specific exemplars of objects take place in dissociable neural processing subsystems that operate in parallel. In one study (Marsolek, 1999), participants viewed centrally-presented line drawings of objects and printed names of other objects during an initial encoding phase, and then they named objects presented briefly in the left or right visual fields during a subsequent test phase. When test objects were presented directly to the left hemisphere (in the right visual field), repetition priming due to storage of abstract-category information was observed: Priming from previous processing of the same exemplar as shown during test and priming from previous processing of a different exemplar (but one in the same abstract category as the test object) were equivalent, yet both were greater than priming from previous processing of the printed word that names the category of the test object. In contrast, when test objects were presented directly to the right hemisphere (in the left visual field), repetition priming due to storage of specific-exemplar information was observed: Priming from previous processing of the same exemplar as shown during test was greater than priming from previous processing of a different exemplar in the same abstract category as the test object, which in turn was equivalent to priming from previous processing of the printed word that names the category of the test object. Given that abstract and specific forms of priming were evidenced when subsystems in the different hemispheres were advantaged by faster and higher-quality stimulus presentations, dissociable neural subsystems likely supported the two forms of priming. Also, given that abstract priming was observed without accompanying evidence of specific priming in direct left-hemisphere presentations, and vice versa in direct right-hemisphere presentations, the two subsystems appear to operate in parallel rather than in sequence.

Moreover, an integration of neuroimaging and neurocomputational evidence converges with this conclusion (Marsolek *et al.*, 2001). Priming deactivations measured in a rapid event-related functional-magnetic-resonance-imaging study (using the same stimuli as in the divided-visual-field study) revealed different neural locations for abstract-category priming and specific-exemplar priming, as well as different sizes for those neural areas, in both the left and right hemispheres. These results corroborate evidence from a neural-network modeling study (also using the same stimuli as in the divided-visual-field study) indicating that separate and different-sized subnetworks accomplish abstract-category and specific-exemplar recognition (and priming) of objects in ways that mimic human performance, but unified networks do not. We conclude that both abstract and specific subsystems operate in each hemisphere, but the abstract subsystem operates more effectively than the specific subsystem in the left hemisphere, and the specific subsystem operates more effectively than the abstract subsystem in the right hemisphere.

An important property of an abstract-category subsystem is that it appears to use a *features-based* processing strategy (likely through relatively sparse coding; see Marsolek, this volume) to subserve category recognition. To efficiently recognize the category to which an input belongs, such a subsystem should learn and store independent visual features or portions of input forms. Efficient categorization can take place after learning which features are presence-diagnostic for a category (those that almost always are found in the different inputs that belong to one abstract category), which features are absence-diagnostic for a category (those that rarely are found in the inputs belonging to that category), and which features are non-diagnostic for a category (those that sometimes are found and others times are not found in the inputs belonging to that category). In line with this reasoning, after learning novel categories of letter-like figures, participants classified previously unseen prototypes of the newly learned categories (but not previously seen exemplars) more efficiently when they were presented directly to the left hemisphere than to the right. The prototypes contained larger proportions of presence-diagnostic features and smaller proportions of non-diagnostic features than the previously seen exemplars (Marsolek, 1995). Within such a processing scheme, representations of different object features should be stored independently of each other to enable activation of one feature to take place without influencing potential activations of other features.

In contrast, a specific-exemplar subsystem appears to use a *whole-based* processing strategy (likely through relatively distributed coding; see Marsolek, this volume) to subserve exemplar recognition. To efficiently recognize the exemplar to which an input corresponds, such a subsystem should learn and store the relatively complex, whole-based representations that enable even highly similar exemplars to be distinguished from each other as well as from exemplars in other categories. In line with this possibility, after viewing lower-case and upper-case words, participants exhibited exemplar-specific (i.e., letter-case specific) priming of word forms only when the test items were presented in the same visual context as that in which they were presented during initial encoding and when the stimuli were presented directly to the right hemisphere. The exemplar-specific representations involved in the priming effect did not store visual features independently of each other, otherwise exemplar-specific priming would have been observed when the test items were presented in different visual contexts compared with encoding (Marsolek *et al.*, 1996). Within a whole-based processing scheme, features of an object are not represented independently of each other; instead, activation of a distributed pattern across a large number of processing units encodes the whole-based shape of an object. Most important for present concerns, the different processing strategies used by abstract and specific subsystems may be crucial for predicting the effects of stimulus and task demands on processing in those subsystems.

Stimulus and task demands

The parallel architecture of abstract-category and specific-exemplar subsystems raises the important question of what determines which subsystem will recognize an object and support repetition priming in particular circumstances. Apparently, in divided-visual-field experiments, the projection of information directly to one hemisphere or the other often determines which subsystem will be reflected in performance (Marsolek, 1999). However, in more typical, real world situations, objects are viewed in the center of vision with multiple eye fixations. In this situation, stimulus and task demands may be critically important factors. Aspects of the particular stimuli being recognized and aspects of the particular tasks or goals being subserved may influence which subsystem will be reflected in performance in particular situations.

In fact, even when test stimuli are presented directly to one hemisphere or the other, stimulus and task demands have been shown to influence whether abstract or specific priming effects are observed to a greater degree than the hemisphere of direct stimulus presentation. For example, additional object-priming experiments indicate that exemplar-specific priming can be observed following either left- or right-hemisphere test presentations when the prime stimuli are presented in a visually degraded manner or when the test task requires sketching the test object before naming it. In both of those cases, an abstract-category subsystem should be more detrimentally affected by the manipulation than a specific-exemplar subsystem (see Marsolek, 1999). In other words, stimulus and task demands appear to create situations in which one subsystem is more likely than the other to recognize the objects and support the observed priming effects (for additional evidence from word priming studies, see Burgund and Marsolek, 1997; Marsolek and Hudson, 1999). In the next section, we examine why recognition and priming of incomplete objects should take place differently in abstract versus specific subsystems, and then we summarize tests of the hypothesized influence of stimulus and task demands on processing in those subsystems.

Recognition and priming of incomplete objects

How many of the visually recognizable objects around you at the moment are at least partially occluded by other things? It may be a surprisingly large number, especially on a typical desk or shelf. For example, you may recognize a telephone even though a cup or a stack of papers is positioned in your line of sight and occludes portions of the phone. Also, you may recognize the first shape in Figure 7.1 as depicting a piano, despite its missing parts. The ability to compensate for occluded or missing information is critical for visual object recognition in everyday life. We suggest that recognition and priming of incomplete objects may take place differently in abstract-category and specific-exemplar subsystems. The critical difference should be whether the missing information is activated during recognition of an incomplete object.

In an abstract-category subsystem that utilizes a features-based processing scheme, representations of different object features should be stored independently of each other to enable activation of one feature to take place without influencing potential activations of other features. The implication for recognition of incomplete objects is that recognition of the category to which an incomplete stimulus belongs may take place without activation of all the information typically found in that object (i.e., without activation of a representation of what the *whole* object typically contains). We label this theoretical possibility for an object recognition subsystem *sub-whole activation*.

Contrastingly, in a specific-exemplar subsystem that utilizes a whole-based processing scheme, features of an object are not represented independently of each other. Instead, activation of a distributed pattern across a large number of processing units encodes the whole-based shape of an object. The implication for recognition of incomplete objects

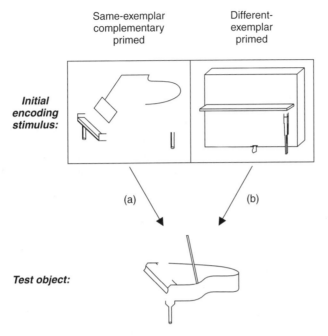

Figure 7.1 Examples of incomplete objects used to measure two types of priming. 'Same-exemplar complementary' primed performance is measured during a test phase when the complementary incomplete version of a test-object exemplar has been processed previously (a) and 'different-exemplar' primed performance is measured during a test phase when a different exemplar with the same name as the test-object exemplar has been processed previously (b).

is that recognition of the exemplar to which an incomplete stimulus corresponds may take place by using the visible information that is present in the image to activate a representation of the entire object, including stored information usually found in the object but not actually present in the input image. This would occur because the information present in the image activates a representation that cannot include only some subset of the information in the whole for a stored exemplar; instead, a representation of the undifferentiated whole configuration for a stored exemplar should be activated. We label this theoretical possibility for an object recognition subsystem *whole activation*. Importantly, evidence for both sub-whole and whole activation can be found in the extant object-priming literature.

Evidence for sub-whole activation and whole activation

In an important study of priming for incomplete objects, Biederman and Cooper (1991) observed an intriguing pattern of results that supports sub-whole activation. They had participants name line drawings of objects with missing volumetric components (see Figure 7.1) in two blocks of trials. The missing components were geons (Biederman, 1987), rather than missing contour information of the sort that preserves evidence of nearly all volumetric components (e.g., Gollin, 1960; Jacoby *et al.*, 1989; Snodgrass and Feenan, 1990). Some of the objects presented during the second block were primed through previous processing during the first block. 'Same-exemplar complementary' primed recognition was measured when the complementary incomplete version of a test-object exemplar was processed during the first block (e.g., see Figure 7.1a), and 'different-exemplar' primed recognition was measured when a different exemplar with the same name as the test-object exemplar was processed during the first block (e.g., see Figure 7.1b). For objects presented in the second block (e.g., see bottom of Figure 7.1), same-exemplar complementary primed recognition and different-exemplar primed recognition were equivalent in efficiency, and both were more efficient than recognition of objects during the first block. An important conclusion that can be drawn from this finding is that no portion of the priming effect could have been due to whole activation of the objects that were processed during the first block. If whole activation had occurred and contributed to priming, then same-exemplar complementary primed performance should have been more efficient than different-exemplar primed performance. Note that these results may reflect processing in an abstract subsystem that underlies sub-whole activation, but could not reflect processing in a specific subsystem that underlies whole activation.

Other studies, including investigations of 'perceptual closure', indicate that whole-activation of incomplete objects can occur. People are biased to (incorrectly) remember a previously seen object as having been viewed in its complete form when it actually was viewed in an incomplete form (e.g., Foley *et al.*, 1997). This sort of closure can influence priming; identification of very incomplete versions of objects is facilitated to a greater degree by previous encoding of moderately incomplete versions of those objects than by previous encoding of the whole versions of those objects (Snodgrass and Feenan, 1990), an effect that is due to perceptual, not conceptual priming (Snodgrass and Kinjo, 1998). An important conclusion that can be drawn from this finding is that the process of activating information that is normally found in the relevant object, but not actually present in the stimulus input, can enhance the subsequently measured priming effect, in line with the idea that whole activation of incomplete objects can occur. Note that this sort of effect may be due to a specific-exemplar subsystem that uses a whole-based processing strategy and operates effectively in the right hemisphere.

Therefore, an interesting, but untested, possibility is that the extant evidence for sub-whole activation may be due to priming in an abstract-category subsystem, whereas the extant evidence for whole activation may be due to priming in a specific-exemplar subsystem. If so, sub-whole activation should be evidenced when test objects are presented directly to the left hemisphere, whereas whole activation should be evidenced when test objects are presented directly to the right hemisphere. Testing these hypotheses will help to clarify whether both abstract and specific subsystems can tolerate missing information yet do so in different ways.

Hemispheric asymmetries for sub-whole and whole activation?

In a recent series of experiments, we tested whether such hemispheric asymmetries would be observed in priming for incomplete objects, as suggested above. In each experiment, 32 right-handed people participated; half were female and half were male (but sex did not enter into any significant effects). The stimuli were 64 line drawings of incomplete common objects, each subtending 4° of widest (horizontal or vertical) visual angle. They included two exemplars from each of 16 abstract categories and two complementary incomplete versions of each exemplar. The different categories had different common names (e.g., piano). Incomplete objects were formed by deleting alternate primitive volumes (geons) (Biederman, 1987) from an original whole image so that approximately 50% of the original contours were deleted for each complementary stimulus. Complementary versions of the same original exemplar were exact in that they shared no overlapping contours and, if overlaid, formed the original intact picture (e.g., see Figure 7.1). These stimuli also were used in Biederman and Cooper (1991, Experiment 2), and detailed rules for creating complementary versions of the exemplars are described there.

During the initial encoding phase, participants named 16 incomplete objects (one from each category), with the list of 16 presented twice in succession to encourage substantial priming. These objects were presented in the central visual field, allowing high quality information to be projected directly to both hemispheres equally quickly. During the subsequent test phase, participants named 32 incomplete objects, 16 of which were same-exemplar complementary versions of the encoding stimuli (half in the left visual field and half in the right) and 16 of which were different-exemplar counterparts of the encoding stimuli (half in the left visual field and half in the right). Participants viewed a central fixation point immediately before viewing and naming each object presented briefly (183 ms) in the left or right visual field (centered 4.57° from the location of the central fixation point, with the inner edge never closer to center than 1.15°). This assured that the subsystems in one hemisphere received higher quality visual input and received that input before subsystems in the other hemisphere. The goal was to create a situation in which subsystems in one hemisphere were given advantages in recognizing the input and guiding acceptable naming responses. The central-field encoding and divided-field test presentations also assured that any observed priming would be due to representations stored post-retinotopically. Thus, four within-participants experimental conditions were created by crossing type of prime (same-exemplar complementary versus different-exemplar) with hemisphere of direct test presentation (left versus right), with eight stimuli representing each of the four conditions. Full counterbalancing of stimuli occurred across participants.

In the analyses, synonyms (e.g., 'phone' and 'telephone') were accepted equally as correct naming responses for a particular object, and outliers (i.e., response times less than 250 ms, greater than 5000 ms, or more than 2.5 standard deviations from the mean of a condition) were excluded from the analyses of response times. Two-way repeated-measures analyses of variance were conducted to examine performance during the test phase, with type of prime (same-exemplar complementary versus different-exemplar) and hemisphere of direct test presentation (left versus right) as within-participants variables. Separate analyses were conducted with mean error rate and mean response time (for correct responses) as the dependent measures.

Priming following brief encoding presentations

We first examined priming for incomplete objects when the initial-encoding presentations were relatively brief. Following Biederman and Cooper (1991), prime objects were presented for a half-second each.

Figure 7.2 depicts the results from this experiment. The relatively brief presentation times during initial encoding of this particular experiment allowed us to verify that repetition priming occurred in all test conditions. We found that same-exemplar complementary primed items were named faster (909 ms) and with fewer errors (7.6%) than objects presented during the first block of initial encoding (1015 ms and 17.4%, respectively), $ps < .001$. Also, different-exemplar primed items were named faster (911 ms) although not with significantly fewer errors (15.2%) than objects presented during the first block of initial encoding (1015 ms and 17.4%, respectively), $p < .001$ and $p > .25$, respectively.

More important, in the analysis of error rates, the interaction between type of prime and hemisphere of direct test presentation did not approach significance, $F < 1$. However, same-exemplar complementary primed objects were named with fewer errors (7.6%) than different-exemplar primed objects (15.2%) in a significant main effect, $F(1, 31) = 13.5$, $MS_e = 137.9$, $p < .001$. The main effect of hemisphere of direct test presentation did not approach significance, $F < 1$. In addition, none of the effects in the analysis of response times approached significance (all $ps > .10$), belying any trade-off between speed and accuracy.

Therefore, the main result from this incomplete-object priming experiment was that same-exemplar complementary primed performance was more accurate than different-

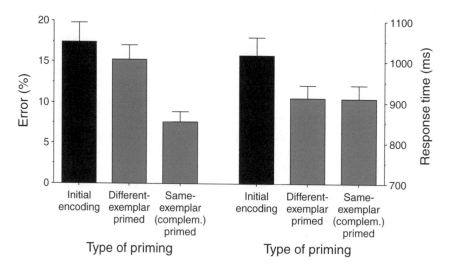

Figure 7.2 Main results from the first experiment, in which initial encoding stimuli were presented for 500 ms each. Mean error rates (on left) and mean response times (on right) for object naming during the test phase are displayed as a function of type of prime (including the unprimed condition of the first block of initial encoding, as a baseline). Error bars indicate standard errors of the mean.

exemplar primed performance, indicative of whole activation of primed objects. That is, when the volumetric parts that were missing during initial encoding of an object were the only parts presented during test, more accurate recognition occurred than when different exemplars with the same name were presented between encoding and test. This suggests that exemplar-specific priming for incomplete objects can be produced by a mechanism that activates representations of whole objects when only a subset of their volumetric information is presented during initial encoding.

Another result was that this effect did not differ depending on whether test objects were presented directly to the left or right hemisphere. This may be surprising initially, because previous results indicate that exemplar-specific priming (of whole objects) is observed when test objects are presented directly to the right hemisphere, whereas no exemplar-specific priming (again of whole objects) is observed when test objects are presented directly to the left hemisphere (Marsolek, 1999). Given these past results, why did the present experiment not produce such a hemispheric difference? One clue may be that the previous hemispheric-asymmetry results were observed in two experiments in which objects were presented for 3 s each during initial encoding, but not in another experiment in which objects were presented briefly (for 500 ms each) during initial encoding. The explanation may be that both specific-exemplar and abstract-category subsystems operate in each hemisphere (albeit with different relative efficiencies across hemispheres, under normal circumstances), and a specific subsystem is relatively less detrimentally affected overall than an abstract subsystem by 'degrading' visual inputs through brief presentations (see Marsolek, 1999; see also Marsolek and Hudson, 1999). This may be due to a lesser ability of features-based processing (in an abstract subsystem) compared with whole-based processing (in a specific subsystem) to utilize the power of distributed representations to effectively recognize 'distorted' sensory inputs (see Hinton *et al.*, 1986). Hence, contributions from a specific subsystem in both hemispheres may have outweighed contributions from an abstract subsystem in both hemispheres under the conditions of the first experiment. Objects were presented for only 500 ms during initial encoding, following the procedure used by Biederman and Cooper (1991).

Priming following longer encoding presentations

Given that brief encoding presentations in the previous experiment may have created a situation in which an abstract-category subsystem did not contribute substantially to performance, we conducted a second experiment to test this possibility. We examined whether the pattern of incomplete-object priming results would differ when stimuli were presented for 3 s each during initial encoding. If so, stimulus demands may play a critical role in the priming effects obtained. This experiment was conducted in the same manner as the first, but with the following exception. During the initial encoding phase, each line drawing was presented for 3 s rather than 500 ms, and we encouraged participants to look at each drawing for the full 3 s (requiring them to respond *after* the disappearance of the encoding stimulus). Thus, we again examined whether whole activation is supported by a subsystem that normally operates effectively in the right hemisphere, whereas sub-whole activation may be supported by a subsystem that normally operates effectively in the left hemisphere, but perhaps only when information is not presented briefly during initial encoding.

Figure 7.3 depicts the results from this experiment. As in the first experiment, the interaction between type of prime and hemisphere of direct test presentation did not approach significance, $F < 1$. Also as before, same-exemplar complementary primed objects were named with fewer errors (9.0%) than different-exemplar primed objects (17.0%) in a significant main effect, $F(1,31) = 16.2$, $MS_e = 126.6$, $p < .001$. The main effect of hemisphere of direct test presentation did not approach significance, $F < 1$. Finally, none of the effects in the analysis of response times approached significance (all $ps > .15$), belying any trade-off between speed and accuracy of responses.

Therefore, the main result from this experiment was that brief encoding presentations were not solely responsible for the lack of a hemispheric asymmetry in the first experiment. Stimuli were presented for a relatively long time during encoding in this second experiment, yet performance did not differ from that of the first experiment, in which encoding-phase stimuli were presented briefly. Same-exemplar complementary primed performance was more accurate than different-exemplar primed performance, again suggesting that exemplar-specific priming for incomplete objects can be produced by a mechanism that activates representations of whole objects when only a subset of their volumetric information is presented during initial encoding. In addition, this effect did not differ depending on whether test items were presented directly to the left or right hemisphere.

How then should the present results (exemplar-specific priming in both left- and right-hemisphere test presentations) be reconciled with the earlier finding in a previous study (exemplar-specific priming following right-hemisphere but not following left-hemisphere test presentations; Marsolek, 1999)? It is possible that only specific-exemplar subsystems contributed substantially to performance in both of the present experiments because of

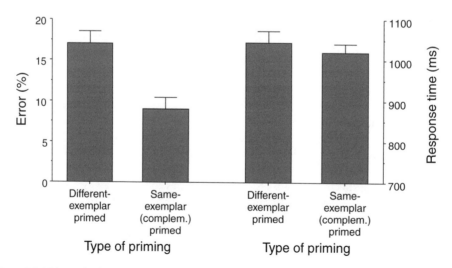

Figure 7.3 Main results from the second experiment, in which initial encoding stimuli were presented for 3 s each. Mean error rates (on left) and mean response times (on right) for object naming during the test phase are displayed as a function of type of prime. Error bars indicate standard errors of the mean.

the nature of the stimuli. *Incomplete* objects are inherently 'degraded', and this degradation of the visual input may have caused contributions from a specific-exemplar subsystem in each hemisphere to outweigh those from an abstract-category subsystem in each hemisphere. Presumably, missing information would degrade a stimulus at least as much as presenting it briefly. Thus, in the third experiment, we tried another approach to more equally balance the contributions from abstract and specific subsystems to priming for incomplete objects.

Another way to increase the relative contributions from a subsystem that recognizes abstract categories may be to refamiliarize participants with the relevant category information before the experiment begins. In the cognitive categorization literature, human participants (as well as neural network models; e.g., Knapp and Anderson, 1984; McClelland and Rumelhart, 1985) tend to learn relatively more information about the abstract and prototypical structure of categories than about the specific exemplars in those categories as the number of training trials increases (e.g., Homa *et al.*, 1973; Marsolek, 1995). Similarly, participants may be more likely to rely on orientation-invariant features (rather than orientation-dependent wholes) to identify disoriented objects *after* they have been familiarized with those objects than before (Murray *et al.*, 1993). Pre-experimental 'training' or refamiliarization trials (during which normal priming changes should occur, as these changes should be ubiquitous in all visual recognition events; see Marsolek, this volume) would be most beneficial to an abstract-category subsystem if multiple exemplars in each category were presented (Marsolek, 1995). This would allow the subsystem to become refamiliarized with the features common to the exemplars in each category before the experiment begins.

Pre-experimental presentations of whole objects

This third experiment was conducted in the same manner as the second, except we presented participants with each of the exemplars from each of the abstract categories of objects (in their whole forms) in a pre-experimental training phase before the encoding phase began. Before the initial encoding phase, participants were presented with the whole versions of each of the 32 exemplars. This pre-experimental 'training' phase was conducted in the same manner as the encoding phase of the second experiment, except complete versions of all 32 exemplars were presented. We hypothesized that the pre-experimental training would increase the contributions from an abstract-category subsystem, relative to a specific-exemplar subsystem, during the rest of the experiment. In this way, we again investigated whether whole activation is performed in a subsystem that operates effectively in the right hemisphere, whereas sub-whole activation is performed in a subsystem that operates effectively in the left hemisphere, under experimental conditions that do not favor one subsystem over the other.

Figure 7.4 depicts the results from this experiment. Unlike the first two experiments, in the error-rate analyses, the interaction between type of prime and hemisphere of direct test presentation was significant, $F(1,31) = 6.37$, $MS_e = 55.4$, $p < .05$. Simple effect contrasts revealed that same-exemplar complementary primed objects were named with fewer errors than different-exemplar primed objects when they were presented directly to the right hemisphere (2.7% vs. 7.4%, respectively), $F(1,62) = 6.69$, $MS_e = 52.6$, $p < .05$, but not

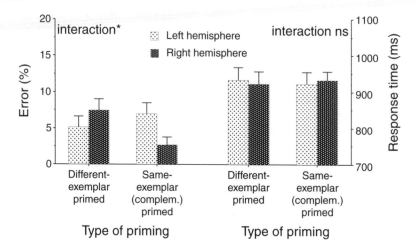

Figure 7.4 Main results from the third experiment, in which initial encoding stimuli were presented for 3 s each, and whole versions of the experimental objects were presented pre-experimentally. Mean error rates (on left) and mean response times (on right) for object naming during the test phase are displayed as a function of type of prime and hemisphere of direct test presentation. Error bars indicate standard errors of the mean.

when they were presented directly to the left hemisphere (7.0% vs. 5.1%, respectively), $F(1,62) = 1.16, MS_e = 52.6, p > .25$. Additional simple effect contrasts revealed that same-exemplar complementary primed objects were named with fewer errors when presented directly to the right hemisphere than to the left (2.7% vs. 7.0%, respectively), $F(1,62) = 6.15, MS_e = 48.0, p < .05$, but different-exemplar primed objects were not named with fewer errors when presented directly to the right hemisphere than to the left (7.4% vs. 5.1%, respectively), $F(1,62) = 1.83, MS_e = 48.0, p > .15$.

In addition, same-exemplar complementary primed objects were not named with significantly fewer errors (4.9%) than different-exemplar primed objects (6.3%) overall; the main effect of type of prime did not approach significance, $F(1,31) = 1.20, MS_e = 49.7, p > .25$. Also, the main effect of hemisphere of direct test presentation also did not approach significance, $F_1 > 1$. In addition, all of the effects that were significant in the analysis of error rates were also significant in an analysis of arcsine-transformed error proportions; this is important because the error rates were relatively low in this experiment and this transform helps to overcome any artificial suppression of variances due to floor effects. Finally, none of the effects in the analysis of response times approached significance (all $ps > .65$). This indicates that the significant effects in error rates were not compromised by any trade-offs between speed and accuracy.

Therefore, the main result from this experiment was that same-exemplar complementary primed recognition was more efficient than different-exemplar primed recognition, but only when test objects were presented directly to the right hemisphere, and not when they were presented directly to the left hemisphere. This pattern of results contrasted with the pattern from the previous two experiments. Although error rates were very low (see the left side of Figure 7.4), any effects of the floor actually worked *against* finding the significant interaction and critical simple effects that were observed (which also were replicated in an analysis of arcsine-transformed data). Thus, under conditions in which both abstract and specific subsystems should contribute substantially to performance, whole activation of incomplete objects appears to take place in a specific-exemplar subsystem that operates independently of another subsystem that performs sub-whole activation of incomplete objects.

Presumably, the critical difference between this experiment and the first two experiments was that participants were refamiliarized with features that are common to the exemplars in each category before this experiment began. They viewed the two exemplars in each category (in their whole forms) in a pre-experimental training phase. This appears to have increased the contributions from an abstract-category subsystem in the left hemisphere compared with the previous experiments, enough to allow expression of equivalent same-exemplar complementary and different-exemplar primed recognition when test stimuli were presented directly to the left hemisphere (reflecting sub-whole activation of the sort that an abstract-category subsystem should underlie). Such an explanation highlights how task and stimulus demands may greatly influence which of two parallel neural subsystems will be evidenced in priming effects in particular situations.

However, one aspect of this explanation requires further testing. The stimuli presented during pre-experimental training were the two exemplars in each category (in their whole forms) that were used in the main experiment. Thus, it is possible that the pre-experimental training served to prime specific exemplars, rather than or in addition to refamiliarizing participants with abstract categories, as was intended in Experiment 3. A more effective way of refamiliarizing participants with the diagnostic features for each category, and only having that effect, would be to present *additional* exemplars in each of the abstract categories during the pre-experimental training phase (ones not used in the main experiment). We used this procedure in the fourth experiment, to more cleanly test the hypothesis that whole activation is performed in a subsystem operating effectively in the right hemisphere whereas sub-whole activation is performed in a subsystem operating effectively in the left hemisphere.

Pre-experimental presentations of whole objects not used during the experiment

This fourth experiment was conducted in the same manner as the third, except the objects presented during the pre-experimental 'training' phase were 32 *additional* exemplars (two from each of the 16 abstract categories) that were not used during the main experiment. The objects presented in the main experiment were the same as those used in the previous three experiments.

Figure 7.5 depicts the results from this experiment. Most important, in the response-time analysis, the interaction between type of prime and hemisphere of direct test presentation was significant, $F(1,31) = 11.0$, $MS_e = 27,410$, $p < .01$. Simple effect contrasts revealed that same-exemplar complementary primed objects were named faster than different-exemplar primed objects when they were presented directly to the right hemisphere (810 vs. 932 ms, respectively), $F(1,62) = 11.1$, $MS_e = 21,258$, $p < .001$, but not

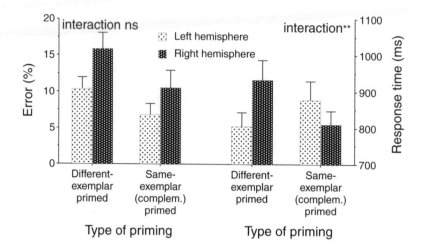

Figure 7.5 Main results from the fourth experiment, in which initial encoding stimuli were presented for 3 s each, and whole versions of additional exemplars (ones not used in the main experiment) were presented pre-experimentally. Mean error rates (on left) and mean response times (on right) for object naming during the test phase are displayed as a function of type of prime and hemisphere of direct test presentation. Error bars indicate standard errors of the mean.

when they were presented directly to the left hemisphere (877 vs. 804 ms, respectively), $F(1,62) = 3.99$, $MS_e = 21{,}258$, $p < .06$. Additional simple effect contrasts revealed that same-exemplar complementary primed objects were named marginally faster when presented directly to the right hemisphere than to the left (810 vs. 877 ms, respectively), $F(1,62) = 2.85$, $MS_e = 24{,}886$, $p < .10$, but different-exemplar primed objects were named significantly faster when presented directly to the left hemisphere than to the right (804 vs. 932 ms, respectively), $F(1,62) = 10.5$, $MS_e = 24{,}886$, $p < .01$. No other effects approached significance in the analysis of response times (other $ps > .25$).

In the analysis of error rates, same-exemplar complementary primed objects were named with significantly fewer errors (8.7%) than different-exemplar primed objects (13.1%), $F(1,31) = 5.44$, $MS_e = 114.3$, $p < .05$, for the main effect of type of prime. In addition, objects were named with significantly fewer errors when presented directly to the left hemisphere (8.6%) than to the right (13.2%), $F(1,31) = 8.84$, $MS_e = 76.4$, $p < .01$, for the main effect of hemisphere of direct test presentation. However, the interaction between type of prime and hemisphere of direct test presentation did not approach significance, $F > 1$. Thus, the important analogous interaction in the analysis of response times was not compromised by a trade-off between speed and accuracy.

Therefore, the main result from this experiment was that same-exemplar complementary primed recognition was more efficient than different-exemplar primed recognition in direct right-hemisphere presentations, but same-exemplar complementary and different-exemplar primed recognition were equivalent in direct left-hemisphere presentations.

This pattern of results was similar to the pattern in the third experiment (but different from the pattern in the first two experiments). Thus, under the present conditions, whole activation of incomplete objects was evidenced in a specific-exemplar subsystem in the right hemisphere, whereas sub-whole activation of incomplete objects was evidenced in a different subsystem in the left hemisphere.

These results are important in part because they may help to explain why Biederman and Cooper (1991) found equivalent same-exemplar complementary primed and different-exemplar primed recognition in their experiment. We suspect that their experimental procedure created a situation in which an abstract-category subsystem was evidenced more than a specific-exemplar subsystem. First, they presented all stimuli in the center of vision, thus visual degradation may have been less than in the divided-visual-field presentations of the present study. Perhaps more important, at the outset of the Biederman and Cooper experiment, participants were familiarized with the names of the object categories that would be used during the subsequent encoding and test phases (the reason was to help standardized names to be produced later in the main experiment). This name familiarization task may have caused participants to anticipate seeing objects with those names (in an object perception study) and to possibly imagine prototypical versions of such objects. If participants imagined *prototypes* of the categories in particular (having no way of knowing what the specific exemplars to be used in the subsequent experiment would actually look like) they would have done an especially good job of activating the prototypical, diagnostic feature information in an abstract-category subsystem. The effect would have been to increase the relative contributions from an abstract-category subsystem during the main experiment.

It is interesting to note that the significant interaction of type of priming with hemisphere of direct test presentation was observed in response times in the fourth experiment but in error rates in the third. In the fourth experiment, the exemplars presented during the pre-experimental training phase were different from the exemplars used in the main experiment (whereas, they were the same in the third experiment). This likely caused the diagnostic-feature information that was activated in an abstract-category subsystem to be more prototypical in the fourth than in the third experiment. Storing prototypical information in the left hemisphere may be reflected more by speed of processing than by accuracy of processing; the effects of storing prototypical information in the left hemisphere were greater in response-time results than in error-rate results in all three prototype-abstraction experiments reported in Marsolek (1995). Thus, the activation of relatively prototypical feature information may be the reason why effects were observed in response times in the fourth experiment.

Conclusions

An important question stems from the theory that priming is caused by small changes in consolidated-memory subsystems in neocortex and that dissociable visual subsystems operate in parallel to underlie recognition and priming of abstract categories of objects versus recognition and priming of specific exemplars of objects (Marsolek, 1999; Marsolek *et al.*, 2001; Marsolek and Burgund, 1997): What factors determine which subsystem will recognize objects and support repetition priming in particular circumstances? Apparently, stimulus and task demands (only one of which stems from the visual field of stimulus presentation) play important roles.

In summary, exemplar-specific priming between complementary versions of incomplete objects was observed in four experiments, supporting the hypothesis that exemplars are recognized through activating representations of a whole object, including stored information usually found in the object but not actually present in the input image. However, this effect was observed when test objects were presented directly to either hemisphere in the first two experiments, and only when test objects were presented directly to the right hemisphere in the third and fourth experiments. These results support the possibility that both specific-exemplar and abstract-category subsystems operate in each hemisphere, however stimulus and task demands greatly influence the relative contributions to performance from these subsystems in different situations. Specific outweighed abstract contributions in the first two experiments, to a point at which specific-exemplar priming was observed in both left-hemisphere and right-hemisphere test presentations (see also Marsolek, 1999, Experiments 2 and 3). In contrast, an abstract subsystem in the left hemisphere was able to overcome the imbalance and contribute substantially to performance in the third and fourth experiments (cf. Marsolek and Hudson, 1999), likely because initial training exposures allowed pre-experimental refamiliarization with the diagnostic features of the relevant object categories.

We conclude that specific-exemplar recognition is supported by a subsystem that performs whole activation of incomplete objects. However, sub-whole activation occurs in another visual subsystem, which helps to explain why sub-whole recognition has been evidenced previously (Biederman and Cooper, 1991). The results summarized in this chapter suggest that the demands on processing that are placed by the stimuli used and by the tasks performed largely determine which subsystem will be evidenced in particular situations. Moreover, the demands on processing that are caused by recognition of *incomplete* objects in particular appear to create a situation in which a specific-exemplar subsystem is benefited at the expense of an abstract-category subsystem. With priming for incomplete objects, additional compensating factors that benefit an abstract subsystem appear to be needed to allow processing in that subsystem to be evidenced in performance. Stimulus and task demands appear to be critical for predicting performance in dissociable subsystems underlying object recognition and priming.

Acknowledgments

We sincerely thank Eric Cooper for the use of his line drawings; Samantha Davis Weida, Todd Hudson, and Kristin McBride, for assistance with data collection and analysis; and Chris Azorson for insightful discussion. This work was supported by the National Institute of Mental Health, Grant MH60442; by the McDonnell-Pew Cognitive Neuroscience Center and the Arizona Cognitive Science Program of the University of Arizona; and by the Center for Cognitive Sciences in conjunction with the National Science Foundation (GER 9454163), the Office of the Vice President for Research and Dean of the Graduate School of the University of Minnesota.

References

Biederman, I. (1987). Recognition-by-components: A theory of human image understanding. *Psychological Review*, **94**, 115–47.

Biederman, I. and Cooper, E. E. (1991). Priming contour-deleted images: Evidence for intermediate representations in visual object recognition. *Cognitive Psychology*, **23**, 393–419.

Burgund, E. D. and Marsolek, C. J. (1997). Letter-case specific priming in the right cerebral hemisphere with a form-specific perceptual identification task. *Brain and Cognition*, **35**, 239–58.

Foley, M. A., Foley, H. J., Durso, F. T., and Smith, N. K. (1997). Investigations of closure processes: What source-monitoring judgments suggest about what is 'closing'. *Memory and Cognition*, **25**, 140–55.

Gollin, E. S. (1960). Developmental studies of visual recognition of incomplete objects. *Perceptual and Motor Skills*, **11**, 289–98.

Hinton, G. E., McClelland, J. L., and Rumelhart, D. E. (1986). Distributed representations. In *Parallel distributed processing: Explorations in the microstructure of cognition* (ed. D. E. Rumelhart and J. L. McClelland), Vol. 1, Foundations, pp. 77–109. Cambridge, MA: MIT Press.

Homa, D., Cross, J., Cornell, D., Goldman, D., and Shwartz, S. (1973). Prototype abstraction and classification of new instances as a function of instances defining the prototype. *Journal of Experimental Psychology*, **101**, 116–22.

Jacoby, L. J., Baker, J. G., and Brooks, L. R. (1989). Episodic effects on picture identification: Implications for theories of concept learning and theories of memory. *Journal of Experimental Psychology: Learning, Memory, and Cognition*, **15**, 275–81.

Knapp, A. and Anderson, J. A. (1984). A signal averaging model for concept formation. *Journal of Experimental Psychology: Learning, Memory, and Cognition*, **10**, 616–37.

Marsolek, C. J. (1995). Abstract-visual-form representations in the left cerebral hemisphere. *Journal of Experimental Psychology: Human Perception and Performance*, **21**, 375–86.

Marsolek, C. J. (1999). Dissociable neural subsystems underlie abstract and specific object recognition. *Psychological Science*, **10**, 111–8.

Marsolek, C. J. and Burgund, E. D. (1997). Computational analyses and hemispheric asymmetries in visual-form recognition. In *Cerebral asymmetries in sensory and perceptual processing* (ed. S. Christman), pp. 125–58. Amsterdam: Elsevier.

Marsolek, C. J. and Hudson, T. E. (1999). Task and stimulus demands influence letter-case specific priming in the right cerebral hemisphere. *Laterality*, **4**, 127–47.

Marsolek, C. J., Schacter, D. L., and Nicholas, C. D. (1996). Form-specific visual priming for new associations in the right cerebral hemisphere. *Memory and Cognition*, **24**, 539–56.

Marsolek, C. J., Andresen, D. R., Westerberg, C. E., Stevenson, W. E., Jax, S. A., Zhuang, J., *et al.* (2001, July). *Integrating neurocomputational and neuroimaging evidence to explain repetition priming*. Presented at the International Conference on Memory III, Valencia, Spain.

McClelland, J. L. and Rumelhart, D. E. (1985). Distributed memory and the representation of general and specific information. *Journal of Experimental Psychology: General*, **114**, 159–88.

Murray, J. E., Jolicœur, P., McMullen, P. A., and Ingelton, M. (1993). Orientation-invariant transfer of training in the identification of rotated natural objects. *Memory and Cognition,* **21**, 604–10.

Snodgrass, J. G. and Feenan, K. (1990). Priming effects in picture fragment completion: Support for the perceptual closure hypothesis. *Journal of Experimental Psychology: General,* **119**, 276–96.

Snodgrass, J. G. and Kinjo, H. (1998). On the generality of the perceptual closure effect. *Journal of Experimental Psychology: Learning, Memory, and Cognition,* **24**, 645–58.

CHAPTER 8

FONT-SPECIFIC MEMORY: MORE THAN MEETS THE EYE?

STEPHEN D. GOLDINGER, TAMIKO AZUMA, HEATHER M. KLEIDER, AND VIRGINIA M. HOLMES

In a classic article, Oldfield (1966) first described the *mental lexicon*, a collection of words in long-term memory that mediates access between perception and lexical knowledge. The lexicon has since been a focus of extensive investigation and theorizing. Within that broader enterprise, a question has arisen regarding the nature of lexical representation, and about the relationship of word recognition to either episodic or semantic memory. Painting in broad strokes, there are two main views on lexical representation: *Abstractionist theories* view the lexicon as a set of ideal, modality-free units (e.g., Morton, 1979), and *episodic theories* assume that groups of detailed memory traces collectively represent individual words (e.g., Goldinger, 1998; Jacoby, 1983a). Naturally, given such poles, there are also intermediate views, including mixed and distributed models (Brown and Carr, 1993; Stark and McClelland, 2000). Putting such compromising positions aside (for now), this chapter is focused on printed word perception and its underlying representations. Our empirical focus is on repetition effects in both implicit and explicit memory, and our theoretical focus begins with the categorical episodic-abstractionist divide (see Bowers, 2000; Tenpenny, 1995).

In some regards, theorizing about lexical representations appears rather schizophrenic, owing to the near-universal application of words as experimental stimuli. Viewed from the perspective of psycholinguistics, words are fairly magical entities, representing the psychological level at which 26 meaningless letters coalesce into thousands of meaningful units. Many choose only to study word-recognition itself, modeling RT data gathered from lexical decision or naming tasks. Others choose to follow the linguistic pathways higher, studying how words are integrated into syntactic or semantic levels of discourse. In either circumstance, words are typically treated in a manner consistent with linguistic theory (e.g., Halle, 1985)—as abstract, canonical units that may be recombined to create endless messages. Word recognition is appreciated for its stability across visual or auditory variations, and is theoretically likened to finding entries in a computer search (e.g., Forster, 1979; Paap *et al.*, 1982) or activating the proper node (or pattern) in a network (e.g., Plaut *et al.*, 1996).

In more general studies of cognition, words are not the investigative focus, but are used as a methodological convenience. Words are commonly presented in studies of short- and long-term memory, category learning, the formation of false memories, etc. Words make excellent stimuli for many reasons—they are already familiar to subjects, they can be manipulated along various dimensions (both perceptual and conceptual), they come with certain 'built-in' manipulations (such as differences in word-frequency or concreteness), and they are plentiful. Such applications often arise in the purview of memory research, and—in many investigations—words are merely objects for memorization, presented to subjects in list format. Indeed, although studies of false-memory formation exploit the semantic relations among words to induce memory illusions (e.g., Roediger and McDermott, 1995), false memories also arise with pictures (Miller and Gazzaniga, 1998) and faces (Homa *et al.*, 2001). Speaking generally, words are often treated as 'cognitive objects', rather than linguistic entities.

Perhaps owing to these different empirical orientations toward words—either as objects of study in their own right, or as generic cognitive stimuli—very different theoretical depictions of words have advanced across fields of research. In psycholinguistics, and the subfield of word perception itself, the abstractionist view is prominent. Perception is typically assumed to involve 'information reduction', matching specific episodes (tokens) to canonical representations (types; Marslen-Wilson and Warren, 1994; Morton, 1979; Posner, 1964). This is a perfectly reasonable stance. People are remarkably robust across perceptual variations in spoken and printed word perception. Moreover, word perception is rarely an end in itself—people most often integrate words into larger linguistic representations. Given these facts, theories focusing on words as abstract or canonical units are patently true, and completely justified (Bowers, 2000). Nobody could reasonably argue against abstraction in the mental lexicon, or in memory at large.

Despite these truisms, researchers focused on other cognitive functions have advanced theories with more dynamic portrayals of long-term memory traces, which easily accommodate lexical representations. As in all scientific fields, theoretical development in various branches of cognitive psychology reflects the specific problems under consideration. For example, researchers studying perceptual classification and categorization have seen a progression of theories, starting from rule-based approaches, moving to prototype models, then to exemplar and connectionist models (see Estes, 1994). At each step of theoretical evolution, researchers try to retain the key elements of previous theories, while allowing the flexibility to accommodate new data. For example, models of long-term memory must allow abstraction and generalization, but must also explain memory for specific episodes (Semon, 1923; see Schacter *et al.*, 1978).

To achieve this balance, many theories of perceptual classification and long-term memory posit episodic representations, collections of instances in memory. Depending upon the model, these instances may be stored separately, or may become blended over time, allowing a full continuum of theories, from purely episodic to purely abstractionist. For example, some global memory models (Gillund and Shiffrin, 1984; Hintzman, 1986; Shiffrin and Steyvers, 1997; Underwood, 1969) and exemplar categorization models (Nosofsky, 1991; Nosofsky and Palmeri, 1997) are strongly episodic. Holographic (Eich, 1982) and distributed (McClelland and Rumelhart, 1985) memory models also assume episodic traces, but blending occurs as a natural product of information storage and retrieval. By allowing some degree of episodic storage, and by allowing stored episodes to influence perceptual and memorial processes, these models successfully blend the stability of abstract representations with the idiosyncratic effects of specific episodes.

Memory for spoken and printed word details

From a general cognitive perspective, printed and spoken word perception are special cases of perceptual classification. The fundamental behavior of content-addressable memory systems (e.g., Kohonen *et al.*, 1989) is to activate stored knowledge by presentation of a stimulus, whether it is an object, a face, or a word. This basic goal may be accomplished across many kinds of lexical representations, as noted above. In abstractionist theories, idiosyncratic features of words may be *normalized* with respect to canonical mental representations; the perceptual system filters surface details that are tangential to word identity (Carr *et al.*, 1989; Green *et al.*, 1991; Jackson and Morton, 1984). In its strongest form (which is not often posed), the normalization assumption suggests that surface features of words will be absent from long-term memory. On the other hand, a strong episodic view would contend that such features are always encoded, and should be retrievable. Naturally, weaker forms of both views are possible (Brown and Carr, 1993; Goldinger, 1998), predicting that surface features of words are incidentally encoded in perception, and may be later recalled if conditions are favorable. We return to such alternatives in the General discussion.

Given these hypotheses, both *implicit* and *explicit* memory for words' surface details have been previously investigated. Whereas explicit memory entails conscious recollection, implicit memory entails facilitation of task performance, possibly without conscious recollection (Musen and Treisman, 1990; Schacter, 1987; Tulving and Schacter, 1990). A common measure of implicit memory—and a central theme of this volume—is the *repetition effect*, improved perception of words with repeated presentations (Jacoby, 1983a; Jacoby and Dallas, 1981; Masson and Freedman, 1990; Roediger and McDermott, 1993).

With respect to memory for stimulus surface details, implicit and explicit memory data differ in several interesting respects: First, memory for surface details is more often (although not exclusively) revealed by implicit measures than by explicit measures (Schacter, 1987; Tenpenny, 1995). Second, the passage of time differentially affects each measure; surface details rapidly fade from explicit memory, but persist in implicit memory (Cave, 1997; Cave and Squire, 1992; Musen and Treisman, 1990). Third, manipulating the levels of stimulus processing (LOP) during study strongly affects explicit memory, but has little effect on implicit memory (Graf and Mandler, 1984; Jacoby and Dallas, 1981; although see Challis and Brodbeck, 1992). In this chapter, we describe experiments that assess both implicit and explicit memory for printed word details, examining different retention intervals and different levels of processing at study.

Memory for voices

In spoken word perception, most theories assume the speech signal is converted to a sequence of discrete segments, which is then compared to abstract lexical entries (McClelland and Elman, 1986; Studdert-Kennedy, 1976; see Pisoni, 1993). These assumptions are motivated by the extremely variable nature of the speech signal (Klatt, 1979; Goldinger *et al.*, 1996). Indeed, a key issue in speech perception concerns *speaker normalization*. Speakers differ in vocal tracts (Joos, 1948; Peterson and Barney, 1952), glottal characteristics (Monsen and Engebretson, 1977), strategies for producing phonemes (Ladefoged, 1980; Remez *et al.*, 1997), and native dialects. Yet, we understand most speakers without difficulty. Speaker normalization presumably allows listeners to follow the lexical-semantic content of speech; voice details used in early phonetic perception are discarded after lexical access (Jackson and Morton, 1984; Krulee *et al.*, 1983). Thus, long-term memory for spoken words should reflect elements of meaning; elements of perception, such as voice details, should be lost.

Despite this view, many data suggest that voices are reliably stored in long-term memory as a side-effect of lexical access, affecting both direct and indirect memory tests (Church and Schacter, 1994; Craik and Kirsner, 1974; Geiselman and Bellezza, 1977; Goldinger, 1996; Goldinger *et al.*, 1991; Palmeri *et al.*, 1993; Schacter and Church, 1992). Detailed episodic traces are apparently created in spoken word perception, affecting later perceptual and memorial tests. Therefore, some authors have suggested that the mental lexicon may consist of episodes, rather than abstract units (Goldinger, 1996, 1997; Jacoby, 1983a). Beyond parsimony, this idea finds empirical support. For example, Goldinger (1998) recently found that single-word shadowing data can be predicted by a pure exemplar model (MINERVA 2; Hintzman, 1986). Moreover, the assumption of episodic storage has found considerable empirical support from researchers using a wide range of experimental procedures and participants (Bradlow *et al.*, 1999; Church and Fisher, 1998; Luce and Lyons, 1998; Meehan and Pilotti, 1996; Nygaard and Pisoni, 1998; Nygaard *et al.*, 1994, 1995; Sheffert, 1998a, b; Sheffert and Fowler, 1995). Taken together, these studies show that repetition effects for spoken words are enhanced when voices remain constant across presentations of any given word. Moreover, they suggest a role of detailed episodes in spoken word perception, supporting the basic premises of an episodic model of lexical access.

Specificity effects with printed words—a mixed bag of results

Given the findings of token-specific repetition benefits in spoken-word perception, it is not surprising that similar effects arise with typographies (or *fonts*) in printed-word perception and memory. However, the accumulated evidence with printed words is less compelling, relative to that with spoken words. As Goldinger (1998) noted, voices carry great ecological value, as they communicate information about a speaker's gender, age, emotional state, etc. Moreover, voice inflections are used paralinguistically, as in sarcasm. Fonts, on the other hand, communicate little information beyond the identity of their intended letters. Although fonts may be used to convey emphasis (as in bold or italics), there is generally little meaningful variation across words or sentences, and the initial choice of font has little communicative value. They are, by definition, superficial details of printed words.

Despite their apparently trivial nature, fonts have been shown to remain in episodic memory, following printed word perception. The literature, however, contains a mixture of positive and null effects. Moreover, the positive effects are generally small, such that repetition priming is robust for repeated words, regardless of fonts, with relatively small 'extra benefits' for words studied and repeated in the same font. For convenience, we may refer to these as 'abstract' and 'episodic' priming effects, although this delineation should not be interpreted too deeply. As we discuss later, the full range of repetition effects may be explained by a single memory system, or by separate systems, with each view having its own benefits. These topics are carefully analyzed by Tenpenny (1995) and Bowers (2000)—we provide a brief, empirical review here.

On the 'abstract' side, repetition effects to words are very robust, even when dramatic changes are introduced between the initial experimental presentation (*study*) and repetition (*test*). Listing just a few relevant examples, priming effects survive changes across synonyms (e.g., *elephant–pachyderm*; Roediger and Challis, 1992). Moreover, priming effects persist across languages and/or scripts, such as switching Japanese words from Kanji to Hiragana (Bowers and Michita, 1998; also Brown *et al.*, 1984; Feldman and Moskovljevic, 1987). Similar abstract priming effects also occur with different pictures of the same nominal object (Biederman and Cooper, 1991) and with ideas conveyed in different sentences (Tardif and Craik, 1989). More generally, in experiments that compare repetition effects to same-format and different-format words, reliable priming nearly always occurs—the only question is whether physical matches will confer any extra benefit. Thus, reliable priming is observed even when repetition voices (Church and Schacter, 1994; Jackson and Morton, 1984; Sheffert, 1998a), modalities (Kirsner and Smith, 1974; Roediger and Blaxton, 1987), or fonts (Hintzman and Summers, 1973; Jacoby and Hayman, 1987; Roediger and Blaxton, 1987) are changed. Clearly, priming reflects more than simple, bottom-up repetition benefits. A basic tenet of cognitive psychology is that observers elaborate upon a stimulus, lending it meaning (as in a word) and purpose (if a response must be selected). Those top-down elaborations clearly convey the potential for priming.

On the 'episodic' side, it is nearly always the case that bottom-up matches *improve* upon the top-down priming effects just described. Although priming effects are strong without specific perceptual matches, they are often stronger when pictures (Snodgrass *et al.*, 1996), modalities (Kirsner and Smith, 1974; Roediger and Blaxton, 1987), or voices (see prior discussion) match. With respect to printed words, both explicit and implicit memory for surface details has been well-documented (see Tenpenny, 1995). For example, Hintzman *et al.* (1972; also Hintzman and Summers, 1973; Kirsner, 1973) found superior recognition memory for words studied and later tested in a constant font, relative to words that changed font between study and test. In a similar implicit memory test, Roediger and Blaxton (1987) found larger repetition effects in word fragment completion for fragments studied and later tested in a constant font, relative to a changed font. This was observed in an immediate test, and after a one-week delay (see also Jacoby and Hayman, 1987; Manso de Zuniga *et al.*, 1991). Many other font-specificity effects have been reported (Blaxton, 1989; Gibson *et al.*, 1993; Graf and Ryan, 1990; Naveh-Benjamin and Craik, 1995; Wiggs and Martin, 1994). These effects are often small, and are sometimes insignificant (Feustel *et al.*, 1983; Scarborough *et al.*, 1977), but they appear generally reliable.

On balance, the foregoing literature can be accurately and concisely summarized as follows: Repetition benefits to words (and other stimuli) reliably occur under a variety of procedures. They occur when conditions are not particularly favorable, including experiments with physical changes to the stimuli between study and test, and experiments with procedural changes between study and test. As a general truism, however, repetition benefits are *stronger*—often to the point of statistical significance—when consistency is maintained. Physical and procedural (bottom-up *and* top-down) matches will produce 'extra' priming, relative to conditions in which the study-test connection is purely conceptual (top-down only). As Bowers (2000) wrote, '...there has been a consistent trend for specificity effects across studies, and if a simple sign test were to be carried out on all these studies, the effect would be significant'. Given this state of affairs, some authors have settled in favor of the episodic view (Goldinger, 1998; Tenpenny, 1995). Bowers (2000) continued from the above statement to defend an abstractionist view. Our Discussion will address this issue again, attempting to move toward a rapprochement. First, however, we will introduce new data that both complicate and clarify the overall picture.

The present research—interesting data under a mantle of failure

This chapter summarizes a series of experiments, conducted in fits and starts over a seven-year period, punctuated by long periods of head-scratching and doing other things. Because book chapters provide some stylistic latitude, we have taken the natural (but uncommon) approach of telling our story chronologically. While this passes for fun in scientific writing, our reason for this approach was more compelling. The present research communicates an object lesson about several common mistakes in cognitive experimentation, including the literal interpretation of null results, failure to consider task demands, and failure to fully examine data. We imagine that similar mistakes characterize many studies, both published and discarded, but ours are sufficient to illustrate the point.

As noted in the foregoing discussion, font-specificity effects have a checkered past, with some null effects. For example, Carr et al. (1989) had volunteers read texts aloud twice. Between readings, half the texts were switched from typed to handwritten format, or vice versa. When equivalent savings were observed despite format changes, Carr et al. suggested that repetition effects reflect priming of abstract word units that are insensitive to surface variability. Similarly, Scarborough et al. (1977) found equivalent repetition effects when words presented in lexical decision were later repeated in old or new typefaces (see also Feustel et al., 1983). Moreover, reliable font-specificity effects are typically small, and are often 'qualified' in some manner. For example, they may only occur with unusual fonts (Jacoby and Hayman, 1987; see Nygaard et al., 2000, for an auditory analogue). From such findings, the potential role of font-specific episodes in lexical processing seems minimal. In the following experiments, we scrutinized such effects in greater detail.

Experiments 1 and 2: good and poor spellers

Like many investigations, our study of font-specific memory began with a sabbatical, when Virginia Holmes visited Arizona State University. One line of her research was on individual differences in spelling ability and associated differences in word-recognition processes (Holmes and Ng, 1993). Combining this focus with our ongoing studies of episodic word perception, we conducted an experiment on font-specific memory in good and poor spellers. We describe the design of this experiment in detail, as it formed the basis for all following experiments.

Experiment 1 entailed one between-subjects comparison, good versus poor spellers. All participants were administered a spelling recognition test, requiring them to select misspelled words in a multiple-choice test (see Holmes and Ng, 1993). To each set of four words, students either identified a misspelling, or selected 'none'. The students also completed a section of the Raven Progressive Matrix test, estimating non-verbal intelligence (see Raven, 2000). Eventually, we distinguished groups of good and poor spellers using the extreme quartiles of the spelling-test scores, with equivalent Raven scores.

In addition to the Group variable, we examined three within-subjects variables. In general, the experiment required subjects to process words in a study phase, and then process them again (differently) in a test phase. During the study phase, we manipulated *levels of processing* (LOP; Craik and Tulving, 1975) for the words: Subjects either completed a 'shallow' or 'deep' two-alternative forced-choice task. For the shallow task, subjects quickly indicated whether words contained the letter E, pressing buttons labeled 'e' and 'no e'. For the deep task, they quickly indicated whether words were abstract or concrete, pressing buttons labeled as such. The second manipulation was *font consistency.* Words were shown in two easily discriminable fonts during both study and test phases. Half the words had consistent fonts across sessions, and half were switched.

The final within-subjects manipulation, in addition to LOP and font consistency, was *test type.* To different subsets of words, subjects either completed direct (explicit) or indirect (implicit) memory tasks during test phases. The direct memory test was simple recognition, as is commonly used. For an indirect memory test, we used lexical decision. Although it is less common than other indirect memory tasks (e.g., stem-completion), lexical decision can reveal repetition effects (Forbach *et al.*, 1974; Masson and Freedman, 1990; Smith *et al.*, 1989). Notably, neither voice-specific nor font-specific repetition effects are easily obtained in lexical decision (Luce and Lyons, 1998; Scarborough *et al.*, 1977). Brown and Carr (1993; also Manso de Zuniga *et al.*, 1991) found such an effect with handwritten words, but our experiment used computer fonts, perhaps calling into question the wisdom of our method.

The results of our experiment were both reassuring and surprising. On the reassuring side, we passed the experimental 'litmus test', replicating major effects in the literature. First, good spellers were uniformly faster and more accurate than poor spellers, replicating findings with many delineations of 'low-verbal' and 'high-verbal' individuals. Indeed, such group differences are often quite large (by the standards of word-perception experiments), far exceeding more heralded effects, such as word frequency (see Butler and Hains, 1979; Chateau and Jared, 2000; Lewellen *et al.*, 1993; Stanovich and West, 1989). Second, we obtained standard LOP effects, more powerfully in recognition than lexical decision. Table 8.1 summarizes the overall results, collapsed across same- and different-font repetitions (reliable contrasts, by rows and columns, are denoted by various symbols).

The surprising side of the data were the font-specificity effects. These are summarized, in several different ways, in Table 8.2. Consider first the aggregate data: When the subjects are combined, there are essentially no font-specificity effects. Indeed, there are no consistent trends, as same-font repetitions occasionally seem better, and occasionally seem worse. When the data are viewed in this standard manner, font-specificity stands as a testament to insignificance, the very embodiment of 'null-ness'. However, when the data are considered

Table 8.1 Overall results from Holmes and Goldinger, collapsed over fonts

	Good spellers		Poor spellers			
Orienting tasks (% correct, RT)						
'e' detection (shallow)	97.7	596	97.5	682		□
abstract/concrete (deep)	92.2	834	91.0	1002		□
	✓	‡	✓	‡		
Recognition memory (% correct, RT)						
Old words (hits)						
Shallow LOP	79.6	777	66.7	1082	§	□
Deep LOP	95.4	790	94.6	824	§	□
	✓		✓	‡		
New words (correct rejections)						
Shallow LOP	86.7	789	75.8	932	§	□
Deep LOP	87.5	878	84.4	1015		□
		‡	✓	‡		
Lexical decision (% correct, RT)						
Words						
Shallow LOP	98.8	624	95.5	722		□
Deep LOP	98.8	626	98.3	756		□
				‡		
Nonwords						
Shallow LOP	97.1	785	93.3	986	§	□
Deep LOP	97.9	794	94.2	1188	§	□
				‡		

Notes: RTs in milliseconds.

§ : Contrast of good vs. poor (% correct), $p < .05.$
□ : Contrast of good vs. poor (RT), $p < .05.$
✓ : Contrast of deep vs. shallow (% correct), $p < .05.$
‡ : Contrast of deep vs. shallow (RT), $p < .05.$

separately for good and poor spellers, a slightly more orderly picture appears. In recognition memory, the good spellers tended to perform better to same-font repetitions, with two reliable effects in four contrasts. Among the poor spellers, the trend is less obvious, but they did show a significant *backwards* effect (in accuracy), following shallow processing. The lexical decision data were similar. Good spellers showed small, occasionally reliable, benefits of font repetition. Poor spellers showed opposite trends, with reliable differences in the RT measures. More formally, we observed reliable two-way interactions (group X font-consistency) in half the possible comparisons.

Taken together, the results of our first experiment were generally encouraging: We both replicated previously reported data (including null font-specificity effects), and by separating our subjects into groups, we found hints that some differences may exist across individuals. Clearly, we never expected font-specificity effects in opposite directions across groups, so the data were exciting. There were, however, several problems. First, even within groups, the font effects were not very uniform. Second, we had no explanation for

Table 8.2 Font-specificity effects from Holmes and Goldinger

	All subjects		Good spellers		Poor spellers			
Recognition memory (hit rate, RT)								
Shallow LOP								
Same font	71.7	922	82.5	767	60.8	1071	§	☐
Different font	74.6	938	75.7	787	72.5	1088		☐
			✓		✓			
Deep LOP								
Same font	96.3	802	95.8	764	96.7	839		☐
Different font	93.8	811	95.0	816	92.5	806		
				‡				
Lexical decision, words (% correct, RT)								
Shallow LOP								
Same font	96.3	689	98.3	616	94.2	746	§	☐
Different font	98.0	657	99.2	632	96.7	698		☐
						‡		
Deep LOP								
Same font	99.2	718	100.0	633	98.3	803		☐
Different font	97.9	664	97.5	816	98.3	708		☐
		‡		‡		‡		

Notes: RTs in milliseconds.

§ : Contrast of good vs. poor (% correct), $p < .05.$

☐ : Contrast of good vs. poor (RT), $p < .05.$

✓ : Contrast of same vs. different font (% correct), $p < .05.$

‡ : Contrast of same vs. different font (RT), $p < .05.$

the font-effect reversal across groups. Third, a follow-up experiment conducted in Melbourne, using very similar methods, did not produce similar results. We all moved on to other projects.

About two years later, we (at Arizona State) conducted a new experiment, again comparing good and poor spellers. Indeed, Experiment 2 was similar to its predecessor in most regards, with just a couple of minor changes. The primary change was to adopt a mixed-model design, rather than an entirely within-subjects design. In Experiment 1, every participant went through multiple blocks of trials, completing the entire design (two levels of LOP for both recognition and lexical decision). Although this reduced the onerous task of screening subjects, it had (at least) two disadvantages. First, it severely limited the data we could collect in each condition. Second, it raised the possibility of cross-task contamination, as people were asked to 'switch gears' every few minutes.

In Experiment 2, the 'secondary' manipulations (shallow versus deep encoding, implicit versus explicit test) were conducted between-subjects. The 'primary' manipulation (font change) was examined within-subjects. This change allowed more trials in each condition, which made it feasible to include 'new' words in lexical decision test sessions. Whereas Experiment 1 included 36 subjects (18 per spelling group), Experiment 2 included 160 subjects, with 20 good and 20 poor spellers in each of the four between-subject conditions. A final change was instrumental; new computers and software were used for Experiment 2. As a result, we had a wide selection of available fonts, and we chose two that were rated (by 15 volunteers) as highly dissimilar, but equally legible.

The overall results of Experiment 2 are shown in Table 8.3. As shown, we replicated the patterns from Experiment 1 (and the prior literature): There were large group differences on nearly all measures, and there were robust LOP effects in recognition. Of greater interest were data from the font manipulation, shown in Table 8.4. As in Experiment 1, a stark contrast emerged when the aggregate data were compared to the separate group data. No font effects were reliable in the aggregate data and the trends were, if anything, backwards.

Table 8.3 Overall results of Experiment 2, collapsed over fonts

	Good spellers		Poor spellers			
Orienting tasks (% correct, RT)						
'e' detection (shallow)	97.2	579	96.8	690	□	
abstract/concrete (deep)	91.6	866	87.5	992	§	□
	✓	‡	✓	‡		
Recognition memory (% correct, RT)						
Old words (hits)						
Shallow LOP	85.7	982	77.5	1087	§	□
Deep LOP	94.7	873	88.5	974	§	□
	✓	‡	✓	‡		
New words (correct rejections)						
Shallow LOP	73.5	1028	68.0	1154	§	□
Deep LOP	90.5	919	86.0	1002	□	
	✓	‡	✓	‡		
Lexical decision (% correct, RT)						
Old words						
Shallow LOP	95.5	583	94.8	629	□	
Deep LOP	98.5	551	96.5	616	□	
New words						
Shallow LOP	92.8	616	91.5	748	□	
Deep LOP	98.8	597	98.8	624	□	
	✓		✓	‡		
Nonwords						
Shallow LOP	95.4	704	94.2	783	□	
Deep LOP	96.2	695	90.2	772	§	□

Notes: RTs in milliseconds.

§ : Contrast of good vs. poor (% correct), $p < .05$.

□ : Contrast of good vs. poor (RT), $p < .05$.

✓ : Contrast of deep vs. shallow (% correct), $p < .05$.

‡ : Contrast of deep vs. shallow (RT), $p < .05$.

Table 8.4 Font-specificity effects in Experiment 2

	All subjects		Good spellers		Poor spellers			
Recognition memory								
(hit rate, RT)								
Shallow LOP								
Same font	82.5	1036	87.5	951	77.5	1121	§	□
Different font	82.3	1033	84.0	1013	80.5	1052		□
			✓		‡			
Deep LOP								
Same font	90.5	935	95.0	833	86.0	1037	§	□
Different font	92.5	923	93.5	910	91.5	935		
			‡	✓				
Lexical decision, words								
(% correct, RT)								
Shallow LOP								
Same font	94.8	628	95.5	565	94.0	690	□	
Different font	95.8	605	96.0	591	95.5	618		
			‡		‡			
Deep LOP								
Same font	97.3	557	98.0	521	96.5	592	□	
Different font	98.3	559	99.0	560	97.5	557		
			‡		‡			

Notes: RTs in milliseconds.
§ : Contrast of good vs. poor (% correct), $p < .05$.
□ : Contrast of good vs. poor (RT), $p < .05$.
✓ : Contrast of same vs. different font (% correct), $p < .05$.
‡ : Contrast of same vs. different font (RT), $p < .05$.

Among the good spellers, however, we observed positive font-specificity effects (i.e., better performance to same-font repetitions), with reliable simple effects emerging once in recognition accuracy, once in recognition RT, and twice in lexical decision RT. Moreover, the non-significant trends in recognition were consistent in direction with the reliable differences. Once again, an opposite pattern was observed for the poor spellers. A general pattern of *backward* font effects was observed, with reliable simple effects emerging once in recognition accuracy, twice in recognition RT, and twice in lexical decision RT. Of eight possible Group X Font interactions, six were reliable, with only accuracy in lexical decision failing to follow suit. As in Experiment 1, font changes had opposite effects across groups, and the pattern was more robust.

Taken together, our experiments on good and poor spellers were both intriguing and worrisome. When the data were collapsed across groups, the potential font-specificity effects appeared completely null. When the data were separated by groups, we found font effects that were often reliable, but in opposite directions across groups. This is easily seen in Figure 8.1, which shows font-specificity effects (displayed as difference scores) in the RT data from Experiment 2.

Multidimensional episodes: a possible explanation?

The results of Experiment 2 were reminiscent of a 'good news–bad news' joke: On the good side, despite methodological changes, our previous data pattern replicated. On the bad side, our previous data pattern replicated, still without a coherent account. Our goal was to answer two questions: First, why might episodic repetition occasionally produce a behavioral penalty, rather than a benefit? Second, why did our repetition effects differ across individuals? As is often the case, we derived a working hypothesis by combining ideas from separate literatures.

To address the first question, we began by closely examining the data from Experiment 2, looking for aberrant stimuli or programming errors. Although such errors would likely cause our 'backward' repetition effects, we found none. We did notice a pattern, however, and it was most evident among the poor spellers: Although Figure 8.1 shows clear negative repetition effects, the poor spellers' raw data looked far less uniform. Specifically, most of the poor spellers had wide RT variations from trial to trial, but only in response to the old words. New words generated fairly clean data, with relatively small standard deviations. By contrast, old words apparently generated either small repetition *benefits* or rather large repetition *costs*, with a clearly bimodal distribution. This was especially true for same-font repetitions. Once added together, these separate populations of trials create an impression of monolithic, negative font effects in the aggregate data.

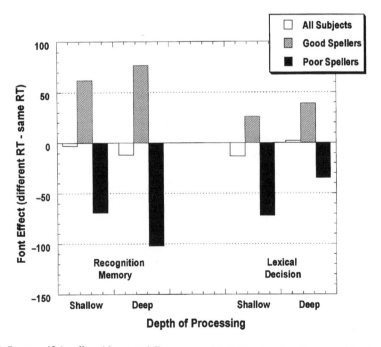

Figure 8.1 Font-specificity effects (shown as difference scores) in the RT data from Experiment 2. The results are shown separately for recognition memory and lexical decision, at each LOP.

Thus, it appeared that some missing factor was modulating the poor spellers' responses to same-font repetitions, leading either to small benefits or large penalties. Because nearly all our experimental factors were counterbalanced, it was not immediately clear what this missing factor could be. For example, all words were used equally often in old or new fonts, words (and fonts) were fully crossed with levels of processing, etc. One aspect of the design, however, was not fully counterbalanced, although few people would have considered it suspicious. Specifically, the assignment of words to *response buttons* was not controlled between study and test. During the study sessions, all words were evenly divided between two possible responses ('e' versus 'no e' or 'abstract' versus 'concrete'). More tangibly, half the words required a *left-button* press and half required a *right-button* press. By contrast, during the test sessions, all 'old' words had their correct responses mapped to the right button, which designated either 'old' or 'word,' depending upon task.

In designing experiments, we generally attempt to place ourselves in the subjects' position, hoping to anticipate possible misunderstandings or sources of error. Nevertheless, certain levels of analysis may elude such introspection. In this case, we had grown so accustomed to thinking about experimental tasks that we forgot the most basic level of analysis—eventually, subjects have to move a finger, either on the right or the left. Although it seemed far-fetched, we were forced to consider the issue: Given our design, the stimulus-response mappings changed for half the 'old' words between study and test. Could our bi-directional font effects indicate that good and poor spellers were differentially sensitive to this factor?

Given this question, we naturally wanted to conduct *post hoc* tests on our data, looking at our effects with a new 'response-button' grouping factor. Unfortunately, this was impossible, given the organization of our data files. Thus we turned to the literature, finding several reports of conceptually analogous findings. Our central hypothesis had not changed, still asserting that word perception and memory rely on detailed episodes. However, to accommodate our data, we had to assume that episodic memory traces are multidimensional, and that various factors may determine which dimensions receive emphasis, leading to stronger encoding. Naturally, this is not a new idea. In a classic article, Underwood (1969) enumerated various dimensions of episodic memory traces, attempting to rank-order their relative strengths in typical memory performance. Moreover, virtually all models of long-term memory assume multidimensional traces, capable of holding at least item-specific and contextual information. Without such dual-coding, performing simple 'old-new' recognition to familiar words would be impossible. Indeed, several studies suggest that environmental context shapes memory traces and may affect performance (e.g., Murnane and Phelps, 1994; Russo *et al.*, 1999).

Beyond the necessary assumption of multidimensional memory traces, a rich literature has developed, focusing on the conditions that maximize recall and recognition of items after various encoding processes. In addition to such explicit memory measures, many studies have similarly focused on repetition priming effects. Generally speaking, a consensus exists, stating that either direct or indirect memory is strongest when similar conditions are maintained across encoding and testing. Variations on basic idea form the principle of *encoding specificity* (Tulving and Thompson, 1973) and the principle of *transfer-appropriate processing* (Blaxton, 1989; Graf and Ryan, 1990; Morris *et al.*, 1977; Srinivas, 1996; see

Franks *et al.*, 2000). Similarly, a key facet of Logan's (1988, 1990) *instance theory* of automaticity is the *attention hypothesis*, which states that episodic content is defined by the focus of attention during encoding. In other words, attention selects which of many possible dimensions (for example, a word's meaning, its appearance, or its context) are most reliably encoded into a new episodic memory trace (or instance).

Although the attention hypothesis is quite general, its emphasis on encoding makes it readily testable and it has considerable support (Logan and Etherton, 1994). Indeed, several researchers have reported that episodic traces are shaped by myriad bottom-up and top-down influences, all of which appear consistent with the attention hypothesis. For example, Masson (1986) found that skill development in reading typographically transformed words was tightly constrained by the visual tokens used, leading him to suggest that specific combinations of tokens and procedures were collected in episodic memory. In research more similar to the present topic, Masson and Freedman (1990) conducted six experiments, all suggesting that repetition effects reflect the context-dependent recruitment of episodic study traces. Their view was quite similar to other episodic views, but with an increased emphasis on cognitive and linguistic processes, rather than superficial perceptual processes.

Most prior studies of episode-specific priming required either degraded displays (e.g., Jacoby, 1983b) or very unusual fonts (e.g., Jacoby and Hayman, 1987). By contrast, Masson and Freedman presented words in a normal manner, but their tasks prompted subjects to derive different conceptual interpretations of the words. That perceptual-conceptual exercise seemed to provide the groundwork for later priming. As they wrote (p. 370), 'Our view is that repeated presentation of a word recruits episodic memories of recent experiences with that word. This recruitment is highly context sensitive and includes operations associated with generating a context-dependent interpretation of the word.' Similar results were reported by MacLeod and Masson (2000), using word naming as a memory index. Also, in experiments using the word-superiority effect, Whittlesea and Cantwell (1987; Whittlesea and Brooks, 1988) found that repetition effects depended upon reinstatement of context-specific interpretations of stimuli. In more precise terms, the unique combinations of stimulus items and their associated tasks form the basis for later episodic effects.

Taken together, studies on encoding specificity, transfer-appropriate processing, the attention hypothesis, and related principles all indicate a bottom line: The observation of clear episodic influences on word perception requires considerable overlap between the study and test encounters with words. This goes beyond obvious overlap in appearance, or even overlap in the assigned tasks. What is required is true 'episodic overlap', wherein test encounters recreate the mental states created in study encounters. When experiments are well-designed, researchers can use study-task data to reasonably infer the mental states generated in each trial (e.g., Masson and Freedman, 1990). It always remains possible, however, that a subject's attention may be focused on situational factors that are orthogonal or redundant to the intended dimensions. If attention is on an orthogonal dimension (e.g., wondering how many trials are left, stealing glances at the attractive experimenter), subjects may generate poor study-task data. Or, given an easy study task, they may appear attentive but have poor memory later. This is an accepted hazard of collecting data from Introductory Psychology students. However, if attention is on a redundant dimension, there may be no obvious empirical marker. From our perspective, our subjects simply classified words according either to letters or meanings. But, as researchers, we are accustomed to experimental programs, booths, and response boxes—from our subjects' perspective, the eventual goals of pressing the left and right buttons may have been a prominent dimension of their mental states. If this were true, test trials requiring concordant or discordant button-presses may be helped or hindered, respectively.

Given this analysis, we return to our second question: If the backwards font effects reflect an undue influence of 'button-press memory', why were the poor spellers more likely to encode such information? Unfortunately, the literature on individual differences in spelling ability offers little insight on this topic. It remains possible, however, that our groups differed along some dimension other than spelling ability. In a study contrasting 'low-verbal' and 'high-verbal' subjects, Lewellen *et al.* (1993) found that spelling scores were correlated with many other metrics used to separate groups, including vocabulary scores and verbal SAT scores. Thus, the spelling delineation used in Experiments 1 and 2 certainly may have incorporated other group differences. Among such possibilities, an interesting candidate is *working-memory (WM) span*, which has been a recent focus of extensive research. Indeed, WM span is known to correlate with many indices of language processing, including several that Lewellen *et al.* associated with spelling ability (Chiappe *et al.*, 2000; Engle *et al.*, 1999).

Recent studies, using various tasks and materials, have shown that individuals with low and high WM spans differ in attentional control. Specifically, lower-span people are relatively poor at *suppressing* irrelevant thoughts or signals (Engle *et al.*, 1999; Gernsbacher, 1993). This has been shown in an impressive array of studies, including many conducted by Engle and his colleagues. Indeed, it often appears that WM capacity is synonymous with suppression ability, either in specific tasks or in general cognition (Rosen and Engle, 1998). Therefore, differences in WM capacity seem like a natural explanation of the data from Experiments 1 and 2: If our poor spellers had generally low WM spans, relative to the good spellers, they would also be less likely to efficiently switch from one set of stimulus-response mappings to another. In other words, they might experience difficulty suppressing a previously correct 'left-button' response when a 'right-button' response is later required.

Experiments 3 and 4: high and low working-memory spans

Because these speculations about Experiments 1 and 2 were impossible to investigate, we conducted Experiments 3 and 4. In these experiments, subjects were delineated according to WM span, and we programmed our procedures to better keep track of the responses required during study and test. In most regards, however, these experiments were similar to the foregoing, using the same words, the same study tasks, and the same test procedures. Experiment 3 was a conceptual replication of Experiment 2, including only the aforementioned changes. Experiment 4 was nearly identical, except some words were encountered once during study, and others were encountered three times. Our expectation was that such multiple encounters would intensify any episodic effects, relative to single exposures. Moreover, examining the study data from repeated items allowed an assessment of repetition effects with total perceptual and behavioral overlap.

In both experiments, subjects were delineated into low and high WM groups according to their performance on an *operation-word span test*. This test of working-memory capacity has proven sensitive and reliable, and it predicts performance differences across many cognitive tasks (Engle *et al.*, 1999; Klein and Fiss, 1999). Subjects received simple mathematical equations for true – false verification, alternating with words for memorization. For example, subjects saw the string $(9/3) + 5 = 8?$, requiring a 'yes' response, followed by the word CHAIR. Correct answers to the equations were evenly divided between 'yes' and 'no'. After responding to each equation, subjects saw a word for memorization. This sequence repeated a varying number of times, until a 'recall' prompt instructed subjects to write all words they could recall, in order, from the preceding set. Memory sets varied from two to seven words, with two trials at each value, creating 12 trials with a maximum score of 54. Span scores were derived by summing the words from all sets that were recalled perfectly (Turner and Engle, 1989). Eventually, we adopted low- and high-span cut-offs corresponding to the lower and upper quartiles of all scores. All subjects completed their entire experiments, data were sorted according to WM afterward. After sorting, each group in Experiment 3 included 36 students. In Experiment 4, each group included 39 students.

The overall results of Experiment 3 are summarized in Table 8.5, following the format of our previous tables. Considering first data from the orienting tasks, there were again robust group differences (low- versus high-span), which were exacerbated by task difficulty. In the test phases, robust group differences emerged in recognition memory. Smaller, occasionally significant trends were observed in lexical decision, mostly in the RT data. And, as one would expect, clear LOP effects were observed in recognition memory, but were generally absent in lexical decision.

The data of primary interest came from the font manipulation, shown in Table 8.6, and they generally replicated the patterns from Experiment 2. As in Experiment 2, a stark contrast emerged between the aggregate data and the separate group data. Whereas no clear font effects were observed in the aggregate data, we again observed opposite font effects in our separate subject groups. The high-span subjects showed modest, but often reliable, benefits of font repetition. The low-span subjects produced relatively large costs of font repetition. Although these effects were smaller in magnitude than those observed with good and poor spellers, the pattern was essentially identical. There was, however, one new aspect to these data that had not emerged in the experiments comparing spelling groups: In Experiment 3, an interaction emerged showing that the asymmetry in font effects between groups grew larger as study LOP increased. Thus, it appeared that low-span subjects who put more effort into their initial responses to words were more constrained by those responses later. This speculation receives support from the response-button analysis, presented next.

As Tables 8.5 and 8.6 show, the previous data patterns from good and poor spellers were quite well replicated by contrasting individuals with high and low WM spans. Having verified this, our main interest was to examine the issue of response buttons, allowing a full assessment of potential episodic memory effects. Figure 8.2 shows font effects ('different' minus 'same' RTs), as a function of group, test task (upper versus lower panels), depth of study processing, and response buttons. On the *x* axis, responses are categorized 'same' and 'different', as a function of the *correct* responses required during study. Occasionally,

Table 8.5 Overall results of Experiment 3, collapsed over fonts

	High WM span		Low WM span			
Orienting tasks (% correct, RT)						
'e' detection (shallow)	98.0	555	96.2	641		□
abstract/concrete (deep)	93.2	790	85.0	1002	§	□
	✓	‡	✓	‡		
Recognition memory (% correct, RT)						
Old words (hits)						
Shallow LOP	88.0	922	85.0	1160		□
Deep LOP	97.2	859	90.2	1085	§	□
	✓	‡	✓	‡		
New words (correct rejections)						
Shallow LOP	80.0	970	78.2	1180		□
Deep LOP	90.2	919	84.2	1114		□
	✓	‡	✓	‡		
Lexical decision (% correct, RT)						
Old words						
Shallow LOP	98.2	560	96.0	615		□
Deep LOP	98.2	555	97.2	589		□
				‡		
New words						
Shallow LOP	95.0	611	93.2	653		□
Deep LOP	98.2	601	96.2	649		□
Nonwords						
Shallow LOP	99.2	695	97.0	738		□
Deep LOP	98.2	701	94.2	749	§	□

Notes: RTs in milliseconds.
§   : Contrast of high- vs. low-span (% correct), $p < .05$.
□ : Contrast of high- vs. low-span (RT), $p < .05$.
✓ : Contrast of deep vs. shallow (% correct), $p < .05$.
‡ : Contrast of deep vs. shallow (RT), $p < .05$.

subjects made mistakes in the study tasks (see Table 8.5); this analysis included no correction for those trials (which could only bias the outcome against our hypothesis).

The data in Figure 8.2 clearly show the three-way interaction we had anticipated: Among the high-span subjects, positive font effects were consistently observed in both tasks and both LOPs.

The high-span subjects showed some sensitivity to response buttons, with slightly larger font effects arising to words requiring the same response button across study and test. Also, their same-font benefits were affected by LOP, such that same-font/same-button trials were most enhanced following deeper study processing. Conversely, the low-span subjects displayed considerable sensitivity to study-test changes in response buttons. Given an old word in its

Table 8.6 Font-specificity effects in Experiment 3

	All subjects		High WM span		Low WM span			
Recognition memory								
(hit rate, RT)								
Shallow LOP								
Same font	87.4	1041	89.8	917	85.0	1165	§	□
Different font	85.6	1034	86.2	927	85.0	1140	□	
Deep LOP								
Same font	94.0	975	98.0	847	92.0	1102	§	□
Different font	92.5	965	96.6	871	88.4	1058	§	□
					‡			
Lexical decision, words								
(% correct, RT)								
Shallow LOP								
Same font	96.4	591	98.0	554	94.8	627	§	□
Different font	97.8	580	98.4	566	97.2	593		
Deep LOP								
Same font	98.2	601	99.0	538	97.4	664		
Different font	97.2	586	97.4	572	97.0	599	□	
			‡		‡			

Notes: RTs in milliseconds.

§   : Contrast of high- vs. low-span (% correct), $p < .05$.

□ : Contrast of high- vs. low-span (RT), $p < .05$.

✓ : Contrast of same vs. different font (% correct), $p < .05$.

‡ : Contrast of same vs. different font (RT), $p < .05$.

original font, low-span subjects reaped modest benefits (comparable to high-spans) if the required response button was the same, but they also incurred large penalties if the response button was different. High-span subjects showed no evidence of such costs, although their positive font effects were somewhat larger when the response button was unchanged. In both groups, font effects (positive or negative) were increased following the deeper LOP.

Experiment 3 provided strong support to a version of the transfer-appropriate processing (TAP) hypothesis, a version that is tailored to individuals with different WM spans. According to TAP, repetition benefits should be greatest when test processes overlap with study processes. Generally, we think of such processes in 'cognitive' terms, such as perceptual and conceptual processes. Clearly, however, more concrete sensory-motor processes are also involved (when subjects are required to generate study-task responses), and those processes may impose themselves on episodic traces, and therefore on later performance. A common observation with low-span individuals is their difficulty in suppressing irrelevant signals or thoughts (Engle *et al.*, 1999). In a task like ours, people are encouraged to quickly map cognitive states onto speeded button-presses, a process that clearly takes learning. Apparently, lower-span individuals either encode such information more strongly, or they have extra difficulty suppressing it later. Thus, when a previously seen stimulus (same word, same font) is encountered, the previous response causes interference. These were not

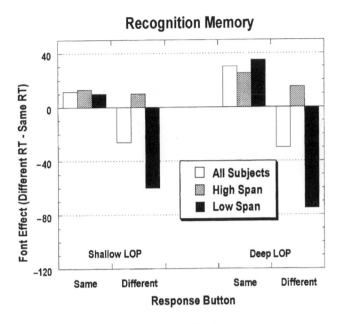

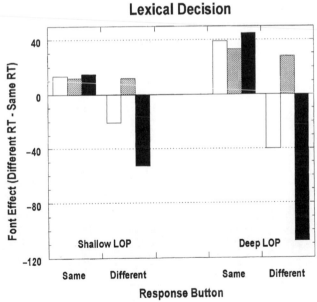

Figure 8.2 Font-specificity effects in the RT data from Experiment 3. The upper panel shows recognition memory data; the lower panel shows lexical decision data. Both panels show font effects as a function of LOP and response buttons.

symmetric effects: The benefits caused by matching old stimuli to their previous buttons was far smaller than the costs of mismatch. Similarly, words in different fonts displayed only minor linkages to their previous responses.

In Experiment 4, we tested this pattern further by strengthening the study-task experience for some words. In Experiment 3, all words were encountered once at study, which already created sizeable repetition effects (positive and negative). In Experiment 4, half the study words were encountered once and half were encountered three times. The orienting-task data are shown in Table 8.7; the recognition and lexical decision data (collapsed over fonts) are shown in Tables 8.8 and 8.9, respectively. These follow the format of previous tables, but new information has been added, showing the effects of repeated word exposures. The assignment of words to repetition values (one versus three) was counterbalanced, so all words are shown in Table 8.7 as having three exposures. In practice, each subject had single exposures for half the words.

The study-task data (Table 8.7) were generally similar to our previous data with respect to group differences. On the shallow encoding task (e-detection), high-span subjects were faster than low-span subjects, without any differences in mean accuracy. As expected, there were clear repetition benefits for both groups, although more so for the low-span group (110 ms) than the high-span group (59 ms). Indeed, the group difference shrank to insignificance after three word repetitions. On the deep encoding task (abstract/concrete), high-span subjects were again faster than low-span subjects, with an accuracy difference only arising upon first exposure. Again, clear repetition benefits occurred for both groups, with greater benefit to the low-span group (110 ms) than the high-span group (59 ms). Despite this asymmetrical improvement, the groups still differed reliably after three exposures.

As shown in Tables 8.8 and 8.9, the overall recognition memory and lexical decision data (i.e., irrespective of font effects) followed their expected patterns. Unlike previous tables,

Table 8.7 Orienting-task data, Experiment 4

	High WM span		Low WM span			
Orienting tasks (% correct, RT)						
'e' detection (shallow)						
first exposure:	97.0	571	96.2	649		□
second exposure:	99.2	544	99.2	585		□
third exposure:	99.2	512	100	539		
		‡		‡		
abstract/concrete (deep)						
first exposure:	94.0	801	86.8	1050	§	□
second exposure:	96.2	777	95.0	981		□
third exposure:	98.6	716	97.0	901		□
	✓	‡	✓	‡		

Notes: RTs in milliseconds.

§   : Contrast of high- vs. low-span (% correct), $p < .05$.

□   : Contrast of high- vs. low-span (RT), $p < .05$.

✓   : Repetition effect (% correct), $p < .05$.

‡   : Repetition effect (RT), $p < .05$.

Table 8.8 Recognition memory data (% correct, RT) from Experiment 4, collapsed across fonts

Old words (hits)	High WM span				Low WM span			
	Number of exposures							
	One		Three		One		Three	
Shallow LOP	86.4	940	98.8	839	88.8	1066	97.6	881
Deep LOP	95.8	882	99.2	770	93.4	1005	97.8	822
New words (correct rejections)								
	High WM span				**Low WM span**			
Shallow LOP	84.8	991			80.2	1137		
Deep LOP	93.8	920			88.6	1017		

Notes: RTs in milliseconds.

Table 8.9 Lexical decision data (% correct, RT) from Experiment 4, collapsed across fonts

Old words	High WM span				Low WM span			
	Number of exposures							
	One		Three		One		Three	
Shallow LOP	96.8	561	98.2	499	93.0	659	95.8	561
Deep LOP	96.0	543	96.4	515	95.4	638	95.8	545
New words								
	High WM span				**Low WM span**			
Shallow LOP	97.2	590			95.0	634		
Deep LOP	96.8	618			94.2	637		
Nonwords								
Shallow LOP	95.8	659			96.4	708		
Deep LOP	97.4	661			92.0	729		

Notes: RTs in milliseconds.

we did not include symbols to indicate statistically reliable contrasts, as the tables became too cluttered. The general patterns, however, are easily seen: The high-span group was consistently faster than the low-span group in both tasks. In terms of accuracy, the groups were generally comparable, with a few contrasts favoring the high-span group. Regarding the new repetition manipulation, both groups showed improved performance to 'old' words following multiple exposures. However, as with the study-task data, the low-span group enjoyed larger benefits of repetition, relative to the high-span group.

As before, our primary interest in Experiment 4 was to examine font effects, and possible response-button effects, comparing the words as a function of repetition. The font-specificity data are shown in Tables 8.10 and 8.11; the data broken down by response buttons (for lexical decision) are shown in Figure 8.3. As before, symbols denoting statistical comparisons have been excluded from these tables, but the patterns of reliable effects are easily seen. Beginning with the recognition memory data (Table 8.10), an interesting contrast emerged, relative to Experiment 3. For words that were seen only once during

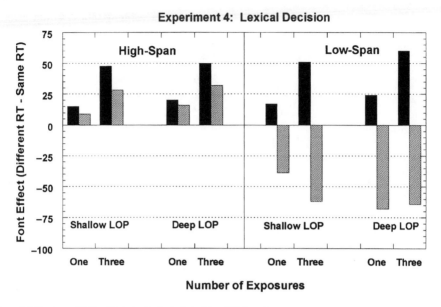

Figure 8.3 Font-specificity effects in the lexical-decision RT data from Experiment 4. Separate panels represent high- and low-span groups; bars within each panel represent each LOP and number of study exposures per word. Dark bars represent same-button trials; light bars represent different-button trials.

Table 8.10 Font-specificity effects in recognition memory, Experiment 4

	All subjects		High WM span		Low WM span	
Shallow LOP						
One exposure						
Same font	87.9	1007	87.2	929	88.6	1085
Different font	87.1	999	85.6	951	88.6	1047
Three exposures						
Same font	98.4	861	98.6	837	98.2	885
Different font	98.0	859	99.0	841	97.0	877
Deep LOP						
One exposure						
Same font	94.9	948	96.8	870	93.0	1026
Different font	94.3	939	94.8	894	93.8	984
Three exposures						
Same font	99.2	770	100.0	774	98.3	826
Different font	99.2	770	98.4	765	97.3	818

Note: Each entry shows percent correct, followed by RT in milliseconds.

Table 8.11 Font-specificity effects in lexical decision, Experiment 4

	All subjects		High WM span		Low WM span	
Shallow LOP						
One exposure						
Same font	95.2	613	97.4	555	93.0	670
Different font	94.5	608	96.0	567	93.0	648
Three exposures						
Same font	97.0	523	99.0	480	94.9	565
Different font	97.1	537	97.4	518	96.7	556
Deep LOP						
One exposure						
Same font	94.9	946	96.9	534	96.8	660
Different font	94.3	936	95.1	552	93.8	616
Three exposures						
Same font	96.2	521	96.2	495	96.2	547
Different font	96.0	539	96.6	534	95.4	543

Note: Each entry shows percent correct, followed by RT in milliseconds.

study, the RT data closely resembled those from Experiment 3, as one would certainly expect. Thus, we observed the same effects of Group and LOP. We also observed similar font effects, such that high-span subjects showed small benefits and low-span subjects showed costs. Moreover, the analysis of font effects conditionalized by response buttons also resembled the previous experiment.

With respect to the words encountered three times, however, a different pattern of recognition memory RTs emerged. Although there remained clear effects of Group and LOP, there were only insignificant trends toward font effects in each group. When these RT data were broken down by response buttons, the previously seen interaction (Group × Font × Button) was no longer apparent. The low-span group *was* still sensitive to study-test changes in response buttons, responding 41 ms faster to same-button items, but there was no conditionalizing influence of fonts. Thus, multiple study repetitions apparently eliminated font effects in explicit memory, at all levels of analysis.

In lexical decision (Table 8.11), a somewhat different pattern was observed. As before, main effects of Group and LOP were observed, along with a main effect of repetition. With respect to font-specific priming, the group profiles now changed as a function of repetition. With one exposure per study word, the earlier data patterns were replicated—modest positive font effects for the high-span subjects and negative font effects for low-span subjects. With three repetitions, however, the font effect grew *larger* for the high-span group and it nearly vanished for the low-span group. Looking at the data in this manner, it is impossible to appreciate the underlying patterns that arise in connection to response buttons, and a variety of hypotheses are viable.

Figure 8.3 shows font effects in lexical decision RTs, as a function of group and response buttons, providing a less ambiguous picture. For clarity, the 'all subjects' data are not included, but are easily derived. Examining the data in this manner, we see a pattern similar to that in Experiment 3. The high-span subjects produced positive font effects in all cases, with larger benefits arising when there were more study repetitions and when the response buttons were held constant. The low-span subjects generated a very different profile, again showing considerable sensitivity to the assignment of response buttons to words. For words requiring identical button-presses across study and test, we observed font and repetition effects that closely mirrored data from the high-span group. But, for words requiring a different button-press across study and test, an equal and opposite pattern emerged: Same-font words again imposed rather large penalties on performance.

Empirical summary: hidden effects hiding other effects

Although complex in design, the major results of the foregoing experiments are easily summarized: In all four experiments, font effects were observed (to differing degrees) in both subject groups, but the 'disadvantaged' groups (i.e., the poor spellers or people with low WM spans) displayed their font-sensitivity in contradictory directions. Those directions of effect were apparently determined by compatibility of the response buttons required for certain words across study and test. Specifically, when presented old words in their original fonts, these groups either showed strong benefits, or stronger penalties, as a function of study-to-test constancy of the indicated response buttons for each word. Note that, despite its complexity, this pattern remains a font effect—old words in new fonts produced relatively small 'button effects'.

In the latter experiments, these data patterns were accentuated by deeper LOP at study. Thus, the harder low-span participants worked to select their study response, the more influence it had during test. Finally, although these effects were generally shared across implicit and explicit memory measures, Experiment 4 produced a dissociation: When words received multiple study exposures, font and response-button effects were eliminated in recognition, but they remained strong in lexical decision.

Implications of the experiments can be also summarized in a few main points: First, all four experiments demonstrated that interpretation of repetition effects is a tricky business, especially when null effects are observed. This point has certainly been raised elsewhere (e.g., Brown and Carr, 1993; Craik *et al.*, 1994; Graf and Ryan, 1990; MacLeod and Masson, 2000; Whittlesea, 1990), but it bears reiteration. In all four of our experiments, different potential interpretations of the data would have arisen, depending upon the chosen levels of analysis. For example, if we ignored group differences (either in spelling ability or WM span), the results of our font manipulations would appear completely null. This is clear in the data presented above, and in the data we omitted. With respect to presented data, consider the tables of font-specificity effects (Tables 8.2, 8.4, 8.6, 8.10, and 8.11)—in every one, the aggregate data (labeled 'all subjects') reveal small, usually unreliable font effects. With respect to omitted data, recall that every experiment originally included about twice as many subjects as the final sample sizes would suggest; potential subjects whose spelling or memory scores fell in the middle quartiles were dropped from later analyses. When their data were included in omnibus analyses, a very common pattern was observed: Small, occasionally significant, benefits for font-specific repetitions were observed in about half the design cells of every experiment. In either case, consideration of the aggregate data would provide little or no evidence for font-specificity (episodic) effects.

Having designed our experiments with an eye toward individual differences, we naturally avoided the most general level of analysis. Nevertheless, our early experiments produced baffling results, and it was essentially luck that we found trends worth following. (And, even with such luck, it took us over five years to understand our own data.) In Experiment 4, after three study repetitions, the low-span subjects produced approximately symmetrical positive and negative font effects, depending upon response buttons. If a similar symmetry had occurred in Experiment 1, our bottom-line would have been very different: We would have reported small, positive font effects for the good spellers, and no font effects for the poor spellers. Without doubt, we could have accounted for such data, perhaps hypothesizing that good spellers have superior encoding skills, leading to greater episodic fidelity. Luckily, the poor spellers produced positive and negative font effects to unequal degrees, providing a trail we eventually followed. Had that not occurred, we would have avoided one null effect (in the aggregate data), only to erroneously accept another. Although this point about interpreting null effects is hackneyed, the present data seem to demand its expression.

Before turning to more theoretical discussion, it is imperative that we clarify two matters of potential miscommunication. First, please note that we do *not* contend that previously reported null font-specificity effects (see Bowers, 2000; Tenpenny, 1995) are hiding similar patterns. Although this is possible, we cannot reasonably speculate on such matters—many reported null effects may be truly null, without any patterns hidden within. Of course, even those outcomes are not easily interpreted, and require conservative conclusions. Second, we should note that we have conducted more experiments than the four described in this chapter, and the results have not been equally uniform. Our other experiments produced interesting data, but without the clearly opposite patterns across groups. We discuss the likely reason for this momentarily. For the time being, we simply wanted to explicitly note that these striking data patterns seem to require a specific balance of factors.

This observation leads to the second, more theoretical implication of the present research. The data reported here, along with the non-replications just noted, strongly suggest that the potential of any study event to affect later test behavior will be determined by the psychological overlap between those experiences. This is the idea behind TAP, and has been the focus of recent articles (e.g., Franks *et al.*, 2000; MacLeod and Masson, 2000). For simplicity, the ill-defined concept of 'psychological overlap' is often treated as a dichotomy, contrasting perceptual and conceptual processing (e.g., Craik *et al.*, 1994). Supporting this approach, memory dissociations have been reported, wherein different retrieval tasks are denoted as data-driven or conceptually-driven, and different manipulations are found to have opposite effects on each (e.g., Hashtroudi *et al.*, 1988).

As is often the case with strong distinctions, however, exceptions gradually emerged, showing that most memory tests contained some mixture of processes (MacLeod and Masson, 1997; Masson and MacLeod, 1992; Weldon, 1991). More generally, a common theme of many recent articles is that episodic content can be shaped by perceptual factors, task requirements, conceptual knowledge, and the focus of selective attention (e.g., Franks *et al.*, 2000; Logan and Etherton, 1994). For example, Johnson (2000) reported two experiments, designed to assess the joint influences of perceptual and attentional factors in long-term repetition priming. In each experiment, subjects made lexical decisions to words, presented either in a typical (horizontal) orientation or a vertical orientation. Control words were presented only once, and were evenly distributed throughout blocks of trials. Other words were presented in each of six successive blocks of trials. Naturally, an RT advantage developed over blocks for repeated words, relative to new words.

The key manipulation occurred in block 6, wherein some repeated words were shown in an orientation that differed from all previous blocks. By strong episodic views of repetition effects, such a change should dramatically reduce priming. In Experiment 1, however, priming remained robust, despite changes in word orientation. This could reflect abstract representation, a poorly chosen stimulus manipulation, or many other possibilities. One such possibility is that word orientation is easily resolved and orthogonal to the task, thus ineffective as a potential aid or disruption to the primary task. In Experiment 2, Johnson required subjects to make responses jointly indicating lexical status and orientation. With that change, an orientation change in block 6 reduced priming by about 50%. Johnson suggested that an episodic account, coupled with a process similar to Logan's attention hypothesis, provided the most coherent account of both experiments. Put simply, focus of attention at study lends unique structure to the episodic traces that are formed; irrelevant dimensions may have little memorial or behavioral impact. A similar stance has been taken by other researchers (e.g., Whittlesea, 1990), and seemingly applies to the present data.

The complexity of episodes: reading is font + mental?

Regarding theoretical approaches to personality, Bem and Funder (1978, p. 485) once wrote:

> Behavior, as everybody knows, is a function of both the person and the situation. But, despite our latter-day obeisance to this truism, we persistently underestimate the influence of the situation. As lay 'intuitive' psychologists, we display this bias so pervasively that it is now known as the 'fundamental attribution error' [...] And, as professional psychologists, we continue to stand bemused as seemingly trivial alterations in experimental procedure continue to produce non-trivial changes in our subjects' behaviors.

Although Bem and Funder were considering behavioral domains more complex than word reading or memory tasks, their observation applies to the present discussion. If nothing else, the foregoing experiments certainly verify that behavior is jointly determined by people and situations, perhaps to degrees we should find discomfiting. In a sense, espousing an episodic view of cognition requires one to relinquish, at least partly, a central goal of cognitive research—the discovery of general rules governing perception, memory, and other domains of information processing. By our view (shared with many other researchers), numerous cognitive functions operate by tapping memory traces for similar prior episodes. No matter the domain—perception, categorization, recognition, problem solving—cognition is guided by similarity between the current mental state and prior states, with memory acting as a content-addressable, resonant system (Kirsner and Dunn, 1985; Kirsner *et al.*, 1987; Kohonen *et al.*, 1989; Shepard, 1984). Given this view, predicting and explaining behavior may be synonymous with knowing the content of someone's relevant episodic trace(s).

In this context, the present data may paint a rather bleak view, giving a nearly chaotic appearance to such memory traces. It is naturally unnerving to see two groups of students, chosen from one population, producing opposite data patterns. Like many cognitive researchers, we are simultaneously interested in individual differences, but are also loathe to imagine a field of scientific inquiry that cannot safely generalize beyond experimental participants. Looking beyond the surface, however, our data were actually quite orderly—we simply overlooked the potential for response buttons to affect behavior. As in any experiment with student volunteers, it is likely for attention to wander, inviting noise into memory traces. Such lapses, however, are likely to be normally distributed within and across individuals (to a degree), and to affect all experimental conditions equally, given a counterbalanced design.

Beyond such unavoidable lapses, we believe that researchers can usually exercise ample control over the episodic traces created in their experiments. As a field, we are skilled in selecting stimuli that vary along specific dimensions, developing tasks that engage attention, and incorporating checks into experimental designs to verify that people followed directions. From the perspective of TAP and the attention hypothesis, the challenge is merely to remain sensitive to the subjects' perspective, from the experimental instructions all the way down to the response buttons. Individuals may vary in their ability to switch sets, suppress inappropriate responses, or simply follow directions, but that imposes no fundamental limits on meaningful experimentation. By extension, adopting an episodic perspective on perception does not consign one to a barren theoretical wasteland, where no explanations exist beyond the episode. It just means you have to be careful.

Coming full circle—episodes or abstractions?

In fashion and cognitive psychology, the classics never go out of style. Although we intended to study word perception and memory, with a hint of individual differences added for flavor, we ended up studying stimulus-response compatibility (Hull, 1943) and proactive interference (e.g., Keppel and Underwood, 1962). Once the data were sorted out, however, they strongly suggested episodic memory as an organizing principle of the subjects' behavior. The episodes were more complex than we initially imagined, but their structures were sensible and their influences were clear. Given such data, we return to the original question: Are words represented in memory as abstract codes, or as collected episodes? Or, more practically, which form of representation confers the most benefit to models of word perception?

Upon reading the foregoing discussion, an astute and irascible defender of abstract representations may notice an apparently unfair double-standard: By its nature, at least as indicated by much of the literature, the hypothesis of abstract representation is tethered to the prediction (and therefore interpretation) of null results. Many studies, for example, are based on logic of the following variety: 'If all repeated words show equivalent priming, regardless of changes (in fonts, voices, etc.), then word perception must rely on abstract representations, insensitive to surface variability.' In other words, if a manipulation of surface features has *no effect*, one theory prevails. On the other hand, the episodic theory allows far more flexibility. Given the caveats about TAP, data-driven versus conceptual tests, and others (including those introduced here), the episodic perspective is allowed to predict positive effects, while seemingly having protection against null effects. This does not constitute a level playing field.

This state of affairs is actually quite common—one theory makes an inherently stronger claim, and is thus answerable to a higher standard of evidence. An excellent example from the field of word recognition is the debate between dual-route and connectionist (single-route) theories of reading, a topic that has generated an enormous literature without resolving the core question (Van Orden and Goldinger, 1994). In that forum, dual-route theory is essentially forced to predict null results, such that phonology effects will be absent in certain words, languages, or experimental conditions. This is a scientifically tenuous position, even if the core hypothesis is correct, because the opposite standard of evidence is so concrete—many studies have shown phonology effects that seemingly violate the theory (Carello *et al.*, 1992). It is much easier to prove a positive than a negative.

Essentially the same situation exists in the case of abstract versus episodic representations, and is evident in long-standing debate between prototype and exemplar models of categorization (e.g., Nosofsky and Zaki, in press; Smith and Minda, 2000). Exemplar models generally 'win' the debate because they can mimic the data considered hallmarks of abstraction (e.g., Hintzman, 1986; Hintzman and Ludlam, 1980), while retaining the ability to account for more idiosyncratic effects. In the present context, we believe that episodic models of word perception are preferable because they account for both 'abstract' and 'exemplar' effects. Others (e.g., Bowers, 2000) have a different view. Given the histories of dual-route theory, prototype theory, and other seemingly endless debates, we are motivated to seek a rapprochement.

In all likelihood, despite the apparent dichotomy drawn between episodic and abstract views, most theorists probably agree that both types of representations exist. The evidence in support of episodic traces is considerable, and they have prima facie psychological validity. Abstract representations also have psychological validity—the hallmark of successful models in learning and memory is the ability to generalize beyond specific instances. In this pluralistic spirit, we will close by considering three different ways that abstract and episodic representations might coexist. This is intended only as a sample, not an exhaustive list of possibilities.

The first possibility comes directly from the architecture of episodic models, which were virtually all designed to create abstraction from substrates of individual traces (Hintzman, 1986; Semon, 1909). In most episodic models, collections of traces are simultaneously activated (to varying degrees) by stimulus input, undergoing some combining function to create a singular experience. By itself, that mental state is an abstraction which constitutes the basis of behavior and conscious experience. Even if those states were entirely transient, mental life would still be a constant blend of episodic and abstract representations, with

Stimuli

Set A	Set B
Practice words (1/2 per font)	**Practice words (1/2 per font)**
1. reform	1. wealth
2. disorder	2. disaster
3. elephant	3. trousers
4. ritual	4. utopia
5. affinity	5. stoicism
6. kitten	6. princess
7. *circus*	7. *pillow*
8. *leather*	8. *freeway*
9. *triumph*	9. *faction*
10. *mahogany*	10. *postcard*
11. *treason*	11. *destiny*
12. *uranium*	12. *tractor*

Experiment Words	Experiment Words
Subset A'	**Subset B'**
1. peanut	1. cherry
2. cushion	2. balloon
3. merchant	3. cemetery
4. hazard	4. vanity
5. penance	5. decency
6. scrutiny	6. disposal
7. lagoon	7. potato
8. mustard	8. buffalo
9. umbrella	9. antelope
10. equity	10. revolt
11. neglect	11. consent
12. humanism	12. aviation
13. sailor	13. salami
14. antenna	14. servant
15. charcoal	15. sandwich
16. denial	16. regret
17. gravity	17. caution
18. conquest	18. tenacity
19. thread	19. sleeve
20. feather	20. trumpet
21. fountain	21. corridor
22. climax	22. custom
23. tuition	23. scandal
24. nonsense	24. distress

Subset A"	Subset B"
25. *string*	25. *locust*
26. *dentist*	26. *steeple*

27.	*overcoat*		27.	*forehead*
28.	*fusion*		28.	*horror*
29.	*fantasy*		29.	*assault*
30.	*fidelity*		30.	*metaphor*
31.	*insect*		31.	*cheese*
32.	*caravan*		32.	*curtain*
33.	*passport*		33.	*sunlight*
34.	*hatred*		34.	*entity*
35.	*secrecy*		35.	*geology*
36.	*dominion*		36.	*validity*
37.	*meadow*		37.	*hostel*
38.	*coconut*		38.	*hammock*
39.	*blizzard*		39.	*ballroom*
40.	*legacy*		40.	*misery*
41.	*poverty*		41.	*revenge*
42.	*sanction*		42.	*duration*
43.	*cowboy*		43.	*button*
44.	*athlete*		44.	*lantern*
45.	*elevator*		45.	*chestnut*
46.	*option*		46.	*sorrow*
47.	*privacy*		47.	*paradox*
48.	*interval*		48.	*heritage*

Nonwords (for LDT test sessions)

Practice nonwords

1. rebivor
2. solofony
3. ensiloge
4. disube
5. crunda
6. asaledo

Experiment nonwords

1.	bealut		49.	provate
2.	doshion		50.	subar
3.	derching		51.	flazicky
4.	rozard		52.	sharlin
5.	fetonce		53.	batoon
6.	prostiny		54.	gultane
7.	jadoon		55.	hinsup
8.	mostand		56.	modge
9.	ungresse		57.	fauze
10.	ethily		58.	lavasult
11.	seblect		59.	manuge
12.	cudanism		60.	ostremate
13.	vaulir		61.	lapek
14.	ingetta		62.	lactain

15.	shirnoal	63.	sorneg
16.	hegial	64.	bewillant
17.	sluvity	65.	trool
18.	conshelt	66.	daver
19.	scrend	67.	roaken
20.	mensher	68.	remond
21.	dountair	69.	acknazzle
22.	plivax	70.	meegon
23.	suigion	71.	stramet
24.	nalsenge	72.	arbeshaw
25.	*sheppy*	73.	*slamp*
26.	*calloot*	74.	*danterly*
27.	*beletery*	75.	*cubble*
28.	*dasity*	76.	*morple*
29.	*welenge*	77.	*humax*
30.	*hispogal*	78.	*noast*
31.	*wistote*	79.	*behick*
32.	*muttalo*	80.	*vorgo*
33.	*ongelipe*	81.	*gultaride*
34.	*befolt*	82.	*blukin*
35.	*hongent*	83.	*persoy*
36.	*abiosion*	84.	*colpane*
37.	*galoni*	85.	*implaret*
38.	*perlant*	86.	*lexel*
39.	*fandlish*	87.	*miglen*
40.	*mogret*	88.	*floak*
41.	*sontion*	89.	*duforst*
42.	*fenaxity*	90.	*unsqueet*
43.	*gleece*	91.	*jandy*
44.	*prunget*	92.	*nucade*
45.	*barrinor*	93.	*gastan*
46.	*fustor*	94.	*grubine*
47.	*spondial*	95.	*bilanork*
48.	*dostrell*	96.	*hesting*

degrees of abstraction determined by the situation and the contents of memory (see Goldinger, 1998).

This idea leads naturally to the second possibility, discussed by Hintzman (1986), that derived abstractions—echoes in MINERVA 2—are themselves stored as new traces. Indeed, with respect to an episodic model of word perception, and many other applications of episodic models, this is a logical necessity. Presumably, word perception requires a reader (or listener) to bestow meaning upon a string of letters (or phonemes). Word perception is obligatory, but does not appear automatic (Goldinger *et al.*, 1997; Herdman, 1992). Moreover, most English words are ambiguous, but correct meanings are typically ascribed to words (in context) without any appreciation that other inter-pretations were available (Azuma and Van Orden, 1997). To achieve such flexibility, word perception must operate by combining the bottom-up information in letter strings with top-down interpretations. By elaborating on the stimulus in this manner, word percep-tion is an act of abstraction. If memory for words entails elements of meaning and interpretation, those traces are more abstract than their original stimulus episodes. Indeed, most of the episodic theories considered our review make the fundamental assumption that memory traces combine perceptual, conceptual, and behavioral elements. This idea is the cornerstone of the attention hypothesis (Logan and Etherton, 1994) and it is the central thesis of articles by MacLeod and Masson (2000), Whittlesea and Brooks (1988), and others.

Put in other words, the second possibility is that all traces are hybrids, falling upon a con-tinuum from strongly episodic to strongly abstract, depending primarily upon attention at the time of encoding. When people read for meaning, they likely create memory traces emphasizing top-down contributions to perception (e.g., sentence and story-level repre-sentations). When they perform specific study tasks in experiments, those traces may assume a variety of forms (see Jacoby *et al.*, 1992). Technically, all traces in such a system would be 'episodic', but the episodic-abstract distinction would become rather empty.

The third possibility is a bit more concrete, assuming that abstract and episodic traces both exist, as separate entities. This approach was taken by Ans *et al.* (1998) in an interest-ing model combining connectionist word reading with episodic traces. The former side of the model was based on the connectionist model by Plaut *et al.* (1996), and the latter side of the model was based on MINERVA 2. This approach gave the model stability in reading behavior (conferred by the 'abstract' side), while allowing it to quickly adapt to new experi-ences (using the 'episodic' side). Taking this idea a step further, one might hypothesize that episodic and abstract representations—and the behaviors they support—are reflections of hippocampal and neocortical memory systems (Eichenbaum and Cohen, 2001; O'Keefe and Nadel, 1978; Tulving and Markowitsch, 1998). It has been frequently suggested, and recently modeled (McClelland *et al.*, 1995; O'Reilly and Rudy, 2001), that the hippocampus quickly stores episodic traces, pulling together the contributions of remote brain areas into singular traces. While remaining in the hippocampus, such traces are highly detailed and episodic. Over time, however, those stored episodes slowly become consolidated into cor-tical memory networks, losing many of their unique or idiosyncratic attributes along the way. Such a dual memory system would require both forms of representation, and would have many adaptive benefits.

In summary, the data reviewed in this chapter—and many other data—are most com-patible with episodic memory views. As Jacoby (1983a) wrote, '[t]here is a great deal of unexploited similarity between theories of episodic memory and theories of perception. [...] The difference...is largely removed if it is assumed both types of task involve parallel access to a large population of memories for prior episodes' (pp. 35–6). By combining episodic traces with an attention hypothesis, we can explain data that at various times appeared either null or chaotic. However, the very nature of our account—the hypothesis that episodes are shaped by combined bottom-up and top-down forces—leads us full cir-cle, back to the concept of abstraction.

Acknowledgments

Support was provided by NIDCD Grant R01-DC04535–01 to S. D. Goldinger and NIDCD Grant R03-DC04231–01 to T. Azuma, both at Arizona State University. We thank Marianne Abramson, Brian Smith, Vanessa Hendrichs, Kristin Magin, David Rogett, Amy Trainor, and Paige Long for assistance in preparing and conducting the experiments.

References

Ans, B., Carbonnel, S., and Valdois, S. (1998). A connectionist, multiple-trace memory model for poly-syllabic word reading. *Psychological Review*, **105**, 678–723.

Azuma, T. and Van Orden, G. C. (1997). Why SAFE is better than FAST: The relatedness of a word's meanings affects lexical decision times. *Journal of Memory and Language*, **36**, 484–504.

Bem, D. J. and Funder, D. C. (1978). Predicting more of the people more of the time: Assessing the personality of situations. *Psychological Review*, **85**, 485–501.

Biederman, I. and Cooper, E. E. (1991). Evidence for complete translation and reflectional invariance in visual object priming. *Perception*, **20**, 585–93.

Blaxton, T. A. (1989). Investigating dissociations among memory measures: Support for a transfer-appropriate processing framework. *Journal of Experimental Psychology: Learning, Memory, and Cognition*, **15**, 657–68.

Bowers, J. S. (2000). In defense of abstractionist theories of repetition priming and word identification. *Psychonomic Bulletin and Review*, **7**, 83–99.

Bowers, J. S. and Michita, Y. (1998). An investigation into the structure and acquisition of orthographic knowledge: Evidence from cross-script Kanji-Hiragana priming. *Psychonomic Bulletin and Review*, **5**, 259–64.

Bradlow, A., Nygaard, L., and Pisoni, D. B. (1999). Effects of talker, rate, and amplitude variation on recognition memory for spoken words. *Perception and Psychophysics*, **61**, 206–19.

Brown, J. and Carr, T. (1993). Limits on perceptual abstraction in reading: Asymmetric transfer between surface forms differing in typicality. *Journal of Experimental Psychology: Learning, Memory, and Cognition*, **19**, 1277–96.

Brown, H. L., Sharma, N. K., and Kirsner, K. (1984). The role of script and phonology in lexical representation. *Quarterly Journal of Experimental Psychology*, **36A**, 491–505.

Butler, B. and Hains, S. (1979). Individual differences in word recognition latency. *Memory and Cognition*, **7**, 68–76.

Carello, C., Turvey, M. T., and Lukatela, G. (1992). Can theories of word recognition remain stubbornly nonphonological? In *Orthography, phonology, morphology, and meaning* (ed. R. Frost and L. Katz), pp. 211–26. Amsterdam: North-Holland.

Carr, T., Brown, J., and Charalambous, A. (1989). Repetition and reading: Perceptual encoding mechanisms are very abstract but not very interactive. *Journal of Experimental Psychology: Learning, Memory, and Cognition*, **15**, 763–78.

Cave, C. B. (1997). Very long-lasting priming in picture naming. *Psychological Science*, **8**, 322–5.

Cave, C. B. and Squire, L. R. (1992). Intact and long-lasting repetition priming in amnesia. *Journal of Experimental Psychology: Learning, Memory, and Cognition*, **18**, 509–20.

Challis, B. H. and Brodbeck, D. R. (1992). Level of processing affects priming in word fragment completion. *Journal of Experimental Psychology: Learning, Memory, and Cognition*, **18**, 595–607.

Chateau, D. and Jared, D. (2000). Exposure to print and word recognition processes. *Memory and Cognition*, **28**, 143–53.

Chiappe, P., Hasher, L., and Siegel, L. S. (2000). Working memory, inhibitory control, and reading disability. *Memory and Cognition*, **28**, 8–17.

Church, B. and Fisher, C. (1998). Long-term auditory word priming in preschoolers: Implicit memory support for language acquisition. *Journal of Memory and Language*, **39**, 523–42.

Church, B. and Schacter, D. L. (1994). Perceptual specificity of auditory priming: Memory for voice intonation and fundamental frequency. *Journal of Experimental Psychology: Learning, Memory, and Cognition*, **20**, 521–33.

Craik, F. and Kirsner, K. (1974). The effect of speaker's voice on word recognition. *Quarterly Journal of Experimental Psychology*, **26**, 274–84.

Craik, F. and Tulving, E. (1975). Depth of processing and the retention of words in episodic memory. *Journal of Experimental Psychology: General*, **104**, 268–94.

Craik, F., Moscovitch, M., and McDowd, J. M. (1994). Contributions of surface and conceptual information to performance on implicit and explicit memory tasks. *Journal of Experimental Psychology: Learning, Memory, and Cognition*, **20**, 864–75.

Eich, J. M. (1982). A composite holographic associative recall model. *Psychological Review*, **89**, 627–61.

Eichenbaum, H. and Cohen, N. J. (2001). *From conditioning to conscious recollection. Memory systems of the brain.* Oxford, England: Oxford University Press.

Engle, R. W., Tuholski, S. W., Laughlin, J. E., and Conway, A. R. (1999). Working memory, short-term memory, and general fluid intelligence: A latent variable approach. *Journal of Experimental Psychology: General*, **128**, 309–31.

Estes, W. K. (1994). *Classification and cognition.* Oxford University Press.

Feldman, L. B. and Moskovljević, J. (1987). Repetition priming is not purely episodic in origin. *Journal of Experimental Psychology: Learning, Memory, and Cognition*, **13**, 573–81.

Feustel, T., Shiffrin, R. M., and Salasoo, A. (1983). Episodic and lexical contributions to the repetition effect in word recognition. *Journal of Experimental Psychology: General*, **112**, 309–46.

Forbach, G. B., Stanners, R. F., and Hochhaus, L. (1974). Repetition and practice effects in a lexical decision task. *Memory and Cognition*, **2**, 337–9.

Forster, K. I. (1979). Levels of processing and the structure of the language processor. In *Sentence processing: Psycholinguistic studies presented to Merrill Garrett* (ed. W. Cooper and E. C. T. Walker), pp. 27–86. Hillsdale, NJ: Erlbaum.

Franks, J. J., Bilbrey, C. W., Lien, K. G., and McNamara, T. P. (2000). Transfer-appropriate processing (TAP) and repetition priming. *Memory and Cognition*, **28**, 1140–51.

Geiselman, R. and Bellezza, F. (1977). Incidental retention of speaker's voice. *Memory and Cognition*, **5**, 658–65.

Gernsbacher, M. A. (1993). Less skilled readers have less efficient suppression mechanisms. *Psychological Science*, **4**, 294–8.

Gibson, J. M., Brooks, J. O., Friedman, L., and Yesavage, J. A. (1993). Typography manipulations can affect priming of word stem completion in older and younger adults. *Psychology and Aging*, **8**, 481–9.

Gillund, G. and Shiffrin, R. M. (1984). A retrieval model for both recognition and recall. *Psychological Review*, **91**, 1–67.

Goldinger, S. (1996). Words and voices: Episodic traces in spoken word identification and recognition memory. *Journal of Experimental Psychology: Learning, Memory, and Cognition*, **22**, 1166–83.

Goldinger, S. D. (1997). Speech perception and production in an episodic lexicon. In *Talker variability in speech processing* (ed. K. Johnson and J. W. Mullennix), pp. 33–66. New York: Academic Press.

Goldinger, S. D. (1998). Echoes of echoes? An episodic theory of lexical access. *Psychological Review*, **105**, 251–79.

Goldinger, S. D., Pisoni, D. B., and Logan, J. S. (1991). On the nature of talker variability effects on serial recall of spoken word lists. *Journal of Experimental Psychology: Learning, Memory, and Cognition*, **17**, 152–62.

Goldinger, S. D., Pisoni, D. B., and Luce, P. A. (1996). Speech perception and spoken word recognition: Research and theory. In *Principles of experimental phonetics* (ed. N. J. Lass), pp. 277–327. St. Louis, MO: Mosby Year-Book.

Goldinger, S. D., Azuma, T., Abramson, M., and Jain, P. (1997). Open wide and say 'blah!' Attentional dynamics of delayed naming. *Journal of Memory and Language*, **37**, 190–216.

Graf, P. and Mandler, G. (1984). Activation makes words more accessible but not necessarily more retrievable. *Journal of Verbal Learning and Verbal Behavior*, **23**, 553–68.

Graf, P. and Ryan, L. (1990). Transfer-appropriate processing for implicit and explicit memory. *Journal of Experimental Psychology: Learning, Memory, and Cognition*, **16**, 978–92.

Green, K., Kuhl, P., Meltzoff, A., and Stevens, E. (1991). Integrating speech information across talkers, gender, and sensory modality: Female faces and male voices in the McGurk effect. *Perception and Psychophysics*, **50**, 524–36.

Halle, M. (1985). Speculation about the representation of words in memory. In *Phonetic linguistics* (ed. V. Fromkin), pp. 101–14. New York: Academic Press.

Hashtroudi, S., Ferguson, S. A., Rappold, V. A., and Chrosniak, L. D. (1988). Data-driven and conceptually driven processes in partial-word identification and recognition. *Journal of Experimental Psychology: Learning, Memory, and Cognition*, **14**, 749–57.

Herdman, C. M. (1992). Attentional resource demands of visual word recognition in naming and lexical decisions. *Journal of Experimental Psychology: Human Perception and Performance*, **18**, 460–70.

Hintzman, D. L. (1986). 'Schema abstraction' in a multiple-trace memory model. *Psychological Review*, **93**, 411–28.

Hintzman, D. L. and Ludlam, G. (1980). Differential forgetting of prototypes and old instances: Simulation by an exemplar-based classification model. *Memory and Cognition*, **8**, 378–82.

Hintzman, D. L. and Summers, J. J. (1973). Long-term visual traces of visually presented words. *Bulletin of the Psychonomic Society*, **1**, 325–7.

Hintzman, D. L., Block, R., and Inskeep, N. (1972). Memory for mode of input. *Journal of Verbal Learning and Verbal Behavior*, **11**, 741–9.

Holmes, V. M. and Ng, E. C. (1993). Word-specific knowledge, word-recognition strategies, and spelling ability. *Journal of Memory and Language*, **32**, 230–57.

Homa, D., Smith, C., Macak, C., Johovich, J., and Osorio, D. (2001). Recognition of facial prototypes: The importance of categorical structure and degree of learning. *Journal of Memory and Language*, **44**, 443–74.

Hull, C. L. (1943). *Principles of behavior*. New York: Appleton-Century.

Jackson, A. and Morton, J. (1984). Facilitation of auditory word recognition. *Memory and Cognition*, **12**, 568–74.

Jacoby, L. L. (1983a). Perceptual enhancement: Persistent effects of an experience. *Journal of Experimental Psychology: Learning, Memory, and Cognition*, **9**, 21–38.

Jacoby, L. L. (1983b). Remembering the data: Analyzing interactive processes in reading. *Journal of Verbal Learning and Verbal Behavior*, **22**, 485–508.

Jacoby, L. L. and Dallas, M. (1981). On the relationship between autobiographical memory and perceptual learning. *Journal of Experimental Psychology: General*, 110, 306–40.

Jacoby, L. L. and Hayman, C. A. G. (1987). Specific visual transfer in word identification. *Journal of Experimental Psychology: Learning, Memory, and Cognition*, 13, 456–63.

Jacoby, L. L., Levy, B., and Steinbach, K. (1992). Episodic transfer and automaticity: Integration of data-driven and conceptually-driven processing in rereading. *Journal of Experimental Psychology: Learning, Memory, and Cognition*, 18, 15–24.

Johnson, D. N. (2000). Task demands and representation in long-term repetition priming. *Memory and Cognition*, 28, 1303–9.

Joos, M. A. (1948). Acoustic phonetics. *Language*, 24, Suppl.2, 1–136.

Keppel, G. and Underwood, B. (1962). Proactive inhibition in short-term retention of single items. *Journal of Verbal Learning and Verbal Behavior*, 1, 153–61.

Kirsner, K. (1973). An analysis of the visual component in recognition memory for verbal stimuli. *Memory and Cognition*, 1, 449–53.

Kirsner, K. and Dunn, J. (1985). The perceptual record: A common factor in repetition priming and attribute retention? In *Attention and performance XI* (ed. M. Posner and O. Marin), pp. 547–65. Hillsdale, NJ: Erlbaum.

Kirsner, K. and Smith, M. C. (1974). Modality effects in word identification. *Memory and Cognition*, 2, 637–40.

Kirsner, K., Dunn, J., and Standen, P. (1987). Record-based word recognition. In *Attention and performance XII* (ed. M. Coltheart), pp. 147–67. Hillsdale, NJ: Erlbaum.

Klatt, D. (1979). Speech perception: A model of acoustic-phonetic analysis and lexical access. *Journal of Phonetics*, 7, 279–312.

Klein, K. and Fiss, W. H. (1999). The reliability and stability of the Turner and Engle working memory task. *Behavior Research Methods, Instruments and Computers*, 31, 429–32.

Kohonen, T., Lehtiö, P., and Oja, E. (1989). Storage and processing of information in distributed associative memory systems. In *Parallel models of associative memory* (ed. G. E. Hinton and J. A. Anderson), pp. 129–67. Hillsdale, NJ: Erlbaum.

Krulee, G., Tondo, D., and Wightman, F. (1983). Speech perception as a multilevel processing system. *Journal of Psycholinguistic Research*, 12, 531–54.

Ladefoged, P. (1980). What are linguistic sounds made of? *Language*, 56, 485–502.

Lewellen, M. J., Goldinger, S. D., Pisoni, D. B., and Greene, B. G. (1993). Lexical familiarity and processing efficiency: Individual differences in naming, lexical decision and semantic categorization. *Journal of Experimental Psychology: General*, 122, 316–30.

Logan, G. D. (1988). Toward an instance theory of automatization. *Psychological Review*, 95, 492–527.

Logan, G. D. (1990). Repetition priming and automaticity: Common underlying mechanisms? *Cognitive Psychology*, 22, 1–35.

Logan, G. D. and Etherton, J. L. (1994). What is learned during automatization? The role of attention in constructing an instance. *Journal of Experimental Psychology: Learning, Memory, and Cognition*, 20, 1022–50.

Luce, P. and Lyons, E. (1998). Specificity for memory representations for spoken words. *Memory and Cognition*, 26, 708–15.

MacLeod, C. M. and Masson, M. E. J. (1997). Priming patterns are different in masked word identification and word fragment completion. *Journal of Memory and Language*, 36, 461–83.

MacLeod, C. M. and Masson, M. E. J. (2000). Repetition priming in speeded word reading: Contributions of perceptual and conceptual processing episodes. *Journal of Memory and Language*, 42, 208–28.

Manso de Zuniga, C., Humphreys, G., and **Evett, L.** (1991). Additive and interactive effects of repetition, degradation, and word frequency in the reading of handwriting. In *Basic processes in reading* (ed. D. Besner and G. Humphreys), pp. 10–33. Hillsdale, NJ: Erlbaum.

Masson, M. E. J. (1986). Identification of typographically transformed words: Instance-based skill acquisition. *Journal of Experimental Psychology: Learning, Memory, and Cognition*, **12**, 479–88.

Masson, M. E. J. and **Freedman, L.** (1990). Fluent identification of repeated words. *Journal of Experimental Psychology: Learning, Memory, and Cognition*, **16**, 355–73.

Masson, M. E. J. and **MacLeod, C. M.** (1992). Reenacting the route to interpretation: Enhanced perceptual identification without prior perception. *Journal of Experimental Psychology: General*, **121**, 145–76.

McClelland, J. L. and **Elman, J. L.** (1986). The TRACE model of speech perception. *Cognitive Psychology*, **18**, 1–86.

McClelland, J. L. and **Rumelhart, D. E.** (1985). Distributed memory and the representation of general and specific information. *Journal of Experimental Psychology: General*, **114**, 159–88.

McClelland, J. L., McNaughton, B. L., and **O'Reilly, R. C.** (1995). Why there are complementary learning systems in the hippocampus and neocortex: Insights from the successes and failures of connectionist models of learning and memory. *Psychological Review*, **102**, 419–57.

Meehan, E. and **Pilotti, M.** (1996). Auditory priming in an implicit memory task that emphasizes surface processing. *Psychonomic Bulletin and Review*, **3**, 495–8.

Miller, M. B. and **Gazzaniga, M. S.** (1998). Creating false memories for visual scenes. *Neuropsychologia*, **36**, 513–20.

Monsen, R. B. and **Engebretson, A. M.** (1977). Study of variations in the male and female glottal wave. *Journal of the Acoustical Society of America*, **62**, 981–93.

Morris, D., Bransford, J. D., and **Franks, J. J.** (1977). Levels of processing versus transfer appropriate processing. *Journal of Verbal Learning and Verbal Behavior*, **16**, 519–33.

Morton, J. (1979). Word recognition. In *Structures and processes* (ed. J. Morton and J. C. Marshall), pp. 109–56. Cambridge: MIT Press.

Murnane, K. and **Phelps, M. P.** (1994). When does a different environmental context make a difference in recognition? A global activation model. *Memory and Cognition*, **22**, 584–90.

Musen, G. and **Treisman, A.** (1990). Implicit and explicit memory for visual patterns. *Journal of Experimental Psychology: Learning, Memory, and Cognition*, **16**, 127–37.

Naveh-Benjamin, M. and **Craik, F. I. M.** (1995). Memory for context and its use in item memory: Comparisons of younger and older persons. *Psychology and Aging*, **10**, 284–93.

Nosofsky, R. M. (1991). Tests of an exemplar model for relating perceptual classification and recognition memory. *Journal of Experimental Psychology: Human Perception and Performance*, **17**, 3–27.

Nosofsky, R. M. and **Palmeri, T. J.** (1997). An exemplar-based random walk model of speeded classification. *Psychological Review*, **104**, 266–300.

Nosofsky, R. M. and **Zaki, S. R.** (in press). Exemplar and prototype models revisited: Response strategies, selective attention, and stimulus generalization. *Journal of Experimental Psychology: Learning, Memory, and Cognition*.

Nygaard, L. C. and **Pisoni, D. B.** (1998). Talker-specific learning in speech perception. *Perception and Psychophysics*, **60**, 355–76.

Nygaard, L. C., Sommers, M. S., and **Pisoni, D. P.** (1994). Speech perception as a talker-contingent process. *Psychological Science*, **5**, 42–6.

Nygaard, L. C., Sommers, M. S., and **Pisoni, D. P.** (1995). Effects of stimulus variability on perception and representation of spoken words in memory. *Perception and Psychophysics*, **57**, 989–1001.

Nygaard, L. C., Burt, S. A., and Queen, J. S. (2000). Surface form typicality and asymmetric transfer in episodic memory for spoken words. *Journal of Experimental Psychology: Learning, Memory, and Cognition*, **26**, 1228–44.

O'Keefe, J. and Nadel, L. (1978). *The hippocampus as a cognitive map.* Oxford, England: Oxford University Press.

Oldfield, R. C. (1966). Things, words, and the brain. *Quarterly Journal of Experimental Psychology*, **18**, 340–53.

O'Reilly, R. C. and Rudy, J. W. (2001). Conjunctive representations in learning and memory: Principles of cortical and hippocampal function. *Psychological Review*, **108**, 311–45.

Paap, K., Newsome, S., McDonald, J., and Schvaneveldt, R. (1982). An activation-verification model for letter and word recognition: The word-superiority effect. *Psychological Review*, **89**, 573–94.

Palmeri, T. J., Goldinger, S. D., and Pisoni, D. B. (1993). Episodic encoding of voice attributes and recognition memory for spoken words. *Journal of Experimental Psychology: Learning, Memory, and Cognition*, **19**, 309–28.

Peterson, G. E. and Barney, H. L. (1952). Control methods used in a study of the vowels. *Journal of the Acoustical Society of America*, **24**, 175–84.

Pisoni, D. B. (1993). Long-term memory in speech perception: Some new findings on talker variability, speaking rate, and perceptual learning. *Speech Communication*, **13**, 109–25.

Plaut, D. C., McClelland, J. L., Seidenberg, M. S., and Patterson, K. E. (1996). Understanding normal and impaired word reading: Computational principles in quasi-regular domains. *Psychological Review*, **103**, 56–115.

Posner, M. (1964). Information reduction in the analysis of sequential tasks. *Psychological Review*, **71**, 491–503.

Raven, J. (2000). Psychometrics, cognitive ability, and occupational performance. *Review of Psychology*, **7**, 51–74.

Remez, R. E., Fellowes, J. M., and Rubin, P. E. (1997). Talker identification based on phonetic information. *Journal of Experimental Psychology: Human Perception and Performance*, **23**, 651–66.

Roediger, H. L. and Blaxton, T. A. (1987). Effects of varying modality, surface features, and retention interval on priming in word-fragment completion. *Memory and Cognition*, **15**, 379–88.

Roediger, H. L. and Challis, B. H. (1992). Effects of exact repetition and conceptual repetition on free recall and primed word-fragment completion. *Journal of Experimental Psychology: Learning, Memory, and Cognition*, **18**, 3–14.

Roediger, H. L. and McDermott, K. B. (1993). Implicit memory in normal human subjects. In *Handbook of neuropsychology* (ed. F. Boller and J. Grafman), Vol. 8, pp. 63–131. Elsevier.

Roediger, H. L. and McDermott, K. B. (1995). Creating false memories: Remembering words not presented in lists. *Journal of Experimental Psychology: Learning, Memory, and Cognition*, **21**, 803–14.

Rosen, V. M. and Engle, R. W. (1998). Working memory capacity and suppression. *Journal of Memory and Language*, **39**, 418–36.

Russo, R., Ward, G., Geurts, H., and Scheres, A. (1999). When unfamiliarity matters: Changing environmental context between study and test affects recognition memory for unfamiliar stimuli. *Journal of Experimental Psychology: Learning, Memory, and Cognition*, **25**, 488–99.

Scarborough, D., Cortese, C., and Scarborough, H. (1977). Frequency and repetition effects in lexical memory. *Journal of Experimental Psychology: Human Perception and Performance*, **3**, 1–17.

Schacter, D. L. (1987). Implicit memory: History and current status. *Journal of Experimental Psychology: Learning, Memory, and Cognition*, **13**, 501–18.

Schacter, D. L. and Church, B. (1992). Auditory priming: Implicit and explicit memory for words and voices. *Journal of Experimental Psychology: Learning, Memory, and Cognition*, **18**, 915–30.

Schacter, D. L., Eich, J. E., and Tulving, E. (1978). Richard Semon's theory of memory. *Journal of Verbal Learning and Verbal Behavior*, **17**, 721–43.

Semon, R. (1909/1923). *Mnemic psychology*. (B. Duffy, translator) London: George Allen and Unwin.

Sheffert, S. (1998a). Voice-specificity effects on auditory word priming. *Memory and Cognition*, **26**, 591–8.

Sheffert, S. (1998b). Contributions of surface and conceptual information to recognition memory. *Perception and Psychophysics*, **60**, 1141–52.

Sheffert, S. and Fowler, C. (1995). The effects of voice and visible speaker change on memory for spoken words. *Journal of Memory and Language*, **34**, 665–85.

Shepard, R. (1984). Ecological constraints in internal representation: Resonant kinematics of perceiving, imagining, thinking, and dreaming. *Psychological Review*, **91**, 417–47.

Shiffrin, R. M. and Steyvers, M. (1997). A model for recognition memory: REM – Retreiving effectively from memory. *Psychonomic Bulletin and Review*, **4**, 145–66.

Smith, J. D. and Minda, J. P. (2000). Thirty categorization results in search of a model. *Journal of Experimental Psychology: Learning, Memory, and Cognition*, **26**, 3–27.

Smith, M. C., MacLeod, C. M., Bain, J. D., and Hoppe, R. B. (1989). Lexical decision as an indirect test of memory: Repetition priming and list-wide priming as a function of type of encoding. *Journal of Experimental Psychology: Learning, Memory, and Cognition*, **15**, 1109–18.

Snodgrass, J. G., Hirshman, E., and Fan, J. (1996). The sensory match effect in recognition memory: Perceptual fluency or episodic trace? *Memory and Cognition*, **24**, 367–83.

Srinivas, K. (1996). Size and reflection effects in priming: A test of transfer-appropriate processing. *Memory and Cognition*, **24**, 441–52.

Stanovich, K. and West, R. (1989). Exposure to print and orthographic processing. *Reading Research Quarterly*, **24**, 402–33.

Stark, C. E. L. and McClelland, J. L. (2000). Repetition priming of words, pseudowords, and nonwords. *Journal of Experimental Psychology: Learning, Memory, and Cognition*, **26**, 945–72.

Studdert-Kennedy, M. (1976). Speech perception. In *Contemporary issues in experimental phonetics* (ed. N. J. Lass), pp. 243–93. New York: Academic Press.

Tardif, T. and Craik, F. I. M. (1989). Reading a week later: Perceptual and conceptual factors. *Journal of Memory and Language*, **28**, 107–25.

Tenpenny, P. L. (1995). Abstractionist versus episodic theories of repetition priming and word identification. *Psychonomic Bulletin and Review*, **2**, 339–63.

Tulving, E. and Markowitsch, H. J. (1998). Episodic and declarative memory: Role of the hippocampus. *Hippocampus*, **8**, 198–204.

Tulving, E. and Schacter, D. L. (1990). Priming and human memory systems. *Science*, **247**, 301–6.

Tulving, E. and Thompson, D. M. (1973). Encoding specificity and retrieval processes in episodic memory. *Psychological Review*, **80**, 359–80.

Turner, M. L. and Engle, R. W. (1989). Is working memory capacity task dependent? *Journal of Memory and Language*, **28**, 127–54.

Underwood, B. (1969). Attributes of memory. *Psychological Review*, **76**, 559–73.

Van Orden, G. C. and Goldinger, S. D. (1994). Interdependence of form and function in cognitive systems explains perception of printed words. *Journal of Experimental Psychology: Human Perception and Performance*, **20**, 1269–91.

Weldon, M. S. (1991). Mechanisms underlying priming on perceptual tests. *Journal of Experimental Psychology: Learning, Memory, and Cognition*, **17**, 526–41.

Whittlesea, B. W. A. (1990). Perceptual encoding mechanisms are tricky but may be very interactive: Comment on Carr, Brown, and Charalambous (1989). *Journal of Experimental Psychology: Learning, Memory, and Cognition*, **16**, 727–30.

Whittlesea, B. W. A. and Brooks, L. (1988). Critical influence of particular experiences in the perception of letters, words, and phrases. *Memory and Cognition*, **16**, 387–99.

Whittlesea, B. W. A. and Cantwell, A. (1987). Enduring influences of the purpose of experiences: Encoding-retrieval interactions in word and pseudoword perception. *Memory and Cognition*, **15**, 465–72.

Wiggs, C. L. and Martin, A. (1994). Aging and feature-specific priming of familiar and novel stimuli. *Psychology and Aging*, **9**, 578–88.

CHAPTER 9

ABSTRACTNESS AND SPECIFICITY IN SPOKEN WORD RECOGNITION: INDEXICAL AND ALLOPHONIC VARIABILITY IN LONG-TERM REPETITION PRIMING

PAUL A. LUCE, CONOR M^CLENNAN, AND JAN CHARLES-LUCE

Introduction

Speech scientists frequently make a subtle, and often unspoken, distinction between two closely allied areas of research: speech perception and spoken word recognition (Jusczyk and Luce, 2002). Research on *speech perception* is typically concerned with consonants, vowels, and syllables, and focuses on such fundamental problems as *invariance* (are there acoustic events that consistently signal a given speech sound?) and *variability* (how does the listener cope with the diverse acoustic manifestations of phonetic segments?). Research on *spoken word recognition* focuses primarily on issues concerning the *activation of* and *discrimination among* form-based (i.e., sound-based) lexical representations. For the sake of tractability, researchers examining spoken word recognition have often side-stepped the fundamental problems that have been the provenance of speech perception. Indeed, most current models of spoken word recognition have little to say about the still unresolved problems of invariance and variability that have occupied speech perception research for over 60 years (Luce and Pisoni, 1998; McClelland and Elman, 1986; Norris, 1994).

The distinction between research on speech perception and spoken word recognition, while never neat, has recently become less clear, owing in part to the realization that the longstanding problem of variability has deep and important implications for models of lexical representation and process. Because of variability in the sex, age, and dialect of talkers, as well as differences in speaking rates, emotional states, and a host of other variables, listeners must cope with the myriad ways in which spoken words are uttered. Understanding how the perceptual system maintains perceptual constancy in the face of this pervasive variability may lead to fundamental insights in the nature and organization of the form-based lexicon, as well as the processes by which memory representations of spoken words are contacted (Martin *et al.*, 1989; Mullennix *et al.*, 1989).

Recent advances in our understanding of variability and its implications for lexical representation and process have come in large part from research using the long-term repetition priming paradigm (Church and Schacter, 1994; Goldinger, 1996; Luce and Lyons, 1998; Schacter and Church, 1992; Sheffert, 1998a, 1998b). This paradigm has enabled investigators to examine the degree of specificity and abstractness of form-based representations, which in turn has provided insights into the architecture of the word recognition system. Briefly, investigators have used the phenomenon of long-term, form-based repetition priming to determine the degree to which lexical representations encode the variability inherent in spoken words.

The logic of the repetition paradigm is simple: Processing of a spoken word is typically facilitated when it is repeated exactly (as measured by accuracy, processing time, or both). However, if the first and second presentations (*prime* and *target*, respectively) mismatch on some dimension—for example, one is spoken by a male and the other by a female—the priming effect is often attenuated. We may infer from this reduction in priming that the prime and target activate somewhat different *specific* form-based lexical representations. If, on the other hand, the priming effect is *not* attenuated by any differences between the prime and target, we might conclude that the prime and target activate the same underlying *abstract* representations.

Our intent in this chapter is to explore the nature of form-based representations of spoken words, as revealed by variability (or specificity) effects in long-term repetition priming. We focus on two sources of variability—indexical and allophonic—each of which provides different clues about the specificity and abstractness of sound-based lexical representations. Based on a number of recent findings, we argue for the existence of both specific and abstract codes in spoken word recognition. Moreover, we argue that the data in favor of abstract lexical codes also implicate the activation of intermediate representations in the mapping of the acoustic-phonetic waveform onto lexical items in memory. Finally, we hypothesize that there is a time-course to specificity effects in spoken word recognition, such that immediate processing is dominated by abstract codes, whereas specific information takes time to percolate through the system and have its effects on perception.

We begin by drawing distinctions between indexical and allophonic variability and between episodic and abstractionist theories of lexical form. As we will argue, evidence for episodic theories comes primarily—although not exclusively—from research on indexical variability, whereas research on allophonic variability suggests the operation of more abstract codes. We conclude by arguing for a mixed representational model in which differential effects of abstract and episodic codes are predictable based on the processing time considerations.

Indexical and allophonic variability

Throughout the course of our discussion, we will distinguish between two sources of variability in spoken word recognition (see Remez *et al.*, 1997). *Indexical variability* refers to variations in a spoken word that arise from differences among talkers, differences in speaking rates, differences in affective states, and so on (Pisoni, 1997). Typically, the indexical variability for a given word has no consequences for its denotation. Whether the noun *telephone* is spoken by a male or female, at a fast or slow rate of speech, or in a happy or sad emotional state has no implication for the fact that the word refers to a device used for communication over distances. The indexical property of speech receiving the most attention in research examining long-term priming has been talker identity (typically male versus female).

Allophonic variability (or, more commonly, allophonic *variation*) refers to articulatory and acoustic differences among speech sounds belonging to the same phonemic category (Ladefoged, 2000). The stop consonant /t/ is articulated somewhat differently—and hence has a different acoustic manifestation—before a vowel (as in *top*), after a vowel (as in *pot*), and in a consonant cluster (as in *stop*). Each of these different versions are referred to as allophones of the phoneme /t/.

We will refer to both indexical and allophonic variability as *surface variation*. Surface variation, whether indexical or allophonic, does *not* result in different lexical items. For example, the word *telephone* spoken by a male or female (indexical variability) still refers to a communicative device (or the act of using such a device). Likewise, allophonic variation cannot, by definition, result in different words, although it may produce lexical ambiguities (see below). In contrast to surface variation, *underlying variation* has direct consequences for lexical discrimination. For example, featural changes in the putatively underlying abstract phoneme /t/ in *top* will result in a change in phonemic category, and hence a new lexical item (e.g., *pop*). In short, surface variants are *tokens*; underlying variants are *types*.

Although indexical and allophonic variation are both examples of surface variation, allophonic variation is in large part constrained by the phonological system of a given language. In general, allophonic variation is highly predictable based on purely linguistic considerations, such as syllable position and phonetic context. On the other hand, the effects of indexical variability are constrained by extra-linguistic factors and are generally predictable only by reference to vocal tract size, emotional disposition, and so on. Consider a monolingual English speaker listening to various speakers of Thai. Our English speaker may be able to distinguish among male and female, fast and slow, and even angry and happy Thai speakers. However, it is unlikely that our English speaker would be able to distinguish among allophonic variants of Thai phonemes. Coping with allophonic variation is a uniquely linguistic skill acquired through extensive exposure to a given language.

The observation that allophonic variability is linguistic, whereas indexical variability is not, raises the possibility that the spoken word recognition system may treat these two sources of variability differently. Perhaps the more predictable effects of allophonic variation are represented more generally or abstractly in memory, whereas the less predictable, highly variable indexical properties are represented in a more specific format. Perhaps both abstractionist *and* episodic accounts of form-based lexical representations may be needed to account for how listeners cope with pervasive variability in the speech signal.

Abstractionist and episodic theories of form-based lexical representation

The conventional assumption among theories of spoken word recognition is that lexical items are represented in memory by *abstract* phonological codes that only preserve information relevant for lexical discrimination (e.g., Jackson and Morton, 1984; Luce and Pisoni, 1998; McClelland and Elman, 1986; Norris, 1994). In most current models of word recognition, stimulus variation—both indexical and allophonic—is treated as irrelevant information that is discarded early in the encoding process (see, however, Luce *et al.*, 2000). The extraction of information that is solely relevant for identification is referred to as *normalization*, and it is during the normalization phase that representations that vary in physical detail but fall within a given perceptual category are equated by processes that abstract defining information.

For example, feature-based accounts of spoken word recognition (Klatt, 1989; Pisoni and Luce, 1987; Stevens, 1998) have proposed that speech sounds and words are processed using the elemental features of linguistic description (e.g., [vocalic], [consonantal], [sonorant]). Because spoken words may differ on many physical dimensions not captured by these features, the normalization process is responsible for winnowing the information in the speech signal and extracting only the featural information that is necessary and sufficient for unique identification of a word. This process thereby serves a substantial data reduction function that may ultimately result in considerable economy of process and representation.

Despite the arguments that have been made for abstract lexical representations in memory, recent research (Church and Schacter, 1994; Goldinger, 1996, 1998; Luce and Lyons, 1998; Schacter and Church, 1992; Sheffert, 1998a, 1998b) has suggested that putatively irrelevant surface details of words—such as information specific to a given talker—are preserved in some form in memory. These findings regarding specificity effects, which we review below, have led to the proposal that lexical representations are episodic (Goldinger, 1992, 1998). One episodic account proposes that form-based lexical representations are exemplars that preserve, rather than discard, much of the physical detail of the stimulus. Indeed, according to the most extreme episodic models (Hintzman, 1986), a unique *instance* is stored in memory each time a new token is encountered.

One advantage of episodic models is that they have the potential for solving the longstanding problem of normalization by dispelling the notion that the ultimate goal of the perceptual process is to map acoustic-phonetic information onto *abstract* form-based representations of words in memory. In episodic models, the representational currency of the perceptual encoding process is more-or-less true to the details of the stimulus itself. In an application of this general theoretical approach to spoken word recognition, Goldinger (1992, 1998) has proposed an exemplar-based lexicon in which the individual memory traces themselves may encode both abstract and surface information, with the degree of stimulus specificity depending on attentional factors during encoding.

Note that episodic theories of the lexicon need *not* be exemplar- or instance-based. For example, distributed models are capable of representing specificity without laying down a separate trace for each encounter with a spoken word. Instead, specificity is encoded in minor changes in convolved feature vectors (Weber and Murdock, 1989) or in connection weights among nodes in the network that makes up the distributed representation (Gaskell and Marslen-Wilson, 1997). Furthermore, episodic models may behave *as if* they contain abstract representations, via emergent generalizations over episodes (Hintzman, 1986; Tenpenny, 1995).

There has been considerable recent debate over the distinction between episodic and abstractionist theories (Bowers, 2000; Tenpenny, 1995). The crux of this debate concerns whether abstract representations emerge from averaging over instances, or whether they have their own status and are different in kind from episodic representations (Tenpenny, 1995). Despite the potential importance of resolving this issue, we will remain agnostic regarding the form and origin of abstract form-based lexical representations, although we will argue throughout the remainder of our discussion for some type of mixed representational model (with both abstract and episodic formats).

Indexical variability and representational specificity

Evidence for representational specificity in spoken word recognition comes from a variety of long-term repetition priming experiments that have examined indexical variability. In general, these studies have demonstrated that under certain circumstances, changes in the surface details of stimuli between study (prime) and test (target) attenuate the repetition priming effect. For example, Church and Schacter (1994) and Schacter and Church (1992) observed effects of talker variability in *implicit* tasks such as fragment completion and identification of low-pass filtered stimuli.[1] Subjects were more likely to complete a fragment of a target word if the fragment was repeated in the same voice as the prime. Subjects were also more accurate at identifying low-pass filtered target words that were primed by stimuli sharing similar surface characteristics. However, these researchers failed to observe effects of stimulus specificity in *explicit* tasks. When subjects performed cued recall or old/new recognition of previously presented items, changing surface characteristics between study and test had no detectable effects on performance.

Goldinger (1996) also performed a series of experiments examining the effects of voice on memory for spoken words. In one of his experiments, he presented words in explicit (old/new recognition) and implicit (perceptual identification in noise) tasks with varying delays between study and test. He found significant effects of voice in both the recognition memory and identification tasks, demonstrating that voice effects are not, in fact, restricted to implicit tasks. In another experiment, Goldinger manipulated levels of processing and voice in the study-test implicit-explicit format. His results demonstrated that effects of voice varied with level of processing, such that strongest effects of stimulus

---

[1] Schacter (1987) defines implicit memory as improved performance on a task following previous experience when the task itself does not depend upon conscious recall or recollection of the previous experience. In contrast, explicit memory is defined as performance on a task requiring conscious recollection of a previous event. We will focus more heavily on results from *implicit* tasks because they tend to be less reflective of conscious, strategy-based processing (although there is probably no pure process; see Bowers, 2000; Jacoby, 1991).

specificity were observed in the shallower processing conditions, especially for recognition memory.

Despite some differences in the circumstances under which specificity effects were observed, the Church and Schacter and Goldinger results demonstrate that implicit long-term repetition priming is attenuated by surface variation between prime and target, strongly suggesting that form-based representations of spoken words are indeed specific. However, the specificity effects observed in these studies may have been amplified by processing difficulties introduced by the use of degraded stimuli (in the form of noise-masked, low-pass filtered, or gated stimuli), which may have encouraged subjects to interrogate memory representations of previously encountered items when they might not have normally done so. Moreover, the use of degraded stimuli in untimed tasks raises the possibility that *speeded* processing of *non-degraded* spoken stimuli may be less susceptible to effects of stimulus variability.

Luce and Lyons (1998) attempted to establish more clearly the degree to which surface variation of *non-degraded* spoken stimuli plays a role in the identification process itself. In particular, they examined the effects of changing voice on stimulus repetition in both auditory lexical decision and recognition memory tasks (Biederman and Cooper, 1992; Cooper *et al.*, 1992). They first presented subjects with a list of stim-uli spoken by two talkers in a lexical decision task. They then followed this first block of lexical decision trials with either (1) another block of lexical decision trials (implicit task) or (2) a block of old/new recognition trials (explicit task). The stimuli in the second block of the experiment were either repeated in the same voice, a new voice, or were new items that had not appeared in the first block. They hypothesized that if memory representations of spoken words are abstract, repetition effects for words repeated in the same voice should be equivalent to repetitions of words repeated in a different voice. That is, changing the voice of the speaker for an item between blocks should have no effect on performance in the second block. On the other hand, if the representations of spoken words used in on-line processing are episodic, words repeated in the same voice should show greater advantages in terms of processing speed than words repeated in a different voice.

Luce and Lyons' results demonstrated that repetition priming for spoken words might not always be sensitive to changes in the surface characteristics of the stimuli (see Figure 9.1). In the implicit lexical decision task, response times to repetitions in the same voice were not statistically different from response times to repetitions in the different voice, although over-all effects of repetition priming were robust. However, in the explicit recognition memory experiment, Luce and Lyons obtained significant effects of voice: Subjects responded *old* more quickly to words repeated in the same voice than to words repeated in the different voice. Thus, they observed no detectable effects of voice on response time in the implicit task using lexical decision but large effects on old/new recognition time in the explicit task.

The failure to observe specificity effects in lexical decision is actually consistent with cer-tain episodic models (Hintzman, 1986). According to Hintzman's model, each stimulus activates an aggregate of memory traces referred to as an *echo*. Because the echo is com-prised of a weighted average of multiple traces, the influence of features that *differ* among the stored exemplars will be minimized, whereas features that are *shared* will be strength-

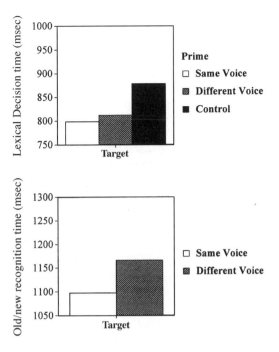

Figure 9.1 Lexical decision times (upper panel) and old/new recognition times (lower panel) to target words as a function of prime type. Target words in the second block of trials were repeated in the same voice, repeated in a different voice, or were not repeated (control). In the implicit task (lexical decision) equivalent effects of long-term repetition priming were obtained for repeated words regardless of voice, whereas in the explicit task (old/new recognition), pronounced effects of specificity were observed. (From Luce and Lyons, 1998.)

ened. With decay of individual features over time, information regarding the central tendency of a category will tend to be more robust. Such a memory system will give the appearance of abstraction, although the representations from which this abstraction emerges are themselves specific (see, however, Bowers and Kouider, this volume). Thus, even within strictly episodic models of memory, both abstract and specific information may coexist (at least functionally).

Time-course of processing and representational specificity

The results of Luce and Lyon's explicit old/new recognition task are consistent with a number of previous demonstrations that voice matters in recognition memory (Goldinger, 1996; Palmeri *et al.*, 1993). However, the failure to observe specificity effects in the implicit priming task does *not* replicate previous work. The reasons for this discrepancy may lie in either stimulus or task differences among the studies, or both. In Church and Schacter's and Goldinger's work, voice effects were typically observed in implicit priming tasks using degraded (filtered or noise-masked) stimuli, which may have amplified the effects of voice by either slowing processing or encouraging activation of specific previous memory traces to aid in identification. In addition, compared to off-line identification, responses in the lexical decision task may be so rapid as to precede potentially slower acting effects of stimulus specificity in processing (Hintzman and Caulton, 1997; Hintzman and Curran, 1997). We refer to the proposal that the rapidity of responding may mediate the presence or absence of specificity effects as the *time-course hypothesis*.

Goldinger (1996) reports one of the only other spoken word recognition studies that has examined response latencies in an implicit task in which voice was manipulated. Response latencies to classify stimuli in his fastest condition were almost 100 ms longer than the latencies that Luce and Lyons observed in their implicit priming task. Thus, it may be that if subjects are capable of making an identification decision quickly enough, effects of stimulus specificity will be small. Conversely, when responses are slower, as in Luce and Lyons' old/new recognition experiment or in Church and Schacter's and Goldinger's studies, effects of voice emerge. Despite the rapidity of the response, however, Luce and Lyons obtained significant overall effects of repetition priming, suggesting that although specific effects of voice failed to develop strongly in the time window within which responses were made, effects of prior lexical activation were still in evidence.

Thus, task and stimulus differences may have enabled faster responding in the Luce and Lyons study, potentially circumventing effects of specificity. Further support for this hypothesis comes from a study by McLennan *et al.* (2002). In contrast to the stimuli used by Luce and Lyons, which were short consonant–vowel–consonant words with a fairly high average frequency, McLennan *et al.* examined specificity effects for longer, lower-frequency bisyllabic spoken words. All things considered, Luce and Lyons' short, higher-frequency stimuli should have been recognized faster than McLennan *et al.*'s longer, lower-frequency stimuli. If our time-course hypothesis is viable, specificity effects should have emerged for those stimuli requiring longer processing times.

McLennan *et al.* presented primes and targets in an implicit long-term repetition-priming paradigm. Items in the first and second blocks either matched or differed on the manner in which they were articulated. (The same talker produced all stimuli.) Half of the stimuli were *hypoarticulated*, or produced in a casual manner, and half were *hyperarticulated*, or carefully produced. Subjects performed a speeded single-word shadowing task in both the first and second blocks.

The average shadowing times to target stimuli in McLennan *et al.*'s study was 65 ms longer than the average lexical decision times reported by Luce and Lyons, despite the fact that single-word shadowing typically produces appreciably faster response times than lexical decision (see, for example, Luce and Pisoni, 1998; Vitevitch *et al.*, 1999). Also, even though the differences in surface variation (i.e., casual versus careful articulation) in McLennan *et al.*'s study were more subtle than those examined by Luce and Lyons, large effects of specificity were observed: Relative to the appropriate baseline, carefully articulated spoken words only primed other carefully articulated spoken words and casually articulated words only primed other casually articulate words (see Figure 9.2). Thus, when stimuli mismatched on the manner in which they were articulated, no long-term priming was observed.

Taken together, the Luce and Lyons and McLennan *et al.* results suggest that specificity effects may take time to develop. If we are able to tap the perceptual process early, by

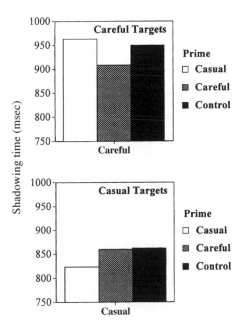

Figure 9.2 Single-word shadowing times to carefully and casually produced target words (upper and lower panels, respectively) as a function of prime type. Target words in the second block of trials were repeated in the same style of articulation (e.g., casual–casual; careful–careful), repeated in a different style of articulation (e.g., casual–careful; careful–casual), or were not repeated (control). Long-term repetition priming effects were obtained only for target words repeated in the same style of articulation. (From McLennan *et al.*, 2001.)

examining processing of short, high-frequency words in a speeded task, no effects of indexical variability are observed. However, specificity effects on long-term priming are clearly in evidence when perception is slowed, even in a speeded perceptual task.[2]

We speculate that either weakly abstractionist or episodic models may be able to account for the effects of time-course on specificity. Abstractionist theories need only assume that the abstract codes respond or resonate more strongly, and hence more quickly, to stimulus input. This is not an unreasonable or untenable assumption: Abstract representations may code the most frequent features of objects. Thus, the time-course of specificity effects in spoken word recognition may simply be yet another example of frequency effects at a sublexical or featural level of processing (see Vitevitch and Luce, 1999). Episodic theories may likewise be able to account for temporal specificity effects. For example, although Hintzman (1986) makes no explicit claims about time-course, he does note that the most frequent features will be most strongly represented in the echo. It is a small leap to assume

---

[2] The absence of priming between mismatching tokens of the same words suggests that specific form-based representations may actually dominate (or, perhaps, inhibit) abstract codes later in processing. We have proposed elsewhere (Gaygen and Luce, 2002; Newman and Luce, 2002) that abstract codes may be immediately inhibited once recognition has been accomplished (in a manner similar to Grossberg *et al*.'s 1997 mismatch reset principle). If correct, this hypothesis predicts that only slower-acting specific codes may be in play during later phases of processing.

that the response of the echo to stimulus input may take time, with more robust or frequent features responding more rapidly.

To summarize, our working hypothesis is that a mixed model best characterizes representation of lexical form in spoken word recognition, be it either episodic or weakly abstractionist. Research on indexical variability has demonstrated that form-based representations preserve much more detail than traditional models of speech perception had previously postulated or current models of spoken word recognition have acknowledged. However, we argue that understanding the nature of abstract and specific form-based lexical representations requires an appreciation of the time-course of processing. In particular, we propose that under optimal processing conditions when identification is easy and fast, abstract codes will dominate spoken word processing, or at least dominate the initial contact of sensory input with memory representations. On the other hand, more specific information may exert its influence on processing over a somewhat longer time frame. We furthermore propose that time-course differences in the processing of abstract and specific form-based information derive directly from the frequency with which the system has encountered features of the input.

Allophonic variability and representational abstractness

Thus far, we have devoted our attention to one kind of variability and its representation, namely indexical variability. However, there is reason to believe that not all variability is equivalent, at least from a processing standpoint. As we discussed, allophonic variability, unlike its indexical counterpart, is tightly constrained by the linguistic system. Consequently, variation at the allophonic level is generally highly predictable. Indeed, some might argue that it is rule-governed (although the rules may be optional, Kentowicz and Kisseberth, 1979). In short, given a constrained and predictable set of allophones, a limited number of highly frequent features in memory may be able to robustly capture and encode this form of systematic phonetic variation.

If our speculation regarding feature frequency is correct, we expect that allophonic variation would be handled under optimal processing conditions by abstract codes. To evaluate this hypothesis, Luce et al. (1999; see also McLennan et al., 2001) examined the phenomenon of flapping in American English. A flap is an allophone of /t/ and /d/. When /t/ or /d/ occurs between two vowels in casual speech, as in *writer* or *rider*, the speaker often produces a segment that has acoustic properties that do not correspond exactly to either /t/ or a /d/ (see Charles-Luce, 1997; Fox and Terbeek, 1977). The resulting intermediate articulation is referred to as a flap (/ɾ/) and has acoustic properties that are ambiguously /t/ or /d/. Under a traditional phonological analysis, flaps are neutralized surface realizations of the underlying phonemic forms /t/ and /d/.[3] According to abstractionist linguistic theories of representation (Kentowicz and Kisseberth, 1979), *only* forms containing fully specified /t/ and /d/ are represented in memory. However, according to an episodic view of

---

[3] The phonemes /t/ and /d/ differ on the dimension of voicing, /t/ being voiceless and /d/ being voiced. A flap is said to *neutralize* this voicing distinction by blurring the distinction between the two voicing categories.

lexical representation, flapped tokens of spoken words should have full representational status as well.

In a long-term repetition priming experiment, Luce *et al.* presented bisyllabic words (e.g., *writer, rider*) containing both carefully articulated /t/s and /d/s and flaps.[4] (See Table 9.1 for a description of the experimental conditions.) Subjects shadowed the primes and targets as quickly as possible. Luce *et al.* attempted to determine if flapped primes facilitate processing of carefully articulated targets, and vice versa. Failure to observe equivalent levels of priming between flapped and carefully articulated stimuli would indicate that the carefully articulated and flapped primes and targets do *not* share a common underlying representation. This result would be consistent with episodic models of lexical representation. However, equivalent facilitation of target processing by both flapped and careful primes would indicate the existence of a shared, and presumably abstract, representation.

Luce *et al.*'s results revealed that flapped and carefully articulated words were equally effective primes for flapped and carefully articulated targets (see Figure 9.3). That is, both types of primes produced equivalent levels of facilitation for each type of target. If effects of priming were restricted to veridical, surface representations of primes and targets—as predicted by a strict exemplar, or strongly episodic, model—markedly different patterns of priming between flapped and carefully articulated words should have been observed. In particular, facilitative priming between *identical* items (i.e., flap to flap and careful to careful) should have been greater than facilitative priming between *different* versions of the stimuli (i.e., flap to careful and vice versa). Instead, Luce *et al.* observed statistically equivalent degrees of facilitative priming for flapped and careful primes and targets. It appears that flapped stimuli activate representations containing both /t/ and /d/, which in turn serve to facilitate subsequent processing of flapped and carefully articulated targets.[5] These results suggest that both

Table 9.1 Stimulus conditions for flap priming experiment (Luce *et al.*, 1999)

Condition	Block 1: Primes	Block 2: Targets
1	Flap (ɹaɪɾɚ)	Flap (ɹaɪɾɚ)
2	Flap (ɹaɪɾɚ)	Careful /t/ (ɹaɪtɚ)
3	Flap (ɹaɪɾɚ)	Careful /d/ (ɹaɪdɚ)
4	Careful /t/ and /d/ (ɹaɪtɚ)/(ɹaɪdɚ)	Flap (ɹaɪɾɚ)
5	Careful /t/ (ɹaɪtɚ)	Careful /t/ (ɹaɪtɚ)
6	Careful /d/ (ɹaɪdɚ)	Careful /d/ (ɹaɪdɚ)
7	None (control)	Flap (ɹaɪɾɚ)
8	None (control)	Careful /t/ (ɹaɪtɚ)
9	None (control)	Careful /d/ (ɹaɪdɚ)

[4] In a screening experiment, Luce *et al.* determined that the flapped stimuli were perceived to be ambiguous.

[5] An alternative interpretation of these results is that no intermediate *form-based* representations are involved. Instead, the ambiguous flapped stimuli activate both lemmas of the word, which in turn mediate the priming effect. However, no mediating semantic representations were in evidence in the McLennan *et al.* (2001) study of unflapped, bisyllabic words that were also carefully and casually articulated, demonstrating that lemma activation is not responsible for the repetition effect in this task.

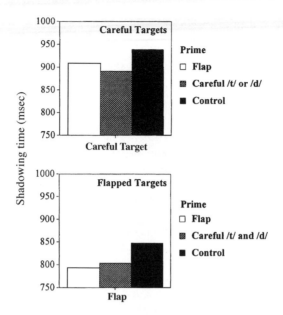

Figure 9.3 Single-word shadowing times to carefully produced and flapped target words (upper and lower panels, respectively) as a function of prime type. Target words in the second block of trials were repeated in the same style of articulation (e.g., flap–flap; careful–careful), repeated in a different style of articulation (e.g., flap–careful; careful–flap), or were not repeated (control). Equivalent effects of long-term repetition priming were obtained for repeated words regardless of the presence or absence of intervocalic flapped consonants. (From Luce *et al.*, 1999.)

underlying and surface forms are activated, at least for the type of allophonic variation examined in this study. To identify a flapped word uniquely, the listener must map the potentially ambiguous word (e.g., ɹaɪɾɚ) onto one of two lexical representations (*writer* or *rider*). Because of this ambiguity, we propose that form-based representations corresponding to clearly delineated voicing categories (i.e., /t/ and /d/) are contacted during the perceptual process. In short, our results suggest that—at least in the perception of flapped items in American English—the surface manifestation of the flap is mapped onto representations in which underlying abstract voicing categories are well specified.

Indexical variability, allophonic variability, and the time-course of processing

We have now discussed a number of pieces of evidence concerning the representation of both indexical and allophonic variability that support the operation of both specific and abstract representations in spoken word recognition. To review:

1. Church and Schacter and Goldinger demonstrated that indexical variability attenuates long-term repetition priming effects.
2. Luce and Lyons demonstrated that indexical variability does *not* attenuate priming effects for short, high-frequency words in a lexical decision task. They hypothesized

that when targets are responded to quickly, specificity effects do not have time to develop (the *time-course hypothesis*).

3. McLennan *et al.* demonstrated that indexical variability attenuates priming effects for longer, lower-frequency words in a speeded shadowing task, providing further evidence for the time-course hypothesis.

4. Luce *et al.* demonstrated that allophonic variability does *not* attenuate priming effects in a speeded shadowing task: Flapped and carefully produced stimuli prime one another equivalently, providing evidence for underlying abstract representations.

Thus, recent research on both indexical and allophonic variability suggests the operation of both abstract and episodic codes in spoken word recognition. In general, indexical variability gives rise to specificity effects whereas allophonic variability results in activation of abstract codes.[6] Although as we have seen, specificity effects arising from indexical variability may be circumvented under certain circumstances. Nonetheless, questions now arise as to why and under what circumstances one of the two codes dominate perception, and why indexical and allophonic variability tend to produce divergent effects of specificity in long-term priming. We propose two answers. The first concerns ambiguity in allophonic variation and attempts to account for the specific effects observed in the flap priming experiment. The second, more general account of the operation of abstract and episodic codes concerns the related issues of predictability, feature frequency, and the time-course of processing. We consider each in turn.

Ambiguity

One crucial difference between indexical and allophonic variability lies in the fact that the type of allophonic variability that we have examined produces ambiguity, which may require the system to generate multiple interpretations of the input. Intervocalic flapped consonants often produce a word that is lexically ambiguous (e.g., something halfway between *writer* and *rider*). Indexical variability rarely results in this kind of lexical ambiguity (see, however, Peterson and Barney, 1952). Luce *et al.* demonstrated that in dealing with this ambiguity, the system appears to activate the alternative underlying *form-based* representations corresponding to the two possible interpretations of the stimulus. Thus, lexical ambiguity may force the activation of abstract codes to enable the recognition system to identify a given lexical item uniquely.

---

[6] Remez *et al.* (1997) dispute the notion that indexical properties alone are responsible for talker differences. Indeed, they provide compelling evidence that allophonic (or idiolectical) information also conveys information about the identity of a talker. Although we have adopted the more traditional view that indexical properties are primarily responsible for talker identification, the possibility that differences among talkers may be signaled at the allophonic level does not undermine our hypothesis that certain aspects of allophonic variation, as well as lexical discrimination, may be handled by abstract codes.

Predictability, frequency, and time-course of processing

The more general predictor of the differential roles of specific and abstract codes appears to involve the speed with which the two types of codes respond to the input, which may itself be intimately tied to feature frequency and predictability. As previously discussed, indexical variability may be far less predictable and constrained than allophonic variability. Flapping in American English is restricted to the consonants /t/ and /d/ and occurs (almost) exclusively intervocalically. Although flapping of /t/ and /d/ is optional (albeit common in casual speech), the circumstances under which this type of phonetic neutralization occurs are highly predictable. The phonological system of American English specifies when and under what circumstances allophonic variation can occur. Aside from fairly general biomechanical constraints, indexical variability is typically not so predictable.

The systematicity and predictability of allophonic variability suggests that the recognition system should have robust and abstract representations of allophones. If we equate abstractness with generalization over consistently and frequently occurring feature patterns in the input, allophonic variation is a prime candidate for abstract representational coding. If we further assume that abstract codes represent the most frequent patterns of features encountered by the system, abstract codes should be the first to respond to the input, with specificity percolating through the system over time.

In short, according to our proposal, abstract codes in memory should respond first to sensory input, with specificity effects in evidence shortly thereafter. Thus, when listeners are able to respond quickly, specificity effects may be small (Luce and Lyons, 1998). However, when processing is slowed, because of stimulus or task factors, specificity effects should emerge.

Our time-course hypothesis also makes a specific prediction regarding the effects of flapping: Fast responses—as in single-word shadowing of high-frequency words—should produce attenuated specificity effects. On the other hand, specificity effects should be more strongly in evidence in situations associated with slowed processing times. To further test this time-course hypothesis, McLennan *et al.* examined long-term repetition priming in an auditory lexical decision task for the same flapped and unflapped stimuli used by Luce *et al.* As previously discussed, lexical decision typically produces appreciably longer reaction times than shadowing. If our time-course hypothesis is correct and specificity effects emerge *after* the response of the abstract allophonic codes, a task such as lexical decision should produce effects of indexical variability for the same stimuli that failed to produce specificity effects in shadowing. This is in fact the case. In lexical decision, which produced reaction times approximately 120 ms longer than single-word shadowing, effects of specificity were clearly in evidence, such that priming effects were attenuated when the stimuli mismatched on the dimension of careful-casual articulation.[7] In short, we propose that abstract codes, by virtue of their higher frequency, tend to respond or resonate first to stimulus input. Episodic codes emerge later and may be in evidence when processing is delayed due to task demands or stimulus characteristics.

---

[7] Of particular interest was finding that the specificity effects were almost entirely carried by those stimuli and subjects producing the longest reaction times.

Conclusion: a mixed model of representation of lexical form

The pattern of results reviewed in this chapter support a mixed model of form-based representations in spoken word recognition. Moreover, the available evidence suggests some fairly precise circumstances under which abstract and specific codes will dominate spoken word processing. In particular, if the process of mapping acoustic-phonetic input onto form-based representations is fast and unimpeded, abstract codes should initially dominate processing. More specific, idiosyncratic information—represented by the indexical properties of speech—may exert its influence later in the course of perception. We have also proposed that the distinction between abstract and specific representational codes should be coextensive with the distinction between highly frequent, systematic, and predictable feature patterns (allophonic variability) and less frequent, less predictable information (indexical variability).

The available evidence on the nature of form-based lexical representations in spoken word recognition fails to distinguish between weakly abstract and episodic models. Indeed, it is doubtful that any set of findings will enable this subtle dispute to be reconciled. Moreover, if episodic theories prevail, the evidence thus far does little to help us distinguish among episodic accounts based on exemplars or distributed representations. Although both sets of theories may account for specificity effects in spoken word recognition, they also may behave *as if* abstract codes are operative in perception.

Despite these as yet unanswered questions, it is clear that the next generation of spoken word recognition models must incorporate mechanisms for accounting for the growing body of research demonstrating representational specificity. Although existing models of spoken word identification (Luce *et al.*, 2000; McClelland and Elman, 1986; Norris, 1994) may be correct in their focus on immediate processing of spoken words as abstract entities, they are ultimately inadequate as representational theories of lexical form. Moreover, they may fail to explain how the recognition system behaves in less than ideal circumstances in which perception is impeded by limitations on data or process. In short, recent work on long-term repetition priming of spoken words has provided important new insights into the nature of form-based representations, insights that may ultimately usher in a new generation of models of spoken word recognition.

Acknowledgments

This work was supported (in part) by research grant number R01 DC 0265801 from the National Institute on Deafness and Other Communication Disorders, National Institutes of Health.

References

Biederman, I. and Cooper, E. E. (1992). Size invariance in visual object priming. *Journal of Experimental Psychology: Human Perception and Performance*, **18**, 122–33.

Bowers, J. S. (2000). In defense of abstractionist theories of repetition priming and word identification. *Psychonomic Bulletin and Review*, 7 (1), 83–99.

Bowers, J. S. and **Kouider, S.** (In press). Developing theories of priming with an eye on function. In *Rethinking implicit memory* (ed. J. Bowers and C. Marsolek). Oxford: Oxford University Press.

Charles-Luce, J. (1997). Cognitive factors involved in preserving a phonemic contrast. *Language and Speech*, 40, 229–48.

Church, B. A. and **Schacter, D. L.** (1994). Perceptual specificity of auditory priming: Implicit memory for voice intonation and fundamental frequency. *Journal of Experimental Psychology: Learning, Memory, and Cognition*, 20 (3), 521–33.

Cooper, L. A., **Schacter, D. L., Ballesteros, S.,** and **Moore, C.** (1992). Priming and recognition of transformed three-dimensional objects: Effects of size and reflection. *Journal of Experimental Psychology: Learning, Memory, and Cognition*, 18, 43–57.

Fox, R. A. and **Terbeek, D.** (1977). Dental flaps, vowel duration and rule ordering in American English. *Journal of Phonetics*, 5, 27–34.

Gaskell, M. G. and **Marslen-Wilson, W. D.** (1997). Integrating form and meaning: A distributed model of speech perception. *Language and Cognitive Processes*, 12, 613–56.

Gaygen, D. and **Luce, P. A.** (2002). Troughs and bursts: Probabilistic phonotactics and lexical activation in the segmentation of spoken words in fluent speech. In C. T. McLennan, P. A. Luce, G. Mauner, and J. Charles-Luce (eds.), University at Buffalo Working Papers on Language and Perception, Vol. 1, 496–549.

Goldinger, S. D. (1992). *Words and voices: Implicit and explicit memory for spoken words* (Technical Report 7). Bloomington, IN: Indiana University Speech Research Laboratory, Department of Psychology.

Goldinger, S. D. (1996). Words and voices: Episodic traces in spoken word identification and recognition memory. *Journal of Experimental Psychology: Learning, Memory, and Cognition*, 22, 1166–83.

Goldinger, S. D. (1998). Echoes of echoes? An episodic theory of lexical access. *Psychological Review*, 105 (2), 251–79.

Grossberg, S., **Boardman, I.** and **Cohen, M.** (1997). Neural dynamics of variable-rate speech categorization. *Journal of Experimental Psychology: Human Perception and Performance*, 23, 481–503.

Hintzman, D. L. (1986). 'Schema abstraction' in a multiple-trace memory model. *Psychological Review*, 93 (4), 411–28.

Hintzman, D. L. and **Caulton, D. A.** (1997). Recognition memory and modality judgments: A comparison of retrieval dynamics. *Journal of Memory and Language*, 37, 1–23.

Hintzman, D. L. and **Curran, T.** (1997). Comparing retrieval dynamics in recognition memory and lexical decision. *Journal of Experimental Psychology: General*, 126, 228–47.

Jackson, A. and **Morton, J.** (1984). Facilitation of auditory recognition. *Memory and Cognition*, 12, 568–74.

Jacoby, L. L. (1991). A process dissociation framework: Separating automatic from intentional uses of memory. *Journal of Experimental Psychology: General*, 30, 306–40.

Jusczyk, P. W. and **Luce, P. A.** (2002). Speech perception. In *Stevens' handbook of experimental psychology* (ed. S. Yantis and H. E. Pashler), 3rd edn, Vol. 1, pp. 493–536. New York: John Wiley and Sons.

Kentowicz, M. and **Kisseberth, C.** (1979). *Generative phonology.* New York: Academic Press.

Klatt, D. H. (1989). Review of selected models of speech perception. In *Lexical representation and process* (ed. W. D. Marslen-Wilson), pp. 201–62. Cambridge, MA: MIT Press.

Ladefoged, P. (2000). *A course in phonetics*, 5th edn. San Diego: Harcourt, Brace, and Jovanovich.

Luce, P. A. and Lyons, E. A. (1998). Specificity of memory representations for spoken words. *Memory and Cognition*, **26**, 708–15.

Luce, P. A. and Pisoni, D. B. (1998). Recognizing spoken words: The neighborhood activation model. *Ear and Hearing*, **19**, 1–36.

Luce, P. A., Charles-Luce, J., and McLennan, C. (1999). *Representational specificity of lexical form in the production and perception of spoken words.* Paper presented at the Proceedings of the 1999 International Congress of Phonetic Sciences.

Luce, P. A., Goldinger, S. D., Auer, E. T. and Vitevitch, M. S. (2000). Phonetic priming, neighborhood activation, and PARSYN. *Perception and Psychophysics*, **62**, 615–25.

Martin, C. S., Mullennix, J. W., Pisoni, D. B. and Summers, W. (1989). Effects of talker variability on recall of spoken word lists. *Journal of Experimental Psychology: Learning, Memory, and Cognition*, **15**, 676–84.

McClelland, J. L. and Elman, J. L. (1986). The TRACE model of speech perception. *Cognitive Psychology*, **18**, 1–86.

McLennan, C., Luce, P. A. and Charles-Luce, J. (2002). Representation of lexical form in spoken word recognition. *Submitted.*

Mullennix, J. W., Pisoni, D. B. and Martin, C. S. (1989). Some effects of talker variability on spoken word recognition. *Journal of the Acoustical Society of America*, **85**, 365–78.

Newman, R. N. and Luce, P. A. (2002). Radical activation in spoken word recognition. *Submitted.*

Norris, D. (1994). Shortlist: A connectionist model of continuous speech recognition. *Cognition*, **52**, 189–234.

Palmeri, T. J., Goldinger, S. D. and Pisoni, D. B. (1993). Episodic encoding of voice attributes and recognition memory for spoken words. *Journal of Experimental Psychology: Learning, Memory, and Cognition*, **19**, 309–28.

Peterson, G. E. and Barney, H. L. (1952). Control methods used in a study of the vowels. *Journal of the Acoustical Society of America*, **24**, 175–84.

Pisoni, D. B. (1997). Some thoughts on 'normalization' in speech perception. In *Talker variability in speech processing* (ed. K. Johnson and J. W. Mullenix), pp. 9–32. San Diego, CA: Academic Press.

Pisoni, D. B. and Luce, P. A. (1987). Acoustic-phonetic representations in word recognition. *Cognition*, **25**, 21–52.

Remez, R. E., Fellowes, J. M. and Rubin, P. E. (1997). Talker identification based on phonetic information. *Journal of Experiment Psychology: Human Perception and Performance*, **23**, 651–66.

Schacter, D. L. (1987). Implicit memory: History and current status. *Journal of Experimental Psychology: Learning, Memory, and Cognition*, **13**, 501–18.

Schacter, D. L. and Church, B. A. (1992). Auditory priming: Implicit and explicit memory for words and voices. *Journal of Experimental Psychology: Learning, Memory, and Cognition*, **18**, 915–30.

Sheffert, S. M. (1998a). Contributions of surface and conceptual information on spoken word and voice recognition. *Perception and Psychophysics*, **60**, 1141–52.

Sheffert, S. M. (1998b). Voice-specificity effects on auditory word priming. *Memory and Cognition*, **26** (3), 591–8.

Stevens, K. N. (1998). *Acoustic phonetics.* Cambridge, MA: MIT Press.

Tenpenny, P. L. (1995). Abstractionist versus episodic theories of repetition priming and word identification. *Psychonomic Bulletin and Review*, **2**, 339–63.

Vitevitch, M. S. and Luce, P. A. (1999). Probabilistic phonotactics and neighborhood activation in spoken word recognition. *Journal of Memory and Language*, **40**, 374–408.

Vitevitch, M. S., Luce, P. A., Pisoni, D. B. and Auer, E. T. (1999). Phonotactics, neighborhood activation, and lexical access for spoken words. *Brain and Language*, **68**, 306–11.

Weber, E. U. and Murdock, B. B. (1989). Priming in a distributed memory system: Implications for models of implicit memory. In *Implicit memory: Theoretical issues* (ed. S. Lewandowsky, J. C. Dunn, and K. Kirsner), pp. 87–98. Hillsdale, NJ: Lawrence Erlbaum Associates.

CHAPTER 10

SPEECH PERCEPTION AND IMPLICIT MEMORY: EVIDENCE FOR DETAILED EPISODIC ENCODING OF PHONETIC EVENTS

LORIN LACHS, KIPP MCMICHAEL, AND DAVID B. PISONI

Nearly every aspect of human speech—our accents, word choice, and even the very language we utter—is influenced by past experience. The perceptual process occurs very quickly and often appears to be carried out almost automatically. For the most part, we rarely, if ever, have any conscious awareness of our linguistic knowledge or our previous experience during speech production or perception. These general observations about speech perception suggest that implicit memory processes may play a pervasive and perhaps undissociable role in both speech perception and production. Yet despite a widespread acceptance by researchers that all behavior is ultimately grounded in prior, long-term experience, the role of implicit memory in speech production and perception has only been the focus of experimental inquiry by cognitive psychologists within the last few years.

To explain why implicit memory research in speech perception has only recently emerged, we begin this chapter with a review and discussion of the theoretical and meta-theoretical notions that underlie the traditional, abstractionist characterization of speech perception. Once we have described the traditional framework, we move on to an emerging view of speech processing and memory where both explicit and implicit effects find a unified, straightforward explanation. Finally, we will expand this emerging view to show that it is highly compatible with a seamless, undichotomized human memory system that incorporates both implicit and explicit memory components.

Speech perception: the abstractionist perspective

At its inception, the field of speech science borrowed many of its constructs and conceptualizations about language from formal linguistics. Perceptual units such as phonemes, allophones, morphemes, and even words themselves were simply direct transplantations from linguistic theory. Even after extensive analysis of speech spectrograms made it clear that speech was nothing like a discrete sequence of idealized segments (Liberman, 1957;

Liberman *et al.*, 1967), researchers continued to maintain that speech was, in essence, a discrete, symbolic signal (Licklider, 1952).

Under this view, then, speech is reduced to spoken text. The viewpoint was so widely accepted that Morris Halle, the noted linguist, went so far as to say:

> 'There can be no doubt that speech is a sequence of discrete entities, since in writing we perform the kind of symbolization just mentioned, while in reading aloud we execute the inverse of this operation; that is, we go from a discrete symbolization to a continuous acoustic signal.' (1956)

Not all views of speech perception have had such a literalist reading of the 'speech as spoken text' hypothesis, but accepted meta-theoretical notions about the discrete, idealized, symbolic nature of speech have been the dominant influence on research in speech perception and production for more than 50 years. Under this view, outlined quite explicitly in early work by phoneticians like Abercrombie (1967), a fundamental distinction is drawn between the *language* and the *medium* that mediates between speech production and reception. For example, the written word is a visible medium that transfers the 'language' produced by a writer to that received by the reader. Likewise, the audible signal generated by the talker's vocal tract during speech production transfers 'language' via acoustic medium to the listener. Because a physical medium has properties that are not related to the communication of language, a dichotomy arises concerning information contained in the physical signal:

> '...all that is necessary for linguistic communication is that the contrasts on which the patterns are based should not be obscured. Usually, therefore, many things about a medium which is being used as vehicle for a given language are not relevant to linguistic communication. Such 'extra-linguistic' properties of the medium, however, may fulfill other functions which may sometimes even be more important than the linguistic communication, which can never be completely ignored.' (Abercrombie, 1967, p. 5)

While certainly acknowledging the utility of 'extra-linguistic' variation in the speech signal, this passage illustrates two very important aspects of the traditionalist view of speech and language. First, the passage states clearly that the primary function of any language pattern is the communication of contrast, which can be used to recover the linguistic content of a message. Second, and more importantly, the extra-linguistic properties of the signal are *defined* as the exclusive complement to linguistic properties encoded in the signal. That is, any property of a medium that was *not relevant* to signaling the linguistic content was considered to be extra-linguistic. By this view, extra-linguistic information is simply a source of undesirable 'noise' created in the physiological realization of the idealized speech signal.

Linguistic content, then, is information specifying the underlying, linguistic representation of an utterance, such as segments, phonemes, syllables, or other idealized, symbolic units like words. Extra-linguistic content is everything else in the signal. Abercrombie (1967) describes the importance of extra-linguistic content, pointing out that it may contain signs or indices of other, non-linguistically important information about the talker. These *indexical* features of the speech signal—as opposed to linguistic features—might include such things as the talker's gender, dialect, or affect. However, it is precisely the dissociation between linguistic and extra-linguistic information in speech that, in our view, makes this traditional account of spoken language questionable at the present time. Over the last few years, many new findings about the contribution of extra-linguistic information to speech perception have been reported in the literature. These findings suggest that the traditional dichotomy between linguistic and extra-linguistic information in the speech signal may be somewhat misleading and possibly an incorrect characterization of the sensory information that human listeners perceive, encode, and store about their language.

Reconstruction and abstraction

The notion that speech is a noisy and highly degraded signal that fails to perfectly transmit the intended utterance of the speaker led to reconstructionist accounts of speech perception. In the words of Neisser (1967, p. 196), 'There must be a kind of filtering, of feature-detection, which precedes the active construction of detail.' According to this view, the impoverished acoustic signal is processed extensively to uncover the underspecified linguistic message that is encoded in the speech waveform. Based on rules or schema derived from acquired linguistic knowledge, the speech signal is further processed to construct an accurate perception of the intended utterance. This view of speech was extremely compatible with the information processing framework of early cognitive psychology (Studdert-Kennedy, 1974, 1976), even as J. J. Gibson's approach to perception challenged the notions of underspecification and reconstruction in the field of perception more generally (Gibson, 1966).

The process of speech perception is, according to traditional accounts, a cleaning up or filtering mechanism that uncovers sequences of idealized units such as phonemes, or words. These abstractionist accounts of speech (Pisoni, 1997) make extra-linguistic information unavailable for encoding into memory for speech events—unless some *ad hoc* reintegration process is proposed before storage. Thus, the long-term memory store of spoken words and knowledge about words—the mental lexicon—necessarily becomes a formalized, idealized, abstract database of linguistic information, a large collection of symbolic representations of words in the language.

This view of speech has motivated a very specific set of research questions and encouraged the development of experimental methodologies that have been prevalent over the last 50 years. Because extra-linguistic variation was thought to obscure the 'real' objects of speech perception—the underlying, abstract, symbolic linguistic units—factors related to the talker's voice, speaking rate, dialect, and affect were either eliminated from experimental designs or explicitly controlled so that effects of these 'irrelevant' factors would not obscure the 'interesting' phenomena more directly related to linguistic communication. Hundreds of experiments on speech perception have studied the perception of utterances spoken by a single talker or the perception of highly controlled 'minimal' units of language, like features or phonemes, in CV nonsense syllables using highly controlled synthetic speech signals (see Liberman *et al.*, 1967).

As a consequence, this research paradigm has provided very little information relating to the human listener's remarkable ability to perceive speech accurately and robustly under a wide variety of conditions and circumstances. We take this ability to deal with enormous stimulus variability in the signal to be of paramount importance to the process of spoken word recognition (Klatt, 1989). Indeed, the usefulness of a linguistic system is severely, if not totally, called into question if it is highly susceptible to drastic and unrecoverable interference as a result of the seemingly limitless conditions under which spoken language is used. Ironically, the lack of research into speech variation and variability and the ways in which listeners deal with these perceptual problems is potentially quite damaging to our understanding of spoken communication. In our view, the traditional abstractionist, symbolic, or 'symbol-processing' framework can no longer be accepted without serious question as to its utility. We now turn to an alternative theoretical framework in which the importance of stimulus variation is acknowledged and made explicit: the detailed encoding perspective.

Speech perception: a detailed encoding perspective

The time-varying acoustic signal that impinges upon the ears of the listener is not one that is neatly divided into linguistic and extra-linguistic information. The acoustic signal of speech simultaneously carries information about the linguistic utterance as well as information about the source of the utterance and the listener's communicative circumstances. In other words, linguistic and extra-linguistic information are mixed together and fundamentally inseparable in their initial acoustic form.

In contrast to the traditional views of speech and speech perception, then, one can consider the object of speech processing as a very rich, detailed representation of the original articulatory events that created the signal (Fowler, 1986; Goldinger, 1998). Since this representation incorporates both linguistic and extra-linguistic information, we need not puzzle over how the abstract, idealized, and formalized units of language are first separated from the extra-linguistic information in the speech signal and later recombined for subsequent semantic processing, where information such as gender, dialect, or affect become relevant.

Rather than viewed as a filtering or abstracting mechanism, the nature of speech perception and processing in a detailed encoding framework is variation-preserving. Under this novel view, speech processing yields a representation of the speech signal much like the original signal itself: a very rich, interleaved collection of information about the underlying events that generated the acoustic signal, in which linguistic and extra-linguistic variation are both inextricably linked.

Detailed encoding and stimulus variability

The acoustic signal that carries linguistic and extra-linguistic information provides a rich and very detailed source of information about the speaker, speaking environment, and the linguistic message. This proposal is nicely illustrated in Figure 10.1, a schematic diagram taken from Hirahara and Kato (1992). The figure describes some of the encoding processes that take place when an incoming acoustic signal is processed by the nervous system. Of particular interest to the present discussion is the top level of the figure, where the composite form of linguistic and extra-linguistic information is illustrated by two transformations of the incoming signal. On the left, particular frequencies in the signal are

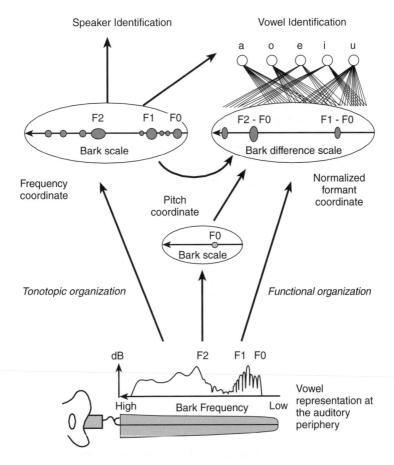

Figure 10.1 Information for talker and vowel identity is carried in parallel by an acoustic signal. Absolute frequencies contain information useful in talker identification, represented here along a Bark scale. Simultaneously, relative frequencies provide information useful in vowel identification. (Taken from Hirahara and Kato, 1992.)

represented using a Bark scale. These frequencies correspond to the resonances of the vocal tract and can be grouped into three primary clusters, commonly referred to as formants. The location and absolute frequency of these formants provide the distinctive cues to talker identification, an 'extra-linguistic' feature of the signal. On the right, the same acoustic signal is transformed and represented on a Bark difference scale, showing the relationships between these formants. These relative differences are necessary and sufficient for vowel identification, which is based on the 'linguistic' features of the signal. Thus, different analyses of the same acoustic signal yield two distinct sources of information about its production. It is important to point out here that both of these analyses are based on a frequency analysis of the components of the acoustic signal. It is not that there are two different sources of information buried in the signal for each of these sets of attributes.

Rather, the two properties of speech—the linguistic and indexical—are carried simultaneously and in parallel by the same acoustic signal.

By conceptualizing the speech signal as a rich source of information, we adopt an ecological approach to speech perception (Fowler, 1986; Gaver, 1993). According to this view, speech is neither underspecified nor noisy; potentially, all of the variation in the acoustic signal can be utilized during the process of speech perception and spoken word recognition. Variation is assumed to be lawful and highly informative about the articulatory events that underlie the production of speech (Fowler, 1986; Pisoni, 1997).

The initial stages of speech perception within such a framework are then stages of information detection and recognition rather than reconstruction and rule application. Essentially, the detailed-encoding framework embraces the fact that any dichotomy between linguistic and extra-linguistic information in the speech signal is arbitrary. The distinction between linguistic and extra-linguistic information becomes merely a convenient way of discussing the different kinds of tasks that can be carried out on an acoustic speech signal by a listener. Moreover, the increased emphasis on processing of the variation in the speech signal intuitively explains the retention of this information in memory—without the need for re-integration of separate sources of linguistic and extra-linguistic information. Because extra-linguistic information is not lost or filtered from the incoming signal, it is encoded in memory and available for use at later levels of processing.

This fundamental reconceptualization of the distinctive information available in the speech signal is not simply convenient or philosophically intriguing. This emerging view was necessitated by the results of a variety of novel experiments conducted over the last 10 years. In the next section, we summarize some of these findings and place them in a somewhat broader framework. We consider perceptually-based phenomena in speech and describe how they affect both implicit and explicit memory processes.

Processing dependencies: effects of stimulus variation in speech perception

Although early work in speech perception suggested that the effects of extra-linguistic variation on the perception of spoken language were minimal (Creelman, 1957; Peters, 1955), these conclusions must be interpreted in light of the meta-theoretical notions that influenced the research agenda of the day. For example, although Creelman (1957) found that the accuracy of spoken word recognition under three different signal-to-noise ratios decreased with an increased number of talkers, he dismissed this effect as 'relatively minor'—only a difference in performance of 7%. A difference of this size probably seemed like a small effect back in the middle 1960s. In an analogue, magnetic audio tape era, large corpora of stimuli spoken by multiple talkers were difficult to create and use in behavioral experiments with human listeners. The complex presentation schemes required to uncover effects of stimulus variation were likewise virtually intractable before the advent of computer controlled experiments. Computer control and the digital audio format have provided the tools to examine and understand the nature of stimulus variation in speech processing and encoding.

Of course, much of this discussion on the composite nature of linguistic and extra-linguistic information in memory for speech would be moot if there were not evidence that the two forms of information show demonstrable effects upon each other during processing. Early studies showed that simply changing the voice of the talker from one trial to the next affected the identification of vowels (Verbrugge *et al.*, 1976), consonants (Fourcin, 1968), and words (Creelman, 1957; Mullennix *et al.*, 1989). In addition, changes in the talker's voice also affect speed of processing. In one study, Cole *et al.* (1974) had participants make same–different judgments on pairs of syllables. The items in each pair were spoken either by the same talker or by different talkers. Despite the fact that the task required access to and use of what would traditionally be called 'linguistic' information, Cole *et al.* found that reaction times were slower when different talkers spoke the two syllables in a pair than when the same talker was used. Obviously, then, variation along an extra-linguistic dimension affects the performance in even the simplest of linguistic tasks like determining if a pair of words is the same or different.

A more detailed investigation was carried out by Mullennix and Pisoni (1990) to assess the co-dependencies of processing linguistic and extra-linguistic information. Using a Garner speeded classification task (Garner, 1974), they constructed sets of stimuli that varied along two dimensions. One dimension, the 'word' dimension, varied the cues to phonetic categorization of the initial segment of a word (e.g., 'b' vs. 'p'). The other dimension, the 'voice' dimension, varied the cues to the identity of the talker uttering the word (e.g., 'male' and 'female'). Mullennix and Pisoni asked subjects to make several judgments about the stimuli using one dimension at a time, while manipulating the variation along the irrelevant dimension. In the 'orthogonal' conditions, the irrelevant dimension was varied randomly from trial to trial. Subjects were asked to classify stimuli as either 'b' or 'p', while the stimuli varied in terms of the gender of the talker speaking the token. For example, in this condition, sometimes the 'b' token would be spoken by the male talker, and sometimes by the female talker. In the 'correlated' conditions, the irrelevant dimension varied consistently along with the relevant dimension. In other words, a male talker might always speak the 'b' tokens, while a female talker would always speak the 'p' tokens. Finally, in the 'control' conditions, the irrelevant dimension was always held constant, while subjects made judgments about the relevant dimension (i.e., the male or the female spoke all the tokens). Response latencies were collected so that patterns of processing speed could be assessed across these different conditions.

Mullennix and Pisoni found consistent differences in reaction time that depended on the variation in the irrelevant dimensions. Response times were fastest in the correlated conditions, slower in the control conditions, and slowest in the orthogonal conditions. Correlated variation along the irrelevant dimension produced a 'redundancy gain' and facilitated classification times, while orthogonal variation along the irrelevant dimension inhibited classification and slowed down response times. The pattern of speeded classification data was consistent with the proposal of mutually dependent processing of the two stimulus dimensions. In other words, the perceptual aspects of a spoken word that are associated with phonetic information and those attributes that are associated with talker information are not analyzed independently, but rather are perceived and processed in a mutually dependent fashion. Interestingly, Mullennix and Pisoni also manipulated the 'extent' of variation along each dimension in several additional experiments in which the number of response alternatives along each dimension was varied from 2 to 4, 8 or 16. While the general pattern of results was similar across all four conditions, they found that the amount of interference in the orthogonal condition increased as a function of stimulus variability. The results of Mullennix and Pisoni's study provide further evidence that increases in stimulus variation produce reliable effects on perceptual processing time and suggest that fine details of the stimulus patterns are not lost or discarded in a speeded classification task.

Thus, stimulus variability has an effect on speech processing. More importantly, the information about a talker's voice in an acoustic signal is processed in a dependent or contingent fashion along with the information specifying the linguistic content of the message. But precisely what kind of information about a talker's voice is available, and how does that information contribute to speech perception? In a measurement study of the acoustic correlates of talker intelligibility, Bradlow *et al.* (1996) found that while global characteristics of speech such as fundamental frequency and speaking rate had little effect on speech intelligibility, detailed changes in the acoustic-phonetic properties of a talker's voice, such as the amount of vowel space reduction and the degree of 'articulatory precision', were strong indicators of overall speech intelligibility. Their findings suggest that the indexical properties of a talker may be completely intermixed with the phonetic realization of an utterance and there may be no real dissociation between the two sources of information in the speech signal itself.

More direct evidence for the parallel encoding of linguistic and extra-linguistic information in the speech signal comes from other studies using sinewave replicas of speech. Sinewave speech is created by generating independent sinusoidal signals that trace the center frequencies of the three lowest formants in naturally produced utterances. The resulting pattern sounds perceptually unnatural, but the signal can be perceived by listeners as speech and the original linguistic message can be recovered (Remez *et al.*, 1981). Indeed, not only is the linguistic content of the utterance perceptible, but specific aspects of a talker's unique individual identity and speaking style are also preserved in sinewave replicas of speech.

Remez *et al.* (1997) reported that listeners could explicitly identify specific familiar talkers from sinewave replicas of their utterances. Their findings on familiar talker recognition are remarkable because sinewave speech patterns preserve none of the traditional 'speech cues' that were thought to support the perception of vocal identity, such as fundamental frequency, or the average long-term spectrum. In creating sinewave speech patterns, an utterance is essentially stripped of all of the redundant acoustic information in an utterance except the time-varying properties of the vocal resonances generated by articulatory motion. While these skeletonized versions of speech have been shown to be sufficient for accurate identification of the linguistic content of a message, the new findings by Remez and colleagues demonstrates that sinewave speech patterns are also sufficient for the accurate identification of extra-linguistic information about familiar voices as well. These time-varying sinewave speech patterns preserve individual, talker-specific cues needed for voice recognition.

Thus, even in its most basic forms, linguistic and extra-linguistic sources of information appear to be inextricably bound to one another. Because sinewave speech patterns preserve little of the original signal other than the acoustic variation corresponding to the kinematics of articulatory motion, we suggest that the link between linguistic and extra-linguistic information derives from the common underlying articulatory events and movements of the speech articulators that produce speech. As we have argued, these links produce consistent effects on speech perception. But do the links between linguistic and extra-linguistic sources of information affect the memory processes that are so crucial to spoken word recognition and lexical access? We suggest they do in the next section.

Detailed encoding effects in implicit and explicit memory

The integration of linguistic and extra-linguistic attributes in the speech signal and the mutually dependent perceptual processes that encode and process these cues has several important implications for the representation of speech in memory. According to the detailed encoding perspective, the mental representation of speech preserves the same sorts of information found in the original speech event (Goldinger, 1998). Rather than a static word-store of idealized, abstract, formalized units, Goldinger (1998) has proposed that the mental lexicon should be viewed as an extremely detailed set of instance-specific episodes. Extra-linguistic and linguistic information are preserved in the lexicon just as they are encoded in the auditory signal—in an integrated, holistic composite of linguistic and extra-linguistic properties. Evidence supporting this 'episodic' view of the lexicon comes from a series of recent memory experiments that show effects of extra-linguistic variation, even when the specific task only requires access to and use of linguistic information alone. The specific memory demands of the task—whether the task measures or assesses explicit or implicit memory—should not matter. If the basic representation of speech events in memory is highly detailed and episodic in nature, then any behavior that requires access to these memory representations should show contingent effects of these detailed composite representations.

While written words have been the primary focus in implicit memory research (Bowers, 2000), *spoken* words have received much less attention in the implicit memory literature. In the next section, we review some of the recent work that has been done on implicit effects of extra-linguistic variation in speech. We take as our starting point the operational definition summarized by Schacter (1987, p. 501) that 'implicit memory is revealed when previous experience facilitates performance on a task which does not require conscious or intentional recollection of those experiences'. The results of experiments using different memory paradigms are important in establishing the generality of these findings. Thus, we summarize experiments that examine the role of variability in both implicit and explicit memory for speech events.

Effects of stimulus variation on implicit memory

In a perceptual identification experiment conducted by Goldinger (1992), several groups of subjects were first asked to repeat words spoken to them in the quiet over headphones. The original set of stimuli was spoken by pools of two, six, and ten talkers. Subjects then returned five minutes, one day, or one week following the initial exposure and again identified spoken words in the quiet. Goldinger found that subjects were faster and more accurate in repeating words spoken by old talkers who were used at the time of the initial presentation than new talkers. Figure 10.2 shows the difference between test phase and study phase accuracy for words in the three talker pools across the three delay periods. Overall, Goldinger's data show evidence for a 'repetition effect'. That is, the identification

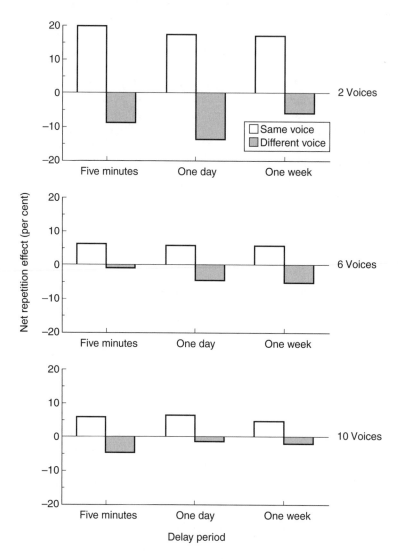

Figure 10.2 Net repetition effects observed in perceptual identification as a function of delay between sessions and repetition voice. The *y* axis shows the difference in word identification accuracy for the original and subsequent presentation of the word. There was a benefit to word identification if the word was repeated in the same voice as it was presented with originally. This effect did not dissipate over time. Increasing the number of voices in the experiment decreased the effect somewhat, due to a decrease in the perceptual distinctiveness of the voices used. (From Goldinger, 1992.)

of words was more accurate when those words were repeated in the same voice that spoke them at the time of study than in a novel voice. In addition, the advantage conferred by a repeated voice did not significantly decline as the delay between training and testing increased from five minutes to one day to one week. Goldinger's findings demonstrate that long-term memory representations of speech events not only include extra-linguistic information, but also preserve these instance-specific details for long periods of time. For talker similarity to have any effects on repetition accuracy, a record or memory trace of the extra-linguistic attributes of the talkers' speech had to persist in memory along with the more abstract, symbolic linguistic information encoded in the signal.

Goldinger also found that the differences in repetition accuracy for old and new voices were related to the perceptual similarity of the talker's voices. Words produced by talkers who had perceptually distinctive voices resulted in larger repetition effects for repeated talkers than words produced by talkers who had less distinctive voices. These latter lists showed smaller, but still significant, effects for repeated talkers. The 'graded' effects that similarity had on the repetition effect was interpreted by Goldinger as evidence for an episodic view of memory for spoken items. Even when subjects were not instructed to attend to the voices of the stimuli, their memories for these speech events were detailed enough for the relative similarity among the talkers' voices to produce differential effects on performance in this task. Such findings are inherently compatible with exemplar models of categorization, in which similarity is represented continuously as distance in a perceptual space (Nosofsky, 1986, 1987). Because points in the perceptual space represent individual tokens and not prototypical, idealized, abstract categories, the exemplar view of the lexicon provides a representational basis for making predictions sensitive to the graded similarity between voices.

In another study, Schacter and Church (1992) found consistent effects of voice information on implicit memory for words. In their experiments, subjects completed a study phase in which they made simple judgments about the enunciation or intonation of lists of words spoken by multiple talkers. Subjects then completed several implicit and explicit memory tasks in a test phase. Test stimuli were composed of tokens from the original study phase and 'new' tokens derived from study stimuli by changing the voice, intonation, or fundamental frequency of old items used in the study phase. In both an auditory identification task and a stem completion task, Schacter and Church found that study-to-test changes in all three of these stimulus attributes yielded significant reductions in subjects' accuracy.

The impairment in performance observed in the implicit memory tasks from this experiment is particularly interesting because performance on explicit recall and recognition tasks showed little, if any, effects of study-to-test changes. Similar effects had previously been observed by Church and Schacter (1994) for word identification when stimuli were presented in white noise and for stem completion tasks when stimuli were presented in the clear. As with the Goldinger experiment reported above, the findings of Schacter and Church show that extra-linguistic variation in speech is encoded and retained in memory for speech events and is an important enough component of this representation to produce reliable implicit effects on the recognition of spoken words even when such tasks do not mention these extra-linguistic dimensions at the time of initial encoding or even call attention to these attributes of the stimulus materials.

The long-term storage of extra-linguistic information about a talker's voice in implicit memory has also been demonstrated in a series of studies that examined the learning of unfamiliar voices (Nygaard and Pisoni, 1998; Nygaard *et al.*, 1995). In one experiment, Nygaard and Pisoni (1998) trained participants to identify a set of novel talkers from their voices alone. Once the participants had learned the names of the voices using a set of training stimuli, Nygaard and Pisoni found that the knowledge of talker characteristics obtained under these conditions also generalized to new stimuli that were never used in training. More importantly, Nygaard and Pisoni found that the perceptual learning of the trained voices transferred to a novel task: words spoken by familiar voices were recognized in noise more accurately than words spoken by unfamiliar voices. Thus, performance on the transfer task was facilitated by prior experience with the voices of the talkers with whom the participants were trained. Because there was no explicit reference to previous episodes or to recognizing words during training, Nygaard and Pisoni's findings provide evidence for the implicit encoding and use of information about a talker's voice in an entirely different task—recognizing spoken words.

Further evidence for implicit encoding and storage of extra-linguistic variation in speech perception comes from a study on the learning of English [r] and [l] by native speakers of Japanese. In a series of perceptual learning experiments in which Japanese listeners were trained to recognize the English /l/ and /r/ distinction, Logan *et al.* (1991) showed implicit effects for variation in the original training sets. In a follow-up study, Lively *et al.* (1992) found that the English /l/ and /r/ contrast was better retained by Japanese listeners when they were exposed to a large corpus of stimuli spoken by many different talkers during training. Compared to a group of listeners who had been trained using stimuli spoken by a single talker, listeners who had been trained using tokens produced by multiple talkers were better able to distinguish /l/ and /r/ in the speech of entirely new speakers. Although not originally designed to study implicit memory effects, these perceptual learning results satisfy the standard definition of implicit memory since it is unlikely that subjects explicitly recalled their earlier training experience when required to identify novel speech samples. Moreover, the subjects were never explicitly told to attend to the different voices used in the training phases of the experiment. All they were required to do was categorize each word they heard as having an /r/ or /l/ in it.

Effects of stimulus variation on explicit memory

Although research findings on implicit memory for speech are limited, a variety of other experimental paradigms have uncovered effects that parallel the results of these implicit memory experiments. These experiments do not measure implicit memory in the standard sense laid out above. Although most of these experiments did require subjects to consciously recall their previous experiences, the results from these experiments are important because they demonstrate the same kinds of effects of encoding detail in speech memory that were revealed in implicit memory research.

In one study, Goldinger *et al.* (1991) examined the effects of talker variability on explicit memory for spoken words using a serial recall task. They manipulated the number of talkers used to create the stimulus lists and the rate at which items within a list were presented.

They measured recall accuracy for items at the various serial positions in the list. The results showed that presentation rate interacted with the number of talkers used in the stimulus lists. At the fastest presentation rates, talker variability caused a decrease in accuracy across all serial positions in the list. Recall of single talker lists was better than recall of multiple talker lists. But, as the presentation rate decreased and the items were presented more slowly, however, the original pattern reversed. At the slowest presentation rates, subjects were more accurate at recalling lists of words spoken by multiple talkers than by a single talker, especially in the earlier portions of the list. Goldinger *et al.* concluded that information about voices must be incidentally encoded in memory at the time of presentation. At faster rates, this incidental encoding of voice features interferes with the perceptual encoding of items, leading to lower recall performance. At slower presentation rates, however, multiple talker lists contain additional distinctive cues that can be used to retrieve items from memory, thus yielding higher recall scores at test.

In another experiment that examined the encoding of extra-linguistic information in memory, Palmeri *et al.* (1993) used a continuous recognition memory procedure in which subjects listened to long lists of words spoken by multiple talkers. In this recognition task (see Shepard and Teghtsoonian, 1961), participants are required to judge each stimulus item in a list as 'old', if they have previously experienced the stimulus in the list, or 'new', if they have not. By varying the lag between the initial stimulus and its subsequent presentation, the effects of time and decay can be measured. In their experiment, Palmeri *et al.* added a variant to the standard recognition memory paradigm by repeating old words in either the same voice or in a different voice from the initial presentation.

Palmeri *et al.*'s results were consistent with the findings we have reported thus far. Subjects showed the highest recognition accuracy for words that were presented in a repeated voice. Interestingly, subjects also showed the worst performance when talkers of a different gender repeated the words, indicating that highly dissimilar voices (as in cross-gender talker changes) were unable to function as reliable 'cues' to recognition of the words. The effects of lag between study and test in this experiment were surprising. As expected, recognition accuracy decreased overall with increasing lags between initial and subsequent presentations of the stimulus. However, the advantage for 'same voice' repetition did not interact with the lag between initial and subsequent presentations of an item. In other words, the encoding of extra-linguistic information facilitated the recognition of words regardless of the time between the initial encoding of the word and test. This pattern of results indicates that extra-linguistic information is preserved in memory to the same extent that linguistic information is preserved. Although the memory trace for a word may decay over time, many of the fine details of the memory representation are not lost over time and can be used to facilitate subsequent recognition.

In another study, Lightfoot (1989) reported that subjects who had previously been trained to identify a set of talkers using common names showed better cued recall scores for lists of words when the words were spoken by multiple talkers compared to single talkers. Unlike the interaction observed by Goldinger *et al.* (1991), however, Lightfoot found that multiple talkers helped recall even at relatively fast presentation rates. Because the listeners in Lightfoot's experiment had been explicitly trained for several days to learn the voices of the talkers to a criterion beforehand, they were more familiar with these voices than participants in Goldinger's experiment. Both experiments provide support for the same conclusion. Detailed information about the talker's voice is encoded in memory along with the more abstract, symbolic linguistic content of the signal, and these instance-specific attributes facilitate the later recall and recognition of spoken words.

Explicit memory research using sentences has also revealed effects that suggest that detailed encoding of linguistic and extra-linguistic information is retained in memory. Geiselman and Bellezza (1977) presented one group of subjects with a set of sentences spoken by a male and a female talker. They also presented a control group with a set of sentences spoken only by the male talker or only by the female talker. Subjects were instructed either to attend only to the content of the sentences ('incidental gender encoding' condition) or to remember *both* the content and gender of the sentences ('explicit gender encoding' condition) for a subsequent memory test. Geiselman and Bellezza found that recall of the sentences was not significantly different for the experimental and control groups even though experimental subjects remembered the gender of sentences at higher than chance levels under both incidental and explicit gender encoding instructions.

Geiselman and Bellezza considered two possible explanations for how gender information could be encoded without detrimental effects on encoding of the linguistic content of the sentences. According to their 'voice-connotation' hypothesis, the meaning of a sentence may be encoded such that information about the speaker's voice is automatically encoded without increasing demands on processing resources. In contrast, their 'dual-hemisphere parallel-processing hypothesis' explained the encoding of gender information without increased processing costs by positing that both content and gender information are encoded in parallel by the left and right hemispheres of the brain. In subsequent research, Geiselman and Bellezza replicated their initial results (unpublished experiment mentioned in Geiselman and Bellezza, 1977) and found support for the voice-connotation hypothesis: the 'voice attribute is not 'attached' to the code for the item in memory. Rather, it may become an integral part of the code itself...' (Geiselman and Bellezza, 1977). These findings are important because they show that the composite encoding in memory of linguistic and extra-linguistic information is not constrained to isolated spoken words, but generalizes to larger linguistic units, like sentences.

Recently, McMichael and Pisoni (2000) obtained additional evidence for implicit encoding and retention of voice information in sentence-length stimuli. In a series of four discrete recognition memory experiments, they presented listeners with a list of 40 sentences in a 'study' phase. In the 'Intentional encoding' conditions, subjects were specifically told that their memory for sentences would be tested following the study phase. In the 'Incidental encoding' conditions, subjects received a surprise recognition memory test. During the study phase, five male and five female talkers spoke the list of sentences. In the test phase, listeners were asked to judge a list of 80 sentences as 'old' (i.e., heard at the time of study) or 'new' (i.e., not heard at the time of study). The 40 'old' sentences were spoken by either the same talker used during study ('Repeated Voice') or an entirely new talker that had not been heard during the study phase ('Non-repeated Voice'). The 40 'new' sentences were also spoken by either a talker that had been heard during the study phase or by an entirely new talker.

McMichael and Pisoni also manipulated the encoding task during the study phase, in order to determine whether instructions focusing attention on voice attributes would affect recognition memory performance. In one task, subjects simply hit the 'enter' key on a keyboard after hearing each sentence. In the other task, subjects indicated the gender of the speaker by typing in 'm' or 'f' after each sentence was played. Both study tasks were run under either 'incidental encoding' instructions or 'intentional encoding' instructions, producing four combinations of instructions and study task.

Figure 10.3 shows the recognition memory results from these experiments. Each set of four columns within a panel represents the probability of a correct response for the four different types of sentences at the time of test. The pattern of results shows consistent repetition effects based on the voice of the talker. Sentences were recognized more accurately as 'old' when they were presented at test in the same voice that was used at study ('Old/Repeated') than when they were presented in a different voice ('Old/Non-repeated'). This voice repetition effect was statistically significant across all four experiments, showing

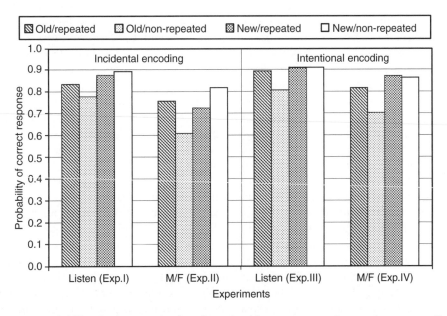

Figure 10.3 Probability of correct response from four recognition memory experiments using sentences. Each group of columns represents the results from a different experiment. In the 'Intentional Encoding' experiments, participants were instructed that there would be a test of recognition memory following the 'study' task. In 'Incidental Encoding' experiments, participants received a surprise recognition test after study. The four columns associated with each experiment show the various conditions under which the sentences were presented. 'Old' sentences are items that were presented during the study phase; 'New' sentences were not presented during the study phase. 'Repeated' voices were voices used during the study phase; 'Non-repeated' voices were novel voices that were not presented during study. The results show that across all four experiments, old sentences were more accurately identified as old when they were repeated in the same voice as original presentation than when they were presented in a new voice. (Adapted from McMichael and Pisoni, 2000.)

that even for sentences, voice information is encoded and stored in memory along with linguistic information.

Surprisingly, new sentences—those that were never presented during study—also showed a voice repetition effect in one of the four experiments. Under the 'incidental encoding' instructions, when the study task involved identifying the gender of the speaker in Experiment II, new sentences spoken in non-repeated voices ('New/Non-repeated') were more accurately identified as new than new sentences spoken by repeated voices ('New/Repeated'). These recognition memory results suggest that listeners did encode information about the specific attributes of the talkers used at the time of study—even when the instructions used at the time of study never mentioned there would be a subsequent recognition memory test for the sentences.

These results indicate that specific details regarding the voice of the talker were encoded at the time of study and this information was later retrieved and utilized in the test phase recognition task. Additionally, the fact that these effects for voice information were observed for both sets of instructions—one that explicitly focused attention on the talker's voice at study, and one that did not—demonstrates that these recognition memory effects were not simply a result of instructions that encouraged voice information encoding. Even without the explicit intention of the listeners to encode voice information, details of the talker's voice were encoded that were sufficient to facilitate performance in the recognition memory task. Thus, the earlier results obtained with isolated words clearly generalized to sentence length materials as well.

The effects of stimulus variation uncovered in these experiments, although obtained under what would traditionally be called explicit memory paradigms, are notable because subjects were never explicitly instructed to pay attention to the talker's voice during study or test. Although subjects were required to explicitly recall or recognize the words or sentences they heard, they might not have been consciously aware of incidental variation in voice information while performing these tasks. To the extent that specific details of the original speech events affected performance in these explicit memory tasks, the results have a clear and direct relationship with the implicit memory effects summarized above.

The range of stimuli investigated in these experiments runs from isolated phonemes to words to sentence length speech samples. The fact that comparable effects of extra-linguistic variation are observed across these different stimulus materials suggests that similar perceptual and memory processes may be involved in the encoding and storage of phonemes, words, and sentences. The similarity of the effects of talker variability in these experiments suggests a close link between implicit and explicit memory and raises important theoretical issues about how to explain and account for the pattern of these findings in a unified and coherent fashion.

Some final thoughts about implicit memory and detailed encoding

Although the history of research on speech perception has been dominated by abstractionist, information-processing approaches that consider extra-linguistic information irrelevant to the primary task of uncovering the idealized linguistic signal from beneath a wide range of noisy transformations, an emerging line of research suggests that extra-linguistic information and variation actually plays an important role in the process of speech perception. Several results of this line of research are particularly important to emphasize here.

Scale invariance

Whether the experiment used phonemes, words, or sentences, similar effects of variation in linguistic and extra-linguistic information have been obtained with units of differing lengths. The similarity of these findings suggests that all levels of speech representation may rely on a common substrate that incorporates both linguistic and extra-linguistic information. If the mental lexicon is conceived of as an abstract word-store that encodes only word 'types' and not word 'tokens', then current accounts of lexical memory will have great difficulty in explaining why units of differing length show effects of extra-linguistic variation. Effects for stimuli that are shorter and longer than words are difficult to explain since it is unclear how an abstracted store of word information could generate episodic effects for phoneme or sentence length stimuli if the fine instance-specific details of speech events are lost or discarded from memory at the time of initial encoding via the process of normalization.

Rather, a conceptualization of the mental lexicon as an integrated, functionally-identical subsection of a larger, more general memory system, in which all experience with speech is encoded and preserved in a detail-rich, complex, and multidimensional representation, seems more appropriate as a way to account for these results.

Parallel transmission

In contrast to the traditional view of speech, in which linguistic and extra-linguistic sources of information were viewed as separate components of the speech signal (Abercrombie, 1967), the research summarized in this chapter suggests that these two sets of attributes may be inseparable. In both speech perception and memory tasks, subjects are consistently affected by variation in both sources of information even when they are not explicitly instructed to attend to one set of attributes or the other.

It is important to keep in mind that the dissociation between linguistic and extra-linguistic information in speech is arbitrary and has been handed down to speech scientists from pre-existing meta-theoretical notions inherited from the study of linguistics, where human performance had been explicitly ruled as irrelevant to the study of language by Chomsky's competence/performance distinction (Chomsky, 1965).

The finding that human listeners encode and retrieve both linguistic and extra-linguistic information is not surprising—after all, how else could we learn to recognize and identify the voices of our friends, or the slight nuances of affect that allow us to negotiate the complex rules of pragmatic discourse, unless we encode and retain very detailed extra-linguistic information in memory. It is precisely the inseparable relationship between linguistic and extra-linguistic information that is important—that is, variation in linguistic and extra-linguistic information is not simply a helpful source of information when listeners happen to have access to it. It is rather an integral part of understanding and remembering the meaning and intent of speech events. Variation in speech is so important that even when listeners are explicitly instructed to ignore differences in linguistic or extra-linguistic information, their performance in speech perception and memory tasks appears to be influenced by all aspects of the original signal, including attributes not relevant to the specific task at hand. The processing of extra-linguistic detail without conscious awareness sounds much like the obligatory or mandatory processing needed for module status under Fodor's modularity hypothesis (Fodor, 1981). However, we do not wish to imply that speech processing is undertaken by a specialized module. Rather, we think it more reasonable to claim that the conjoint processing of linguistic and extra-linguistic attributes follows naturally from their simultaneous and inextricable production by the vocal articulators.

Parallels in explicit and implicit memory

In both implicit and explicit memory paradigms, similar effects of stimulus variation in the speech signal have been obtained across a variety of tasks. Utterances spoken in the same voice as earlier presentations increase accuracy in explicit memory for words and reduce response latencies in implicit tasks such as word identification.

That the same variation in the original speech signal can have parallel effects in both explicit and implicit tasks suggests that these two memory systems rely on the same types of representations for speech events. These representations are not based on abstract, idealized, contrastive linguistic units, but rather carry with them detailed episodic, instance-specific information about the circumstances of vocal articulation that produce speech. Furthermore, the similarity of these effects suggests that the traditional separation of these two types of memory may not be a valid conceptualization of memory for spoken language.

A detailed encoding, or 'exemplar', perspective provides an alternative view that can account for findings. With regard to scale invariance, the specific, rich detail with which speech events are retained in memory preserves information about the dialect, gender, or other indexical properties of the talker at any scale, whether the units are phonemes, words, sentences, or even units like discourse segments. Just as speech is perceived and produced in a consistent manner across scales from words to extended discourse, the memory representation for speech may be similar across different sized chunks of speech. Whether these units are phonemes or sentences, the detail of these speech events in memory would allow for the observed effects of stimulus variability.

The approach advocated here is consistent with a composite form of mental representations for speech. Since speech is produced and perceived as a unitary event that carries both linguistic and extra-linguistic information, the composite representation of a detailed memory representation falls out naturally from the physics of speech motor control and behavior. The intended message of a speaker preserves a form of parity with the production of that message via vocal articulation. Rather than being a source of noise, however, the complex interaction of the speech articulators lawfully varies the speech signal in ways that are informative and distinctive to the listener. We need not posit that different 'entries' for information about linguistic content, gender, dialect, and affect are stored in a complex associative memory system. Rather, the fact that this information arrives encoded and packaged in a unitary speech signal provides a *de facto* explanation of its storage together in speech memory. Since our memories for speech events are integrated, unitary composites of both linguistic and extra-linguistic information, behavioral tasks that assess these memories may also be affected by the rich, redundant information stored therein. Just as the detailed encoding perspective questions the validity of a distinction between linguistic and extra-linguistic information, so too does this perspective challenge the distinction between implicit and explicit memory.

For the purposes of speech research, implicit and explicit memory have largely been distinguished based on the kinds of speech information relevant to each memory system. Extra-linguistic information such as speaking rate or gender has been the traditional focus of implicit memory for speech experiments (Church and Schacter, 1994; Goldinger, 1992; Schacter and Church, 1992), while explicit memory research has focused on the more abstract, idealized linguistic information such as phonemes or words (Liberman, 1957; Peters, 1955). The result of this divergence of research has been the tacit assumption that implicit and explicit memory for speech events reflect the operation of functionally distinct, separate memory systems that deal with different types of speech information.

In a detailed encoding perspective, however, there is no valid distinction between linguistic and extra-linguistic information. Without this information-based distinction, the difference between implicit and explicit memory for speech events begins to blur. If the same memory representation underlies behavior in both implicit and explicit memory tasks and if behavior in these tasks shows similar effects of variation in the speech signal, then we can rightly question whether these two memory systems are, in fact, separate and distinct.

To apprehend the meaning of a given speech event and to recover the talker's intended message, it is necessary for the listener to know who is speaking, what they said, and under what conditions the articulatory events that produced an utterance occurred. The traditional perspective on speech perception, as well as the accepted distinction between implicit and explicit memory, assumes that the information in these representations is processed, stored, and accessed separately. The episodic view of speech perception, which is intimately tied to a description of the underlying events and their consequences, takes the integration of this information as an important constraint on the way speech events are processed and stored in memory. This approach incorporates both implicit and explicit memory phenomena as reflecting aspects of a single complex memory system that retains highly detailed, instance-specific information in a perceptual record containing all of our experiences—speech and otherwise.

Acknowledgments

This work was supported by NIH Research Grant DC00111 and Training Grant DC00012 to Indiana University.

References

Abercrombie, D. (1967). *Elements of general phonetics*. Chicago, IL: Aldine Publishing Company.

Bowers, J. S. (2000). In defense of abstractionist theories repetition priming and word identification. *Psychonomic Bulletin and Review*, **7** (1), 83–99.

Bradlow, A. R., Torretta, G. M., and **Pisoni, D. B.** (1996). Intelligibility of normal speech I: Global and fine-grained acoustic-phonetic talker characteristics. *Speech Communication*, **20**, 255–73.

Chomsky, N. (1965). *Aspects of a theory of syntax*. Cambridge, MA: MIT Press.

Church, B. A. and **Schacter, D. L.** (1994). Perceptual specificity of auditory priming: Implicit memory for voice intonation and fundamental frequency. *Journal of Experimental Psychology: Learning, Memory, and Cognition*, **20**, 521–33.

Cole, R. A., Coltheart, M., and **Allard, F.** (1974). Memory of a speaker's voice: Reaction time to same- or different-voiced letters. *Quarterly Journal of Experimental Psychology*, **26**, 1–7.

Creelman, C. D. (1957). Case of the unknown talker. *Journal of the Acoustical Society of America*, **29**, 655.

Fodor, J. A. (1981). The mind-body problem. *Scientific American*, **224**, 114–23.

Fourcin, A. J. (1968). Speech-source interference. *IEEE Transactions in Audio Electroacoustics, ACC*, **16**, 65–7.

Fowler, C. A. (1986). An event approach to the study of speech perception from a direct-realist perspective. *Journal of Phonetics*, **14**, 3–28.

Garner, W. R. (1974). *The processing of information and structure*. Potomac, MD: Erlbaum.

Gaver, W. W. (1993). What in the world do we hear?: An ecological approach to auditory event perception. *Ecological Psychology*, **5** (1), 1–29.

Geiselman, R. E. and **Bellezza, F. S.** (1977). Incidental retention of speaker's voice. *Memory and Cognition*, **5**, 658–65.

Gibson, J. J. (1966). *The senses considered as perceptual systems*. Boston, MA: Houghton Mifflin.

Goldinger, S. D. (1992). Words and voices: Implicit and explicit memory for spoken words. *Research on Speech Perception Technical Report No. 7*. Bloomington, IN: Indiana University.

Goldinger, S. D. (1998). Echoes of echoes? An episodic theory of lexical access. *Psychological Review*, **105** (2), 251–79.

Goldinger, S. D., **Pisoni, D. B.**, and **Logan, J. S.** (1991). On the nature of talker variability effects on recall of spoken word lists. *Journal of Experimental Psychology: Learning, Memory, and Cognition*, **17** (1), 152–62.

Halle, M. (1956). *For Roman Jakobson: essays on the occasion of his sixtieth birthday, 11, Oct 1956*. The Hague: Mouton.

Hirahara, T. and **Kato, H.** (1992). The effects of F0 on vowel identification. In *Speech perception, production, and linguistic structure* (ed. Y. Tohkura, E. Vatikiotis-Bateson, and Y. Sagisaka), pp. 89–112. Tokyo: Ohmsha Publishing.

Klatt, D. H. (1989). Review of selected models of speech perception. In *Lexical representation and process* (ed. W. D. Marslen-Wilson), pp. 201–62. Cambridge, MA: MIT Press.

Liberman, A. M. (1957). Some results of research on speech perception. *Journal of the Acoustical Society of America*, **29**, 117–23.

Liberman, A. M., Cooper, F. S., Shankweiler, D. P., and **Studdert-Kennedy, M.** (1967). Perception of the speech code. *Psychological Review*, **74**, 431–61.

Licklider, J. C. R. (1952). On the process of speech perception. *Journal of the Acoustical Society of America*, **24**, 590–4.

Lightfoot, N. (1989). Effects of talker familiarity on serial recall of spoken word lists. *Research on speech perception, progress report No. 15*. Bloomington, IN: Indiana University.

Lively, S. E., **Pisoni, D. B., Yamada, R. A., Tohkura, Y.**, and **Yamada, T.** (1992). Training Japanese listeners to identify English [r] and [l]: III. Long-term retention of the new phonetic categories. *Research on Speech Perception Progress Report No. 18*, pp. 185–216. Bloomington, IN: Indiana University.

Logan, J. S., Lively, S. E., and **Pisoni, D. B.** (1991). Training Japanese listeners to identify the English [r] and [l]: A first report. *Journal of the Acoustical Society of America*, **89** (2), 874–86.

McMichael, K. and **Pisoni, D. B.** (submitted) Effects of talker-specific encoding on recognition memory for spoken sentences. *Memory and Cognition*.

Mullennix, J. W. and **Pisoni, D. B.** (1990). Stimulus variability and processing dependencies in speech perception. *Perception and Psychophysics*, **47** (4), 379–90.

Mullennix, J. W., **Pisoni, D. B.**, and Martin, C. S. (1989). Some effects of talker variability on spoken word recognition. *Journal of the Acoustical Society of America*, **85** (1), 365–78.

Neisser, U. (1967). *Cognitive psychology*. New York: Appleton-Century-Crofts.

Nosofsky, R. M. (1986). Attention, similarity, and the identification-categorization relationship. *Journal of Experimental Psychology : General*, **115** (1), 39–57.

Nosofsky, R. M. (1987). Attention and learning processes in the identification and categorization of integral stimuli. *Journal of Experimental Psychology: Learning, Memory, and Cognition*, **13**, 87–108.

Nygaard, L. C. and **Pisoni, D. B.** (1998). Talker-specific learning in speech perception. *Perception and Psychophysics*, **60** (3), 355–76.

Nygaard, L. C., Sommers, M. S., and **Pisoni, D. B.** (1995). Effects of stimulus variability on perception and representation of spoken words in memory. *Perception and Psychophysics*, **57**, 989–1001.

Palmeri, T. J., Goldinger, S. D., and **Pisoni, D. B.** (1993). Episodic encoding of voice attributes and recognition memory for spoken words. *Journal of Experimental Psychology: Learning, Memory, and Cognition*, **19** (2), 309–28.

Peters, R. W. (1955). *The relative intelligibility of single-voice and multiple-voice messages under various conditions of noise* (Joint Project Report No. 56). Pensacola, FL: US Navel School of Aviation Medicine.

Pisoni, D. B. (1997). Some thoughts on 'Normalization' in speech perception. In *Talker variability in speech processing* (ed. K. Johnson and J. W. Mullennix), pp. 9–32. San Diego: Academic Press.

Remez, R. E., Rubin, P. E., **Pisoni, D. B.**, and Carrell, T. D. (1981). Speech perception without traditional speech cues. *Science*, **212**, 947–50.

Remez, R. E., Fellowes, J. M., and Rubin, P. E. (1997). Talker identification based on phonetic information. *Journal of Experimental Psychology: Human Perception and Performance*, **23** (5), 651–66.

Schacter, D. L. (1987). Implicit memory: History and current status. *Journal of Experimental Psychology: Learning, Memory, and Cognition*, **13**, 501–18.

Schacter, D. L. and Church, B. A. (1992). Auditory priming: Implicit and explicit memory for words and voices. *Journal of Experimental Psychology: Learning, Memory, and Cognition*, **18**, 915–30.

Shepard, R. N. and Teghtsoonian, M. (1961). Retention of information under conditions approaching a steady state. *Journal of Experimental Psychology*, **62** (3), 302–9.

Studdert-Kennedy, M. (1974). The perception of speech. In *Current trends in linguistics* (ed. T. A. Sebeok), Vol. XII, pp. 2349–85. The Hague: Mouton.

Studdert-Kennedy, M. (1976). Speech perception. In *Contemporary issues in experimental phonetics* (ed. N. J. Lass), pp. 243–93. New York: Academic Press.

Verbrugge, R. R., Strange, W., Shankweiler, D. P., and Edman, T. R. (1976). What information enables a listener to map a talker's vowel space? *Journal of the Acoustical Society of America*, **60**, 198–212.

PRIMING AND MEMORY

ON THE CONSTRUCTION OF BEHAVIOR AND SUBJECTIVE EXPERIENCE: THE PRODUCTION AND EVALUATION OF PERFORMANCE

BRUCE W. A. WHITTLESEA

Two stars came out. The mind, tirelessly inventing its fictions, announced them as points on a straight line. But they were indeterminate messes, unrelated, save through some one thing, at some one time (Innes, 1941, p. 41).

In an anecdote related by Stoppard (1978), Wittgenstein is said to have asked a colleague why, historically, people assumed that the sun revolved around the earth, rather than realizing that the earth was rotating. His colleague replied that it must just have looked as though it did. To which Wittgenstein replied, 'Well, what would it have looked like, if it had looked as if the earth was rotating?' The anecdote points to a fundamental problem in understanding the phenomena of nature. The phenomena themselves, like the change in location of the sun relative to the sky, may be clear and obvious. Nevertheless, the relationship among the parts, the underlying chain of cause and effect that produces the phenomena, may be fundamentally ambiguous; and the fact that some interpretation of the relationship appears simple, sensible, and obvious is no guarantee that it is correct.

Psychologists have a similar problem in understanding the underlying organization and mechanism of memory. After more than a century of empirical work, many of the phenomena of memory are now clear: the differences between recollection and recognition, between remembering and knowing, between unconscious influence of prior experience and performance that is accompanied by awareness of source. However, a synthesis of memory as a whole has proved elusive.

The Wittgenstein anecdote is revealing in several ways. First, the error made by our forebears was in miscasting the function of the sun, thinking of it as 'that which sheds light on the world'. Thinking of the sun in this way made it easy to understand the sun simply as part of what makes the world work, and therefore as secondary in the which-rotates-around-what relationship. Although that is part of what the sun is and does, and although that function is of prime importance to us, it is incidental to the fundamental nature of the sun and does not contribute to a critical understanding. Our forebears were led into this error by focusing on the significance of the sun for its consumers, on its contribution to their well-being. I will argue that psychologists have made a similar error, treating incidental by-products of memory as its primary functions. Because remembering and knowing are of importance for us as conscious, interactive social beings, we, the consumers of memory's products, have been led into the error of assuming that memory is designed to perform those functions, and that its primary mechanisms must be devoted directly to those activities. However, the fact that we could not perform as we do if memory did not in some way serve those functions does not mean that memory serves them directly, or that its fundamental structure and mode of operation are directly related to them. I will argue that qualitative differences in remembering versus knowing, or in reflective versus non-reflective tasks, do not reveal the operation of qualitatively different memory systems.

The anecdote also illustrates what I think is the fundamental function of memory, namely construction of a mental model of the stimulus environment. It further demonstrates the relationship between that function and consciousness. What appears to the observer to be a mere apprehension of a relationship, of a direct, unmediated registration of what is out there, is actually the product of an inferential and attributive process that imposes organization and meaning on the stimulus world, without the person becoming aware of performing those acts. For the observer, the sky remains stable, fixed within the confines of the hills, trees, and other features of the horizon; the sun is seen to change location with respect to these markers; therefore the sun moves across an unmoving earth and sky. But this chain of inference is performed unconsciously; consciously the observer only becomes aware of perceiving the sun to move around the earth. The idea that perception is the product of an unconscious interpretive process is very old, going back at least to Helmholtz (1910/1962). Similarly, Bartlett (1932) argued that remembering and knowing are also products of a fundamentally inferential and attributional process. Those ideas are given little prominence in most contemporary theories of memory. However, they form the basic premise of the SCAPE account (Whittlesea, 1997; Whittlesea and Leboe, 2000).[1]

Separate systems versus SCAPE

The *separate systems account* is based on the idea that people have certain primary functions to perform, namely remembering events in the past, knowing the identity and meaning of objects, and being able to perform skilled cognitive and motoric actions appropriately. These functions appear to require qualitatively different kinds of knowledge: specific versus general, and knowing what versus knowing how. The separate systems account thus begins with the assumption that people have different kinds of knowledge: it

---

[1] SCAPE is an acronym for Selective Construction And Preservation of Experiences. This account is a synthesis of ideas from many sources, including instance theory (e.g., Brooks, 1978; Medin and Schaffer, 1978; Jacoby and Brooks, 1984), the episodic-processing account of concept acquisition (e.g., Whittlesea and Dorken, 1993), the attribution theory of remembering (e.g., Jacoby and Dallas, 1981; Jacoby *et al.*, 1989; Whittlesea, 1993), skill transfer (e.g., Kolers and Smythe, 1984), and transfer-appropriate processing (e.g., Morris *et al.*, 1977; Roediger and Challis, 1992; Masson and MacLeod, 1992).

seeks to discover the unique principles by which these forms of knowledge are acquired, stored, and applied selectively in different tasks. That account is fundamentally structural: it assumes that each qualitatively different aspect of performance is supported by a different module of memory.

The separate systems account is based on observations of dissociations between tasks, caused by trauma or task variables. For example, amnesics may lose the ability to discriminate between old and new items in a direct task, such as recognition, while preserving the ability to perform other memory-based activities, such as repetition priming (Warrington and Weiskrantz, 1970) or implicit learning (Knowlton and Squire, 1994). Similarly, within intact subjects, variables such as levels of processing in training (Jacoby and Dallas, 1981) or delay of test (Tulving *et al.*, 1982) can have a large impact on recognition without affecting identification of the same stimuli. Such dissociations were taken as support for the idea that memory consists of subsystems, preserving qualitatively different kinds of knowledge, that are used selectively in different tasks, acquired and applied by different principles, and preserved in physically distinct stores.

Proponents of this account have proposed three major dichotomies. Tulving (e.g., 1983, 1985) proposed the episodic/semantic distinction, positing memory systems respectively preserving the detail of particular experiences, supporting recognition and recall, and the abstract, context-free, summary properties of those experiences, supporting perception, identification, and conceptual and categorical knowledge. Cohen and Squire (1980) focused instead on dissociations between tasks requiring the person to make a deliberate, conscious statement about the content of their knowledge versus tasks involving motoric or cognitive skills. They proposed that the former tasks are supported by a declarative memory, containing information about the *what* of experience, and a procedural memory, preserving information about the *how*. Graf and Schacter (1985) emphasized the differential role of consciousness in performance, contrasting phenomena such as repetition priming, in which prior experience can affect performance without the person's awareness, against tasks such as remembering, in which awareness of the prior experience is the issue. They proposed a distinction between implicit and explicit forms of memory as the fundamental dichotomy. Together, these three dichotomies form the basis of much current thinking about the structure of memory. I will attempt to demonstrate problems with each of these assumptions, using recent work conducted by myself and colleagues.

In contrast, *processing accounts* propose that memory uses the same knowledge and the same set of principles to perform all activities. They begin with the assumption that people have different kinds of processes that they can apply to stimuli in different situations. They attempt to discover what are the fundamental processes that memory can perform; they then attempt to work out how the application of those processes to the stimulus world results in the differential properties of the categories of behaviors that we call knowing, remembering, and skill. Investigators taking this approach have emphasized various processing dimensions, such as data-driven versus conceptually-driven (e.g., Roediger and McDermott, 1993) and automatic versus controlled (e.g., Jacoby, 1991). The SCAPE account (Whittlesea, 1997) acknowledges the importance of both of those dimensions of processing, but also such dimensions as analytic/non-analytic, broad/selective, unitized/extensive, intentional/incidental, specific/general, and integral/separate processing.

According to the SCAPE account, the central function of memory is construction: of percepts, cognitions, and attitudes. It further suggest that the activity of construction has two aspects:

(a) The production of psychological events, controlled by the interaction of the stimulus, task, and context with the memory base.

(b) The evaluation of the significance of that production, given the stimulus, task, and context.

The former leads to performance, to the occurrence of all manner of perceptual, cognitive, and motoric events; the latter results in phenomenology, the subjective reaction to current processing that causes people to adopt the attitude that they are remembering, or understanding, or identifying an object correctly, or committing an error. The production of behavior is controlled by the principle of transfer-appropriate processing (henceforward TAP); the evaluation of that performance is controlled by what aspects of the current situation are salient given the task and context, and by people's intuitive theories about how general and specific aspects of their past could affect their current performance. By that account, the major difference between remembering and classification is the breadth or specificity of cueing of memory traces; and the major difference between conscious, intentional use of experience and non-conscious, incidental influence of that experience is the attitude that people develop toward their performance.

The episodic/semantic dichotomy

The separate systems account makes a strong distinction between remembering and knowing. The account suggests that the former depends on episodic information, consisting of contextually-bound representations of specific events, whereas the latter depends on semantic knowledge, consisting of abstract, summary representations such as prototypes (Rosch, 1978), logogens (Paap and Noel, 1991), rules (Reber, 1989, 1993), or types (Anderson, 1980; Kanwisher, 1987). Episodic and semantic knowledge are thought to be acquired and applied by qualitatively different principles. Remembering is thought to occur through the encoding and retrieval of specific prior experiences, controlled by the principle of TAP (e.g., Craik and Lockhart, 1972; Kolers, 1973; Morris *et al.*, 1977; Tulving and Thompson, 1973). In contrast, the ability to perform in tasks such as identification and classification is thought to be acquired through automatic, unconscious abstraction of regular or common features across exemplars of a category or repetitions of a stimulus in multiple contexts.

One phenomenon that clearly suggests the use of abstracted, summary knowledge is 'implicit learning' (e.g., Dienes and Berry, 1997; Knowlton and Squire, 1994; Reber and Allen, 1978; Reber, 1989, 1993). In a study phase, subjects are shown stimuli selected by a hidden rule. After the training, the subjects are informed that the training stimuli conformed to a rule; they are asked to discriminate novel stimuli following the rule from items violating it. The usual result is that the subjects succeed in discriminating legal from illegal items above chance, without being able to state the rule. That is, they demonstrate sensitivity to the abstract structure of the domain without becoming aware of that structure.

Such performance is taken as evidence that the subjects must have abstracted information about the rule during the training phase; because they are unaware of doing so, that abstraction must be automatic. The phenomenon of implicit learning is thus argued to demonstrate the existence in memory of an autonomous abstraction mechanism, that proceeds independent of conscious intention or awareness, and supports performance in tasks such as classification and identification.

That conclusion has been criticized by a number of investigators (e.g., Brooks, 1978, 1987; Dulany *et al.*, 1984; Neal and Hesketh, 1997; Perruchet and Pacteau, 1991; Shanks and St. John, 1994; Vokey and Brooks, 1992). These authors point out that a test item that violates the abstract rules of the set will necessarily be less similar on average to training instances (or their parts) than an item that preserves the rules. In consequence, if the subjects simply memorize a few of the training instances and judged test items by their similarity to those instances, the observed success in classification would still occur. By this account, memory need not possess a semantic subsystem: The same memory that is responsible for remembering individual events could also produce sensitivity to the abstract properties of the domain as a whole.

The SCAPE account agrees with those ideas, but adds that it is not just the structural similarity of legal test items to training items that permits people to discriminate them from illegal items. It suggests that memory preserves processing experiences, not stimulus structures, and that a prior experience will affect future processing of a related stimulus only if they are processed in a similar way (Whittlesea and Dorken, 1993, 1997). That is, the account suggests that the principle of TAP will also apply to non-remembering activities such as classification.

Wright and Whittlesea (1998) constructed a set of 16 four-digit stimuli that followed a simple rule, that each must be of the form odd–even–odd–even (e.g., 1274, 5216, 7638, 3458, etc.) The subjects were exposed to these items in a training phase, then given one of several tests. In one study, after the training, subjects were shown new and old stimuli, all of which were legal (e.g., old: 1274 vs. new: 1634), and asked to perform recognition. The subjects judged about 71% of the items accurately. Clearly, the subjects had encoded the training items to some degree; these representations permitted them to discriminate items actually seen from structurally similar items. According to the separate systems account, this is a demonstration of the acquisition and application of episodic knowledge.

In another study, we assessed the subjects' ability to classify items according to the hidden rule. All test stimuli were novel, but half were legal and half violated the rule at some point (e.g., 5831: odd–even–odd–odd). The subjects showed sensitivity to the rule, classifying 68% of the stimuli accurately (about the same level of accuracy as in the recognition task), but none were able to state the rule. This type of performance is taken by many investigators as evidence of automatic, unconscious abstraction of the underlying regularity across the exemplars of the training set. According to the separate systems account, this is a demonstration of the automatic acquisition and application of semantic memory. If that is true, then performance in that task should not be affected by the processing that people perform on training stimuli, so long as they are exposed to the full structure of the training set.

In both studies so far described, the subjects were encouraged to encode training stimuli as two pairs of bigrams, for example reading '1256' as 'Twelve–fifty-six'. In another study, half of the subjects were asked to read training stimuli in this way; the others were asked to read them as single digits, for example as 'One–two–five–six'. In test, both groups were presented the same novel legal and illegal stimuli as in the last study. The bigram-encoding group classified items according to the rule with 70% accuracy, the single-digit group with only 58% accuracy. This result demonstrated that the induction phase of implicit learning experiments is not a neutral opportunity to experience the general structure of the set. Instead, the demands of that task affect the ways in which people encode those items; representations of those particular experiences are preserved, and dictate the degree of transfer not only in 'episodic' tasks like recognition, but also in 'semantic' tasks such as classification.

In a fourth experiment, we again exposed 16 items in a study phase (asking subjects to encode them as bigrams), and again displayed novel legal and illegal items in test. The subjects classified 65% of the test items accurately, but were unable to report the rule. That again seems to suggest automatic, unconscious abstraction of the hidden regularity. However, in this study, all of the training items violated the rule at some point (e.g., 1257, 5824, 7538, 4816, etc.). The subjects therefore could not have become sensitive to the rule by abstracting it from the training items. In fact, had they done so, they would have abstracted a rule dictating either an odd–odd bigram or an even–even bigram in each legal item: in that case, they would have chosen 'illegal' items more often than 'legal' items in test. However, we had constructed the training stimuli so that 'legal' test items would be similar to training stimuli, and 'illegal' items less so: both halves of each 'legal' test item (e.g., 1238) had occurred in several training items (e.g., in 1257, 7312, 7538, and 3826), whereas the bigrams of the 'illegal' items (e.g., 1356) never occurred in any training item. In consequence, the subjects could discriminate 'legal' from 'illegal' items if they had coded the individual training instances, and used the similarity of test instances to training instances to classify them. That is, they could show sensitivity to the hidden odd–even–odd–even rule if and only if they used the same 'episodic' representations that were responsible for their performance in the recognition task.

Although this is an extreme example of implicit learning—learning to classify stimuli according to a non-existent rule—it is also a paradigm case of the implicit learning phenomenon and of semantic memory studies in general. The primary evidence for the existence of a memory system that automatically abstracts and preserves general, context-free aspects of experience is the observation of a correlation of performance in a perceptual, classification, or identification task with the typicality, frequency, or regularity of stimuli. I and my colleagues have examined such correlations in a wide variety of areas, including word identification (Whittlesea and Cantwell, 1987), classification (Whittlesea and Leboe, 2000), repetition blindness (Whittlesea et al., 1995), implicit learning (Whittlesea and Dorken, 1993), prototype learning (Whittlesea, 1987), and semantic priming (Whittlesea and Jacoby, 1990). In each case, it has turned out that the correlation between performance and abstract properties of experience was confounded with variation in similarity of test instances to particular training experiences. When that confound is removed from the studies, it becomes apparent that performance in non-remembering, semantic tasks is controlled by the same principles as performance in remembering tasks, and is based on the same representations. The major difference between remembering and non-remembering tasks is that in the former, subjects are cued to make selective use of particular prior experiences, whereas in the latter, their experiences of a whole category of stimuli may be cued in parallel, causing performance to become correlated with abstract properties of the domain such as typicality.

The procedural/declarative dichotomy

According to the separate systems account, declarative memory supports the acquisition, retention, and retrieval of knowledge that can be consciously and intentionally recollected (Cohen and Squire, 1980).[2] In contrast, procedural memory controls performance in non-reflective tasks, such as skill and repetition priming. Both of these latter phenomena involve changes in the efficiency of sensorimotor, cognitive, or perceptual performance. The major difference is that changes that build up over trials are referred to as 'skill', whereas similar changes resulting from a single prior experience are called 'priming'. For the separate systems account, the major importance of these activities is that they appear to be independent of conscious control or volition: effects are measured through savings in the performance of skilled activities, rather than through the subject's decision about the nature of their knowledge.

Repetition priming can be observed over long periods of time, such as an hour (Jacoby and Dallas, 1981), a day, or a year (Kolers, 1976). Such long-term effects are subject to the principles of TAP: the amount of priming due to a prior experience depends on the structural similarity between a prime and probe, and also on the processing that was applied to the prime and is required on the probe (e.g., Whittlesea and Brooks, 1988; Whittlesea and Cantwell, 1987). That is, long-term priming appears to obey the same principles as recognition and recall.

In contrast, many investigators have argued that short-term or immediate priming is controlled by a different set of principles, namely activation and/or inhibition. For example, the phenomenon of 'negative priming', in which a stimulus ignored during a prime event may be identified more slowly when presented again as a probe than a stimulus that was not presented during the prime event, led many investigators to conclude that people inhibit the representation of to-be-ignored items during the prime event, resulting in a short refractory period for identifying it on a later occasion (e.g., Neill, 1977a; Tipper, 1985).

Alternatively, short-term priming might also be controlled by TAP (Neill, 1997b; Neill and Valdes, 1992; Milliken and Joordens, 1996; Milliken et al., 1998). The critical difference between activation and TAP accounts of priming is that the former asserts that experience of the prime has an unconditional effect on processing the probe, whereas the latter

---

[2] That definition is somewhat strained, inasmuch as declarative memory is thought to consist of both episodic and semantic memory; and representations in the latter store (e.g. prototypes, rules, logogens, etc.) are thought to control performance, without themselves being directly accessible or reportable. That is, people are thought to acquire a concept by abstraction over instances, but that act, and the resultant summary representation, are thought to be automatic and unconscious. Only the USE of the semantic representation is conscious and intentional; and, as in the example of implicit learning, the person may not realize they have acquired a concept, even when performance on a transfer test is above chance.

suggests that the effect of the prime experience is conditional on the need for resources in processing the probe. According to the activation view, priming (positive or negative) occurs because the representation of the probe item was activated/inhibited during processing of the prime; that is, the processing of the prime is unilaterally responsible for extra ease or difficulty in processing the probe. In contrast, according to the TAP view, processing the prime simply establishes a resource which may be called upon on a later occasion. By this view, the occurrence of priming depends not only on the structural similarity of the prime and probe and the task performed on the prime, but also on the difficulty of the probe task and on the similarity of processing performed on the prime and probe. That is, according to the TAP account, priming should be selective, depending on the need for resources in processing the probe, whereas according to the activation account, it should be unselective, based only on the structural relationship between the prime and probe.

Whittlesea *et al.* (2002) investigated the role of TAP in immediate priming. On each trial of the study, subjects were shown two stimuli in rapid succession, each of which was either a word or a nonword. The subject was required to perform a decision on each stimulus of the pair, depending on its color. If a stimulus was presented in black, the subject was to perform lexical decision; if presented in blue or red, the subject was to perform color discrimination. Further, successive stimuli might be orthographically similar (e.g., both selected from the set CARBON, CARTON, CARGON, and CARMON), or orthographically different (one taken from the former set and one from the set RANDOM, RANSOM, RANTOM, RANCOM). Thus, between the prime and probe on a trial, the subject might be required to change tasks or perform the same task twice, on items that were of the same or different lexical status, and of similar or different orthographic structure. The subjects each performed about 2500 trials.

Lexical decision is a relatively abstract and difficult task compared to color naming: it takes longer, and requires the person to process aspects of the stimulus that are not physically present. The question was whether requiring these different tasks on the probe would cause differential priming, as suggested by the TAP account, or whether the amount and direction of priming would be controlled only by the structural relationship between the prime and probe, as suggested by the activation account.

The subjects judged the color of the probe about 150 ms faster when the prime task was also color naming rather than lexical decision. In addition, when color naming was required on both stimuli, performance on the probe was about 50 ms faster when the colors matched. However, neither the orthographic nor the lexical match between prime and probe had much influence on naming the color of the probe. Judging the lexical status of the probe was also affected by the prime task, being about 25 ms faster when the prime task was also lexical decision rather than color naming. However, in this case, the effect of matching tasks was mediated by the orthographic similarity of the prime and probe (about 15 ms faster when similar), but especially by lexical match (about 50 ms faster when the items were of the same lexical status). That is, positive priming occurred for both test tasks, but was mediated only by those aspects of the stimuli that were relevant to performing the demanded judgment on the probe.

In a second study, we included a condition in which the prime and probe were identical. That condition had little effect when the probe task was color naming. However, when the probe task was lexical decision, and the prime task was also lexical decision, identical prime and probe caused even greater positive priming (about 100 ms faster than even the similar-orthography, same-lexical-status condition, such as CARBON–CARTON). More important, when the probe task was lexical decision and the prime task was instead color naming, identical prime and probe instead caused negative priming (about 25 ms slower than the similar-orthography, same-lexical-status condition). That negative priming occurred without selection between stimuli in either the prime event or the probe event, and without a task on the prime that would cause the subjects to ignore or otherwise attempt to suppress its representation.

These results demonstrate TAP in immediate priming. The occurrence of priming was not dependent just on the structural relationship between prime and probe; instead, it depended on the similarity of the tasks performed on those stimuli, and on the specific demands of those tasks (to perform a superficial or abstract judgment). Color naming of the probe was facilitated when the prime task focused the subject on that dimension, and especially when the prime and probe matched on that dimension, regardless of the orthographic and lexical relationship between them. In contrast, lexical decision on the probe was facilitated when the prime task was also lexical decision; and that effect depended on the similarity of the prime and probe in orthography and lexical status. The most impressive aspect of these data was the observation that presenting the identical items as prime and probe had no effect when the probe task was color naming; had the greatest positive priming effect when the probe task was lexical decision and the prime task was the same; and caused the greatest negative priming when the probe task was lexical decision and the prime task was different. We concluded that all of the observed priming effects could be explained through the subjects selectively accessing components of the prime experience, depending on those aspects of the probe experience that were made salient by the demands of the probe task: the magnitude and the direction of the priming depended on the appropriateness of the cued components of the earlier experience for performing the demanded task on the probe. Thus, when the probe task was shallow, performing the same task on the prime facilitated performance on any probe item, regardless of their abstract similarity; whereas when the probe task was deep, requiring the person to identify more particular, idiosyncratic characteristics of the stimulus, the priming was dependent on the specific similarity between prime and probe on orthography, lexical status, and identity.

Such studies demonstrate that the principles of TAP control performance in a 'procedural' task such as immediate priming, just as they do in the 'declarative' tasks of remembering and classification. In turn, this suggests that the procedural/declarative dichotomy does not reveal any fundamental difference in processing or in the types of representation supporting performance. Instead, that dichotomy only points to the fact that people sometimes become aware of the source of their performance and sometimes not.

The implicit/explicit dichotomy

In many tasks, such as remembering and classification, people often become aware of specific or general aspects of their past. On other occasions, performance exhibits an influence of the past that is not accompanied by awareness. The difference in awareness is also sometimes accompanied by a difference in the success of the performance. This kind of dissociation led a number of investigators to propose that memory has separate stores, containing qualitatively different kinds of information, that are differentially accessible in explicit and implicit tasks (e.g., Graf and Schacter, 1985; Knowlton and Squire, 1994).

One example of the implicit/explicit issue is the 'mere exposure' effect. In this paradigm, people are exposed to a set of stimuli, presented very rapidly. In a subsequent test, they are shown pairs of items, one old and one new, and asked either which is more pleasant (preference) or which is old (recognition). The phenomenon is that people select the old item from the pair above chance in the preference test, but may be at or near chance in the recognition test. This effect seems to show that people can be influenced by prior experience in an indirect test of memory, whereas they are not able to be sensitive to that experience in a direct test. The effect has been interpreted by numerous authors to mean that there are two forms of memory, one explicit and the other implicit: not just two ways of accessing the same memory, but two separate memory systems, selectively controlling performance in direct and indirect tests (Seamon *et al.*, 1995, Schacter, 1990; Schacter *et al.*, 1991). The effect of prior experience on pleasantness judgments is thought to be mediated by repetition priming (an implicit form of memory), resulting in augmented perceptual fluency; in contrast, the failure of recognition is attributed to failure to encode adequate representations in explicit (episodic) memory (Seamon *et al.*, 1984; Bornstein and D'Agostino, 1994).

The problem with this interpretation is that recognition can be performed on either of two bases, recollection of the prior event or a feeling of familiarity (e.g., Jacoby and Dallas, 1981; Mandler, 1991). Because stimuli are presented very briefly in this paradigm, it is understandable that people usually cannot claim recognition through recollection of detail. However, the other basis of recognition, a feeling of familiarity, is now generally thought to be based on a perception of extra fluency of processing, resulting from the priming effect of a prior presentation of the item (e.g., Jacoby *et al.*, 1989; Lindsay and Kelley, 1996; Rajaram, 1993; Whittlesea, 1993). That perception of extra fluency is also thought to be the basis of the preference effect in mere exposure studies (e.g., Bonnano and Stillings, 1986; Bornstein and D'Agostino, 1994). Thus the puzzle presented by the mere exposure effect is why people can experience augmented fluency as pleasantness, permitting them to discriminate between new and old items in a preference test, when that same fluency is not experienced as a feeling of familiarity strong enough to allow them to discriminate new from old items in a recognition test.

Whittlesea and Price (2001) speculated that the effect is based not on two forms of memory but instead on two ways of accessing the same memory representations, as suggested by the SCAPE account. We noted that the stimuli used in studies of the mere exposure effect are usually taken from a single category, such as geometric figures or pseudo-ideographs. Taking the stimuli from a single category is not definitional to the effect. However, it has the consequence that the stimuli share a family resemblance: they all generally look alike. We argued that in response to this problem, people adopt different strategies in the preference and recognition tests. In judging pleasantness, we suspected that they adopt a non-analytic strategy, examining each stimulus as a whole. In doing so, they process the old stimulus more fluently than the other, resulting in an attribution of pleasantness. In contrast, when faced with the recognition discrimination, we suspected that they adopt an analytic strategy, attempting to isolate some recognizable feature in one of the stimuli. This strategy does not succeed, because the training presentation is too restricted to support recollection of parts of the stimulus. But it also has another consequence: because the person focuses on specific, local aspects of the stimulus, they are prevented from experiencing fluency of re-processing the whole. That is, the strategic response to the old–new discrimination problem causes the person to process the old stimuli in a way that prevents them from experiencing differential fluency, and hence prevents them from experiencing a differential feeling of familiarity.

To test that hypothesis, Whittlesea and Price (2001) assembled large sets of pictures, all pictures within a set being taken from a single category, such as chairs, mountains, or geometric patterns. Half of these pictures were presented in RSVP format in a study phase; one-third were presented once, one-third three times, and one-third five times. In test, subjects were shown pairs of pictures, one old and one new on each trial, and asked to select either the old picture or the more pleasant picture. Recognition performance was at chance, regardless of the number of training presentations of the old picture, but old items were selected above chance in the preference judgment. These observations replicated the basic mere exposure effect. We then repeated each of those studies, with altered instructions. In the new recognition test, subjects were told that all test stimuli were new, but that one item in each pair would globally resemble one of the training items: they were to select that item. This was an attempt to cause the subjects to process test stimuli non-analytically, examining them as whole pictures rather than searching for a critical, recognizable feature. The result was that the subjects selected the old item reliably above chance in all three presentation conditions. In the new preference task, we asked the subjects to select the more pleasant picture, but also to justify their selection by pointing to a feature of that stimulus. This was an attempt to cause the subjects to focus analytically on parts of the pictures. The result was that subjects were now at chance in selecting the old item, regardless of the frequency of presentation in the study phase.

The reversal of the usual mere exposure effect in these experiments demonstrates that that effect is not produced by presenting direct and indirect tests that selectively tap into explicit and implicit memory systems. Instead, we concluded that the difference in the challenge presented to subjects, to judge which picture is more pleasant or which is old, caused the subjects to use different strategies, which permitted or prevented experiencing priming. When those strategies were reversed through an instructional manipulation, sensitivity to prior experience in direct and indirect tests reversed as well. In subsequent experiments, we demonstrated that the motive to perform analytic processing in the direct (recognition) test was the family resemblance of the stimulus sets used to test the mere exposure effect. When that motive was removed (by presenting pictures from different sets in the same RSVP procedure), subjects spontaneously performed well above chance in the recognition test. Thus the failure of recognition in the standard mere exposure paradigm does indeed appear to be due to adopting an analytic strategy as a response to the perceived difficulty of discriminating between new and old items of family-resemblance categories.

According to the separate systems account, awareness of the source of one's performance depends on the type of task one is performing, and the type of memory system (explicit or implicit) that that task accesses. In contrast, according to the SCAPE account, awareness of the source of performance is constructed through a process of generation, inference, and attribution, in the same way that the performance itself is constructed. Explicit versus implicit is a description of the outcome of this process, not a description of the knowledge on which it is based or the process that controls performance and creates awareness. As illustrated in the next section, one consequence of this constructive process is that one can become aware of sources of performance that do not exist.

Feelings of familiarity: the synthesis of implicit and explicit

The above chance pleasantness and recognition judgments observed in the experiments just reported likely occurred because prior exposure caused the old member of test pairs to be processed with greater fluency than the novel member (i.e., repetition priming), at least when subjects performed non-analytically. That is, these subjects appear to have used a simple decision heuristic such as 'if fluent then old/pleasant'. However, the evaluation process that leads to a subjective reaction can be considerably more complex than that. In four recent articles, Whittlesea and Williams (1998, 2000, 2001a, 2001b) investigated the source of the feeling of familiarity. We concluded that people chronically examine their cognitive and perceptual processing at a variety of levels, attempting to integrate various aspects of that processing with other aspects. In doing so, they come to perceive their current processing as falling into one of three basic categories: that it is coherent, or discrepant, or incongruous. The former occurs when all aspects of the current experience seem to fit well with others; the chief reaction to that perception is to accept the current processing event and move on. The latter perception occurs when some aspect of current processing is clearly inconsistent with others, for example when a speech error is made or when stimulus elements conflict semantically or at some other level (e.g., on reading 'The hunter sat quietly on the dog'). The chief reaction to the perception of incongruity is to stop processing the inflow of environmental stimuli and to focus on the source of the incongruity, resulting in error correction.

In contrast, the perception of discrepancy occurs when various aspects of a situation fit surprisingly well or surprisingly poorly, for a reason that is not immediately clear. Like the perception of incongruity, this reaction interrupts ongoing processing of the environment and causes a re-focusing on the stimulus event that provoked that reaction. However, in this case, the source of the surprise cannot be identified within the event itself. A common reaction to this situation is to perform an attribution to a source external to the event. Variously, the person may infer that the cause of the unexpected processing is in some covert characteristic of the stimulus itself ('There's something odd/interesting about that item'), or their own current state ('I must be tired or something'), or some aspect of their past ('That feels familiar'). According to the 'discrepancy-attribution hypothesis' (Whittlesea and Williams, 1998, 2000), the feeling of familiarity occurs when people perceive their current processing to be discrepant, rather than coherent or incongruous, and attribute the source of that perception to the past.

To demonstrate that hypothesis, we created a set of natural words (e.g., DAISY), orthographically regular nonwords (e.g., HENSION), and irregular nonwords (e.g., STOFWUS). Half of each type were presented in a study session, and all items were presented in a recognition test. We observed that words and regular nonwords were pronounced more fluently than irregular nonwords; we also observed that the regular nonwords were falsely claimed old 20% more often than either the words or irregular nonwords. We concluded that the subjects had experienced their fluency of processing natural words as being consistent with the fact that they knew those items, and their non-fluent processing of irregular nonwords as being consistent with not knowing those units. In contrast, the regular nonwords were both meaningless (unknown units) but also fluently processed. We concluded that the subjects, evaluating the coherence of their processing, experienced a perception of discrepancy in this case; unable to attribute the fluency to knowledge of those units, they instead attributed it to a prior experience of those items in the training phase. This unconscious attribution to a source in the past produced a conscious feeling of familiarity.

Three points must be made clear to understand the significance of this result. First, the illusion of familiarity caused by the HENSION items was not due to the subjects responding to the fluency of their processing *per se*. Had that been the case, they would have produced even more false alarms for natural words, which were actually somewhat more fluently processed. Instead, the subjects apparently reacted to the surprisingness of the fluency of the regular nonwords, given that they were unknown entities. Second, the illusion of familiarity for those items was based on a misinterpretation of the real coherence of those processing experiences. The regular nonwords were fluently processed because they were orthographically regular: there was no actual discrepancy between the lexical status and fluency of those items. The subjects, not taking this factor into account, but simply thinking of those items as meaningless and unknown, erroneously perceived their processing as discrepant. This demonstrates that it is the interpretation that the subject places on their processing in evaluating it, given what is salient to them, not the actual coherence of that processing, that determines their consequent subjective reaction. Third, the subjects could not identify any source within the processing event itself to explain the apparent lack of match between their fluency and the items' lexical status. They therefore perceived their processing as discrepant, and made an external attribution to explain it, rather than perceiving it as incongruous, and making an attribution internal to the event.

The separate systems account is most impressive when priming influences performance in an indirect test but not a direct test of memory, as in the standard 'mere exposure' effect discussed earlier. However, it has some difficulty with feelings of familiarity that are based on surprising fluency of processing. Priming is supposed to be the archetypical example of implicit memory. That people can readily use variations in processing fluency to make explicit recognition decisions suggests, at minimum, that implicit memory is not all that implicit. Defenders of the separate systems account argue that it is not always easy to distinguish between implicit and explicit memory tests, and that some implicit tests invoke declarative memory processes and some explicit tests invoke implicit memory (e.g., Gabrieli, 1998). But if there is no criterion for deciding a priori whether a certain test should require implicit or explicit memory, then performance in those tests cannot be used to claim that there really are two such qualitatively different systems.

The SCAPE account suggests instead that every processing episode involves explicit and implicit processing. In the familiarity experiment just described, there are two kinds of implicit processing:

(a) Productive processes that enhance the fluency of processing test items, based on skill (the effects of orthographic regularity on fluency of pronouncing different kinds of items) and on repetition priming (the effects prior exposure to test items in the training phase).

(b) The evaluative processes that cause the person to experience their processing as coherent, discrepant, or incongruous.

In this study, enhanced fluency that was evaluated as discrepant resulted in an explicit, conscious feeling of familiarity. In other cases, it may cause the person to conclude that they actually recall something or know it.

The constructive nature of awareness

According to the separate systems account, remembering and knowing rely on explicit, declarative knowledge, consisting of that information that can be consciously and deliberately retrieved. In contrast, according to the SCAPE account, knowledge is not retrieved, but constructed. To give a simple example, imagine that a recognition study begins with a training phase consisting of paired associates, such as onion–carrot, milk–cheese, bread–cake, etc. In test, when asked 'Did you see ONION in the list?', one subject may reply 'Onion: h'm, oh yeah, CARROT: yes, I recall seeing ONION'. That performance seems to indicate that the subject has used ONION as a cue to retrieve the episodic representation of the training experience, and that, in doing so, they have now become aware of a prior experience. However, that description of the process is too simple. Another subject might respond 'ONION—h'm, CARROT: no, that's just a common associate: I don't remember ONION'. That subject's initial performance duplicates that of the first, but although the content of the earlier experience comes to mind, this subject does not become aware of the prior experience. A third subject might respond 'ONION—oh yeah, SOUP: sure, I remember seeing ONION in the list'. This subject's performance is influenced by a source other than the training experience, yet this subject experiences awareness of encountering that item.

These examples are intended to demonstrate that becoming aware of a prior event is not a matter of retrieval, but instead is caused by two interlinked processes: the production of some performance in response to a stimulus, and a decision about the significance of that performance with respect to one's prior knowledge. As illustrated by the examples, an idea may come to mind in response to a stimulus either because the two were associated on some particular occasion, or because both are associated through one's general background knowledge. The coming-to-mind of an associate in a remembering experiment is thus not itself awareness of the prior event, but instead only awareness of the current occurrence of the associate. The person must now perform an evaluation of the significance of that event, attributing it to whatever source appears most likely. The decision one reaches in the course of that evaluation determines whether or not one becomes aware of the prior event. Thus becoming aware of a prior event consists of adopting an attitude toward current performance, that its source is in some particular occurrence in one's past.

The difference between these two aspects of the construction of awareness is illustrated in a study by Leboe and Whittlesea (2000). In a training phase, subjects were exposed to a series of words, one-third paired with a strong associate (e.g., LION–TIGER), one-third paired with a non-associated word (e.g., ROAD–NAVY), and one-third each paired with a row of Xs (e.g., FORK–XXXX). Each associate in the former two cases occurred only once in the study, whereas XXXX occurred with many stimuli. At test, the subjects were shown each stem word (the first word of each training pair) and asked to recall the item with which it had been paired. They were allowed to report nothing, if nothing came to mind; on occasions on which they reported some item as a potential recall, they were asked to state their confidence that that report was a genuine act of recall.

The subjects reported the correct paired item on 48% of trials when the stimulus had been paired with a close associate, on 41% of trials on which the pair item was XXXX, and on only 13% of trials when the pair item was an unrelated word. In contrast, the confidence rating accompanying those same trials was 78% for recall of an associate, only 45% for XXXX, but 91% for recall of an unrelated word. We concluded that the differential rates of accuracy and confidence of recall reflect the interaction of two principles: the production of a response to the test stimulus (the coming-to-mind of a strong associate, XXXX, or an unrelated word), and the subject's consequent evaluation of the significance of each of those types of response coming to mind. It was easy for the subjects to generate XXXX in test, because of their knowledge that one-third of training items had had that associate: but equally, the subjects were unimpressed with the coming-to-mind of that response, because they were aware that they could easily generate it for spurious reasons. Thus, they often produced XXXX correctly, but even when accurately reduplicating their earlier experience, they were not confident that they were actually recalling. Generating a strong associate was also easy, and resulted in about the same degree of successful recall. However, unlike the XXXX case, generation of an associate for a word could potentially result in many different outcomes (e.g., LION: TIGER, JUNGLE, CAT, TAMER, etc.). The coming-to-mind of a particular associate was therefore more impressive than production of XXXX. The subjects responded to this difference, reporting higher confidence that they were recalling the word when they generated an associate than when producing XXXX. In contrast, reproducing an unrelated word was difficult, in part because the association formed during training would often be of low quality (e.g., the association between ROAD and SPOON). In consequence, accurate recall was low in this condition. However, when an unrelated word did come to mind, that occurrence was very impressive: the subjects could think of no other reason why is should come to mind other than that those words had been paired in training. Such productions were thus experienced as true recall, with very high confidence estimates.

Awareness of the contents of previous experiences is thus the product of a heuristic decision, not direct access to a representation of the past. People are always in the position of having to infer the nature of their past from the quality and content of their current processing. There are always multiple possible reasons why a particular mental event occurs: because it actually happened in one's experience, exactly as it is recalled; because one experienced a similar event, with a different stimulus; because that event occurred in the life of friend, who told you about it; or because one has experienced many similar events, which in parallel contribute to the ease and detail of the current mental event. Although some mental events occur with great clarity, coherence and extensiveness, and simply feel like remembering, the conclusion that one is now aware of an aspect of the past is always a decision, the adoption of an attitude toward current processing, not a simple retrieval of the past.

This heuristic relationship between awareness and experience is not limited to remembering. It is also true of knowledge in general. This is not often apparent to the user of knowledge. For example, if a person is asked 'What does the word ONION mean?', they may respond 'A pungent vegetable, used in many flavourful dishes'; and in doing so, they feel that they are simply reporting knowledge. However, they are in fact performing the same two-part operation of production and evaluation that was illustrated for remembering. Stimulated by the question, a meaning comes to mind, supported by many prior interactions with the word ONION. That production is then evaluated for quality (ease, completeness, etc.) and informational coherence. That knowing consists of the adoption of an attitude toward performance can be illustrated when the person makes an error. For example, a person reading the word ETYMOLOGY may think 'the study of insects; their forms and behaviour'. That is of course an error, caused by the similarity of that word with ENTOMOLOGY; but because that meaning comes to mind readily, and with mutually consistent parts, the person may pass on, thinking that they know the meaning communicated by the word. The point is that, however immediate the feeling that one is simply aware of the meaning of a stimulus, that awareness is always a construction, based on the production of some response to the stimulus, an evaluation of the goodness of that production, and a decision to adopt an attitude towards it: an attitude that one knows that stimulus, or remembers it, or has made an error in responding to it.

Whittlesea and Leboe (2000) demonstrated three heuristics that people use in developing the attitude of knowing. We generated a set of nonword stimuli, all of which had a B or D in the fourth location (e.g., BARDEN, GOMBUF). The subjects were exposed to a set of these stimuli, then told that they all conformed to a simple rule and asked to classify new but structurally similar items as legal or illegal. The subjects could perform this decision by abstracting the B–D rule during training, either explicitly or implicitly. However, they could also perform that judgment on the basis of similarity to training items, because legal test items differed from training items by only one letter (e.g., BALDEN) and illegal items by two letters (e.g., BALTEN). In a series of studies, we observed that the subjects could discriminate above chance between legal and illegal test items.[3]

However, the interest in the study was the subjects' use of heuristics in making classification decisions. Orthogonal to the manipulation of legality (similarity to old), half of the test items contained a glide transition (e.g., BARDEN or BALDEN) and were consequently easy to pronounce, and half contained a non-glide transition (e.g., BAGDEN or BATDEN) and were consequently more difficult to pronounce. Thus, supposing that the person had seen BARDEN in training, we could show them BALDEN (legal, glide), BALTEN (illegal, glide), BATDEN (legal, non-glide), or BATPEN (illegal, non-glide). Our interest was in whether or not this factor of pronunciation fluency would affect the subjects' classification decisions.

---

[3] It is likely that subjects' sensitivity to the hidden rule was based on the differential similarity of legal and illegal items to training items, rather than on implicit abstraction of the rule. There does not seem to be any positive evidence that people can abstract such a rule unconsciously (cf. Cock *et al.*, 1994; Whittlesea and Wright, 1997; Wright and Whittlesea, 1998).

In the study phase of one experiment, the subjects were exposed to a set of items, all of which contained glide transitions. In the subsequent test, they were 23% more likely to claim legal items to be legal than illegal items; they were also 15% more likely to claim glide items legal than non-glide items. That effect of the ease of pronunciation could occur for either of two reasons. First, legal items (similar to old) were easier to pronounce than illegal items (less similar to old): having seen a similar item previously speeded naming by about 50 ms. The subjects could thus normatively use the ease of naming as a basis of claiming items to be legal. Glide items were also pronounced faster than non-glide items, by about 60 ms, regardless of legality. Use of the *fluency heuristic* would thus lead the subjects to claim glide items to be legal more often than non-glides, as observed. However, the same outcome would occur if the subjects used a *resemblance heuristic*, judging items old if they were easy to say because the training items were also all easy to say (all having glide transitions). To disambiguate those possibilities, in another study, all training items were made to contain non-glide transitions. In that case, the subjects again classified legal and illegal items above chance, but also judged non-glide items to be legal about 17% more often than glide items. We concluded that the subjects used the resemblance heuristic to judge legality.

We then investigated whether people can also use the fluency heuristic to make such judgments. To prevent use of resemblance, we adopted two strategies. First, we presented half glide and half non-glide items in training, so that neither type of test item resembled the training list more than the other: use of the resemblance heuristic would thus result in no net bias. Second, to prevent the subjects from thinking of training items as easy or hard, we included English words in the training, thus causing the subjects to characterize the training items as words or nonwords. No natural words were shown in test: the subjects were shown the same set of nonwords as in other studies, and asked to classify them as legal or illegal according to the hidden rule. The subjects classified legal items above chance; but they were also about 15% more likely to claim glide items legal than non-glide items. We concluded that those subjects had used the fluency heuristic to judge legality.

Next, we investigated whether the subjects might also use a *generation heuristic* in classification. This heuristic consists of deciding that some piece of information that comes to mind is a valid indicator of the decision to be made, because there seems to be no other reason for it to come to mind. This heuristic was the basis of subjects' high-confidence recall judgments for unrelated pair words in the remembering experiment described earlier. To examine this heuristic in classification, we split the training lists used in other studies into two categories, respectively those items having a D and those having a B in the fourth position. We paired all items of one category with male names and items of the other category with female names, presenting the nonwords as surnames (e.g., Jerry Barden and Diane Gombuf). At test, we presented new items, all of which differed by one letter from a training item (e.g., BALDEN, GORBUF), asking subjects to classify them as names belonging to males or females according to the hidden rule of the training set. All training and test items of both categories were made to contain glide transitions. In consequence, the subjects were prevented from using either the fluency or resemblance heuristics to discriminate between categories. However, they could still discriminate between the categories by using the generation heuristic. That is, if we presented an item such as BALDEN, and the name Jerry came to mind, the subject could classify BALDEN as a male's name even if they could not recall the original training item

(BARDEN). The outcome was that the subjects were able to classify the novel items above chance, at 58% accuracy. We then re-analyzed the data, basing the new analysis only on trials when the subjects either reported an incorrect associate (e.g., reporting Adam as the associate for BALDEN rather than Jerry) or claimed to be unable to recall anything useful. In that case, the subjects were still at 55% accuracy, reliably above chance. We concluded that people can use the generation heuristic to classify stimuli, and may be able to do so even when the generation is inaccurate or produces no definite conscious response.

All three decision heuristics used to classify stimuli in these studies (fluency, resemblance, and generation) depend on the same two-part process demonstrated in the recall and familiarity experiments earlier. In all cases, some aspects of experience (either characteristics of particular prior experiences, of the mass of past experience in parallel, or of the current processing context) drive current performance, resulting in production of mental events with some degree of quality, coherence, and extensiveness; the person then evaluates that performance, attempting to argue back from the outcome to the source. In doing so, they apply intuitive theories about how prior specific experiences or the general properties of classes of stimuli should affect their current performance; they consequently develop an attitude toward their performance, that it is caused by general knowledge (in the case of concepts or categories) or specific knowledge (in the case of remembering events). This attitude, that what is in mind now is the product of a certain kind of knowledge, is as close as people can come to being aware of what they know. Contrary to the separate systems account, knowing is an essentially heuristic, constructive activity, not an act of retrieval.

Summary

In the experiments described in this article, I have demonstrated implicit learning occurring without abstraction of general structure; positive and negative priming occurring without activation or inhibition; a dissociation between an implicit memory task (preference) and an explicit task (recognition) that is reversible by a change in processing; variations in the feeling of familiarity caused by the unconscious perception of discrepancy; a dissociation between accuracy and confidence of recall; and classification that is based on three separate heuristics. Among them, these tasks provide examples of the range of behaviours that the separate systems account was intended to explain. However, as I have attempted to demonstrate, that account is unnecessary to explain the variety of phenomena observed with such tasks, and has difficulty in explaining many of them. Instead, the assumptions of the SCAPE account, consisting of constructive production, controlled by TAP, and constructive evaluation, controlled by the application of intuitive theories of cause and effect to those aspects of the current processing made salient by the current stimulus, task, and context, seem to provide a more adequate account.

References

Anderson, J. R. (1980). *Cognitive psychology and its implications*. San Francisco, CA: W. H. Freeman.

Bartlett, F. C. (1932). *Remembering: A study in experimental and social psychology*. Cambridge: Cambridge University Press.

Bonnano, G. A. and **Stillings, N. A.** (1986). Preference, familiarity and recognition after repeated brief exposures to random geometric shapes. *American Journal of Psychology*, **99**, 403–15.

Bornstein, R. F. and **D'Agostino, P. R.** (1994). The attribution and discounting of perceptual fluency: Preliminary tests of a perceptual fluency/attributional model of the mere exposure effect. *Social Cognition*, **12**, 103–28.

Brooks, L. R. (1978). Non-analytic concept formation and memory for instances. In *Cognition and categorization* (ed. E. H. Rosch and B. B. Lloyd), pp. 169–211. Hillsdale, NJ: Erlbaum.

Brooks, L. R. (1987). Decentralized control of categorization: The role of prior processing episodes. In *Concepts and conceptual development: Ecological and intellectual factors in categorization* (ed. U. Neisser), pp. 141–74. Cambridge, England: Cambridge University Press.

Cock, J. J., Berry, D. C., and **Gaffan, E. A.** (1994). New strings for old: The role of similarity processing in an incidental learning task. *Quarterly Journal of Experimental Psychology*, **47A**, 1015–34.

Cohen, N. J. and **Squire, L. R.** (1980). Preserved learning and retention of pattern-analyzing skill in amnesia: dissociation of knowing what and knowing how. *Science*, **210**, 207–10.

Craik, F. I. M. and **Lockhart, R. S.** (1972). Levels of processing: A framework for memory research. *Journal of Verbal Learning and Verbal Behavior*, **11**, 671–84.

Dienes, Z. and **Berry, D.** (1997). Implicit learning: Below the subjective threshold. *Psychonomic Bulletin and Review*, **4**, 1–23.

Dulany, D. E., Carlson, R. A., and **Dewey, G. I.** (1984). A case of syntactical learning and judgment: How conscious and how abstract? *Journal of Experimental Psychology: General*, **113**, 541–55.

Gabrieli, J. D. E. (1998). Cogntive neuroscience of human memory. *Annual Review of Psychology*, **49**, 87–115.

Graf, P. and **Schachter, D. L.** (1985). Implicit and explicit memory for new associations in normal and amnesic subjects. *Journal of Experimental Psychology: Learning, Memory, and Cognition*, **11**, 501–18.

Helmholtz, H. (1962). Concerning the perceptions in general. In *Helmholtz on perception: Its physiology and development* (ed. N. Warren and R. Warren), pp. 171–203. New York: Riley.

Innes, M. (1941). *Appleby on Ararat.* Harmondsworth, Middlesex: Penguin.

Jacoby, L. L. (1983). Remembering the data: Analyzing interactive processes in reading. *Journal of Verbal Learning and Verbal Behavior*, **22**, 485–508.

Jacoby, L. L. (1991). A process dissociation framework: separating automatic from intentional uses of memory. *Journal of Memory and Language*, **30**, 513–41.

Jacoby, L. L. and **Brooks, L. R.** (1984). Nonanalytic cognition: Memory, perception and concept formation. *Psychology of Learning and Motivation*, **18**, 1–47.

Jacoby, L. L. and **Dallas, M.** (1981). On the relationship between autobiographical memory and perceptual learning. *Journal of Experimental Psychology: General*, **110**, 306–40.

Jacoby, L. L., Kelley, C. M., and **Dywan, J.** (1989). Memory attributions. In *Varieties of memory and consciousness: Essays in honor of Endel Tulving* (ed. H. L. Roediger and F. I. M. Craik), pp. 391–422. Hillsdale, NJ: Erlbaum.

Kanwisher, N. G. (1987). Repetition blindness: Type recognition without token individuation. *Cognition*, **27**, 117–43.

Knowlton, B. J. and **Squire, L. R.** (1994). The information acquired during artificial grammar learning. *Journal of Experimental Psychology: Learning, Memory, and Cognition*, **20**, 79–91.

Kolers, P. A. (1976). Remembering operations. *Memory and Cognition*, **12**, 347–55.

Kolers, P. A. and **Smythe, W. E.** (1984). Symbol manipulation: Alternatives to the computational view. *Journal of Verbal Learning and Verbal Behavior*, **21**, 289–314.

Leboe, J. P. and **Whittlesea, B. W. A.** (2002). The inferential basis of familiarity and recall: Evidence for a common underlying process. *Journal of Memory and Language*, **46**, 804–29.

Lindsay, D. S. and **Kelley, C. M.** (1996). Creating illusions of familiarity in a cued recall remember/know paradigm. *Journal of Memory and Language*, **35**, 197–211.

Mandler, G. (1991). Your face looks familiar but I can't remember your name: A review of dual process theory. In *Relating theory and data: essays on human memory in honor of Bennett B. Murdock* (ed. W. E. Hockley and S. Lewandowsky), pp. 207–25. Hillsdale, NJ: Erlbaum.

Masson, I. E. J. and **MacLeod, C. M.** (1992). Re-enacting the route to interpretation: Enhanced perceptual identification without prior perception. *Journal of Experimental Psychology: General*, **121**, 145–76.

Medin, D. L. and **Schaffer, M. M.** (1978). Context theory of classification learning. *Psychological Review*, **85**, 07–38.

Milliken, B. and **Joordens, S.** (1996). Negative priming without overt prime selection. *Canadian Journal of Experimental Psychology*, **50**, 333–46.

Milliken, B., Joordens, S., Merikle, P. M., and **Seiffert, A. E.** (1998). Selective attention: A re-evaluation of the implications of negative priming. *Psychological Review*, **105**, 203–29.

Morris, C. D., Bransford, J. D., and **Franks, J. J.** (1977). Levels of processing versus transfer-appropriate processing. *Journal of Verbal Learning and Verbal Behavior*, **16**, 519–33.

Neal, A. and **Hesketh, B.** (1997). Episodic knowledge and implicit learning. *Psychonomic Bulletin and Review*, **4**, 24–37.

Neill, W. T. (1977). Inhibition and facilitation processes in selective attention. *Journal of Experimental Psychology: Human Perception and Performance*, **3**, 444–50.

Neill, W. T. (1997). Episodic retrieval in negative priming and repetition priming. *Journal of Experimental Psychology: Learning, Memory, and Cognition*, **23**, 1291–305.

Neill, T. and **Valdes, L. A.** (1992). Persistence of negative priming: Steady state or decay? *Journal of Experimental Psychology: Learning, Memory, and Cognition*, **18**, 565–76.

Paap, K. R. and **Noel, R. W.** (1991). Dual-route models of print to sound: Still a good horse-race. *Psychological Research*, **53**, 13–24.

Perruchet, P. and **Pacteau, C.** (1991). Synthetic grammar learning: Implicit rule abstraction or explicit fragmentary knowledge? *Journal of Experimental Psychology: General*, **119**, 264–75.

Rajaram, S. (1993). Remembering and knowing: Two means of access to the personal past. *Memory and Cognition*, **21**, 89–102.

Reber, A. S. (1989). Implicit learning and tacit knowledge. *Journal of Experimental Psychology: General*, **118**, 219–35.

Reber, A. S. (1993). Implicit learning and tacit knowledge: An essay on the cognitive unconscious. New York: Oxford University Press.

Reber, A. S. and **Allen, R.** (1978). Analogic and abstraction strategies in synthetic grammar learning: A functionalist interpretation. *Cognition*, **6**, 193–221.

Roediger, H. L. and **Challis, B. H.** (1992). Effects of exact repetition and conceptual repetition on free recall and primed word fragment completion. *Journal of Experimental Psychology: Learning, Memory, and Cognition*, **18**, 3–14.

Roediger, H. L. and **McDermott, K. B.** (1993). Implicit memory in normal human subjects. In *Handbook of neuropsychology* (ed. F. Boller and J. Grafman), Vol. 8, pp. 63–131. New York: Elsevier.

Roediger, H. L. and **McDermott, K. B.** (1995). Creating false memories: Remembering words not presented in lists. *Journal of Experimental Psychology: Learning, Memory, and Cognition*, **21**, 803–14.

Rosch, E. H. (1978). Principles of categorization. In *Cognition and categorization* (ed. E. H. Rosch and B. B. Lloyd), pp. 27–48. Hillsdale, NJ: Erlbaum.

Schacter, D. L. (1990). Perceptual representation systems and implicit memory: Toward a resolution of the multiple memory systems debate. In *Development and neural bases of higher cognitive functions* (ed. A. Diamond). *Annals of the New York Academy of Sciences*, **608**, 543–72.

Schacter, D. L., Cooper, L. A., Delaney, S. M., Peterson, M. A., and Tharan, M. (1991). Implicit memory for impossible and possible objects: Constraints on the construction of structural descriptions. *Journal of Experimental Psychology: Learning, Memory, and Cognition*, **17**, 3–19.

Seamon, J. G., Marsh, R. L., and Brody, N. (1984). Critical importance of exposure duration for affective discrimination of stimuli that are not recognized. *Journal of Experimental Psychology: Learning, Memory, and Cognition*, **10**, 465–9.

Seamon, J. G., Williams, P. C., Crowley, M. J., Kim, I. J., Langer, S. A., Orne, P. J., *et al.* (1995). The mere exposure effect is based on implicit memory: Effects of stimulus type, encoding conditions, and number of exposures on recognition and affect judgments. *Journal of Experimental Psychology: Learning, Memory, and Cognition*, **21**, 711–21.

Shanks, D. R. and St. John, M. F. (1994). Characteristics of dissociable human learning systems. *Behavioral and Brain Sciences*, **17**, 367–95.

Stoppard, T. (1978). *Jumpers*. London: Faber.

Tipper, S. (1985). The negative priming effect: Inhibitory priming by ignored objects. *Quarterly Journal of Experimental Psychology*, **37A**, 571–90.

Tulving, E. (1983). *Elements of episodic memory*. Oxford: Clarendon Press.

Tulving, E. (1985). How many memory systems are there? *American Psychologist*, **40**, 385–98.

Tulving, E. and Thompson, D. M. (1973). Encoding specificity and retrieval processes in episodic memory. *Psychological Review*, **80**, 352–73.

Tulving, E., Schacter, D. L., and Stark, H. A. (1982). Priming effects in word-fragment completion are independent of recognition memory. *Journal of Experimental Psychology: Learning, Memory, and Cognition*, **8**, 336–42.

Vokey, J. R. and Brooks, L. R. (1992). The salience of item knowledge in learning artificial grammars. *Journal of Experimental Psychology: Learning, Memory, and Cognition*, **18**, 328–44.

Warrington, E. K. and Weiskrantz, L. (1970). The amnesic syndrome: consolidation or retrieval? *Nature*, **228**, 628–30.

Whittlesea, B. W. A. (1987). Preservation of specific experiences in the representation of general knowledge. *Journal of Experimental Psychology: Learning, Memory, and Cognition*, **13**, 3–17.

Whittlesea, B. W. A. (1993). Illusions of familiarity. *Journal of Experimental Psychology: Learning, Memory, and Cognition*, **19**, 1235–53.

Whittlesea, B. W. A. (1997). Production, evaluation and preservation of experiences: Constructive processing in remembering and performance tasks. In *The psychology of learning and motivation* (ed. D. L. Medin), **37**, 211–64. New York: Academic Press.

Whittlesea, B. W. A. and Brooks, L. R. (1988). Critical influence of particular experiences in the perception of letters, words, and phrases. *Memory and Cognition*, **16**, 387–99.

Whittlesea, B. W. A., Brooks, L. R., and Westcott, C. (1994). After the learning is over: Factors controlling the selective application of general and particular knowledge. *Journal of Experimental Psychology: Learning, Memory, and Cognition*, **20**, 259–74.

Whittlesea, B. W. A. and Cantwell, A. L. (1987). Enduring influence of the purpose of experiences: Encoding-retrieval interactions in word and pseudoword perception. *Memory and Cognition*, **15**, 465–72.

Whittlesea, B. W. A. and Dorken, M. D. (1993). Incidentally, things in general are particularly determined: An episodic-processing account of implicit learning. *Journal of Experimental Psychology: General*, 122, 227–48.

Whittlesea, B. W. A. and Dorken, M. D. (1997). Implicit learning: Indirect, not unconscious. *Psychonomic Bulletin and Review*, 4, 63–7.

Whittlesea, B. W. A., Dorken, M. D., and Podrouzek, K. W. (1995). Repeated events in rapid lists, Part 1: Encoding and representation. *Journal of Experimental Psychology: Learning, Memory, and Cognition*, 21, 1670–88.

Whittlesea, B. W. A. and Jacoby, L. L. (1990). Interaction of prime repetition with visual degradation: Is priming a retrieval phenomenon? *Journal of Memory and Language*, 29, 546–65.

Whittlesea, B. W. A. and Leboe, J. P. (2000). The heuristic basis of remembering and knowing: Fluency, generation, resemblance and coherence. *Journal of Experimental Psychology: General*, 129, 84–106.

Whittlesea, B. W. A., Leboe, J. P., and Milliken, B. (2002). Selective and non-selective transfer: Positive and negative priming in a multiple task environment. Manuscript submitted.

Whittlesea, B. W. A. and Price J. R. (2001). Implicit/explicit memory versus analytic/nonanalytic processing: Re-thinking the mere exposure effect. *Memory and Cognition*, 29, 234–46.

Whittlesea, B. W. A. and Williams, L. D. (1998). Why do strangers feel familiar, but friends don't? The unexpected basis of feelings of familiarity. *Acta Psychologica*, 98, 141–66.

Whittlesea, B. W. A. and Williams, L. D. (2000). The source of feelings of familiarity: The discrepancy-attribution hypothesis. *Journal of Experimental Psychology: Learning, Memory, and Cognition*, 26, 547–65.

Whittlesea, B. W. A. and Williams, L. D. (2001a). The discrepancy-attribution hypothesis, Part I: The heuristic basis of feelings of familiarity. *Journal of Experimental Psychology: Learning, Memory, and Cognition*, 27, 3–13.

Whittlesea, B. W. A. and Williams, L. D. (2001b). The discrepancy-attribution hypothesis, Part II: Expectation, uncertainty, surprise and feelings of familiarity. *Journal of Experimental Psychology: Learning, Memory, and Cognition*, 27, 14–33.

Whittlesea, B. W. A. and Wright, R. (1997). Implicit (and explicit) learning: Acting adaptively without knowing the consequences. *Journal of Experimental Psychology: Learning, Memory, and Cognition*, 23, 1–20.

Wright, R. and Whittlesea, B. W. A. (1998). Implicit learning of complex structures: Active adaptation and selective processing in acquisition and application. *Memory and Cognition*, 26, 402–20.

CHAPTER 12

ASSOCIATIVE REPETITION PRIMING: A SELECTIVE REVIEW AND THEORETICAL IMPLICATIONS

RENÉ ZEELENBERG, DIANE PECHER, AND
JEROEN G. W. RAAIJMAKERS

Introduction

An extensive body of research in the last two decades has shown that recent experiences can affect performance even when subjects are not instructed to remember these earlier experiences and even when subjects are not aware of these experiences. These so-called implicit memory phenomena are usually demonstrated by the *repetition priming* effect. Repetition priming refers to the finding that responses are faster and more accurate to stimuli that have been encountered recently than to stimuli that have not been encountered recently. For example, in a perceptual word identification task (Jacoby and Dallas, 1981; Salasoo *et al.*, 1985) subjects can more often correctly identify the briefly flashed target word if they have recently studied the target than if they have not studied the target. Comparable effects have been obtained in tasks such as picture identification (e.g., Rouder *et al.*, 2000), word stem completion (e.g., Graf *et al.*, 1984), and lexical decision (e.g., Bowers and Michita, 1998; Scarborough *et al.*, 1977), to name but a few.

The large majority of studies in the domain of implicit memory have concentrated on the effect of repeating stimuli in isolation. In the common repetition priming paradigm stimuli are presented one-by-one both during the study phase and the test phase. A question that has received relatively little attention is whether repetition priming can be obtained not only for single stimuli but also for *pairs* of stimuli. In other words, is there an advantage of repeating a stimulus pair over and above the effect of repeating the individual stimuli? Such an effect might be obtained if an associative bond between the members of a pair is formed (or strengthened) and if this bond is accessed at the time of test. Research in other domains of psychology indicates that associative relations between stimuli affects performance in a variety of tasks. For example, a large number of studies in the field of *associative priming* (e.g., Balota and Lorch, 1986; Evett and Humphreys, 1981; Meyer and Schvaneveldt, 1971; Neely, 1977) have shown that responses are faster and/or more accurate to targets that follow related words (e.g., *lion–tiger*) than to targets that follow unrelated words (e.g., *sand–tiger*). In a similar vein, a response to a target stimulus might be facilitated if the target is preceded by a stimulus with which it has been studied recently. A typical experiment investigating priming for pairs of words consists of a study phase in which a list of word pairs (e.g., *sand–tiger*) is presented. The study phase is followed by a test phase in which word pairs are presented in a priming paradigm. In the priming task, the prime words are presented either immediately prior to the target word or simultaneously with the target word. Priming is assessed by comparing performance for prime-target pairs that were studied together during the study phase to performance for pairs that were not studied together. In the remainder of this chapter we will refer to such a priming effect due to the repetition of a stimulus pair as *associative repetition priming*.[1]

As we will argue in this chapter, associative repetition priming is of interest not only from an empirical perspective, but also from a more theoretical perspective. In the second part of this chapter we will discuss some examples of how the finding of associative repetition priming can be used to answer some fundamental questions concerning the representation of knowledge in memory and the retrieval of knowledge from memory. More specifically, we will address three issues that have been raised in the literature. The first issue is whether or not the findings from the associative priming literature provide evidence supporting the hypothesis that there are separate episodic and semantic memory systems. Several researchers have proposed that associative repetition priming depends on the formation of new semantic traces. The most important difference between episodic and semantic memory is that episodic memories depend on the overlap in contextual information between study and test. Semantic memories on the other hand are assumed to be abstract and therefore contain no contextual information from the study episodes. By investigating the extent to which associative repetition priming is sensitive to contextual overlap between study and test we obtain evidence regarding the distinction between episodic and semantic memory.

The second issue is whether associative priming is subject to interference. Specifically, we will ask the question whether strengthening a word pair (e.g., *lion–mane*) interferes with priming for other word pairs (e.g., *lion–tiger*) sharing the same prime. This question touches on the fundamental issue whether activation processes in memory depend on relative or absolute associative strength (see Anderson and Bjork, 1994, for a discussion of different accounts of interference). As we will discuss, this question is difficult to answer using other methods. One problem is that there is no adequate method of assessing the strengths of the associations between words in memory. The finding of associative

---

[1] In previous research, associative repetition priming has often been termed *episodic priming* or *priming for new associations*. However, we prefer to use the term associative repetition priming (this term was to the best of our knowledge first used by Goshen-Gottstein and Moscovitch, 1995b). The term episodic priming might seem to suggest that different mechanisms are responsible for semantic and episodic priming effects which is not necessarily the case. The term priming for *new* associations seems to suggest that associative repetition priming is studied only for pre-experimentally unrelated word pairs. However, in some studies priming due to the repetition of word pairs is studied for both pre-experimentally unrelated (e.g., *sand–tiger*) and pre-experimentally related (e.g., *lion–tiger*) word pairs.

repetition priming, however, allows us to manipulate the structure of the associative network and hence to address the question whether activation depends on relative or absolute associative strength.

A final issue concerns the question whether priming in the standard associative priming paradigm (i.e., priming for related pairs such as *lion–tiger*) depends on associative or on semantic relations between words. Some researchers (e.g., Shelton and Martin, 1992) have argued that priming depends on associative relations between words that are the result of co-occurrence in natural language. Other researchers (e.g., Thompson-Schill *et al.*, 1998) have argued, however, that priming is not mediated by associative relations between words. According to these researchers, priming depends on semantic similarity which is usually defined as overlap in featural descriptions. We argue that the finding of associative repetition priming is problematic for those accounts proposing a strong distinction between associative and semantic relations, while arguing that associative relations do not cause priming.

It is important to first establish whether or not associative repetition priming in implicit memory tasks can be obtained before these theoretically more interesting questions can be answered. There is considerable disagreement among researchers whether or not truly implicit associative repetition priming occurs. Although associative repetition priming has been obtained in a number of studies (e.g., McKoon and Ratcliff, 1979, 1986) these results have often been dismissed on the ground that they were due to contamination by explicit retrieval attempts. In the first part of this chapter we will review the existing literature on associative repetition priming. Contrary to what is argued by many researchers we will argue that there is convincing evidence to support the notion that automatic associative repetition priming can be obtained. In the second part of the chapter will discuss how associative repetition priming can be used as a tool to provide some new insights in the theoretical issues mentioned above.

Associative repetition priming: a selective review of experimental results

Methodological issues

Before we turn to a review of the literature we will discuss two methodological concerns that have been raised by researchers investigating associative repetition priming. The first concern is the possible contamination of associative repetition priming effects with *explicit retrieval*. The second concern is the choice of an *appropriate baseline condition* against which associative repetition priming can be assessed.

Studies that investigate associative repetition priming usually consist of some sort of study phase in which word *pairs* are studied. After the study phase, word pairs are presented in an implicit memory task. The question of interest is whether responses to the target word are facilitated by presentation of the prime word with which the target was presented during study. Associative repetition priming effects have been studied in a number of different tasks including word stem completion (Graf and Schacter, 1987), lexical decision (Ratcliff and McKoon, 1979), and perceptual identification (Pecher and Raaijmakers,

1999). One complicating factor in the interpretation of associative repetition priming effects is that the effects might be due to contamination by explicit retrieval strategies (Carrol and Kirsner, 1982; Durgunoglu and Neely, 1987). The use of a word stem completion task in particular has been criticized (see for example, Reingold and Goshen-Gottstein, 1996) for its susceptibility to contamination by explicit retrieval strategies. In a word stem completion task word pairs (e.g., *sand–tiger*) are presented at study. At test the prime word is presented along with the word stem (i.e., *sand–ti_*). In an attempt to come up with a word to complete the stem subjects might try to remember the studied word pairs and hence the resulting priming effect could be due to contamination by explicit retrieval. In the present review of the literature we will therefore limit discussion to those studies that have used priming tasks such as lexical decision and perceptual identification in which contamination by explicit retrieval processes can be minimized or eliminated.[2]

It is important to note that the use of a priming task such as lexical decision in itself does not eliminate the use of explicit retrieval strategies that can cause priming effects. A large number of studies have been dedicated to investigate the nature of strategies that affect priming and the conditions under which these strategies occur in the 'standard' associative priming paradigm in which the effect of a semantically related prime on the processing of a subsequently presented target is investigated. One strategy that has been proposed is the *predictive* or *expectancy-based generation* strategy. The idea is that participants generate expectancies about the target after reading the prime (Becker, 1980; Neely, 1977; Posner and Snyder, 1975) and that the response to the target will be facilitated if the target matches the expectancy of the participant. In standard associative priming experiments the expectancy that is generated will be a semantic associate of the prime (e.g., the subject will expect the target *tiger* after reading the prime *lion*), however, expectancies may also play a role in associative repetition priming. After reading the prime the participant may try to generate the target with which the prime was paired during study. If the target is indeed the word with which the prime was paired during study such a strategy might result in facilitation for recently studied word pairs.

It is generally assumed that expectancy-based strategies are effective only at longer SOAs (Stimulus Onset Asynchrony: the time interval between the onset of the presentation of the prime and the onset of the presentation of the target), when participants have enough time to generate expectancies (e.g., Neely, 1977; den Heyer *et al.*, 1983). Therefore, the influence of these strategies can be eliminated by using a short SOA (i.e., an SOA of about 250 ms or shorter). Because the present paper is concerned primarily with fast-acting automatic priming we will focus on those experiments in which a short SOA was used although we will occasionally discuss results from experiments that used a longer SOA.

The second concern is the choice of an appropriate baseline condition. In order to determine whether study of a word pair results in associative repetition priming, performance

---

[2] Note that we do not argue that associative repetition priming in a task such as word stem completion is necessarily due to contamination by explicit retrieval strategies. However, because many researchers have argued that associative repetition priming effects are due to strategies we will focus on those studies that are least likely to be subject to this criticism.

Table 12.1 Types of conditions used in experiments investigating associative repetition priming

| Type of condition | Example | |
	Study pair	Test pair
Experimental		
Intact	sand–tiger	sand–tiger
Control		
Neutral	house–tiger	xxx–tiger
Non-studied prime	house–tiger	sand–tiger
Recombined	house–tiger	sand–tiger
	sand–chair	

in an *intact* condition (e.g., study: *sand–tiger*, test: *sand–tiger*) must be compared with performance in a *control* condition. Table 12.1 shows three different control conditions that have been used in studies that have investigated associative repetition priming. The first is a control condition in which a studied target is combined with a *neutral* prime such as the letter string *xxx* or the word *blank*. The use of a neutral prime is potentially problematic, because a neutral prime differs in many respects from the prime in the intact condition. First, neutral primes have no (*xxx*) or little (*blank*) meaning and are (in the case of *xxx*) orthographically less complex than prime words in the experimental condition. Second, neutral primes are usually not presented during the study phase. Third, during the test phase, the same neutral prime is used for all targets in the neutral condition while the primes in the experimental condition are unique for each target. Thus, during the test phase, the neutral prime is repeated whereas the prime in the intact condition is presented only once. All these differences between a neutral prime and the prime in the intact condition could potentially affect performance to the target and hence cause a difference in performance between the intact condition and the neutral condition.[3] Such a difference would *not* be due, however, to the *associative* relation between the prime and target in the intact condition but to differences in the processing of the primes between the intact and neutral conditions.

A similar problem occurs for a baseline with *non-studied primes*. In that case, the baseline consists of studied targets that are preceded by primes that were not presented during study. Because the primes in the experimental condition are studied, this non-studied prime condition, like the neutral condition, has the problem that the study status of the prime is confounded with the associative relation between the prime and the target. Therefore we cannot be sure that a difference between the intact condition and the control condition is due to repetition of the *association*. In fact, any difference could potentially be due to a difference in the study status of the prime between the two conditions. A study by

---

[3] A detailed discussion of the advantages and disadvantages of a neutral condition is beyond the scope of the present chapter. The reader is referred to Jonides and Mack (1984) for a review of possible problems in interpreting performance relative to a neutral condition.

Smith *et al.* (1989) shows that this concern is not purely hypothetical and that the study status of the prime can affect response times to the target. Smith *et al.* obtained a so-called *list wide priming* effect. Responses were faster to studied targets that were preceded by a studied prime than to studied targets preceded by a non-studied prime, irrespective of whether or not the studied prime and studied target were presented together (i.e., as a pair) during study.

We argue that to make the claim that associative repetition priming is obtained, the use of a *recombined* condition is preferable. In the recombined condition both the prime and target are presented during study although not as members of the same pair. This ensures that repetition status for individual words is identical for the intact condition and the control condition and that any difference between the two conditions is due to the repetition status of the *pair*. We will now turn to a selective review of empirical results related to the phenomenon of associative repetition priming.

Does automatic associative repetition priming exist?

We have identified 14 studies that have investigated associative repetition priming in paradigms that used a relatively short SOA so that the possibility of contamination by predictive strategies was minimized. As we will show, studies that have investigated associative repetition priming have produced somewhat mixed results. Several studies reported in the literature have failed to obtain consistent evidence for associative repetition priming and this has lead researchers to argue that automatic associative repetition priming does not occur. However, as we will argue, in most of these studies there are alternative explanations for the absence of associative repetition priming. Thus, our conclusion is that the currently available data support the notion that automatic associative repetition priming can be obtained.

Early evidence for associative repetition priming: McKoon and Ratcliff (1979, 1986)

The first study, to our knowledge, that investigated associative repetition priming was performed by McKoon and Ratcliff (1979). They used a repeated study-test procedure in which subjects studied short lists of paired-associates (e.g., *city–grass*) that were immediately followed by short lists of lexical decision trials with words presented one at a time. McKoon and Ratcliff obtained consistent evidence for associative repetition priming. Several researchers (Carrol and Kirsner, 1982; Durgunoglu and Neely, 1987; Goshen-Gottstein and Moscovitch, 1995b) have, however, argued that interpretation of the results is problematic because of methodological problems and that therefore the results do not unambiguously support the hypothesis that automatic associative repetition priming can be obtained.

One problem mentioned by those who criticized the McKoon and Ratcliff study is that the SOA was relatively long and that therefore the effect could be due to strategic recollective processes (i.e., predictive strategies). McKoon and Ratcliff used a continuous presentation paradigm in which participants respond by making a lexical decision to each stimulus in a long continuous sequence of stimuli. In this paradigm the stimulus on the previous presentation acts as a prime for the stimulus on the current presentation. McKoon and Ratcliff used a 250 ms and a 150 ms response stimulus interval (i.e., the time between the response to the stimulus on trial *n–1* and the onset of the presentation of the stimulus on trial *n*) in Experiments 1 and 2, respectively. Since response times were in the order of 550–600 ms this means that the nominal SOA was about 700–850 ms. It should be noted, however, that although the nominal SOA was indeed quite long it is difficult to compare it to the SOA in a standard presentation procedure in which a prime is briefly presented and followed by a target. The task demands are quite different in both tasks because in the standard paradigm subjects do not respond to the primes. To our knowledge, there are no available data that show that subjects use a predictive strategy in a continuous presentation paradigm. Thus, it is an open question whether under the conditions used by McKoon and Ratcliff (1979) subjects were able to employ predictive strategies. More important, in Experiment 3 McKoon and Ratcliff (1979) used a standard presentation procedure with a 300 ms SOA and again obtained an associative repetition priming effect. In order to provide further evidence against the claim that associative repetition priming depends on predictive strategies McKoon and Ratcliff (1986) performed a follow-up study in which they used a standard presentation paradigm with an even shorter SOA (i.e., 150–250 ms). In a series of experiments they consistently obtained evidence for associative repetition priming. Because associative repetition priming was obtained at a short SOA these results can not easily be attributed to predictive strategies.

A second problem mentioned by some researchers (e.g., Goshen-Gottstein and Moscovitch, 1995a) is that the McKoon and Ratcliff studies (1979, 1986) confounded associative repetition priming and standard associative priming. McKoon and Ratcliff chose the word pairs in the intact condition so that they would be easy to learn (e.g., *city–grass*, *angel–nurse*), but not associated according to free association norms. Although McKoon and Ratcliff used a recombined control condition, the intact and control condition were not completely counterbalanced. Thus, in the intact condition the word pair *angel–nurse* would be presented both at study and at test. In the recombined control condition, however, the word pairs *table–house* and *paper–nurse* would be presented at study and the recombined word pair *table–nurse* would be presented at test. Thus, the word pairs in the intact and control condition were *not* identical and therefore the difference between the intact condition and the recombined condition might have been due to a weak pre-existing relation between the prime and target in the intact condition instead of to a newly learned association (i.e., the 'associative repetition' priming effect might in fact have been a disguised standard associative priming effect). However, this possibility was ruled out by Experiment 3 of the McKoon and Ratcliff (1979) study that showed that a priming effect was obtained only for studied pairs and not for non-studied pairs (i.e., the priming effect was due to the recent study of the word pair and not to a pre-existing relation between the prime and the target). To summarize, the studies of McKoon and Ratcliff seem to provide solid evidence for automatic associative repetition priming.

Evidence against automatic associative repetition priming?

As we mentioned earlier, the conclusion of McKoon and Ratcliff (1979) that automatic associative repetition priming can be obtained has been questioned by several researchers.

In a number of studies that followed the McKoon and Ratcliff (1979) study researchers have failed to obtain consistent evidence for associative repetition priming. In one such a study Carroll and Kirsner (1982) presented word pairs in a lexical decision task. Each prime and target were presented twice. On the second presentation word pairs were either intact (i.e., the same pairing as on the previous presentation) or recombined (i.e., a different pairing). Carrol and Kirsner obtained significant associative repetition priming for intact pre-experimentally related word pairs (e.g., *lion–tiger*) but not for intact pre-experimentally unrelated word pairs (e.g., *sand–tiger*).

In another study, Den Heyer (1986) presented word pairs six times in a lexical decision task and observed that the associative repetition priming effect for repeated pairs depended on the SOA used in the experiment. Den Heyer obtained priming for repeated pairs compared to a neutral condition (in which the prime was the word *blank*) at a long SOA (550 ms) was used, but not at a short SOA (100 ms) and argued that the different results might be due to the use of predictive strategies at a long SOA. However, as we argued the use of neutral primes as a baseline is problematic. In one experiment, Den Heyer studied associative repetition priming with a recombined control condition using a long SOA and obtained a significant priming effect for both related and unrelated intact pairs. Unfortunately, Den Heyer did not use a recombined control condition at a short SOA. Therefore the results of this study are difficult to interpret.

Neely and Durgunoglu (1985) and Smith *et al.* (1989) also studied associative repetition priming, but contrary to the above mentioned studies used a paired-associate learning task during study. This made their study procedures more similar to those used by McKoon and Ratcliff (1979, 1986). However, both Smith *et al.* and Neely and Durgunoglu failed to find any evidence for associative repetition priming. Durgunoglu and Neely (1987) did obtain associative repetition priming but only under very specific conditions. Durgunoglu and Neely studied associative repetition priming at both a short (150 ms) SOA and a long (950 ms) SOA. We limit discussion to the results obtained at a short SOA. Durgunoglu and Neely manipulated a number of factors that might affect the occurrence of associative repetition priming and only obtained associative repetition priming when all word targets had been studied during the study phase and all nonwords had not been studied during the study phase (i.e., when there was perfect confounding between the study status and lexical status of the stimuli). This finding was attributed to a decision bias. Durgunoglu and Neely argued that the confounding of episodic status and lexical status encouraged participants to use episodic information in making a lexical decision to the target. For targets recognized as being presented during the study phase the participant would be biased towards a 'word' response and for targets not recognized as being presented during the study phase the participant would be biased towards a 'nonword' response.

In a further attempt to obtain associative repetition priming Dagenbach *et al.* (1990) presented word pairs in a very long study phase. Word pairs were studied extensively, especially in Experiments 3 and 4 in which word pairs were presented in a study phase that lasted five weeks. Every week subjects visited the laboratory and studied the same word pairs until they could correctly recall all pairings (i.e., until they could produce the target word upon presentation of the prime). This was followed by 10 additional practice trials for each word pair. Furthermore, during each week, between their visits to the laboratory, subjects were required to make sentences using the two words of the pair in a meaningful way. Dagenbach *et al.* obtained associative repetition priming only in Experiment 3 in which the primes were new *unfamiliar* words (i.e., very low frequency words that were not known to most subjects) learned in the experiment and the targets were familiar synonyms of the primes (e.g., *drupe–cherry*). In Experiment 4 using unrelated word pairs consisting of familiar words (e.g., *sand–tiger*) no significant associative repetition priming was obtained.

The studies just described all failed to obtain consistent evidence for associative repetition priming. A few remarks are in order, however, when evaluating these studies since the evidence against associative repetition priming provided by these studies is not as solid as it might seem at first sight. First, the studies of Carrol and Kirsner (1982) and Dagenbach *et al.* (1990) did not obtain significant associative repetition priming for semantically unrelated prime-target pairs (e.g., *sand–tiger*), but they did obtain associative repetition priming for semantically related prime-target pairs (e.g., *lion–tiger*). Thus, they did obtain some evidence for associative repetition priming. Moreover, even for semantically unrelated pairs there was an effect in the expected direction in both the Carrol and Kirsner and the Dagenbach *et al.* studies. However, given that the number of observations were quite small in both studies (12 observations per condition in both studies and only 14 subjects in the Carrol and Kirsner study and 12 subjects in the Dagenbach *et al.* study) the power to detect an effect was probably not very high.

Smith *et al.* (1989) failed to obtain associative repetition priming at both a short and a long SOA. Although we have not been able to come up with a good explanation for their failure to obtain an effect, the absence of associative repetition priming in their study at a long SOA is somewhat troublesome because other researchers (den Heyer, 1986, Durgunoglu and Neely, 1987) that did not obtain associative repetition priming at a short SOA obtained at least some indication of such an effect at longer SOAs.

Durgunoglu and Neely (1987) performed a large number of experiments and as mentioned above obtained evidence for associative repetition priming only under a limited set of conditions. It should be noted, however, that in *none* of the experiments they succeeded in obtaining standard associative priming (i.e., priming for semantically related prime-target pairs such as *lion–tiger*) at a short SOA. The absence of standard associative priming is quite puzzling and indicates that one should be cautious interpreting the absence of associative repetition priming in this study.

To conclude, the studies discussed in this section are often cited as providing evidence against the notion of automatic associative repetition priming. We argue, however, that failure to find consistent evidence for associative repetition priming might have been due to methodological problems and do not provide convincing evidence against the occurrence of automatic associative repetition priming. We will now turn to more recent studies that succeeded in obtaining associative repetition priming.

Recent evidence for associative repetition priming

Goshen-Gottstein and Moscovitch (1995b) argued that automatic associative repetition priming can be obtained but that it depends on the preservation of the presentation format between study and test. During study, pairs of words were presented and subjects were asked to form sentences with the two words of each pair. During test, the words of a pair were presented simultaneously, and subjects responded 'yes' if *both* words were existing words and 'no' otherwise. With this procedure Goshen-Gottstein and Moscovitch (1995a, Experiment 1) obtained associative repetition priming for pre-experimentally unrelated pairs. Encoding instructions during study did not affect associative repetition priming: under both shallow (vowel counting) and deep (sentence generation) instructions an associative repetition priming effect was obtained. In Experiment 2 (Goshen-Gottstein and Moscovitch, 1995a), the presentation procedure at test was changed so that the prime and the target were presented sequentially. As in Experiment 1, subjects decided if both words (i.e., the prime *and* the target) were existing words or not. Consistent with the idea that preservation of the perceptual format is important, no associative repetition priming was obtained when the prime and target were presented sequentially at test. Another experiment (Goshen-Gottstein and Moscovitch, 1995b, Experiment 1) provided further evidence that preservation of the perceptual format affects associative repetition priming. At test word pairs were presented visually and associative repetition priming was present for word pairs that were also presented visually during study but absent for word pairs that were presented auditorily during study. In sum, the experiments of Goshen-Gottstein and Moscovitch show that reliable associative repetition priming can be obtained after a single study trial if the perceptual format is maintained from study to test.

In our laboratory we have obtained associative repetition priming in a variety of priming tasks. The experiments in our laboratory differ from most other studies in that word pairs are usually presented *multiple* times during the study phase. In most of our experiments word pairs are presented in both an explicit paired-associate learning task and in a priming task (e.g., lexical decision) during study. At test, responses to intact studied pairs are compared to a baseline of recombined pairs. We have been especially concerned with using procedures to prevent strategies that might influence the associative repetition effect. In addition to lexical decision we have also investigated associative repetition priming in perceptual identification and animacy decision. This was done because some researchers have argued that 'standard' associative priming effects might be (partially) due to a so-called relatedness checking strategy, even with a short SOA (Balota and Lorch, 1986; Shelton and Martin, 1992). That is, in the lexical decision task, subjects make a binary decision about the lexical status of the target stimulus. An important characteristic of the primed lexical decision task is that there is a correlation between the relatedness of prime and target and the correct response. If the prime and target are semantically related the target must be a word, because nonwords are not related to words. The relatedness checking strategy account assumes that subjects use this correlation in the decision process. Subjects will be biased to give a 'word' response if they detect a relation between prime and target. It is further assumed that the absence of a relation will bias subjects to give a 'nonword' response. A similar strategy might play a role in producing associative repetition priming when there is a correlation between the study status of a word pair and the response. As we mentioned earlier, consistent with such a strategy, Durgunoglu and Neely (1987) obtained associative repetition priming only when there was a confounding between the study status and lexical status of the stimuli (i.e., when all words were studied and all nonwords were not studied).[4]

In a number of recent studies we have investigated associative repetition priming in tasks in which the influence of possible relatedness checking strategies is eliminated. One such a task that we have used is the animacy decision task. In this task subjects decide whether a word refers to a living entity (e.g., *tiger*) or a non-living entity (e.g., *sand*). The presentation procedure in this task is similar to that of lexical decision. In one study (Pecher and Raaijmakers, 2001) we used a 260 ms SOA and responses were made to the target (but not to the prime). Relatedness checking strategies are not effective in an animacy decision task, because relatedness is not correlated with the response to the target. That is because related word pairs can be animate (*doctor–nurse*), inanimate (*thread–needle*), or mixed (*baker–bread, school–teacher*). Consequently a relation between prime and target gives no information about which response should be given (see McRae *et al.*, 1997, for a similar argument). The same applies to studied word pairs. Targets of studied word pairs can be animate or inanimate, hence study status and response are not confounded. We obtained associative repetition priming in several experiments using the animacy decision task (Pecher and Raaijmakers, 2001).

Another task that we used is masked perceptual identification. Our presentation procedure was based on the four-field paradigm developed by Evett and Humphreys (1981). In this paradigm four stimuli are presented on each trial: a forward pattern mask, the prime, the target, and a backward pattern mask. The task of the subject is to try to identify both the prime and target. However, subjects are usually unable to identify the prime. The presentation time is adjusted individually and set at a duration at which the subject can correctly identify the target on approximately 40% of the trials. In this task a standard associative priming effect is obtained: the probability of correctly identifying the target is higher if it is preceded by an associatively related prime than if preceded by an unrelated prime. This priming effect is not likely contaminated by strategies because the prime is masked (Pecher *et al.*, 2001 obtained experimental evidence supporting this claim). Using the perceptual identification task we also obtained an associative repetition priming effect (Pecher and Raaijmakers, 1999; Zeelenberg, 1998, Chapter 3). These results from the animacy decision and the perceptual identification experiments provide additional evidence that associative repetition priming can be obtained under conditions that eliminate contamination by explicit retrieval strategies.

In a series of experiments Schrijnemakers and Raaijmakers (1997), and Pecher and Raaijmakers (1999) studied whether there was transfer of associative repetition priming from a particular study task to another test task. Schrijnemakers and Raaijmakers (1997, Experiment 3) presented prime-target pairs nine times distributed over three different sessions with time intervals of one or two days. On each presentation the subject first made

---

[4] It should be noted, however, that McKoon and Ratcliff (1979, Experiment 2) did find associative repetition priming even when nonwords were presented during study. Evidence obtained in our laboratory (Zeelenberg, 1998, Chapter 3) also shows that associative repetition priming can be obtained when there is no perfect correlation between the study status and lexical status of stimuli.

a lexical decision to the target, and then studied the complete word pair for a later cued recall test. At the end of the experiment associative repetition priming was tested in both lexical decision and perceptual identification. Schrijnemakers and Raaijmakers observed associative repetition priming in both tasks. However, only for the pre-experimentally unrelated word pairs did they use the correct recombined baseline. Therefore, Pecher and Raaijmakers (1999, Experiment 1) tried to replicate their results, this time using a recombined baseline for all types of word pairs. They obtained associative repetition priming only for pre-experimentally unrelated word pairs in lexical decision. In the perceptual identification task there was a small associative repetition priming effect, but it was only marginally significant. In Experiment 2, Pecher and Raaijmakers (1999) used a perceptual identification task during study. Word pairs were presented four times in the perceptual identification task and four times in a paired-associate study task. In the test phase, reliable associative repetition priming was obtained in perceptual identification but not in a lexical decision task with masked primes (although there was a small effect in the expected direction). In a recent study, Pecher and Raaijmakers (2001) used an animacy decision task at study. During the study phase word pairs were presented in animacy decision, paired-associate study, or both. They observed associative repetition priming only for word pairs that had been presented in the animacy decision task during study, but not for word pairs that had been presented only in a paired-associate learning task. In sum, these experiments suggest that the associative repetition priming effect depends on the overlap in processes at study and test.

Concluding remarks regarding experimental findings

Our review shows that associative repetition priming has been obtained in a large number of experiments. Although associative repetition priming has not been obtained in every single experiment we have argued that in many such cases the absence of associative repetition priming might have been due to methodological problems. All in all there is plenty of evidence that associative repetition priming can be obtained under conditions in which it is unlikely that the results were due to contamination with explicit retrieval strategies. This is an important conclusion because many researchers have argued that associative repetition priming effects are the result of strategies.

Although we do argue that automatic associative repetition priming can be obtained, this is not to say, however, that the effect is as easy to find as 'standard' word repetition priming. Two factors may be important in obtaining associative repetition priming. The first factor is the amount of study given to a word pair in the study phase. We have generally been successful in obtaining associative repetition priming in our laboratory using multiple study trials. In other studies (with the exceptions of the studies by Dagenbach et al., 1989 and den Heyer, 1986) word pairs are presented only once. It seems reasonable to assume that the effect of prior study is larger after several study trials then after one study trial.

The second factor that may enhance the likelihood of finding associative repetition priming is the overlap between study procedure and test procedure. Goshen-Gottstein and Moscovitch (1995a, b) showed that associative repetition priming was present when the spatio-temporal configuration of the word pair was identical at study and test. Associative repetition priming was obtained when both words of the pair were presented simultaneously at study and test, but not when they were presented simultaneously at study and sequentially at test. Associative repetition priming was also absent when the study modality changed from auditory presentation at study to visual presentation at test.[5] In our laboratory we have always presented word pairs at study both in a paired-associate learning task as well as in a priming task (e.g., lexical decision). Our consistent success in obtaining associative repetition priming might be (partially) due to the presentation of the word pairs in the priming task. Consistent with this idea is the finding that the associative repetition priming effect is reduced when the priming task changed from study to test (Pecher and Raaijmakers, 1999, 2001; Schrijnemakers and Raaijmakers, 1997).

Goshen-Gottstein and Moscovitch concluded from their studies that associative repetition priming is perceptually based. According to their perceptual contiguity hypothesis associative repetition priming should be obtained only when the two words of a pair are presented simultaneously. However, in several studies (Pecher and Raaijmakers, 1999, 2001; Zeelenberg, 1998) we did obtain reliable associative repetition priming, despite the fact that prime and target were presented sequentially. Thus, it is not the case that associative repetition priming relies *solely* on perceptual factors. Recently, we (Pecher and Raaijmakers, 2001) have shown that *semantic* variables can also influence the associative repetition priming effect. In this experiment we studied associative repetition priming in an animacy decision task and manipulated the type of processing that was done during the study task. The study task focused on either semantic or on orthographic features of the word pairs, and we manipulated whether the study task was aimed at forming a unitized representation or not. Associative repetition priming was obtained only if the study task focused on semantic features and promoted forming a unitized representation of the prime-target pair. These results show the importance of the type of processing that is done during study for the occurrence of an associative repetition priming effect.

Theoretical implications

In the first part of this chapter we have reviewed the literature on associative repetition priming and concluded that associative repetition priming effects can be obtained even under conditions that eliminate contamination by explicit retrieval strategies. Our aim in the second part of this chapter is to indicate how the associative repetition priming effect might be used as a tool to find an answer to some theoretical questions that have been difficult to answer with other procedures.

---

[5] Note, however, that this study confounded modality of presentation and temporal aspects of the presentation because for the auditory presentation condition words were presented sequentially at study and simultaneously at test whereas for the visual presentation condition the words of a pair were presented simultaneously both at study and test.

The distinction between episodic and semantic memory

The associative repetition effect has been used to study how new information is added to semantic memory. There are basically two views on the storage of information in semantic memory. One is the multiple memory systems view, which assumes that semantic knowledge is stored separate from other types of knowledge such as episodic or procedural knowledge (Tulving, 1984; Tulving and Schacter, 1990). These theories usually do not specify the exact processes that are involved in storing information, but the idea seems to be that whenever there is an experience, two separate memories are stored, one in episodic and one in semantic memory. Episodic memory consists of memories for specific events that are organized according to their temporal and spatial characteristics. Semantic memory consists of more abstract knowledge such as word meanings and the relations among words. Episodic memory is used in tasks such as recognition and recall, where explicit reference is made to the study episode. Semantic memory is used in tasks such as lexical decision, perceptual identification, or animacy decision, where there is no reference to the study episode. Another version of the multiple memory systems theory has distinguished yet another memory system, the perceptual representation system (Tulving and Schacter, 1990). This system is assumed to be responsible for repetition priming or implicit memory effects. However, according to Tulving and Schacter, priming in conceptual tests is not explained by this system and thus has to be located in semantic memory.

The opposite view is that only one type of knowledge is stored in memory (Anderson and Ross, 1980; Hintzman, 1986; McKoon et al., 1986) and that more general or abstract information is calculated by the system as it is needed. For example, in Hintzman's model, a memory trace is stored for each experience. If an item, for example a word, is encountered several times it is stored on each occurrence together with some context features. If memory is probed with a cue that includes context, a specific trace that matches the context will be activated. However, if the cue only includes the word, all traces that contain the word are activated and the resulting content is more abstract (i.e., is averaged over different prior contexts). Thus, the system calculates more or less abstract information according to the cue that is used to access memory. There are no separate memory systems for episodic and semantic knowledge.

Dagenbach et al. (1990) studied associative repetition priming from the multiple memory systems view. They argued that associative repetition priming is found if these new associations have been added to semantic memory. They assumed that automatic priming in lexical decision is the result of associations in semantic memory and that automatic priming will not be found if the words are associated only in episodic memory. Thus, if priming is found for new associations, this is evidence that these new associations are integrated into semantic memory. McKoon and Ratcliff (1979, 1986), however, argued that if priming is found for new associations, this should be considered as evidence against the *distinction* between episodic and semantic memory. According to them if the two memory systems are separate it should be possible to access episodic and semantic information independently. Therefore, a semantic memory task such as lexical decision should not be affected by episodic information (i.e., there should be no priming for new associations). On the other hand, McKoon and Ratcliff argued that a theory that assumes that episodic and semantic information are stored in the same memory system does predict that both episodic and semantic information can affect performance in the same task.

The multiple memory systems view in which associative priming is mediated by the semantic system predicts that the associative repetition effect should not be sensitive to context. It has been assumed that semantic memory is an abstraction of specific episodes, in other words, that semantic memory develops out of repeated experiences (Dagenbach *et al.*, 1990). If information in semantic memory is abstract, retrieval should be context-independent. If a word is activated, its associates also become activated to some degree, and this should not depend on the context in which that word is presented. Similarly, information that is strongly related to a specific context should not be integrated into semantic memory. However, our results show that this is not always true. Our finding of automatic associative repetition priming in semantic memory tasks indicates that these new associations are integrated in semantic memory. Yet, we (Pecher and Raaijmakers, 1999, 2001; Schrijnemakers and Raaijmakers, 1997) found that prior context plays an important role in finding associative repetition priming. These results pose problems for theories that assume that semantic knowledge is abstract and does not contain information about the context in which it is encountered (Dagenbach *et al.*, 1990; Tulving, 1983, 1984). Rather, the results suggest that semantic memory does not consist of abstract information that is retrieved whenever a word is activated, but that it is more flexible. Storage and retrieval of information from semantic memory is dependent on the context in which a word is encountered. Other studies have also shown that both the present context (McKoon and Ratcliff, 1995) and recent experiences with words (Dagenbach *et al.*, 1989; Pecher *et al.*, 1998) affect what aspects of a word's meaning are activated at a certain moment.

We (Pecher and Raaijmakers, 1999, 2001) have argued that associative repetition priming is obtained because the prime affects the interpretation of the target. Thus, for intact pairs the interpretation of the target is more similar at study and test than for recombined pairs. The task in which a word pair is presented will also affect this interpretation. If the word pair has been presented in the same task during study and test, the effect of the prime on the interpretation of the target during study is more relevant to the test task. In general, the more similar the study and test task are, the larger the overlap in interpretation of the target between study and test. Such a mechanism goes against the view of semantic memory as abstract and context-independent, and might be easier to accommodate into theories that do not make a distinction between semantic and episodic information.

Associative priming and interference

Interference effects have been obtained in a variety of memory tasks. The best known example is probably that of interference in paired-associate learning. In the retroactive interference paradigm participants first learn a list of A–B pairs. Participants in the interference group then learn a list of A–C pairs involving the same stimulus words as the pairs on the first list. For the participants in the control group the second list consists of C–D pairs having no stimulus words in common with the pairs on the first list. Participants are tested on their memory for the pairs on the first list. The stimulus term of each pair is presented and participants are required to produce the corresponding first-list response. Cued recall performance is typically lower for participants in the interference group than for participants in the control group (McGovern, 1964; also see Barnes and Underwood, 1959). Although there are important differences between paired-associate learning and associative priming they are similar in that both depend on the existence of associations between words. An interesting question is whether interference effects analogous to those obtained in paired-associate learning are also obtained in associative priming.

The dominant theory of associative priming, the spreading activation theory does indeed predict such an interference effect. According to spreading activation theories (Anderson, 1983; Collins and Loftus, 1975) words are represented by nodes in an associative network. The nodes representing related words are connected to each other by links. When a word is presented, the node representing that word is activated and activation spreads out in a parallel fashion along the links from the source node to related nodes. Associative priming occurs because the node representing the target receives activation from the node representing the prime. This results in an enhanced activation level of the target representation which speeds responding. In the ACT* model (Anderson, 1983), the amount of activation spreading from the source node to a related node depends on two factors, the strength of the node (which is a function of the number of presentations) and the number of other nodes connected to the source node. The stronger the association between two nodes A–B the more activation will spread from the source node A to the related node B. The larger the number of other nodes that are connected to the source node and the larger the strength of these nodes the *less* activation will spread from A to B. Thus, spreading activation theories predict that the amount by which word A activates word B depends on the strength of the association A–B *relative* to all associations A–X.

The assumption that activation processes depend on relative associative strength is difficult to test in the context of associative priming because how are we to know the associative strengths in the network that supports the occurrence of priming? Associative strengths are usually inferred from free association norms. However, these norms are inherently based on the relative strength of the association. An example will help to explain the problem in assessing the absolute associative strength of a word pair. Suppose a word pair A–B has an association frequency of 25%, that is in a free association task 25% of the participants respond with word B when asked to provide the first word that comes to mind when given the cue word A. Suppose another word pair D–E also has an association frequency of 25%. Does this mean that the *absolute* associative strengths of both word pairs are identical? Not necessarily! The absolute associative strength of the word pair A–B might in fact be considerably stronger than that of D–E, but the association *frequencies* of A–B and D–E might be equally large because A–B has *more* or *stronger* competitors that D–E. In the example shown in Figure 12.1 the absolute associative strength A–B is five times larger than that of D–E (this might for example be due to the fact that the words of the pair A–B have been encountered more often in close proximity than the words of the pair D–E). However, A–B has a stronger competitor than D–E. Free association does not reflect the absolute associative strength of an association because whenever a cue word is presented for free association multiple words might be activated. In order to emit a response one of the words has to be selected. Assuming that the probability of producing a certain word in free association depends on the strength of the association between the cue word (e.g., A) and the related word (e.g., B) relative to the other words (e.g., C) related to the cue, the

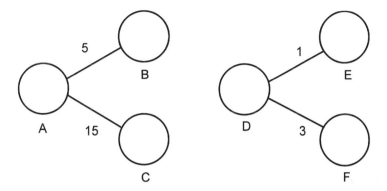

Figure 12.1 Example showing associative structures for word A, B, C and D, E, F. The numbers indicate the absolute associative strengths between two words.

probability of generating B to A is identical to that of generating E to D (i.e., 25% in both cases). Thus even though in the example the absolute associative strength of A–B is much larger than that of D–E, the association frequencies of B and E are identical. Thus, testing the relative strength assumption by using word pairs based on their association frequency is a troublesome enterprise.

An alternative approach to test the assumption that activation processes depend on relative associative strength is by manipulating the strengths in the associative network. The advantage of such an approach is that one has experimental control over the structure of the associative network and does not have to rely on measures of associative strength that are inherently based on the relative associative strength. We tested the relative strength assumption in a series of experiments. In our experiments, the interfering association A–C was strengthened in the study phase of the experiment. In the test phase, the effect of strengthening an interfering association on the priming effect for the test pair A–B was assessed. As a result of strengthening the association A–C the *relative* strength of A–B decreases. The prediction therefore is that if the activation process depends on relative associative strength the priming effect for the pair A–B (e.g., *lion–tiger*) should decrease if the association A–C (e.g., *lion–mane*) is strengthened.

We (Zeelenberg, 1998) tested the relative strength assumption in several experiments, using a lexical decision task with a short 200 ms SOA and a masked perceptual identification task. In both experiments a regular associative priming effect was found (i.e., performance was better for the word pair *lion–tiger* than for the pair *sand–tiger*). We also obtained an associative repetition priming effect (i.e., performance was better for repeated intact word pairs then for recombined word pairs). However, we did not obtain an interference effect. Thus strengthening the word pair *lion–mane* did not affect the priming effect for the pair *lion–tiger*. This finding is problematic for the claim that activation processes depend on the relative associative strength and seems to indicate that automatic activation processes depend on the absolute associative strength.

One might wonder how this finding might be reconciled with the finding of interference in a number of other paradigms. A detailed description of such an explanation is clearly beyond the scope of this chapter, but a brief discussion of it is in order. An important feature of this explanation is the distinction between activation and selection processes. Our explanation assumes that in many tasks performance does not directly reflect the activation level. For example, in a standard cued-recall task a stimulus cue (usually a word) is provided and the subject has to generate the word corresponding to the stimulus (i.e., the word with which the cue was paired during study). One problem the subject faces in a cued-recall task is that the cue might activate several words instead of only one, especially if the cue was studied with more than one response word as is the case in an interference paradigm. If it is assumed that one of the activated words must be selected for further processing (see for example Raaijmakers and Shiffrin, 1981) then the fact that other words are associated with the cue will decrease the chance of selecting the correct word and hence impair performance. Such a decrease in performance does not, however, mean that the activation level of the words associated to the cue decreases. Instead if it is assumed that *selection* depends on the relative associative strength than the probability of selecting a particular word will decrease as more words are associated to the cue. Thus, there is no need to assume that the *activation* depends on relative associative strength.

In a priming task such as naming, lexical decision, or perceptual identification the influence of selection processes is greatly reduced because subjects do not have to respond to the target on the basis of the prime information alone (which is the case in a task like cued-recall). Instead the target is presented and the subject has to respond to the target. The prime-target association may facilitate responding to the target, but the subject's task is to respond to the target and the associative relation does not have to be verified. Thus, on a theoretical level the absence of interference effects in associative priming is not inconsistent with the finding of interference in other paradigms. It suggests that *activation* processes are dependent on the *absolute* strength of associations, whereas *selection* processes are dependent on the *relative* strength.

The critical difference between the above proposal and spreading activation theory is the point in processing at which relative strength comes into play. In this respect it is useful to discuss a taxonomy proposed by Anderson and Bjork (1994) in some detail. Anderson and Bjork distinguished between resource diffusion models and occlusion models. In resource diffusion models such as ACT*, a limited amount of activation spreads out from the source node to related nodes. Strengthening an association results in more activation spreading from the source node to the strengthened node at the expense of less activation spreading to the other nodes. Thus, in resource diffusion models the relative strength exerts its influence at a very early stage in the retrieval process. Interference is, therefore, an almost inevitable prediction of resource diffusion models, because the cause of interference is located in a very early stage of processing. In occlusion models such as SAM (Mensink and Raaijmakers, 1988; Raaijmakers and Shiffrin, 1980), however, the cause of interference is located in a later stage of processing. In occlusion models, strengthening an association does not result in less activation going to non-strengthened items. The 'bottleneck' in occlusion models is located in the competition for access to further processing mechanisms. If, however, the competition for access to further processing mechanisms is resolved by the test procedure then occlusion models need not predict interference. The absence of interference in our experiments is therefore not problematic for occlusion models, if it is assumed that the influence of selection processes was greatly reduced by our test procedures. Thus, the lack of interference effects in associative priming tasks suggests that the bottleneck is not in the activation of information in memory, but in the selection of items for further processing.

Priming and the distinction between associative and semantic relations

Several researchers have made a distinction between *associative* or *semantic* relations between words. For example, according to Thompson-Schill *et al.* (1998; see also Shelton and Martin, 1992) associative relations, as measured by free association, reflect word use rather than word meaning. An associative relation between words may develop if two words co-occur relatively frequently in the use of language. It is further assumed that associative relations are represented at a *lexical* level of representation. Semantic relations on the other hand are assumed to reflect similarity in *meaning* or overlap in featural descriptions.

The distinction between associative and semantic relations has led to research investigating whether automatic priming is mediated by associative or semantic relations between words (Fischler, 1977; Lupker, 1984). Recently this issue has regained the interest of the field. Shelton and Martin (1992) reported automatic priming for associatively related word pairs (e.g., *boy–girl*) but not for semantically related word pairs that are not associated according to free association norms (e.g., *nose–hand*). They argued that semantic relations do not support *automatic* priming and that priming in the lexical decision task occurs at a lexical level of representation and not at a semantic level.

Thompson-Schill *et al.* (1998) disputed Shelton and Martin's (1992) claim that semantic relations do not support automatic priming. According to Thompson-Schill *et al.*:

> a closer examination of their stimuli reveals an important confound in their experiments: the unassociated word pairs (e.g., 'dirt–cement', 'bird–fish', 'duck–cow') seem to have far fewer semantic features in common than do the associated word pairs (e.g., 'hill–mountain', 'blanket–sheet', 'road–street'). In other words, the authors did not adequately equate semantic similarity in their two lists of stimuli. (p. 442)

Several other researchers (Lund *et al.*, 1995; McRae and Boisvert, 1998) have also disputed the conclusions of Shelton and Martin on the ground that in their study the associatively related pairs were more semantically similar than the semantically related but associatively unrelated pairs. The common claim of these researchers is that automatic priming effects can be based on semantic relations.

Thompson-Schill *et al.* (1998) went one step further and explicitly argued that automatic priming is mediated by semantic relations, but *not* by associative relations. This claim was based on the results of their Experiment 3. This experiment included word pairs that according to Thompson-Schill *et al.* were associatively related but semantically unrelated (e.g., *foot–note*). No priming was obtained for these word pairs. On the basis of these results, Thompson-Schill *et al.* concluded that a semantic relation between prime and target is not only sufficient to produce automatic priming, but that a semantic relation is *necessary* to produce automatic priming.

Unfortunately, the claim that *associative* relations are not sufficient to produce priming is not very convincing because of a methodological flaw, as is revealed by a closer look at their stimuli. We obtained the free association frequencies of the word pairs used by Thompson-Schill *et al.* (1998) from published free association norms (Nelson *et al.*, 1994). The association norms showed that the word pairs in the associatively related but semantically unrelated condition were in fact not or only very weakly associated (the mean forward associative strength was .03 and the mean backward associative strength was .00). The semantically related word pairs had much stronger associations. These word pairs were unidirectionaly associated and had an mean associative strength of .38 (in either the forward or the backward direction). Thus, the Thompson-Schill *et al.* study was not a particularly fair test of the influence of associative relations on automatic priming. On the basis of these results, the conclusion that a semantic relation between prime and target is *necessary* to produce automatic priming is unwarranted.

The issue of whether associative or semantic relations support automatic priming is related to associative repetition priming because many researchers (e.g., Thompson-Schill *et al.*, 1998) have argued that associative relations are based on co-occurrence. Therefore, if Thompson-Schill *et al.* are correct in their claim that associative relations do not support automatic priming effects associative repetition priming should not be obtained, especially not for pre-experimentally unrelated word pairs. The association between such a pair is mainly based on their co-occurrence in the study task, and not on semantic similarity. However, as we discussed earlier, there are now several studies that show that such effects can be obtained under conditions that are associated with automatic processes. Thus contrary to the claim of Thompson-Schill *et al.* there is ample evidence that associative relations support automatic priming.

Summary and conclusions

In the present chapter we have reviewed empirical studies on associative repetition priming. Although earlier findings of associative repetition priming have been attributed to explicit retrieval strategies we have argued that recent studies provide enough evidence to support the view that the repetition of word pairs results in automatic priming. In the second part of the chapter we have provided some examples that show how the finding of associative repetition priming may be used to answer theoretical questions about the representations and processes involved in memory performance. We have shown how the associative repetition priming effect can be used to study the distinction between episodic and semantic memory. We have argued that although both the multiple memory systems view and the single memory systems view can explain associative repetition priming, the multiple memory systems view will have more difficulty doing so. Especially the influence of context is not a priori predicted by the multiple memory systems view. A second issue we have discussed was the role of relative and absolute associative strengths in priming tasks. The results suggest that whereas *selection* processes are dependent on *relative* associative strength, *activation* processes are dependent on *absolute* associative strength. Finally, we have argued that the finding of associative repetition priming is problematic for theories that make a strong distinction between semantic and associative relations and that argue that semantic relations support priming while associative relations do not support priming.

References

Anderson, J. R. (1983). A spreading activation theory of memory. *Journal of Verbal Learning and Verbal Behavior*, **22**, 261–95.

Anderson, J. R. and Ross, B. E. (1980). Evidence against a semantic-episodic distinction. *Journal of Experimental Psychology: Human Learning and Memory*, **6**, 441–66.

Anderson, M. C. and Bjork, R. A. (1994). Mechanisms of inhibition in long-term memory: A new taxonomy. In *Inhibitory processes in attention, memory, and language* (ed. D. Dagenbach and T. Carr), pp. 265–325. San Diego, CA: Academic Press.

Balota, D. A. and Lorch, R. F. (1986). Depth of automatic spreading activation: Mediated priming effects in pronunciation but not in lexical decision. *Journal of Experimental Psychology: Learning, Memory, and Cognition*, **12**, 336–45.

Barnes, J. M. and Underwood, B. J. (1959). 'Fate' of first-list associations in transfer theory. *Journal of Experimental Psychology*, **58**, 97–105.

Becker, C. A. (1980). Semantic context effects in visual word recognition: An analysis of semantic strategies. *Memory and Cognition*, **8**, 493–512.

Bowers, J. S. and Michita, Y. (1998). An investigation into the structure and acquisition of orthographic knowledge: Evidence from cross-script Kanji-Hiragana priming. *Psychonomic Bulletin and Review*, **5**, 259–64.

Carroll, M. and Kirsner, K. (1982). Context and repetition effects in lexical decision and recognition memory. *Journal of Verbal Learning and Verbal Behavior*, **21**, 55–69.

Collins, A. M. and Loftus, E. F. (1975). A spreading activation theory of semantic memory. *Psychological Review*, **82**, 407–28.

Dagenbach, D., Carr, T. H., and Wilhelmsen, A. (1989). Task-induced strategies and near-threshold priming: Conscious influences on unconscious perception. *Journal of Memory and Language*, **28**, 412–43.

Dagenbach, D., Horst, S., and Carr, T. H. (1990). Adding new information to semantic memory: How much learning is enough to produce automatic priming? *Journal of Experimental Psychology: Learning, Memory, and Cognition*, **16**, 581–91.

den Heyer, K. (1986). Manipulating attention-induced priming in a lexical-decision task by means of repeated prime-target presentations. *Journal of Memory and Language*, **25**, 19–42.

den Heyer, K., Briand, K., and Dannenbring, G. L. (1983). Strategic factors in a lexical decision task: Evidence for automatic and attention-driven processes. *Memory and Cognition*, **11**, 374–81.

Durgunoglu, A. Y. and Neely, J. H. (1987). On obtaining episodic priming in a lexical decision task following paired-associate learning. *Journal of Experimental Psychology: Learning, Memory, and Cognition*, **13**, 206–22.

Evett, L. J. and Humphreys, G. W. (1981). The use of abstract graphemic information in lexical access. *Quarterly Journal of Experimental Psychology*, **33A**, 325–50.

Fischler, I. (1977). Semantic facilitation without association in a lexical decision task. *Memory and Cognition*, **5**, 335–9.

Goshen-Gottstein, Y. and Moscovitch, M. (1995a). Repetition priming effects of newly formed associations are perceptually based: evidence from shallow encoding and format specificity. *Journal of Experimental Psychology: Learning, Memory, and Cognition*, **21**, 1249–62.

Goshen-Gottstein, Y. and Moscovitch, M. (1995b). Repetition priming for newly formed and preexisting associations: perceptual and conceptual influences. *Journal of Experimental Psychology: Learning, Memory, and Cognition*, **21**, 1229–48.

Graf, P. and Schacter, D. L. (1987). Selective effects of interference on implicit and explicit memory for new associations. *Journal of Experimental Psychology: Learning, Memory, and Cognition*, 13, 45–53.

Graf, P., Squire, L. R., and Mandler, G. (1984). The information that amnesic patients do not forget. *Journal of Experimental Psychology: Learning, Memory, and Cognition*, 10, 164–78.

Hintzman, D. L. (1986). 'Schema abstraction' in a multiple-trace memory model. *Psychological Review*, 93, 411–28.

Jacoby, L. L. and Dallas, M. (1981). On the relationship between autobiographical memory and perceptual learning. *Journal of Experimental Psychology: General*, 110, 306–40.

Jonides, J. and Mack, R. (1984). On the cost and benefit of cost and benefit. *Psychological Bulletin*, 96, 411–28.

Lund, K., Burgess, C., and Atchley, R. A. (1995). Semantic and associative priming in high-dimensional semantic space. *Proceedings of the Cognitive Science Society*, pp. 660–5. Hillsdale, NJ: Erlbaum Publishers.

Lupker, S. J. (1984). Semantic priming without association: A second look. *Journal of Verbal Learning and Verbal Behavior*, 23, 709–33.

McGovern, J. B. (1964). Extinction of associations in four transfer paradigms. *Psychological Monographs*, 78, (16, Whole No. 593).

McKoon, G. and Ratcliff, R. (1979). Priming in episodic and semantic memory. *Journal of Verbal Learning and Verbal Behavior*, 18, 463–80.

McKoon, G. and Ratcliff, R. (1986). Automatic activation of episodic information in a semantic memory task. *Journal of Experimental Psychology: Learning, Memory, and Cognition*, 12, 108–15.

McKoon, G. and Ratcliff, R. (1995). Conceptual combinations and relational contexts in free association and in priming in lexical decision and naming. *Psychonomic Bulletin and Review*, 2, 527–33.

McKoon, G., Ratcliff, R., and Dell, G. S. (1986). A critical evaluation of the semantic-episodic distinction. *Journal of Experimental Psychology: Learning, Memory, and Cognition*, 12, 295–306.

McRae, K. and Boisvert, S. (1998). Automatic semantic similarity priming. *Journal of Experimental Psychology: Learning, Memory, and Cognition*, 24, 558–72.

McRae, K., De Sa, V. R., and Seidenberg, M. S. (1997). On the nature and scope of featural representations of word meaning. *Journal of Experimental Psychology: General*, 126, 99–130.

Mensink, G. J. M. and Raaijmakers, J. G. W. (1988). A model for interference and forgetting. *Psychological Review*, 93, 434–55.

Meyer, D. E. and Schvaneveldt, R. W. (1971). Facilitation in recognizing pairs of words: Evidence of a dependence between retrieval operations. *Journal of Experimental Psychology*, 90, 227–34.

Neely, J. H. (1977). Semantic priming and retrieval from lexical memory: Roles of inhibitionless spreading activation and limited-capacity attention. *Journal of Experimental Psychology: General*, 106, 226–54.

Neely, J. H. and Durgunoglu, A. Y. (1985). Dissociative episodic and semantic priming effects in episodic recognition and lexical decision tasks. *Journal of Memory and Language*, 24, 466–89.

Nelson, D. L., McEvoy, C. L., and Schreiber, T. A. (1994). The University of South Florida word association, rhyme, and word fragment norms. Unpublished manuscript.

Pecher, D. and Raaijmakers, J. G. W. (1999). Automatic priming for new associations in lexical decision and perceptual identification. *Quarterly Journal of Experimental Psychology*, 52A, 593–614.

Pecher, D. and Raaijmakers, J. G. W. (2001). Priming for new associations in animacy decision: Evidence for context-dependency. Manuscript submitted for publication.

Pecher, D., Zeelenberg, R., and Raaijmakers, J. G. W. (1998). Does pizza prime coin? Perceptual priming in lexical decision and pronunciation. *Journal of Memory and Language*, 38, 401–18.

Pecher, D., Zeelenberg, R., and Raaijmakers, J. G. W. (in press). Associative priming in a masked perceptual identification task: evidence for automatic processes. *Quarterly Journal of Experimental Psychology*.

Posner, M. I. and Snyder, C. R. R. (1975). Facilitation and inhibition in the processing of signals. In *Attention and performance V* (ed. P. M. A. Rabbit and S. Dornic), pp. 669–82. New York: Academic Press.

Raaijmakers, J. G. W. and Shiffrin, R. M. (1981). Search of associative memory. *Psychological Review*, **88**, 93–134.

Reingold, E. M. and Goshen-Gottstein, Y. (1996). Separating consciously controlled and automatic influences in memory for new associations. *Journal of Experimental Psychology: Learning, Memory, and Cognition*, **22**, 397–406.

Rouder, J. N., Ratcliff, R., and McKoon, G. (2000). A neural network model of implicit memory for object recognition. *Psychological Science*, **11**, 13–19.

Salasoo, A., Shiffrin, R. M., and Feustel, T. C. (1985). Building permanent memory codes: Codification and repetition effects in word identification. *Journal of Experimental Psychology: General*, **114**, 50–77.

Scarborough, D. L., Cortese, C., and Scarborough, H. S. (1977). Frequency and repetition effects in lexical memory. *Journal of Experimental Psychology: Human Perception and Performance*, **3**, 1–17.

Schrijnemakers, J. M. C. and Raaijmakers, J. G. W. (1997). Adding new word associations to semantic memory: Evidence for two interactive learning components. *Acta Psychologica*, **96**, 103–32.

Shelton, J. R. and Martin, R. C. (1992). How semantic is automatic semantic priming? *Journal of Experimental Psychology: Learning, Memory, and Cognition*, **18**, 1191–210.

Smith, M. C., MacLeod, C. M., Bain, J. D., and Hoppe, R. B. (1989). Lexical decision as an indirect test of memory: Repetition priming and list-wide priming as a function of type of encoding. *Journal of Experimental Psychology: Learning, Memory, and Cognition*, **15**, 1109–18.

Thompson-Schill, S. L., Kurtz, K. L., and Gabrieli, J. D. E. (1998). Effects of semantic and associative relatedness on automatic priming. *Journal of Memory and Language*, **38**, 440–58.

Tulving, E. (1983). *Elements of episodic memory*. New York: Oxford University Press.

Tulving, E. (1984). Precis of elements of episodic memory. *Behavioral and Brain Sciences*, **7**, 223–68.

Tulving, E. and Schacter, D. L. (1990). Priming and human memory systems. *Science*, **247**, 301–6.

Zeelenberg, R. (1998). *Testing theories of priming*. Unpublished doctoral dissertation. University of Amsterdam.

CHAPTER 13

FAMILIARITY IN AN IMPLICIT AND EXPLICIT MEMORY TASK: A COMMON MECHANISM

SACHIKO KINOSHITA

Abstract

In this review, I examine the nature of familiarity that has been proposed as a basis for making decisions in an explicit memory task (recognition memory) and an implicit memory task (lexical decision). The review aims to relate the visual word recognition literature with the recognition memory literature, two areas that to date have been linked only occasionally. Empirical findings are reviewed and it is suggested that a common familiarity detection mechanism underlies both lexical decision and episodic recognition judgments. I also argue that this common familiarity is a product of explicit memory, contrary to the view that recognition judgments based on familiarity are inferred from perceptual fluency (a product of implicit memory). The function of a familiarity monitor in a broader theoretical context is also discussed.

Familiarity in an implicit and explicit memory task: a common mechanism?

The lexical decision task (LDT) is one of the most frequently used tasks in the study of visual word recognition. In this task, on each trial, the subject is presented with a letter string, and is asked to respond as quickly as possible whether it is a word or a nonword, with reaction time (decision latency) as the dependent measure.

Less commonly, the LDT is used as a test of implicit memory. Implicit (or indirect) memory tests are those that tap evidence of retention of an episode without requiring conscious recollection of its prior occurrence. It is contrasted with explicit memory tests such as recall or recognition, in which subjects are explicitly asked to recollect the prior occurrence. When the LDT is used as an implicit memory test, decision latency is compared between items that have been presented earlier ('old' items) and items that have not ('new' items). The finding that decision latency is facilitated for old items relative to new items is referred to as the repetition priming effect, and is generally interpreted as an implicit memory phenomenon. That is, because the LDT does not require subjects to recollect the episode in which the repeated items were encountered, the effect of prior exposure is assumed to reflect a process that is different from that tapped in explicit tests of memory such as recall and recognition.

The main aim of this review is to evaluate the status of the LDT as an implicit memory task. This question is important because it is now well recognized that the mere fact that the test instruction does not explicitly require subjects to recollect the prior occurrence of an item does not mean the task is tapping solely 'implicit memory' (the task-purity assumption, see Jacoby, 1991). Against this, however, there is a suggestion that because the LDT is a speeded task, it affords less opportunity for 'contamination' by explicit memory and hence it is a task well suited to investigating implicit memory in non-amnesic subjects (e.g., Goshen-Gottstein and Moscovitch, 1995; McKone and Slee, 1997). I will examine the empirical evidence, and argue that such a position is not warranted: Instead, I will argue that the LDT taps familiarity, which is a product of explicit memory.

The review will be organized as follows. I will first describe what I consider to be key facts about the LDT that indicate that the task involves a familiarity monitoring process. I will then review findings that have been used to interpret the LDT as an implicit memory task. There are two lines of arguments. One uses the findings of dissociative effects of factors on the LDT and recognition memory to argue that they tap different forms of memory, while the other uses the similarity between recognition memory and repetition priming effects to argue that recognition decisions may be based on the output of an implicit memory process. I will argue that support is lacking for both lines of arguments. Finally, I will consider the role of a familiarity monitoring process in a broader theoretical perspective.

Key facts about the LDT as monitoring familiarity

The word frequency effect

Normative word frequency has been known to have a large effect on lexical decision performance: In Whaley's (1978) multiple regression study, its contribution was greater than that of all other variables combined. While word frequency has been known to affect other visual word identification tasks such as naming and semantic categorization, it has been commented that the word frequency effect is disproportionately greater in the LDT (Balota and Chumbley, 1984).

Several researchers have noted this fact and suggested that this sensitivity of the LDT to the effect of word frequency reflects a familiarity monitoring process. For example, Besner (1983; Besner et al., 1984) proposed a distinction between two kinds of recognition: 'One in which the response uniquely specifies a stimulus, and one in which figural familiarity is assessed' (Besner et al., 1984, p. 121). He argued that the LDT involves the latter type of recognition, termed familiarity detection, and that lexical decisions can be made without unique stimulus identification. This claim is based on the way a factor that disrupts figural familiarity (by means of cAsE aLtErAnAtIoN) is modulated by lexicality and word frequency. Because case alternation disrupts the overall word shape (envelope), it is assumed to prevent the effective use of the familiarity detection mechanism. In addition, words are assumed to be more figurally familiar than nonwords, because, they are by definition seen more often than nonwords. Hence in tasks involving familiarity detection, case alternation should impair responses to words more than nonwords. On the other hand, in tasks requiring unique word identification, there is no reason to expect this pattern of interaction between lexicality and case alternation effects, because the output of the familiarity detection mechanism cannot be used to uniquely identify a word. In line with this prediction, Besner (1983) reported that case alternation impaired responses to words more than nonwords in the LDT, but not in the naming task.[1]

Another well-known description of the LDT as a familiarity detection task was given by Balota and Chumbley (1984; also see Balota and Spieler, 1999) in their two-stage decision model. The main tenet of the model is that words and nonwords may be distinguished along the dimension of familiarity/meaningfulness (FM), which is primarily determined by the letter string's orthographic and phonological similarity to actual words, and frequency of usage. Balota and Chumbley suggested that the first stage of the decision process involves a global computation of the FM value of the letter string. It is further assumed that in this stage subjects adopt an upper and lower decision criterion along the FM dimension such that if the letter string's FM value exceeds the upper criterion, a fast 'word' response is made; if it fails to exceed the lower criterion, a fast 'nonword' response is made. On the other hand, if the FM value falls between the lower and upper criteria, then a second-stage decision process will be required. In this stage, a more analytic evaluation of the letter string is carried out, for example, the spelling of the letter string against the spelling of a word contained in the subject's lexicon. Balota and Chumbley explained the larger word frequency effect observed in the LDT relative to other word identification tasks such as the naming task and semantic categorization task in terms of the involvement of this two-stage decision process. The exaggerated word frequency effect in the LDT comes from the fact that a number of low-frequency words, by virtue of their low FM value, fail to reach the upper decision criterion, and hence require the time-consuming second-stage analysis. In tasks that do not involve the assessment of FM value, such as the naming task and semantic categorization task, the word frequency effect is smaller is size, because high-frequency words do not gain an additional advantage by sometimes exceeding the high criterion and producing a fast familiarity-based response.

I should point out that the idea that lexical decision is based on familiarity does not necessarily mean that a decision is made without unique stimulus identification, as implied by these two models just described. For example, Joordens and Becker (1997) have pointed out that in their model of lexical decision, based on the concept of harmony (which is synonymous with familiarity), increases in harmony corresponding to the presentation of a stimulus are directly tied to the active retrieval of information pertaining to that stimulus. To make this point clearer, a reference to the feeling of knowing (FOK) literature would be useful.

In the FOK paradigm, subjects are asked to recall an item, for example, in response to a general knowledge question (e.g., What is the name of India's 'holy' river?). When the

---

[1] However, see also Kinoshita (1987) for a contrary finding. Also see Besner and McCann (1987) regarding the pattern of interaction between the effects of case alternation, word frequency, and task type predicted by this view.

subject is unable to provide an answer, he/she is asked to rate their FOK. Such FOK ratings are generally positively correlated with performance on a subsequent objective memory task, for example, in an eight-alternative recognition test. This ability for subjects to monitor the presence of information in the memory store that they are unable to retrieve has been a puzzle for FOK researchers, and one dominant idea has been that there is a monitoring mechanism that is separate from the memory retrieval process. Contrary to this view, Koriat (1993) has argued that one need not assume a separate FOK monitor. In his model, FOK ratings are based on the accessibility of correct and incorrect information about the target. Thus, for example, if a subject is unable to recall the answer to the question 'Corsica island belongs to what country?', and rates his/her FOK, it may be based on what the subject can recall about the wrong answer 'Italy', rather than the correct answer 'France'. According to Koriat (1993, 1994) then, FOK is based directly on the product of the retrieval attempt, rather than a separate internal monitor that has privileged access to unretrieved information. However, this monitor does not know about the source of information: The high FOK rating may be based on the amount of information retrieved about the wrong answer (in this case, Italy) or the correct answer. In the same way, familiarity used in LDT may be tied directly to the active retrieval of information pertaining to that stimulus. Familiarity is therefore simply a measure of the total amount of information retrieved about the stimulus at that time.

Whether or not the models assume familiarity to be monitored by a separate or the same mechanism as that involved in retrieval of lexical information, the familiarity-based models share the assumption that the familiarity monitor does not know about the source of information contributing to that familiarity. In the word recognition literature, many models of lexical decision share the view that lexical decision involves this familiarity monitoring mechanism (e.g., Balota and Chumbley, 1984; Besner *et al.*, 1984; Gordon, 1985; Grainger and Jacobs, 1996; Stone and van Orden, 1993). It is also relatively uncontroversial that this familiarity is global or multidimensional, as we see in the next section.

Subjective familiarity

A factor closely related to word frequency is word familiarity, as evaluated by subjective ratings. Rated familiarity is correlated with a number of word variables such as age of acquisition (Brown and Watson, 1987) and pronounceability (Rubin, 1980). Brown and Watson (1987) showed in a multiple regression study that factors other than objective frequency measures (e.g., age of acquisition) made independent contributions towards rated familiarity. That is, rated familiarity encompasses more than estimates of experiential frequency.

From the view that lexical decisions are based on 'global' familiarity, rated familiarity may be expected to provide a better measure of this dimension than objective frequency. There is empirical support for this prediction. Gordon (1985) reported that for low-frequency words, rated familiarity accounted for significantly more latency variance in a LDT than objective frequency (29–30% vs. 7.5%). Similarly, Connine *et al.* (1990) showed that rated familiarity affected lexical decisions for words that had the same range of (low) objective frequency. The correlation between word variables such as concreteness and pronounceability and rated familiarity also explains why Gernsbacher (1984) found in an LDT an interaction between objective frequency and other word variables such as concreteness and ortho-graphic regularity but not between these variables and rated familiarity. That is, for low-frequency words, rated familiarity is influenced by factors such as concreteness and pro-nounceability (which would be correlated with orthographic regularity) and hence predicts lexical decision latencies better than objective frequency. In summary, these findings support the view that lexical decision is based on multidimensional familiarity.

Strategic variation

It is important to note that lexical decision latencies to the same items are not invariant, but are affected by list composition. For example, it has been reported (Dorfman and Glanzer, 1988; Glanzer and Ehrenreich, 1979; Gordon, 1985; Stone and van Orden, 1993) that word frequency effects are larger when all the word trials in a block were composed of high-frequency words only or low-frequency words only (blocked condition) compared with when the block contained both high- and low-frequency words (mixed condition). Also, the size of the word frequency effect is affected by the nature of the nonwords. When nonwords are less wordlike, as in when they are unpronounceable or consist of consonant strings, word frequency effects are smaller (Stone and van Orden, 1993); in addition, when nonwords are less wordlike, there is less influence of semantic properties as evidenced by smaller effects of semantic priming (Shulman and Davison, 1977) or concreteness (James, 1975).

These variations in lexical decision latencies as a function of list composition are generally interpreted as evidence that subjects strategically adjust their bases for making lexical deci-sions. While details differ between different decision models (Balota and Chumbley, 1984; Balota and Spieler, 1999; Gordon, 1985), one assumption common to all models is that list composition reflects the separation of word and nonword distributions along the familiarity dimension, with less wordlike nonwords at the low end, and high-frequency words at the high end. The variation in lexical decision latency reflects the strategic placement of the criterion that is sensitive to the degree of separation in the word and nonword distributions.

Given the possibility of such strategic modification of decision process, both the deci-sion latency and the size of the effect of an item factor (e.g., word frequency) can vary depending on the type of foils used. This point is important when evaluating studies that directly compared the LDT and recognition task using the same stimuli.

Frequency attenuation effect

In the LDT, repetition priming effects are greater for low-frequency words than high-frequency words (Forster and Davis, 1984; Scarborough *et al.*, 1977, 1979). To put it another way, the word frequency effect in the LDT is reduced for words that have been pre-sented earlier in the experimental session, an effect termed the *frequency attenuation* effect (Forster and Davis, 1984).

In the (explicit) memory literature, it is well established that the amount of attention an item receives during study has large effects on subsequent memory performance on explicit memory tests such as recall and recognition (Craik *et al.*, 1996; Moscovitch, 1995;

Naveh-Benjamin *et al.*, 1998). Forster and Davis (1984) reported a series of studies investigating how the nature of initial presentation modulates the frequency attenuation effect. They found frequency attenuation when subjects responded to the words on initial presentation but not when the initial presentation was masked and hence the item was not available for conscious report (see also Rajaram and Neely, 1992 for replication). Forster and Davis also reported a weaker frequency attenuation effect for words that were not masked on initial presentation but that did not require responding. A picture that emerges from this is that frequency attenuation effects are modulated by the amount of attention the items receive during study.

It is useful to note also that the longevity of masked and unmasked repetition priming effects is quite different: Whereas the masked repetition effect dissipates after two or three intervening items (Forster and Davis, 1984, Experiment 6) or within 500 ms of presentation (Ferrand, 1996), unmasked repetition effects in the LDT have been known to persist over 24 hours (Scarborough *et al.*, 1977). This difference therefore provides further support for Forster and Davis' (1984) claim that the masked and unmasked repetition effects reflect the operation of different mechanisms. In particular, the finding of frequency attenuation for unmasked, but not for masked repeated items indicates that familiarity is modulated differently for high- versus low-frequency words only when the item was consciously attended to during initial study. Based on these observations, Forster and Davis (1984) suggested that the repetition priming effect accompanied by frequency attenuation observed in the LDT reflects explicit memory.

Section summary

The main conclusion drawn from this brief and selective review is that the LDT involves a familiarity monitoring process, a view that is relatively uncontroversial in the word recognition literature. This familiarity is multidimensional and is predominantly based on (objective) word frequency, but is also affected by such factors as imageability and orthographic regularity. How this familiarity is used to make lexical decisions is strategically controlled by subjects depending on the composition of stimuli. Finally, the repetition priming effect in the LDT is greater for low-frequency words than high-frequency words. Because this pattern of interaction between the effects of word frequency and repetition is observed only for words that can be consciously recognized as having occurred, it has been suggested by Forster and Davis (1984) to reflect explicit recognition of the studied words.

Is the LDT an implicit memory task?

As stated above, within the word recognition literature, the repetition priming effect observed in the LDT is generally regarded as a product of explicit recognition (e.g., Forster and Davis, 1984). In contrast, in the implicit memory literature, it is generally interpreted as reflecting implicit, rather than explicit, memory. In this section, findings that have been interpreted as evidence for this position will be reviewed. In the main, this evidence takes the form of dissociations observed in the LDT and recognition memory task, a task generally accepted as tapping explicit memory (an alternative interpretation will be discussed later under the heading of Perceptual fluency). If a factor is found to have an effect on the LDT but not recognition memory task or vice versa, it is taken as evidence that the LDT does not tap explicit memory. However, as argued by Moscovitch (e.g., Witherspoon and Moscovitch, 1989) and other proponents of the component process approach, empirical dissociations between explicit and implicit memory tasks need not imply that the tasks tap different memory systems. Instead, such dissociations may be explained in terms of different component processes involved in performing the tasks. In the review of the findings presented below, it will be argued that alternative interpretations couched in terms of such component processes are possible in each case.

Dividing attention at study

It is well established that dividing attention at study has detrimental effects on memory performance, whether tested in terms of recall, cued recall, or recognition (Craik *et al.*, 1996; Naveh-Benjamin *et al.*, 1998), but it has little effect on implicit memory performance (Mulligan and Hartman, 1996). Thus the demonstration that dividing attention at study preserves repetition priming effects in LDT (Kinoshita, 1995; Smith and Oscar-Berman, 1990) has been used to argue that the LDT is an implicit memory task (Hintzman and Curran, 1997; McKone and Slee, 1997). However, a closer look at the data shows that the case is not as strong as it initially seems. Specifically, the recognition memory task, which is considered to be an explicit memory task, shows similar imperviousness to the effects of divided attention, as described below.

Although recognition performance has been reported to be impaired by dividing attention at study, it is noteworthy that recognition is not reduced to a chance level. For example, Gardiner and Parkin (1990) manipulated attention during study by requiring subjects to listen to a sequence of high, medium, and low pitched tones and monitoring the pitch (by calling out 'high', 'medium', or 'low'). While this manipulation reduced recognition performance, subjects were nevertheless able to discriminate between old and new words. Further, this experiment used the REMEMBER–KNOW procedure in which subjects are asked to classify an 'old' response either as a REMEMBER response (one in which the subject was able to retrieve contextual aspects of the study episode such as the look of the word or what reaction they had to the word at study), or a KNOW response (one in which contextual aspects of the study episode could not be brought to mind). Dividing attention at study was found to reduce the number of REMEMBER responses, but not KNOW responses. This finding suggests that feeling of familiarity (that is not based on retrieval of context) was not affected by divided attention at study.

Against this, it may be argued that the manipulation of attention was not strong enough in the above study. Indeed, Gardiner and Parkin's (1990) data showed that even for words studied under the divided attention condition, more REMEMBER responses were made to old words than new words, indicating that even recognition based on retrieval of context was well above chance level. However, even studies that used a stronger manipulation of attention at study indicate that dividing attention at study does not completely eliminate recognition memory. Although it was not commented on in the paper, the data reported by Kinoshita (1995) show this to be the case. In that study, subjects were not informed at encoding of the subsequent memory test, each target word was presented only briefly (100 ms), and the manipulation of attention involved flanking each target word with two digits (e.g., 5 sleet 8), and requiring subjects to decide whether the two digits had the same parity (whether they were both odd or both even). Subjects then performed either a lexical decision task or a recognition judgment task. For the low-frequency words studied under this divided attention condition, repetition priming effect was found in the lexical decision task, consistent with the view that divided attention does not eliminate repetition priming effects.[2] For the same words, recognition was at chance for both REMEMBER responses and KNOW responses when recognition was not speeded (Experiment 1). However, when recognition was speeded, subjects made more KNOW responses to old words than new words (Experiment 2), that is, recognition memory was better than chance. To put it another way, when the emphasis is on speed and when judgments do not require the retrieval of context, the explicit recognition memory judgments (as tapped by KNOW responses) behave similarly to lexical decisions with respect to the effects of divided attention. This means that in these previous studies, task dissociation (dissociative effects of dividing attention at study on the recognition memory task and the LDT) has not been demonstrated, and hence, it is premature to argue the LDT as tapping implicit memory on the basis of the effects of dividing attention at study.

Korsakoff patients

Another finding that has been taken to interpret the LDT as an implicit memory test is the observation that amnesic subjects show intact repetition priming effects in the LDT. At least two studies (Smith and Oscar-Berman, 1990; Verfaellie *et al.*, 1991) have reported such findings using Korsakoff patients. The argument is that because these patients perform poorly on tests of explicit memory, the intact repetition priming effects observed with these patients in the LDT must have reflected implicit memory.

However, it should be noted that while these patients generally perform poorly on recall, recognition performance of Korsakoff patients is relatively well-preserved, and is rarely at chance (but see also Haist *et al.*, 1992; Hirst *et al.*, 1986). In particular, the classic studies by Huppert and Piercy (1976, 1978) have shown that when they are not required to retrieve the context in which an item was studied (as in when the stimuli were photographs that subjects would have been unfamiliar with prior to the study episode), Korsakoff patients' recognition performance was just as good as the controls. Hence the finding that repetition priming effects in the LDT are intact in Korsakoff patients is not incompatible with the idea that the LDT taps the same familiarity that is used to make recognition judgments.

---

[2] In contrast to this study, Forster and Davis (1984, Experiment 4) reported finding weak and unreliable repetition priming effects for words that have been studied under poor encoding conditions. It is relevant to note here that in Kinoshita (1995), nonwords were not presented in the study phase, whereas Forster and Davis (1984) presented nonwords as well as words at study. In the latter case, responding on the basis of perceptual familiarity could lead to a high rate of errors to nonwords, and therefore it would not be a useful discriminator of lexical status. It is possible therefore that the absence of repeated nonwords is a necessary condition for observing reliable repetition priming effect for words studied under poor encoding conditions.

Speed–accuracy trade-off studies

Perhaps the most problematic finding for the view that the LDT and recognition task tap the same familiarity is the finding that retrieval dynamics in the two tasks are different. Specifically, the evidence comes from studies that examined speed–accuracy trade-off functions using the response–signal technique in the LDT and recognition task. In this technique, subjects are interrupted at various points of time in a speeded decision task, and the changes in accuracy as a function of processing time is measured.

In a study most relevant to the present question, Hintzman and Curran (1997) used the same word and nonword items in a LDT and recognition memory task, and compared the speed–accuracy trade-off functions for the two tasks. They reported that the intercept of the speed–accuracy trade-off function (i.e., the earliest time at which performance is above chance) was shorter for lexical decisions than for recognition memory. They took this to argue that 'if recognition intercept indexes the point in retrieval when episodic information first becomes available, then it is too late to be the basis of the repetition priming effect (in lexical decisions)' (p. 241). The same argument may be mounted on the basis that (in standard speeded decision conditions) recognition decision latencies are typically much longer than lexical decision latencies.

Initially, this seems to constitute the most damaging evidence against the view that lexical decisions tap episodic familiarity. However, in the same article, Hintzman and Curran (1997) suggested the possibility that 'the same information is used in lexical decision and recognition memory but that it is used in different ways' (p. 244). Consider the fact that the intercept is determined by the items that can be answered correctly the most quickly. In the LDT, this decision involves binary classification of lexical status. In the recognition memory task, this decision involves classification of items into the 'old' versus 'new' category. The intercept in the two tasks would be therefore dependent on what information is required for discriminating between word and nonwords, versus between old and new items, and the speed with which such information becomes available. When both words and nonwords were repeated, recognition would require retrieval of context: The larger intercept in the recognition task may therefore be due to the fact contextual information accumulates more slowly over time. To put it another way, it is not clear whether at any given time, the separation of words and nonwords along the dimension of familiarity is the same as the separation of old and new words. It is therefore argued that the shorter intercept found with lexical decisions relative to recognition judgments does not rule out the possibility that the same familiarity dimension is used as a basis for making recognition memory judgments at an earlier point in time.

Interaction between word frequency and other factors

Neely and colleagues (Duchek and Neely, 1989; Rajaram and Neely, 1992) studied the pattern of interaction between the effects of word frequency and other factors (e.g., type of encoding) in the LDT and recognition memory task and took the dissociation observed between the two tasks as evidence that the LDT was not based on explicit memory. However, as with the retrieval dynamics data discussed in the preceding section, these dissociations observed between the LDT and recognition memory task need not imply that the two tasks do not involve a common familiarity monitoring process: They may simply reflect different component processes.

Rajaram and Neely (1992) reported that the frequency attenuation effect in LDT was observed even when the low-frequency advantage in recognition was not found in a recognition memory task using the identical set of items. Based on this finding, they argued that the frequency attenuation effect in the LDT could not have been due to explicit memory. However, they also found that the recognition advantage for low-frequency words was restored when nonwords were excluded from study. In a recognition memory task, there would be greater reliance on the retrieval of context (source monitoring) when nonwords had been studied than when they were all 'new'. In this case, a more time-consuming search for the context is required, and a recognition judgment may not be produced until this search is complete. In contrast, in a LDT, even when some of the nonwords had been studied, there may still be sufficient separation between the word and nonword distributions based on pre-experimental familiarity for it to be an indicator of lexical status, without the need for a time-consuming source monitoring process. The fact that lexical decision latencies were considerably faster than recognition judgment latencies is consistent with the present argument. Therefore Rajaram and Neely's finding does not rule out the possibility that the frequency attenuation effect in the LDT is mediated by explicit familiarity.

In Duchek and Neely's (1989) study, different patterns of interaction between word frequency and levels-of-processing were observed in the LDT and the recognition memory task. Specifically, whereas semantic processing facilitated lexical decisions for high-frequency words more than low-frequency words (at least when the nonwords were pronounceable), the reverse was true for recognition memory decisions. Duchek and Neely argued that this dissociation presents a problem for the view that episodic memory mediates the frequency attenuation effect in the LDT, because if this is the case, deeper encoding which benefits low-frequency more than high-frequency words in the recognition memory task should have produced the same pattern in the LDT.

It is important to note, however, that in this study, a levels-of-processing effect was observed both for the LDT and the recognition memory task, and that the dissociation (in the pattern of interaction between the effects of word frequency and levels-of-processing) was found only when the nonwords in the LDT were pronounceable. From the perspective that the LDT taps episodic familiarity, it is not surprising to find a levels-of-processing effect in this task. It would also be expected that deeper encoding would benefit low-frequency words more than high-frequency words, given the perspective that relative to high-frequency words, discrimination of low-frequency words from nonwords would rely more on semantic factors. What is difficult to explain within this view, then, is the fact that this pattern was found when the nonwords were non-pronounceable, but not when the nonwords were pronounceable: In the latter condition, deeper processing benefited high-frequency words more than low-frequency words.

Frankly, this latter result is puzzling, and it may reflect some idiosyncratic aspects of this condition. Specifically, in this study, the levels-of-processing effect was greater when the nonwords were non-pronounceable (a 22 ms effect) than when they were pronounceable (a 14 ms effect). This result is contrary to the typical finding that semantic factors make greater contributions when nonwords are pronounceable than non-pronounceable (James, 1975; Shulman and Davison, 1977; Shulman *et al.*, 1978). This odd result may reflect the fact that because the pronounceable nonwords in this experiment were generated by changing a single letter of words they resembled specific words, hence necessitating an extensive spelling check. This possibility is supported by the fact that in this condition the nonwords generated from high-frequency words were responded to faster than the non-words generated from low-frequency words. The primary role played by the spelling check process may have effectively reduced the scope for factors other than orthographic infor-mation to influence latency, thus reducing the levels-of-processing effect. The greater levels-of-processing benefit observed with high-frequency words than low-frequency words in this condition may therefore not be typical of a standard LDT which is largely dependent on familiarity. With the exception of this condition then, overall, the patterns of effects of levels-of-processing and word frequency are similar for recognition test and LDT.

The perceptual fluency account

The previous section evaluated, and argued against, the view that the recognition memory task and LDT tap different forms of memory. In contrast, there are some proponents of the view that familiarity tapped in the recognition memory task is based on perceptual fluency, a product of an implicit memory process (e.g., Gardiner, 1988; Jacoby and Whitehouse, 1989; Johnston *et al.*, 1985). If the familiarity monitored in the recognition memory task and the LDT is the same, then this view presents an alternative approach to arguing that the familiarity monitored in the LDT is a product of implicit memory. In this section, I will consider arguments against this perceptual fluency view.

Perceptual fluency is usually measured in terms of how well an item can be identified under impoverished presentation conditions. Items that have been exposed earlier show enhanced perceptual fluency (i.e., repetition priming effect). The perceptual fluency account is associ-ated with a class of recognition memory models that assume that recognition may be based on one of two processes: Retrieval of contextual information, and feeling of familiarity (e.g., Mandler, 1980). The argument is that subjects can detect the relative ease of perception of an item and can use the fluent perception of old items as part of the basis for recognition mem-ory judgments. That is, the feeling of familiarity is an attribution based on perceptual fluency.

There are both theoretical and empirical problems with the perceptual fluency account. At the theoretical level, the perceptual fluency account will have difficulty accommodating both the frequency attenuation effect in LDT and the greater recognition advantage for low-frequency words, the very two phenomena that motivated the suggestion for a common mechanism. In order to use perceptual fluency as a basis for making recognition memory judgments presupposes some standard against which fluency is judged, since using absolute fluency as a basis for making recognition judgments would result in excessively high false alarm rates for high-frequency word foils. Thus, a test item must be seen as *relatively* fluent (resulting in an 'old' response) or *relatively* non-fluent (resulting in a 'new' response). As pointed out by Hintzman and Caulton (1997), this begs the question, 'relative to what?' (p. 16).

An obvious candidate for such a standard is the subjective frequency of a word ('I perceived this word relatively quickly *considering that it is not a word used frequently*, therefore I must have studied it'). Using such a standard would explain why subjects do not make excessively high false alarms to high-frequency word foils. But note that this explanation creates a chicken-and-egg problem, because it suggests that subjective frequency is computed before recognition memory judgments are made. Recall, however, that the frequency attenuation effect (i.e., the greater repetition benefit for low-frequency words relative to high-frequency words) in the LDT is explained in terms of greater increment in familiarity for low-, relative to high-frequency words. Hence the idea of 'relative perceptual fluency' runs into circularity.[3]

At the empirical level also, the perceptual fluency account has a number of problems. One is that studies that used the REMEMBER–KNOW procedure have found that the low-frequency advantage is associated with REMEMBER responses rather than KNOW responses (Gardiner and Java, 1990; Kinoshita, 1995). This finding is contrary to the view that the low-frequency advantage reflects familiarity that is based on perceptual fluency rather than retrieval of context, because such a view would predict that low-frequency advantage would be associated with KNOW responses. Note that this problem is not eliminated by assuming that REMEMBER and KNOW responses do not tap qualitatively different memory processes but that they are expressions of strong and weak memory traces, respectively (see Donaldson, 1996; Hirshman and Master, 1997). This is because there is no rationale for assuming that a feeling of familiarity based on perceptual fluency necessarily results in strong memory traces. As will be argued below, the evidence in fact suggests the contrary that recognition judgments may be based on perceptual fluency only with poor encoding conditions, that is, only when memory traces are weak. Thus the perceptual fluency account is inconsistent with the pattern of low-frequency word advantage observed with REMEMBER and KNOW responses.

Second, according to the perceptual fluency account of low-frequency advantage in recognition memory, it may be expected that the advantage would be reduced when modality of presentation is changed between study and test. This prediction follows from the transfer-appropriate processing principle (Roediger and Blaxton, 1987) in which the gain in processing fluency would be less when the perceptual operations involved are different between study and test. Such a finding was reported by Jacoby and Dallas (1981, Experiment 6), in which the low-frequency advantage in recognition memory was reduced when the study-test modality differed than when they matched. However, it is important to note that in their study the test modality was always visual and hence match/mismatch of study-test modality was confounded with study modality (auditory vs. visual). In contrast, Lee *et al.* (1978) tested the full combination of study and test modalities and found that the low-frequency advantage was not reduced when study-test modalities did not match, but that the advantage was reduced when the study modality was auditory (irrespective of test modality). This pattern of data therefore argues against the perceptual fluency interpretation of low-frequency advantage in recognition memory.

Third, the evidence linking perceptual fluency and recognition judgments is typically correlational. As pointed out by Watkins and Gibson (1988), studies showing a correlation between judgments of fluency and probability of calling an item 'old' does not constitute

---

[3] See also Rugg and Doyle (1994) for arguments against this 'relative fluency' view based on electrophysiological evidence.

evidence that perceptual fluency *causes* a feeling of familiarity: Only direct manipulation of perceptual fluency can provide such evidence. In this regard, it is important to note that experimenter-manipulated perceptual fluency produces effects on recognition judgments only when the level of recognition is low (Johnston *et al.*, 1991). This, along with the fact that experimenter-manipulated fluency affects recognition when recognition judgments follow immediately after judgments of perceptual fluency (Watkins and Gibson, 1988) suggests a deliberate decision strategy on the part of the subject (e.g., 'I have very little memory for these items; this item looks clearer than other ones, so I must have studied this item'). To put another way, effects of experimenter-manipulated perceptual fluency (when they are found), likely reflect demand characteristics of particular experimental settings, rather than a general mechanism that underlies recognition memory judgments.

Section summary

In the first half, I reviewed the findings reporting empirical dissociation between recognition test and the LDT. It was argued however that in each case the observed dissociation did not rule out the view that recognition decision and lexical decisions involve a common familiarity monitoring process.

In the second half, I discussed the view that perceptual fluency, a product of an implicit memory process, is the basis for computing familiarity used in recognition memory judgments, and argued that there is little support for the view. In this sense, I concur with the view put forward by Moscovitch and Bentin (1993) that 'recognition, even when it is based only on a sense of familiarity, is an explicit test of memory' and that 'the process that gives rise to a sense of familiarity (insofar as that sense is inextricably a product of the process rather than an inferred or attributed by-product of it, Jacoby, 1983; Johnston *et al.*, 1985) is different from the process that is involved in producing repetition effects' (p. 157).

The role of the familiarity monitor

The conclusion that emerges from the preceding sections is that familiarity tapped by the LDT is multidimensional and encompasses both episodic familiarity as well as pre-experimental familiarity. I have also argued that the episodic familiarity is not a product of implicit memory, but is the same as that tapped by a recognition memory task. This last point is hardly surprising from the word recognition perspective that the LDT involves a familiarity monitoring process and that this familiarity is multidimensional: If familiarity is multidimensional, why shouldn't it encompass episodic as well as pre-experimental familiarity? A moral of this chapter is therefore that researchers using a task to tap implicit memory will do well to consider the nature of component processes involved in performing the task. Although broad classification of test tasks such as 'data-driven' versus 'conceptually-driven' has proved (and continues to be) useful in guiding implicit memory research, more theoretical advances would be made by considering the specific component processes that benefit from repetition in each task.

Taking the position that the familiarity tapped by the LDT and recognition memory task is one and the same provides a rationale for relating the literature on word recognition and recognition memory. As pointed out by Hintzman and Curran (1997), there are similarities between the LDT and the recognition memory task in that in both tasks subjects are asked whether the item is in memory: A recognition memory test asks whether the test item is in one's memory of a recent study episode, and a lexical decision asks whether it is in one's lexicon, but otherwise the tasks are alike. However, there has been relatively little contact between the literatures on the two tasks. Future modeling endeavors in each domain would benefit from consideration of theoretical advances made in the other.

In the remainder of this section, I will speculate on the role of the familiarity monitor in a broader theoretical context. The question is *why* there is such a global familiarity monitor. The ubiquitousness of decision processes based on familiarity, the speed with which such familiarity is evaluated, and its resistance to brain impairment are all suggestive of the idea that the familiarity detection mechanism serves some fundamental purpose, rather than that it developed as a specialized decision strategy to specifically carry out the LDT. Here, I concur with previous theorists who suggested that the main rationale for the existence of a global familiarity monitor is that it serves a useful function for facilitating learning. The idea that learning rate is adjusted differently for familiar versus novel stimuli can be found in the traditional learning literature as well as more recent computational modeling literature, as reiterated below.

In the learning literature, latent inhibition refers to the observation that a stimulus that has been pre-exposed without any consequence enters into new associations more slowly than a novel stimulus. This phenomenon is found widely in a variety of mammalian species, including mice, rats, rabbits, cats, and humans, both young children and adults (for a review, see Lubow and Gewirtz, 1995). Lubow and Gewirtz (1995) pointed out the fact that the ubiquity of latent inhibition testifies to its biological significance and adaptive importance: 'Latent inhibition promotes the stimulus selectivity required for rapid, efficient learning' by 'creating a bias in favor of potentially important stimuli by degrading those stimuli that have been registered as inconsequential in the past' (p. 87). A monitor which can rapidly compute the familiarity of a stimulus would be essential for this to work, and it is therefore not surprising that it plays an important role in animals that live in changing environments.[4]

The idea that a global familiarity monitor serves an important function has also been suggested by various computational models of memory (e.g., Carpenter and Grossberg, 1991; Metcalfe, 1993, 1994). Metcalfe (1993) has pointed out that in a model that assumes composite memory traces, that is, where a memory trace consists of distributed elementary features, the activation values of the individual features can increase in magnitude out of bounds and without control, particularly when the to-be-stored event is similar to existing memory traces. Metcalfe's solution is to propose a familiarity monitor which evaluates the

---

[4] It is also useful to note that this assumed role of a familiarity monitor provides a common explanation of the frequency attenuation effect in the LDT, and the recognition memory advantage for low-frequency words. That is, the operation of the familiarity monitor at encoding (the initial presentation) is expected to result in more attention being paid to low-frequency words than high-frequency words, by virtue of the greater familiarity of the latter. The result is enhanced recognition memory for low-frequency words. This interpretation is consistent with the fact that the frequency attenuation effect is not found for items that are not attended to at study (Forster and Davis, 1984), as well as the results of many studies showing that pre-exposure to items prior to the critical study phase eliminates the recognition advantage for novel items (Glanzer and Adams, 1990; Maddox and Estes, 1997; Tulving and Kroll, 1995).

global similarity between the existing trace and the to-be-stored event (i.e., the global familiarity of the to-be-stored event). The computed familiarity is then used to weight (control) the variance of activation values of the features.

Metcalfe (1993) emphasized the idea that the monitored familiarity is global. In her terms, the computed value of familiarity is a 'scalar' which does not require specific retrieval of features: The value does not contain any specific information such as the characteristics of the stored items. This multidimensional nature is necessary for Metcalfe's solution, because as she suggests, it is unlikely that 'the human memory system would solve this problem analytically' (1993, p. 7), presumably because that would take too long. Rather, what is needed is a rapid assessment of overall similarity between the event in question and what is already stored, that is, global (multidimensional) familiarity. Such an assumption is common to a class of recognition memory models referred to as global matching models (for a review, see Clark and Gronlund, 1996).

Viewing the familiarity monitor as an intrinsic part of a learning process offers a new perspective on modeling the lexical decision process. Rather than regarding repetition priming effects in the LDT as reflecting 'explicit contamination', it should be regarded as providing useful information about how individual episodes are incorporated into a stable knowledge network. In particular, a familiarity monitor plays an important role in self-organizing networks that are specifically concerned with how memory mechanisms solve the plasticity-stability dilemma, that is, how a system learns about new events while maintaining stability for already-learned categories (see, for example, Carpenter and Grossberg, 1991). In this way, it offers a way of 'rethinking implicit (more appropriately, explicit) memory'.

Acknowledgments

I am grateful to Ken Paap and Colin Davis for helpful discussions during the preparation of this chapter (although neither should be held responsible for the views expressed here).

References

Balota, D. A. and Chumbley, J. I. (1984). Are lexical decisions a good measure of lexical access? The role of word frequency in the neglected decision stage. *Journal of Experimental Psychology: Learning, Memory, and Cognition,* **10**, 340–57.

Balota, D. A. and Spieler, D. H. (1999). Word frequency, repetition, and lexicality effects in word recognition tasks: Beyond measures of central tendency. *Journal of Experimental Psychology: General,* **128**, 32–5.

Besner, D. (1983). Basic decoding components in reading: Two dissociable feature extraction processes. *Canadian Journal of Psychology,* **37**, 429–38.

Besner, D. and McCann, R. S. (1987). Word frequency and pattern distortion in visual word identification and production: An examination of four classes of models. In *Attention and performance XII: The psychology of reading* (ed. M. Coltheart), pp. 201–20. Hove, UK: Erlbaum.

Besner, D., Davelaar, E., Alcott, D., and Parry, P. (1984). Wholistic reading of alphabetic print: Evidence from the FDM and FBI. In *Orthographies and reading* (ed. L. Henderson), pp. 121–35. Hillsdale, NJ: Erlbaum.

Brown, G. D. A. and Watson, F. L. (1987). First in, first out: Word learning age and spoken word frequency as predictors of word familiarity and word naming latency. *Memory and Cognition,* **15**, 208–16.

Carpenter, G. A. and **Grossberg, S.** (1991). A massively parallel architecture for a self-organizing neural pattern recognition machine. In *Pattern recognition by self-organizing neural networks* (ed. G. A. Carpenter and S. Grossberg), pp. 316–82. Cambridge, MA: MIT Press.

Clark, S. E. and **Gronlund, S. D.** (1996). Global matching models of recognition memory: How the models match the data. *Psychonomic Bulletin and Review,* **3**, 37–60.

Connine, C. M., **Mullennix, J., Shernoff, E., and Yelen, J.** (1990). Word familiarity and frequency in visual and auditory word recognition. *Journal of Experimental Psychology: Learning, Memory, and Cognition,* **16**, 1084–96.

Craik, F. I. M., **Govoni, R., Naveh-Benjamin, M., and Anderson, N. D.** (1996). The effects of divided attention on encoding and retrieval processes in human memory. *Journal of Experimental Psychology: General,* **125**, 159–80.

Donaldson, W. (1996). The role of decision processes in remembering and knowing. *Memory and Cognition,* **24**, 523–33.

Dorfman, D. and **Glanzer, M.** (1988). List composition effects in lexical decision and recognition memory. *Journal of Memory and Language,* **27**, 633–48.

Duchek, J. M. and **Neely, J. H.** (1989). A dissociative word-frequency x levels-of-processing interaction in episodic recognition and lexical decision tasks. *Memory and Cognition,* **17**, 148–62.

Ferrand, L. (1996). The masked repetition priming effect dissipates when increasing the inter-stimulus interval: Evidence from word naming. *Acta Psychologica,* **91**, 15–25.

Forster, K. I. and **Davis, C.** (1984). Repetition priming and frequency attenuation in lexical access. *Journal of Experimental Psychology: Learning, Memory, and Cognition,* **10**, 680–98.

Gardiner, J. M. (1988). Functional aspects of recollective experience. *Memory and Cognition,* **16**, 309–13.

Gardiner, J. M. and **Java, R. I.** (1990). Recollective experience in word and nonword recognition. *Memory and Cognition,* **18**, 23–30.

Gardiner, J. M. and **Parkin, A. J.** (1990). Attention and recollective experience in recognition memory. *Memory and Cognition,* **18**, 579–83.

Gernsbacher, M. A. (1984). Resolving 20 years of inconsistent interactions between lexical familiarity and orthography, concreteness, and polysemy. *Journal of Experimental Psychology: General,* **113**, 256–81.

Glanzer, M. and **Adams, J. K.** (1990). The mirror effect in recognition memory: Data and theory. *Journal of Experimental Psychology: Learning, Memory, and Cognition,* **16**, 5–16.

Glanzer, M. and **Ehrenreich, S. L.** (1979). Structure and search of the internal lexicon. *Journal of Verbal Learning and Verbal Behavior,* **18**, 381–98.

Gordon, B. (1985). Subjective frequency and the lexical decision latency function: Implications for mechanisms of lexical access. *Journal of Memory and Language,* **24**, 631–45.

Goshen-Gottstein, Y. and **Moscovitch, M.** (1995). Repetition priming for newly formed and preexisting associations: Perceptual and conceptual influences. *Journal of Experimental Psychology: Learning, Memory, and Cognition,* **21**, 1229–48.

Grainger, J. and **Jacobs, A. M.** (1996). Orthographic processing in visual word recognition: A multiple read-out model. *Psychological Review,* **103**, 518–65.

Haist, F., **Shimamura, A. P., and Squire, L. R.** (1992). On the relationship between recall and recognition memory. *Journal of Experimental Psychology: Learning, Memory, and Cognition,* **18**, 691–702.

Hintzman, D. L. and **Caulton, D. A.** (1997). Recognition memory and modality judgments: A comparison of retrieval dynamics. *Journal of Memory and Language,* **37**, 1–23.

Hintzman, D. L. and **Curran, T.** (1997). Comparing retrieval dynamics in recognition memory and lexical decision. *Journal of Experimental Psychology: General,* **126**, 228–47.

Hirshman, E. and Master, S. (1997). Modeling the conscious correlates of recognition memory: Reflections on the Remember-Know paradigm. *Memory and Cognition*, 25, 345–51.

Hirst, W., Johnson, M. K., Kim, J. L., Phelps, E. A., Risse, G., and Volpe, B. T. (1986). Recognition and recall in amnesics. *Journal of Experimental Psychology: Learning, Memory, and Cognition*, 12, 445–51.

Huppert, F. A. and Piercy, M. (1976). Recognition memory in amnesic patients: Effects of context and familiarity of material. *Cortex*, 4, 3–20.

Huppert, F. A. and Piercy, M. (1978). The role of trace strength in recency and frequency judgements by amnesic and control subjects. *Quarterly Journal of Experimental Psychology*, 30, 346–54.

Jacoby, L. L. (1983). Remembering the data: Analyzing interactive processes in reading. *Journal of Verbal Learning and Verbal Behavior*, 22, 485–508.

Jacoby, L. L. (1991). A process dissociation framework: Separating automatic from intentional uses of memory. *Journal of Memory and Language*, 30, 513–41.

Jacoby, L. L. and Dallas, M. (1981). On the relationship between autobiographical memory and perceptual learning. *Journal of Experimental Psychology: General*, 110, 306–40.

Jacoby, L. L. and Whitehouse, K. (1989). An illusion of memory: False recognition influenced by unconscious perception. *Journal of Experimental Psychology: General*, 118, 126–35.

James, C. T. (1975). The role of semantic information in lexical decisions. *Journal of Experimental Psychology: Human Perception and Performance*, 104, 130–6.

Johnston, W. A., Dark, V. J., and Jacoby, L. L. (1985). Perceptual fluency and recognition judgments. *Journal of Experimental Psychology: Learning, Memory, and Cognition*, 11, 3–11.

Johnston, W. A., Hawley, K. J., and Elliott, J. M. G. (1991). Contribution of perceptual fluency to recognition memory judgments. *Journal of Experimental Psychology: Learning, Memory, and Cognition*, 17, 210–33.

Joordens, S. and Becker, S. (1997). The long and short of semantic priming effects in lexical decision. *Journal of Experimental Psychology: Learning, Memory, and Cognition*, 23, 1083–105.

Kinoshita, S. (1987). Case alternation effect: Two types of word recognition? *Quarterly Journal of Experimental Psychology*, 39A, 701–20.

Kinoshita, S. (1995). The word frequency effect in recognition memory versus repetition priming. *Memory and Cognition*, 23, 569–80.

Koriat, A. (1993). How do we know that we know? The accessibility model of the feeling of knowing. *Psychological Review*, 100, 609–39.

Koriat, A. (1994). Memory's knowledge of its own knowledge: The accessibility account of the feeling of knowing. In *Metacognition: Knowing about knowing* (ed. J. Metcalfe and A. P. Shimamura), pp. 115–36. Cambridge, MA: MIT Press.

Lee, A. T., Tzeng, O. J. L., Garro, L. C., and Hung, D. L. (1978). Sensory modality and the word-frequency effect. *Memory and Cognition*, 6, 306–11.

Lubow, R. E. and Gewirtz, J. C. (1995). Latent inhibition in humans: Data, theory, and implications for schizophrenia. *Psychological Bulletin*, 117, 87–103.

Maddox, W. T. and Estes, W. K. (1997). Direct and indirect stimulus-frequency effects in recognition. *Journal of Experimental Psychology: Learning, Memory, and Cognition*, 23, 539–59.

Mandler, G. (1980). Recognizing: The judgment of previous occurrence. *Psychological Review*, 87, 252–71.

McKone, E. and Slee, J. A. (1997). Explicit contamination in 'implicit memory' for new associations. *Memory and Cognition*, 25, 352–66.

Metcalfe, J. (1993). Novelty monitoring, metacognition, and control in a composite holographic associative recall model: Implications for Korsakoff amnesia. *Psychological Review*, 100, 3–22.

Metcalfe, J. (1994). A computational modelling approach to novelty monitoring, metacognition, and frontal lobe dysfunction. In *Metacognition: Knowing about knowing* (ed. J. Metcalfe and A. P. Shimamura), pp. 137–56. Cambridge, MA: MIT Press.

Moscovitch, M. (1995). Models of consciousness and memory. In *The cognitive neurosciences* (ed. M. S. Gazzaniga), pp. 1341–56. Cambridge, MA: Bradford.

Moscovitch, M. and Bentin, S. (1993). The fate of repetition effects when recognition approaches chance. *Journal of Experimental Psychology: Learning, Memory, and Cognition*, **19**, 148–58.

Mulligan, N. W. and Hartman, M. (1996). Divided attention and indirect memory tests. *Memory and Cognition*, **24**, 453–65.

Naveh-Benjamin, M., Craik, F. I. M., Guez, J., and Dori, H. (1998). Effects of divided attention on encoding and retrieval processes in human memory: Further support for an asymmetry. *Journal of Experimental Psychology: Learning, Memory, and Cognition*, **24**, 1091–104.

Rajaram, S. and Neely, J. H. (1992). Dissociative masked repetition priming and word frequency effects in lexical decision and episodic recognition tasks. *Journal of Memory and Language*, **31**, 152–82.

Roediger, H. L. and Blaxton, T. A. (1987). Effects of varying modality, surface features, and retention interval on priming in word-fragment completion. *Memory and Cognition*, **15**, 379–88.

Rubin, D. C. (1980). 51 properties of 125 words: A unit analysis of verbal behavior. *Journal of Verbal Learning and Verbal Behavior*, **19**, 736–55.

Rugg, M. D. and Doyle, M. C. (1994). Event-related potentials and stimulus repetition in direct and indirect tests of memory. In *Cognitive electrophysiology* (ed. H.-J. Heinze, T. F. Munte, and G. R. Mangun), pp. 124–48. Boston: Birkhauser.

Scarborough, D. L., Cortese, C., and Scarborough, H. (1977). Frequency and repetition effects in lexical memory. *Journal of Experimental Psychology: Human Perception and Performance*, **3**, 1–17.

Scarborough, D. L., Gerard, L., and Cortese, C. (1979). Accessing lexical memory: The transfer of word repetition effects across task and modality. *Memory and Cognition*, **7**, 3–12.

Shulman, H. G. and Davison, T. C. B. (1977). Control properties of semantic coding in a lexical decision task. *Journal of Verbal Learning and Verbal Behavior*, **16**, 91–8.

Shulman, H. G., Hornak, R., and Sanders, E. (1978). The effect of graphemic, phonetic, and semantic relationships on access to lexical structures. *Memory and Cognition*, **6**, 115–23.

Smith, M. E. and Oscar-Berman, M. (1990). Repetition priming of words and pseudowords in divided attention and in amnesia. *Journal of Experimental Psychology: Learning, Memory, and Cognition*, **16**, 1033–42.

Stone, G. O. and van Orden, G. C. (1993). Strategic control of processing in word recognition. *Journal of Experimental Psychology: Human Perception and Performance*, **19**, 744–74.

Tulving, E. and Kroll, N. (1995). Novelty assessment in the brain and long-term memory encoding. *Psychonomic Bulletin and Review*, **2**, 387–90.

Verfaellie, M., Cermak, L., Letourneau, L., and Zuffante, P. (1991). Repetition effects in a lexical decision task: The role of episodic memory in the performance of alcoholic Korsakoff patients. *Neuropsychologia*, **29**, 641–57.

Watkins, M. J. and Gibson, J. M. (1988). On the relation between perceptual priming and recognition memory. *Journal of Experimental Psychology: Learning, Memory, and Cognition*, **14**, 477–83.

Whaley, C. P. (1978). Word-nonword classification time. *Journal of Verbal Learning and Verbal Behavior*, **17**, 143–54.

Witherspoon, D. and Moscovitch, M. (1989). Stochastic independence between two implicit memory tasks. *Journal of Experimental Psychology: Learning, Memory, and Cognition*, **15**, 22–30.

CHAPTER 14

IMPLICIT MEMORY FOR NEW ASSOCIATIONS: TYPES OF CONCEPTUAL REPRESENTATIONS

BOB UTTL, PETER GRAF, AND STEPHANIE COSENTINO

'Psychologists love to question.' This bumper-sticker claim is affirmed by the myriad of questions that have been asked about implicit and explicit memory phenomena. Nearly two decades of intense research have answered many questions, but others remain as puzzles, fuel for new investigations. In this chapter, we focus on one of these puzzles, the memory representation of newly acquired associations.

We use the phrase 'newly acquired associations' as a shorthand to refer to a specific phenomenon in implicit memory for previously unrelated perceptual wholes such as pairs of unrelated words or pictures. Early compelling demonstrations of this phenomenon were given by the work of Graf and Schacter (e.g., Graf and Schacter, 1985, 1987; Schacter and Graf, 1986a, b, 1989). They required subjects to learn pairs of unrelated words, such as WALLET–CASTLE and MOTHER–RIVER. After a retention interval, memory for the second word from each pair—commonly called the target—was assessed. On the test, targets were presented either paired with the same context word as in the study phase (e.g., WALLET–CASTLE) or paired with a different context word (e.g., MOTHER–CASTLE). The results revealed higher memory for targets that were paired in the same way as at study (i.e., in the same context condition) than for targets paired with different context words (i.e., in the different context condition). The performance advantage in the same versus different context condition provides evidence of memory for the specific pairing of words in the study list. This advantage is assumed to reflect the study phase acquisition of associative information between previously unrelated words.

How is new associative information represented in memory? We do not yet have a clear, compelling answer to this question, despite a substantial number of previous investigations. Previous investigations were designed to document the basic phenomenon (i.e., memory for new associations), and to show various kinds of performance dissociations (e.g., functional, developmental, neuropsychological) between implicit and explicit memory for new associations. The results have inspired a number of theoretical accounts, and they in turn highlight more questions about memory for newly acquired associative information. One of these questions is whether all types of associative information are represented in memory in the same manner. A plausible alternative is that there are distinguishable subtypes of associative representations, for example, for linking concepts represented by words versus for linking concepts with contexts (e.g., spatial, temporal, or emotional contexts). The main goal of the research we report in this chapter was to explore these alternatives.

We begin this chapter with a brief review of previous investigations on implicit memory for new associations and of theoretical accounts that have been offered for their findings. We use the theoretical accounts for making specific predictions about memory for newly acquired associations for two types of materials: word–word pairs and picture–word pairs. The final section of the chapter reports two experiments that tested the predictions.

Core findings

A number of facts are well established about implicit memory for new associations. One of them is that this phenomenon occurs on a variety of different tests. Moscovitch *et al.* (1986) used a test that required reading words shown in degraded displays. In the study phase, subjects had to learn word pairs, and after a retention interval, the same words were re-presented in a visually degraded display, arranged either in the same pairs as in the study list or in different pairs. The task was to read the words aloud. The results showed that subjects were faster at reading words in the same pairs than in different pairs. Paller and Mayes (1994) used a word identification task to explore implicit memory for new associations. At study, their subjects saw unrelated noun pairs each of which was embedded in a meaningful sentence. At test, the nouns were re-presented either in the same pairs as in the study sentences or in different pairs and the task was to identify the second word from each pair. The results showed higher identification of words that were paired as in the study sentences. Graf and Schacter (1985) showed implicit memory for new associations on word-stem completion tests. As described earlier in this chapter, they presented subjects with unrelated words for study, and after a retention interval, implicit memory was assessed with a test that required completing three-letter word stems (e.g., STI___). The stems appeared paired either with the same words as in the study list or with a different word, and the results showed higher completion rates for targets in the same versus different pair condition.

A second core finding about implicit memory for new associations is that at least under some conditions of testing, this phenomenon occurs only following study phase semantic processing of a new connection/association between unrelated words (but see Marsolek *et al.*, 1996). In their seminal work, Graf and Schacter (1985) presented unrelated words either in a condition that required using each word pair in a meaningful sentence or in a condition that required deciding for each pair whether or not the two words had the same number of vowels. Completion test performance showed priming for new associations following semantic study phase processing, but not after the vowel comparison task. Additional investigations clarified this finding. Schacter and Graf (1986a) found implicit memory for new associations only for unrelated noun pairs that were embedded in meaningful sentences, but not for pairs embedded in anomalous sentences (e.g., the new ROCK was returned to the CANDLE). They also showed that semantic processing of the individual words from each pair was not sufficient, that some type of relational processing is necessary for the occurrence of implicit memory for new associations.

Implicit memory for new associations is dissociable from explicit memory for new associations. This claim is supported by experiments that manipulated the degree of semantic elaborative processing at the time of study. For example, Schacter and Graf (1986a) had subjects generate either a meaningful sentence for each to-be-remembered pair or a single word for connecting the two words in each pair. In another experiment, the study task was either to generate a sentence for each pair or to read and rate for meaningfulness a sentence that contained each pair. The results showed the same level of implicit memory for new associations across these study phase activities. By contrast, explicit memory for new associations varied, depending on the degree of semantic elaborative processing required by each study task (see also Graf and Schacter, 1989).

Additional investigations of implicit memory for new associations with young and older adults, and with various patient groups have yielded relevant but inconsistent findings. For example, a handful of studies have focused on age-related changes. Monti *et al.* (1997) used a re-reading task for assessing implicit memory and found similar levels of implicit memory for new associations in young and older adults. Howard *et al.* (1991) also found comparable levels of implicit memory for new associations in young and older adults, but only when study phase learning was self-paced. They assessed implicit memory by means of a word-stem completion test and obtained age-related performance reductions 'under less-than-optimal study conditions'. Yet other studies (see Ergis *et al.*, 1998; Van der Linden *et al.*, 1992) found clear age-effects in implicit memory for new associations. Investigations with amnesic patients have produced similarly conflicting outcomes (Gabrieli *et al.*, 1997; Graf and Schacter, 1985; Musen and Squire, 1993; Schacter and Graf, 1986a; Shimamura and Squire, 1989; for reviews see Bower, 1996; Schacter, 1990, 1994).

Theoretical *accounts*

Several explanations have been proposed for these findings, notably for the fact that the basic phenomenon—implicit memory for new associations—occurs on a variety of different tests, that it is dissociable from explicit memory for new associations, that it occurs (under some methods of testing) only following semantic elaborative study phase processing, that it may or may not vary across the adult life span, and that it may or may not be present in amnesic patients. In this chapter, we focus on two explanations, the structural description view of Schacter and his colleagues (Schacter, 1990; Schacter *et al.*, 1990, 1993; Tulving and Schacter, 1990) and the reactivation view of Bower, Mandler, and their colleagues (Bower, 1996; Johnson, 1994; Graf and Ryan, 1990; Mandler, 1981, 1991, 1994). Despite obvious differences between these two views (for example, their emphasis on systems versus processes respectively), they give closely similar explanations for implicit memory for newly acquired associations. They also offer similar explanations for word priming effects.

By Schacter's view, word 'priming effects on a variety of implicit memory tests rely heavily on a class of modular processors or subsystems that ... I will refer to as a perceptual representation system, or PRS for short' (Schacter, 1990, p. 544). The study phase processing of a word is assumed to create a representation of its particular visual-perceptual features. In the test phase, this representation facilitates the re-processing of words and produces a priming effect. Schacter maintains that the representations that mediate priming capture the form and structure of words, but do not include information about context, thereby explaining why study phase processing manipulations (e.g., semantic versus perceptual) tend not to influence the magnitude of priming effects on such tests as word identification and stem completion (Graf and Mandler, 1984; Graf *et al.*, 1982; for a review see Challis and Roediger, 1993; Challis *et al.*, 1996). Additional assumptions about the PRS and the nature of structural representations account for modality specific priming effects, as well as for priming effects that are specific to physical features of words under some but not other study/test conditions (e.g., Graf and Ryan, 1991).

The activation view by Bower, Mandler, and their colleagues gives a similar explanation for word priming effects. The core assumption, as indicated by Figure 14.1, is that words are represented by a continuum of processes—shown as network nodes—and by interconnections among them. At one end of the continuum are processes recruited for analyzing the physical features of words, and at the other end are the processes engaged for semantic analysis. The figure over-simplifies; it does not show either the many levels of nodes that may sit between visual features and logogens or lexical units (e.g., letter representations, orthographic representations, phonemic representations), nor the rich associative connections among all nodes (see Anderson and Bower, 1973; Bower, 1996). The presentation or study phase encoding of a word is assumed to engage sensory feature processes, and the co-processing of the features that constitute a letter is thought to activate the node for that letter. In turn, activated letter nodes spread activation to orthographic nodes, and from here to word and concept nodes. The subject is thought to perceive that lexical unit whose current level of activation is higher than that of all competing units and is above the awareness threshold level.

The model explains word priming by assuming that whenever a pre-existing node-network is successfully activated, that network is strengthened (i.e., connection weights are

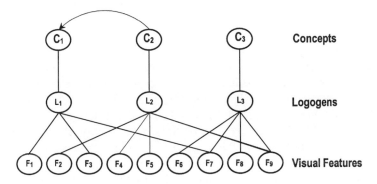

Figure 14.1 Representation of words as a network of nodes and interconnections among them. Physical features (F) of words have associative links to nodes representing their structural configuration called logogens (L). Logogens in turn have associative links to nodes representing concepts (C).

changed), and this elevated strength is maintained for a significant duration. Mandler and his colleagues have used the term integration or intra-unit organization to refer to the strength of connections among the constituents of items. When a studied item is re-presented in the test phase, activation produced by processing its features will spread through the network and will preferentially—because of elevated connection strength or higher integration—reactivate a previously activated representation. By this route, the elevated strengthening of items' representations functions analogously to the structural representations postulated by Schacter.

The structural representation and activation view give equally compatible accounts for priming effects for newly acquired associations. Schacter and his colleagues (Schacter, 1990; Tulving and Schacter, 1990) postulate that acquiring new associations involves semantic learning, more specifically, a modification to or addition of information in semantic or episodic memory. PRS representations are assumed not to contain semantic/associative information. This type of information is part of other representations (i.e., representations in episodic or semantic memory), with PRS representations facilitating access to them.

The network view depicted in Figure 14.1 postulates that priming effects for newly acquired associations are mediated by newly formed connections between concept nodes. It is assumed that prior to being paired in the experiment, there is no connection between the concepts corresponding to two unrelated words (e.g., C_2 and C_1), but such connections are established by semantic-elaborative study phase processing of paired words (e.g., by using paired words in a meaningful sentence). At the time of testing, when a target word is re-presented with the same context word as at study, processing the context word is assumed to activate its concept representation and activation spreads via the newly acquired association to the target's representations. By this route, the target's representations will be pre-activated, and consequently, less data driven processing of the target is required for its successful identification (i.e., for the current level of activation of the target representation to reach the awareness threshold). When a target is presented for testing together with a different context (i.e., not the same as at study), there is no link between the corresponding concept nodes (e.g., from C_3 to C_1) and thus no opportunity for the spreading of activation from the context to the target representations.

More detailed descriptions of the structural representation and activation views are available elsewhere (e.g., Bower, 1996; Schacter and Tulving, 1994). Our purpose here is to give only just enough information in order to highlight similarities between the views, specifically, the fact that both explain priming for newly acquired associations by invoking higher-order—beyond the word level—representations and newly formed connections between them. More critical in the context of this chapter is that both views postulate only one type of representation/associative connection in order to account for priming of newly acquired associations (note: they postulate a variety of representations at or below the word level, such as visual and phonemic feature representations, geon representations, letter representations, letter-pattern representations). By this postulate, this one type of higher-order representation would have to be harnessed for all types of associative learning and remembering, for example, for mediating implicit and explicit memory for newly acquired associations, for associating two paired words and for linking events with contexts. It seems more plausible to us that different types of representations are recruited for different kinds of associative learning and remembering.

The latter possibility seems consistent with previous findings of performance dissociations between implicit and explicit memory for newly acquired associations (e.g., Graf and Schacter, 1985, 1987; Schacter and Graf, 1986a, b, 1989). These types of dissociations might occur, for example, because different types of higher-order representations are recruited for implicit and explicit memory tests. However, performance dissociations may also be explained by postulating only one type of representation that is harnessed to different degrees for different memory tests. Evidence from investigations with young and older adults and with amnesic patients is also inconclusive. If implicit and explicit memory for newly acquired associations were mediated by different types of higher-order representations, we might expect the former—implicit memory for new associations—to be spared in older adults and in amnesic patients, consistent with what is known about spared word priming effects, even in the face of significant declines or impairments in explicit memory for new associations.

Previous attempts to identify performance dissociations between implicit and explicit memory for newly acquired associations are relevant to, but not focused on the central question that motivated our investigation: Whether implicit memory for newly acquired associations is mediated by one type or multiple types of higher-order representation(s)? We favor the multiple-types option, in part because of performance dissociations across different explicit memory tests. The finding that explicit episodic and source memory for items can be dissociated (Jurica and Shimamura, 1999; Schacter, 1990; Schacter et al., 1994) seems to point to two kinds of associative representations. If two different kinds of associative representations are engaged for explicit memory, why not assume the same for implicit memory?

The new research we report in this chapter focused on the representation of newly acquired associations between word–word pairs and picture–word pairs. We considered two possible higher-order representations, as shown in Figure 14.2. The *top* panel reflects the assumption that the representation of a word (i.e., the logogen L_1) and the representation of a depicted object (i.e., the imagen I_1) may connect with the same concept representation (C_1) (see Bower, 1996). The *bottom* panel shows a different higher-order representation for each logogen and imagen. Consistent with the *top* panel, the word-name of an object and a picture of the same object have the same concept representation, and this representation can be activated either via an underlying logogen (L_1) or imagen (I_1) representation. We might expect, therefore, that in an experiment that employs both words and pictures as contexts (with words as targets), we would find the same amount of priming for newly acquired associations.

The *top* panel of Figure 14.2 shows an associative link between I- and L-representations. Consistent with Paivio's (1991) dual code view of picture encoding, this link represents the possibility that a picture of a common object will activate both its imagen and logogen representations. If so, when a picture is used as the context, it might activate two representations (e.g., L_2 and I_2), and in turn, this may cause a greater or faster activation of a target's concept node and thereby yield a larger associative priming effect.

The representation depicted on the *bottom* panel of Figure 14.2 makes the same prediction, albeit by implicating different higher-order representations for words and pictures. However, the *bottom* panel of Figure 14.2 permits a more interesting prediction. It seems plausible that associative links between word concepts (e.g., from ${}_wC_2$ to ${}_wC_1$) are

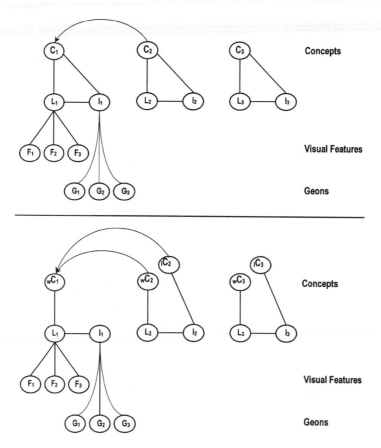

Figure 14.2 Representation of newly acquired associations between word–word pairs and picture–word pairs. The *top* panel reflects the assumption that the representation of a word (i.e., logogen L_1) and the representation of a depicted object (i.e., imagen I_1) may be linked to the same concept representation (C_1). Associative links between imagens and logogens reflect a possibility that a picture of a common object activates both its imagen and logogen representation (Pavio, 1991). Note that geons (G) are parts of objects (Biederman, 1986) analogous to features of words. The *bottom* panel reflects the possibility that higher level concept representations for words and pictures are different (i.e., $_wC$ and $_iC$), with logogens and imagens linked to their corresponding concept representations. Consequently, associative links between target word concepts and context word concepts (i.e., $_wC_2$ to $_wC_1$) are different from associative links between target word concepts and context picture concepts (i.e., $_iC_2$ to $_wC_1$).

different—perhaps stronger or more easily formed—from associative links between picture and word concepts (e.g., from $_iC_2$ to $_wC_1$). It may be that forging a link between two items in the same subsystem is easier than forging a link between two items represented in different subsystems (see Schacter, 1994). By this possibility, we would expect that some experimental manipulations would reveal differences in associative memory for word–word pairs versus picture–word pairs.

Overview of new empirical work

In order to investigate these possibilities, we conducted two experiments that used a method similar to Graf and Schacter (1985). The general strategy was to examine memory across variables that are known to affect explicit test performance, and to track the influence of these variables on implicit memory for both item and associative information. For each experiment, participants first learned a set of paired items, each pair consisting either of two familiar, unrelated words or of a picture of a common object paired with a familiar word (see Table 14.1 for examples). At the time of testing, the right-hand or target words were displayed either in the context of the same item (word or picture) as at study or in the context of a different item. Implicit memory was assessed by means of a word identification test and explicit memory was assessed by means of a word recognition test.

In Experiment 1, memory was assessed either a few minutes after study or after a one week delay. Previous research has shown that similarly long delays decrease explicit memory test performance, while having no effect or only a minimal effect on implicit tests that focus on item information (for reviews see Mitchell *et al.*, 1990; Roediger *et al.*, 1994). Consistent with such findings, the delay manipulation was expected to lower memory for associative but not item information. More importantly, on the assumption that only one type of higher-order representation is involved in memory for associative information, we expected that the delay manipulation would have the same influence on implicit and explicit memory for associative information and on implicit memory for word–word and picture–word pairs. For Experiment 2, the subjects were young and older adults. Previous research has shown that such age manipulations produce large effects in explicit memory but not in implicit memory for item information (for reviews see Gabrieli, 1999; Graf and Masson, 1993). We expected to replicate this finding. More critical, on the assumption that only one type of higher-order representation is involved in memory for associative information, we expected that the age manipulation would have the same influence on implicit and explicit memory for associative information and on implicit memory for word–word and picture–word pairs.

Table 14.1 Examples of study and test pairs

Study pairs	Test pairs
	Same context
glove–quarter	glove–quarter
WHALE–mirror	WHALE–mirror
	Different context
apple–artery	wallet–artery
wallet–mystery	apple–mystery
LEMON–stair	SOCCER–stair
SOCCER–cotton	LEMON–cotton
	New (non-studied)
	ring–bench
	PEANUT–throat

Note: Items in lowercase were presented as words and items in uppercase were presented as pictures.

Experiment 1

Method

Subjects and design

The participants were 144 undergraduate students who received course credit. The design had two between-subjects factors—test type (explicit or implicit) and test delay (a few minutes or one week), and three within-subject factors—study/test condition (same context, different context), context type (word, picture), and history (studied, non-studied). Thirty-two participants were randomly assigned to each of three between-subjects conditions, but 48 participated in the delayed recognition test condition.

Materials

A set of 256 medium frequency words each being the name of a concrete common object was used to construct the critical context-target pairs: 128 targets (word frequency: $M = 36$, $SD = 21$; 4–10 letters in length), 128 contexts (word frequency: $M = 28$, $SD = 23$, 4–10 letters in length). An additional 24 one-word object names were selected for making practice context-target pairs, and 38 concrete word/object names were required for calibrating each subjects' baseline target identification performance.

Two lists of 64 context-target pairs were created by the following procedure. First, two context and two target words were selected randomly from the set of 256, without replacement, and these were arranged to form two pairs. These same words were also used to form two additional context-target pairs, as illustrated in Table 14.1. By this method of constructing pairs, it was possible at testing to present targets either with the same contexts as at study or with different contexts. For quality control, each pair was checked for the presence of familiar, meaningful associations between the context and target; when such associations were present, the selected words were returned to the pool, and a new sample of four was drawn.

The contexts or left-hand member of each pair was either a one-word object name, or it was a color picture of the named object. The color pictures were obtained from two clip art libraries: CorelDraw! 5.0 (CorelDRAW!, 1994) and Charisma 4.0 (Charisma, 1990). Each picture was scaled so as to span approximately 220 pixels on its longest axis, and was centered on a white 320×240 pixel rectangle. For each context, we also prepared an identical display that contained the object name, centered and typed in black ink, in 24 point Dauphin font.

For each subject, one list of 64 pairs was used for assessing performance in the word–word pair condition; the other list was used for the picture – word pair condition. Across subjects, each list was used equally often for each of these conditions. For the purpose of counterbalancing materials across the test context conditions, each list was arranged to form four sets of 16 pairs. Within each set, each target was linked with two contexts, one of which was used for testing the target in the same context condition and the other for testing it in the different context condition. Across subjects, each set was used equally often in each experimental condition (i.e., the conditions listed in Table 14.1).

All contexts were displayed on a 15-inch NEC 4FGe color graphics monitor, driven by an ATI Mach64 Turbo Graphics Pro video card operating in 1024 by 768 resolution, 15 bit color mode, with a 75 Hz refresh rate (i.e., requiring 13.33 ms per refresh). The presentation of materials was controlled by PicBlit3.0 (Uttl, 1995).

Procedure

The experiment was described as examining the influence of different contexts on perception and memory. Participants were tested individually in a session that lasted about 45 minutes. They were seated at a desk about 60 cm from the computer monitor. The session had a study and test phase.

The study phase was the same for all subjects. On each trial, a context—either a word or an object picture—was displayed immediately above the vertical midline of the screen, centered horizontally. Subjects rated how much they liked this item on a 3-point scale (1 = dislike, 2 = neutral, 3 = like) and they registered their ratings by means of a 3-button mouse. Immediately after pressing the mouse button or after 2 seconds had elapsed, a target word was displayed immediately below the vertical midline of the screen, centered horizontally. The subjects were required to create and say aloud a sentence connecting the context and target in a meaningful way, within 15 seconds. The experimenter recorded (via the computer keyboard) whether a meaningful sentence had been generated in the allotted time, and this event blanked the screen for ~ 1 second and initiated the next trial. The context and target remained on the screen until the end of each trial. Subjects were instructed in and they practiced this method until they felt comfortable with it and then 64 critical context-target pairs were presented for study. For each subject, the study list included 32 (two sets of 16) picture–word pairs and 32 (two sets of 16) word–word pairs. Counterbalancing was used to ensure that across subjects, all context-target pairs appeared equally often in each condition.

Immediately following the study phase, subjects assigned to the no-delay implicit test condition were assessed for baseline target identification. The goal was to determine for each individual what target display duration would yield 50% identification accuracy. On each trial, subjects were shown a fixation point—a small square—followed by a 100 ms long tone. After 500 ms, the fixation point was replaced by a 200 ms long pre-mask, a series of line segments and ampersands, immediately followed by the to-be-identified target word and then the post-mask (the same as the pre-mask). Subjects' task was to identify the displayed target word and say it aloud, within 3 seconds. The experimenter entered subjects' responses on the keyboard. This action cleared the post-mask and started the next trial. In order to determine what target display duration would yield 50% identification accuracy, the display duration was set to ten refresh cycles (~133 ms) for the first trial. After two consecutive correct responses, the display duration was reduced by one cycle, and this procedure continued until a subject failed to make a correct response within five consecutive trials. The display duration identified by this method was used for presenting all targets for the implicit word identification test. The average display duration set by this procedure was 44.1 ms (median = 39 ms, range 26 ms to 78 ms).

Implicit memory testing followed immediately after assessing baseline identification performance. The test consisted of presenting, randomly ordered, 128 context-target pairs (two sets of 16 picture–word pairs and two sets of 16 word–word pairs) from the study list, plus 64 non-studied context-target pairs (two sets of 16 picture–word pairs and two sets of 16 word–word pairs). For each type of studied pairs (picture–word, word–word), one set of 16 was used for assessing performance in the same context condition while the other was used for assessing performance in the different context condition (see Table 14.1 for examples). Across subjects, counterbalancing ensured that each pair was used equally often in each experimental condition.

For the test, contexts and targets were presented exactly as at study, except that the display of each target followed the sequence of events used for assessing baseline identification performance. According to the instructions used for study, subjects rated how much they liked each displayed context, and they were required to identify and name out loud each target within 3 seconds of its appearance. Subjects were encouraged to guess if they could not identify a target; alternatively, they responded with the word 'pass'. The experimenter recorded target identification accuracy on the computer keyboard.

For the explicit test, the same list of 128 studied and non-studied context-target pairs was presented for an old/new recognition test. (They were arranged into sets and assigned to conditions in the same manner as for the identification test.) On each trial, the context and target were presented exactly the same way as during the implicit memory test, except that target displays were not masked and they remained on the screen until subjects responded. Subjects' task was to decide, as quickly and accurately as possible, whether or not the target had appeared in the study list, regardless of the context that appeared with it at study. The test was self-paced, with each mouse button response initiating the next trial.

The delayed tests were administered one week after study, according to the exact same procedure as the immediate test.

Results

On the old/new recognition test, the dependent measure was the proportion of hits—words correctly identified as studied—and the proportion of false alarms—non-studied words that were called old. On the word identification test, the dependent measure was the proportion of target words correctly identified in each experimental condition. Target word identification was too easy for some subjects and too difficult for others, thereby limiting the test's sensitivity to priming effects. For this reason, the data from all subjects who identified less than 3% (i.e., where performance was limited by a floor effect) or more than 75%[1] (i.e., where performance was too close to the ceiling and restricted the opportunity for substantial priming to occur) of the non-studied words were excluded from the analysis. We also screened the data for univariate outliers—values that differed by more than two interquartile ranges from their medians, and to reduce their influence on statistical analyses, all outliers were set equal to the value of the largest or smallest non-outlier, respectively. One percent of the data were identified as outliers. Screening for multivariate outliers using the Malanahobis statistics with $\alpha < .01$ revealed no outliers either in old/new recognition or identification test performance.

Identification test performance

The *top* panel of Figure 14.3 shows performance on the word identification test. A preliminary analysis focused on baseline performance, that is, on identification of

---

[1] Consistent with the results from previous investigations, we anticipated priming effects of about 25%. For this reason, for subjects with baseline performance in excess of 75%, their performance on studied items was expected to reach 100%, that is, to be marred by a ceiling effect.

non-studied (new) targets. An ANOVA of baseline performance showed a small overall advantage for targets displayed with word vs. picture contexts, $F(1,62) = 4.30$, $MSe = 0.01$, $\eta^2 = .065$, $p = .04$. No other effects were significant. In view of the significant effect due to context type, all subsequent analyses focused on priming scores defined as the difference between identification of studied (old) versus non-studied (new) target words.

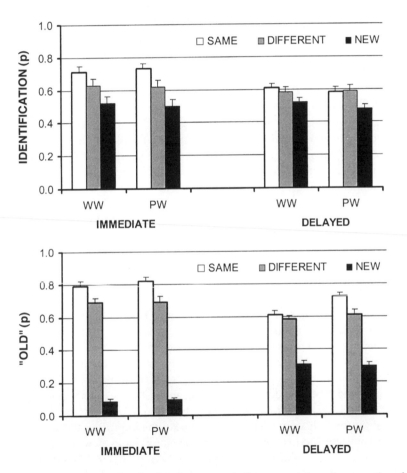

Figure 14.3 The *top* panel shows identification test accuracy; the *bottom* panel shows the proportion of targets called 'old' in Experiment 1. Performance is shown separately for immediate test (i.e., a few minutes after the study phase end) and for delayed test (i.e., one week after the study phase) and for word–word (WW) context-target pairs and picture–word (PW) context-target pairs. Same, different, and new labels refer to context item status (i.e., same context item, different studied context item, new not-studied context item). Performance for word–word context is identified with WW whereas performance for picture–word context is identified with PW. Bars represent standard errors of means.

The figure highlights clear context effects in priming—an influence due to the same/different context manipulation—under immediate but not delayed testing conditions. This observation is supported by an ANOVA of priming scores that had test delay (immediate, delayed) as a between-subjects factor with context type (word, picture) and study/test condition (same, different) as within-subjects factors. The results revealed a significant main effect for study/test condition, $F(1,62) = 18.22$, $MSe = 0.01$, $\eta^2 = .227$, $p < .01$, a marginal main effect for test delay, $F(1,62) = 2.84$, $MSe = 0.12$, $\eta^2 = .043$, $p = .10$, and a marginal main effect for context type, $F(1,62) = 3.93$, $MSe = 0.01$, $\eta^2 = .059$, $p = .06$. More importantly, there was also a significant study/test condition $\times$ test delay interaction, $F(1,62) = 10.83$, $MSe = 0.01$, $\eta^2 = .149$, $p < .01$. No other effects approached significance. A follow-up ANOVA of the priming scores from the immediate test showed a significant main effect due to study/test condition, $F(1,31) = 31.10$, $MSe = 0.01$, $\eta^2 = .500$, $p < .01$. An ANOVA of the priming scores from the delayed test showed no significant effects.

Recognition test performance

The *bottom* panel of Figure 14.3 shows performance on the recognition test. The depicted performance levels show that the delay manipulation affected both hits—correct recognition of studied targets, and false alarms—false recognition on non-studied words. For this reason, we used adjusted recognition scores, defined as hits-minus-false alarms, for all subsequent analyses.

The findings that bear most directly on the present investigation are the study/test condition effects on the immediate recognition test with both word and picture contexts, and the fact that on the delayed test, performance showed an influence due to the same/different manipulation only with picture contexts. This observation is supported by an ANOVA of the adjusted recognition scores. The ANOVA included test delay as a between-subjects factor with context type (word, picture) and study/test condition (same, different) as within-subjects factors. The results showed significant main effects for test delay, $F(1,78) = 101.66$, $MSe = 0.08$, $\eta^2 = .565$, $p < .01$, for context type, $F(1,78) = 7.97$, $MSe = 0.01$, $\eta^2 = .092$, $p < .01$, and for study/test condition, $F(1,78) = 35.91$, $MSe = 0.02$, $\eta^2 = .315$, $p < .01$. There were also two significant interaction effects, one between test delay $\times$ context type, $F(1,78) = 8.62$, $MSe = 0.01$, $\eta^2 = .099$, $p < .01$, and the other between context type $\times$ study/test condition, $F(1,78) = 4.54$, $MSe = .05$, $\eta^2 = .055$, $p = .03$. The three-way interaction among context, study/test condition, and test delay did not reach significance. To clarify further the significant two-way interaction effects, we conducted separate ANOVAs of the immediate and delayed test data. For the immediate test, an ANOVA with context type and study/test condition as within-subjects factors showed a significant main effect due to study/test condition, $F(1,31) = 23.90$, $MSe = 0.02$, $\eta^2 = .435$, $p < .01$. On the delayed test, the same type of ANOVA showed significant main effects for context type, $F(1,47) = 17.92$, $MSe = 0.01$, $\eta^2 = .276$, $p < .01$, for study/test condition, $F(1,47) = 12.95$, $MSe = 0.02$, $\eta^2 = .207$, $p < .01$, and a significant context type $\times$ study/test condition interaction, $F(1,47) = 5.46$, $MSe = 0.01$, $\eta^2 = .104$, $p = .02$. Follow-up simple effects analyses showed a significant effect due to study/test condition for picture contexts, $F(1,47) = 16.30$, $MSe = 0.02$, $\eta^2 = .257$, $p < .01$, but not for word contexts, $F(1,47) = 1.57$, $MSe = 0.01$, $\eta^2 = .033$, $p = .21$.

Discussion

The study/test delay manipulation had a much larger influence on overall recognition test performance than on priming of individual words, consistent with a wealth of prior research. More interesting and new are the findings of same/different effects due to both word and picture contexts. On the identification test, word and picture contexts produced equivalent associative effects under immediate testing conditions, and no evidence of associative priming under delayed testing conditions. By contrast, on the explicit recognition test, word and picture contexts produced equivalent associative effects under immediate testing conditions, and on the delayed test an associative effect was still present but only when targets were tested in the context of pictures.

This pattern of findings is consistent with both panels in Figure 14.2, but it is explained more parsimoniously by the model depicted in the *top* panel. The finding that word and picture contexts yielded equivalent associative memory effects, at least under immediate testing conditions, is consistent with the view that a picture of a common object and its name activate the same higher-order (concept) representation, that the same type of associative link may be used for encoding both picture–word and word–word relational information. This finding may be interpreted without appealing to Paivio's dual code view (1991), that is, without postulating a link between imagen and logogen representations (e.g., between I_2 and L_2 in Figure 14.2).

The finding of an associative effect with picture but not word contexts on the delayed recognition test may be explained in terms of the memory advantage of pictures over words. It is well known that memory for pictures is better (i.e., higher, more enduring) than memory for words, and for this reason, pictures may be more effective as associative retrieval cues. Consistent with this interpretation, we assume that the newly formed associations shown in the *top* panel of Figure 14.2 (e.g., between C_2 and C_1) are still present at the time of the delayed test. They may have lost strength over time (i.e., across the retention interval), and as a consequence, identification performance was facilitated only under intentional retrieval conditions, or only with context cues that evoked a strong feeling of familiarity or recognition.

The finding of an associative effect with picture contexts on the delayed recognition but not identification test provides evidence that performance on these two tests was guided by different retrieval strategies. However, this finding may also be used to argue that all associative memory effects shown in Figure 14.3, including those observed on the immediate identification test, are the product of an intentional memory retrieval strategy. Consistent with the interpretation laid out in the preceding paragraph, this type of strategy would be effective under immediate testing conditions when memory for all contexts was still strong, when subjects were likely to consciously connect up all parts of the experiment. By this view, if all associative priming effects in Experiment 1 reflect the same retrieval strategy, one should never expect to find evidence that would support the representational model shown in the *bottom* panel of Figure 14.2.

We are unable to rule out this kind of 'explicit contamination' interpretation for the associative priming effects observed in Experiment 1. However, this kind of interpretation is weakened by post-experiment interviews that provided no evidence that subjects in the identification test conditions were engaging in explicit retrieval, that they were using contexts as part of an intentional memory retrieval strategy.

Experiment 2

The overall goal of Experiment 2 was the same as for Experiment 1, that is, to find out whether one type or multiple types of higher-order representations are involved in memory for newly acquired associative information. The subjects were adults from different age groups: young and old. Previous research has shown that such age manipulations have large effects on explicit but not implicit memory for item information, and we expected to replicate this finding. More interesting, on the assumption that only one type of higher-order representation is involved in memory for associative information, we expected that the age manipulation would have the same influence on implicit and explicit memory for associative information as well as on implicit memory for word – word and picture – word pairs.

Method

Subjects and design
The participants were 36 young adults (age: M = 22.2 yrs, SD = 2.4) and 36 older adults (age: M = 69.8 yrs, SD = 6.7). All participants were volunteers recruited either via a database at the National Institutes of Health in Bethesda, Maryland, or through newspaper advertisements in Washington, DC. The participants were paid between $30 and $40, according to the time required for completing the experiment. The design had age (young, old) as a between-subjects factor, and it had four within-subjects factors: test type (explicit, implicit), context type (word, picture), study/test condition (same, different), and history (studied, non-studied).

Materials
The critical materials were 512 words/object-names arranged into two equal lists. One of the 256-item lists consisted of the word/object-names from Experiment 1; the other list consisted of new words, selected according to the exact same criteria. The words in the two lists were comparable (i.e., not statistically different from each other) in terms of word frequency, concreteness, and letter length. Each list was arranged to form 128 (eight sets of 16) pairs according to the same method used for Experiment 1. The pairs from the first list were used for assessing performance in the picture–word conditions; the pairs from the second list were used for the word–word condition. All words and pictures were displayed using the same equipment as in Experiment 1 except that we used a 17-inch Sony ST-II monitor with a higher 100 Hz refresh rate (10 ms per refresh cycle).

Procedure
Each subject was tested individually in a session that lasted between 2–2.5 hours. The session consisted of the following task/test sequence: study Phase 1, implicit memory testing, finger tapping (see Graf and Uttl, 1995), making simple reactions (see Graf and Uttl, 1995), card sorting (see Graf and Uttl, 1995), study Phase 2, recognition testing, trail making (see Spreen and Strauss, 1991), speeded word reading and the North American Adult Reading Test (NAART; Spreen and Strauss, 1991). The neuropsychological tests, that is, all but the implicit memory test and the recognition memory test, were administered according to

published procedures. The neuropsychological tests were included in the battery for reasons that are beyond the scope of this chapter, and thus we do not report the findings from these tests.

Each study phase was administered according to the exact same method as in Experiment 1. Each study list had 64 randomly ordered pairs, including 32 picture–word pairs and 32 word–word pairs. Each test list had 128 pairs, including the 64 from the study list plus 32 non-studied picture–word pairs, and 32 non-studied word–word pairs. Across subjects, the pairs were assigned so that each appeared equally often in each study and test list, in each context (same, different) condition, and in each history (studied, non-studied) condition. The identification test and the recognition test were administered as in Experiment 1.

The average display duration set by the adjustment procedure was 35.8 ms (median = 29 ms, range 19 ms to 69 ms) for young adults and 54.5 ms (median = 49 ms, range 29 ms to 89 ms) for older adults.

Results

The critical dependent variables and the methods used for screening outliers were the same as for Experiment 1. In Experiment 2, < 1% of the data were identified as outliers. Two subjects (one young and one old) who were identified as multivariate outliers were replaced.

Identification test performance

The top panel of Figure 14.4 shows performance on the word identification test. A preliminary ANOVA of baseline performance showed a marginal main effect due to context type (words, pictures), $F(1,70) = 3.13$, $MSe = .02$, $\eta^2 >= .043$, $p = .08$. No other effects approached significance. In view of the effect due to context type, all subsequent analyses focused on priming scores.

The means in Figure 14.4 provide clear evidence of associative priming effects, but the size of these effects was influenced by context type (word, picture) and by age group. An ANOVA of priming scores, with age group (young, old) as a between-subjects factor and context type (word, picture) and study/test (same, different) condition as within-subjects factors, showed a significant main effects for study/test condition, $F(1,70) = 16.86$, $MSe = 0.02$, $\eta^2 = .194$, $p < .01$, as well as a significant age group × context type × study/test condition interaction, $F(1,70) = 4.27$, $MSe = 0.01$, $\eta^2 = .058$, $p = .04$. We explored the interaction by means of two follow up analyses. For word contexts, an ANOVA that had age group as a between-subjects factor and study/test condition as a within-subjects factor showed a significant effects for age group, $F(1,70) = 3.94$, $MSe = 0.07$, $\eta^2 = .053$, $p = 0.05$, and a significant effect for study/test condition, $F(1,70) = 13.12$, $MSe = 0.02$, $\eta^2 = .158$, $p < .01$. The study/test condition × age group interaction was not significant, $F < 1$, $\eta^2 = .007$, $p = .49$. For picture contexts, the same kind of ANOVA showed a marginal effect for age group, $F(1,70) = 2.85$, $MSe = 0.07$, $\eta^2 = .039$, $p = 0.10$, and a significant main effect for study/test condition, $F(1,70) = 7.08$, $MSe = 0.02$, $\eta^2 = .092$, $p = 01$. In addition, there was also a significant study/test condition × age group interaction, $F(1,70) = 3.94$, $MSe = 0.02$, $\eta^2 = .053$, $p = .05$. Simple effects analyses showed a

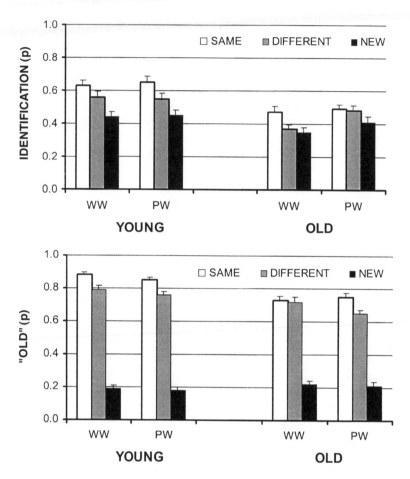

Figure 14.4 The *top* panel shows identification accuracy; the *bottom* panel shows the proportions of targets called 'old' in Experiment 2. Performance is shown separately for young and old adults and for word–word (WW) context-target pairs and picture–word (PW) context-target pairs. Same, different, and new labels refer to context item status (i.e., same context item, different studied context item, new not-studied context item). Bars represent standard errors of means.

significant effect of study/test condition for the young group, $F(1,35) = 9.90$, $MSe = 0.02$, $\eta^2 = .220$, $p < .01$, but not for the old group, $F < 1$, $\eta^2 = .007$, $p = 62$.

Recognition test performance

The *bottom* panel of Figure 14.4 shows performance on the recognition test. The figure shows that overall recognition accuracy decreased with age. More interestingly, for the word contexts, associative effects were absent in the old groups' performance whereas for the picture contexts, both young and old subjects showed evidence of memory for newly acquired associative information.

An ANOVA of hits-minus-false alarm scores, with age group as a between-subjects factor and context type and study/test condition as within-subjects factors, showed significant main effects for age group, $F(1,70) = 26.87$, $MSe = 0.05$, $\eta^2 = .277$, $p < .01$, and study/test condition, $F(1,70) = 26.14$, $MSe = 0.01$, $\eta^2 = .272$, $p < .01$, as well as a significant context type $\times$ study/test condition interaction, $F(1,70) = 4.05$, $MSe = 0.01$, $\eta^2 = .055$, $p = .05$, and a marginal age group $\times$ context type $\times$ study/test condition interaction, $F(1,70) = 3.47$, $MSe = 0.01$, $\eta^2 = .047$, $p = 0.07$. For word contexts, an ANOVA with age group as a between-subjects factor and study/test condition as a within-subjects factor showed a significant effects for age group, $F(1,70) = 20.76$, $MSe = 0.03$, $\eta^2 = .228$, $p < .01$, study/test condition, $F(1,70) = 7.01$, $MSe = 0.01$, $\eta^2 = .091$, $p = .01$, and a significant study/test condition $\times$ age group interaction, $F(1,70) = 4.25$, $MSe = 0.01$, $\eta^2 = .057$, $p = .04$. For picture contexts, an ANOVA showed a significant main effects for age group, $F(1,70) = 22.93$, $MSe = 0.03$, $\eta^2 = .247$, $p < .01$, and study/test condition, $F(1,70) = 31.74$, $MSe = 0.01$, $\eta^2 = .312$, $p < .01$. Importantly, the study/test condition $\times$ age group interaction did not reach significance, $F < 1$, $\eta^2 < .001$, $p = .92$.

Discussion

The critical new finding from Experiment 2 is the older adults' performance on the identification and recognition test. On the identification test, they showed an associative effect on word–word but not picture–word pairs, whereas on the recognition test an associative effect occurred for picture–word but not word–word pairs. Young adults' performance revealed an associative effect for both pair types, on both types of tests.

The pattern of performance by the older adults is strong evidence against an 'explicit contamination' interpretation of the associative effects found on the identification test. A contamination interpretation would have to predict the same pattern of associative effects for identification and recognition test performance. The finding of different associative effects for word–word and picture–word pairs on identification and recognition suggests that different retrieval strategies or processes mediate performance on these tests.

The recognition test results from the young and old groups show the same pattern as found on the immediate and delayed test, respectively, of Experiment 1, and therefore, we offer a similar interpretation. We assume that aging is accompanied by a decrease in the quantity or quality of encoding associative information, and further, that the effect of this age-related change in processing is similar to that brought about by the use of a study/test delay manipulation in Experiment 1. Because the associative connections encoded by older adults are weaker than those of young adults, recognition performance of the older adults showed an associative effect only with context cues that evoked strong feelings of familiarity or recognition (i.e., with picture–word pairs).

The pattern of associative effects on the identification test of Experiment 2 is different from that revealed by the recognition test because identification performance is guided by different (non-intentional) retrieval processes. In the absence of conscious retrieval, performance is determined by the power of the context cues to trigger (in an automatic or bottom-up manner) the spreading of activation from context-concept representations to target-concept representations. The results indicate that this spreading of activation occurred for both word–word and picture–word pairs in young adults, but for older adults, it was effective only with word–word pairs. One reason for this may be that for older adults, the associative connections required for the spreading of activation are stronger for word – word pairs (e.g., from $_wC_2$ to $_wC_1$ in Figure 14.2) than for picture–word pairs (e.g., from $_iC_2$ to $_wC_1$). Another possibility is that the spreading of activation is more easily accomplished when contexts and targets are in the same format (i.e., both words) rather than different formats (i.e., pictures and words). In either case, the findings from Experiment 2 are more supportive of the model shown in the bottom panel of Figure 14.2. The finding that an experimental manipulation (e.g., age) had different influences on the identification and recognition of word–word and picture–word pairs seems in conflict with the view that a single higher-order representation mediates all aspects of implicit memory for newly acquired associative information.

Conclusion

The main goal of the research reported in this chapter was to examine the claim that all aspects of memory for newly acquired associative information are mediated by a single type of higher-order representation (i.e., beyond the logogen or imagen level) versus by two types of such representations. The results from Experiment 1 are consistent with both of these claims. By contrast, the findings from Experiment 2 argue against the single representation view. They suggest that memory for newly acquired associative information may recruit a variety of representation types, just as memory for items is known to involve a variety of different representations.

The findings from Experiment 2 need to be replicated and extended in order to justify strong inferences about the memory representation of newly acquired associative information. However, these findings are suggestive, fuel for interesting speculations. It seems plausible to us that the conceptual domain of memory is arranged into a variety of functional modules, analogous to the large number modules that have been postulated for perception of, for example, visual features, sound features, letters, written words, and spoken words. It seems equally plausible to assume that making associative connections within a module (e.g., word–word associations) would be easier than making associative connections between modules (e.g., picture–word associations). This may be the reason for why the old subjects in our Experiment 2 showed an associative influence on priming for word–word but not picture–word pairs.

The proposal that the conceptual domain of memory is arranged into modules, that a variety of different types of links may be used for the higher-order representation of newly acquired associative information, may illuminate the existing inconsistent findings of associative priming effects in amnesic patients and in older adults. Aging as well as events or diseases that cause amnesia may selectively impair some but not all of conceptual memory modules, resulting in impaired memory for some but not all types of newly acquired associative information. We believe that this possibility needs to be examined by future research, that without such research, any sweeping conclusions about, for example, implicit memory for new associations in amnesic patients or in old age are premature. The research we report in this chapter gives a method for going beyond the narrow conception of implicit memory for newly acquired associative information that has guided most previous investigations.

Acknowledgments

This research was supported by operating grants from Natural Sciences and Engineering Research Council of Canada to P. Graf, by University of British Columbia Graduate Fellowship to Bob Uttl, by Henry M. Jackson Foundation support to Bob Uttl, and by equipment loans from Alfalab Research Inc. Part of this research was conducted while Bob Uttl was at the National Institutes of Neurological Disorders and Stroke, National Institutes of Health, Bethesda, MD. We thank Joy Bonerba, Pilar Santacruz, and Jennifer Shapka for assisting with data collection.

References

Anderson, J. R. and **Bower, G. H.** (1973). *Human associative memory*. Washington, DC: V. H. Winston and Sons.

Bower, G. H. (1996). Reactivating a reactivation theory of implicit memory. *Consciousness and Cognition*, **5**, 27–72.

Charisma [Computer software]. (1990). Richardson, TX: Micrographx, Inc.

CorelDRAW! [Computer software]. (1994). Ottawa, ON, Canada: Corel, Inc.

Challis, B. H. and **Roediger, H. L.** (1993). The effect of proportion overlap and repeated testing on primed word fragment completion. *Canadian Journal of Experimental Psychology*, **47**, 113–23.

Challis, B. H., Velichovsky, B. M., and **Craik, F. I. M.** (1996). Levels-of-processing effects on a variety of memory tasks: New findings and theoretical implications. *Consciousness and Cognition: An International Journal*, **5**, 142–64.

Ergis, A., Van der Linden, M., and **Deweer, B.** (1998). Priming for new associations in normal aging and in mild dementia of the Alzheimer type. *Cortex*, **34**, 357–73.

Gabrieli, J. D. E. (1999). The architecture of human memory. In *Memory: Systems, process, or function? Debates in psychology* (ed. J. K. Foster and M. Jelicic), pp. 205–31. New York: Oxford University Press.

Gabrieli, J. D. E., Keane, M. M., Zarella, M. M., and **Poldrack, R. A.** (1997). Preservation of implicit memory for new associations in global amnesia. *Psychological Science*, **8**, 326–9.

Graf, P. and **Mandler, G.** (1984). Activation makes words more accessible, but not necessarily more retrievable. *Journal of Verbal Learning and Verbal Behavior*, **23**, 553–68.

Graf, P. and **Masson, M. E. J.** (1993). *Implicit memory: New directions in cognition, development, and neuropsychology*. Hillsdale, NJ: Erlbaum.

Graf, P. and **Ryan, L.** (1990). Transfer-appropriate processing for implicit and explicit memory. *Journal of Experimental Psychology: Learning, Memory, and Cognition*, **16**, 978–92.

Graf, P. and **Schacter, D. L.** (1985). Implicit and explicit memory for new associations in normal and amnesic subjects. *Journal of Experimental Psychology: Learning, Memory, and Cognition*, **11**, 501–18.

Graf, P. and **Schacter, D. L.** (1987). Selective effects of interference on implicit and explicit memory for new associations. *Journal of Experimental Psychology: Learning, Memory, and Cognition*, **13**, 45–53.

Graf, P. and **Schacter, D. L.** (1989). Unitization and grouping mediate dissociations in memory for new associations. *Journal of Experimental Psychology: Learning, Memory, and Cognition*, **15**, 930–40.

Graf, P. and **Uttl, B.** (1995). Component processes of memory: Changes across the adult lifespan. *Swiss Journal of Psychology*, **54**, 113–30.

Graf, P., Mandler, G., and Haden, P. E. (1982). Simulating amnesic symptoms in normal subjects. *Science*, **218** (4578), 1243–4.

Howard, D. V., Fry, A. F., and Brune, C. M. (1991). Aging and memory for new associations: Direct versus indirect measures. *Journal of Experimental Psychology: Learning, Memory, and Cognition*, **17**, 779–92.

Johnson, M. K. (1994). Binding complex memories: The role of reactivation and the hippocampus. In *Memory systems 1994* (ed. D. L. Schacter and E. Tulving), pp. 311–50. Cambridge, MA: MIT Press.

Jurica, P. J. and Shimamura, A. P. (1999). Monitoring item and source information: Evidence for a negative generation effect in source memory. *Memory and Cognition*, **27**, 648–56.

Mandler, G. (1981). The recognition of previous encounters. *American Scientist*, **69**, 211–8.

Mandler, G. (1994). Hypermnesia, incubation, and mind popping: On remembering without really trying. In *Attention and performance 15: Conscious and nonconscious information processing. Attention and performance series* (ed. C. Umilta and M. Moscovitch), pp. 3–33. Cambridge, MA: MIT Press.

Mandler, G. (1991). Your face looks familiar but I can't remember your name: A review of dual process theory. In *Relating theory and data: Essays on human memory in honor of Bennet B. Murdock* (ed. W. E. Hockley and S. Lewandowsky), pp. 207–25. Hillsdale, NJ: Lawrence Erlbaum Associates.

Marsolek, C. J., Schacter, D. L., and Nicholas, C. D. (1996). Form-specific visual priming for new associations in the right cerebral hemisphere. *Memory and Cognition*, **24**, 539–56.

Mitchell, D. B., Brown, A. S., and Murphy, D. R. (1990). Dissociations between procedural and episodic memory: Effects of time and aging. *Psychology and Aging*, **5**, 264–76.

Monti, L. A., Gabrieli, J. D., Wilson, R. S., Beckett, L. A., Grinnell, E., Lange, K. L., *et al.* (1997). Sources of priming in text reading: Intact implicit memory for new associations in older adults and patients with Alzheimer's disease. *Psychology* and *Aging*, **12**, 536–47.

Moscovitch, M., Winocur, G., and McLachlan, D. (1986). Memory as assessed by recognition and reading time in normal and memory-impaired people with Alzheimer's disease and other neurological disorders. *Journal of Experimental Psychology: General*, **115**, 331–47.

Musen, G. and Squire, L. R. (1993). On the implicit learning of novel associations by amnesic patients and normal subjects. *Neuropsychology*, **7**, 119–35.

Paivio, A. (1991). *Images in mind: The evolution of a theory*. London, UK: Harvester Wheatsheaf.

Paller, K. A. and Mayes, A. R. (1994). New-association priming of word identification in normal and amnesic subjects. *Cortex*, **30**, 53–73.

Roediger, H. L. III, Guynn, M. J., and Jones, T. C. (1994). Implicit memory: A tutorial review. In *International perspectives on psychological science, 2: The state of the art* (ed. G. d'Ydewalle, P. Eelen, and P. Bertelson), pp. 67–94. Hove, UK: Lawrence Erlbaum Associates.

Schacter, D. L. (1990). Perceptual representation systems and implicit memory: Toward a resolution of the multiple memory systems debate. *Annals of the New York Academy of Sciences*, **608**, 543–71.

Schacter, D. L. (1994). Priming and multiple memory system: Perceptual mechanisms of implicit memory. In *Memory systems 1994* (ed. D. L. Schacter and E. Tulving), pp. 233–68. Cambridge, MA: MIT Press.

Schacter, D. L. and Graf, P. (1986a). Effects of elaborative processing on implicit and explicit memory for new associations. *Journal of Experimental Psychology: Learning, Memory, and Cognition*, **12**, 432–44.

Schacter, D. L. and Graf, P. (1986b). Preserved learning in amnesic patients: Perspectives from research on direct priming. *Journal of Clinical and Experimental Neuropsychology*, **8**, 727–43.

Schacter, D. L. and Graf, P. (1989). Modality specificity of implicit memory for new associations. *Journal of Experimental Psychology: Learning, Memory, and Cognition*, **15**, 3–12.

Schacter, D. L. and Tulving, E. (1994). *Memory systems 1994*. Cambridge, MA: MIT Press.

Schacter, D. L., Cooper, L. A., and Delaney, S. M. (1990). Implicit memory for unfamiliar objects depends on access to structural descriptions. *Journal of Experimental Psychology: General*, **119**, 5–24.

Schacter, D. L., Cooper, L. A., and Treadwell, J. (1993). Preserved priming of novel objects across size transformation in amnesic patients. *Psychological Science*, **4**, 331–5.

Schacter, D. L., Osowiecki, D., Kaszniak, A. W., Kihlstrom, J. F., and Valdiserri, M. (1994). Source memory: Extending the boundaries of age-related deficits. *Psychology and Aging*, **9**, 81–9.

Shimamura, A. P. and Squire, L. R. (1989). Impaired priming of new associations in amnesia. *Journal of Experimental Psychology: Learning, Memory, and Cognition*, **15**, 721–8.

Spreen, O. and Strauss, E. (1991). *A compendium of neuropsychological tests*. New York: Oxford University Press.

Tulving, E. and Schacter, D. L. (1990). Priming and human memory systems. *Science*, **247**, 301–6.

Uttl, B. PicBlit3.0 [Software] Neurexis Research, Cochrane, AB, Canada, 1992–1995.

Van der Linden, M., Bruyer, R., and Dave, B. (1992). Effect of aging on implicit and explicit memory for new associations. *Cahiers de Psychologie Cognitive*, **12**, 223–37.

COMMENTARY

CHAPTER 15

COMMENTARY

FERGUS I. M. CRAIK

My main reactions on reading the chapters in this volume were first, their uniform excellence, and second, my strong personal identification with the underlying assumptions that run through them. This commentary chapter will therefore serve more as a series of endorsements rather than as a critique, but I will organize my remarks under headings that I find personally congenial. I will also attempt to resist the tendency of senior scientists like myself to make too many remarks of the type 'I made much the same point in a poster presented at a meeting of the Rocky Mountain Psychological Association in 1956...' but I will bring in some references to my own work when such temptation is too hard to resist.

The general approach

The point that priming and related phenomena of implicit memory should be considered functional and adaptive is made by several authors, notably by Bowers and Kouider and by Marsolek. This makes excellent sense to me; cognitive processes reflect highly evolved brain processes and mechanisms, and it is a very reasonable assumption that all cognitive processes act to improve the fit between organism and environment. A second general point is that the cognitive system is to be understood as a whole, not as a group of separate functions such as memory, perception, categorization, and so on. The various phenomena associated with priming fit very comfortably into this framework. At first reading priming appears to be a rather specific linguistic mechanism, but the work reported throughout the present volume makes it clear that the effects are also found in object perception (Marsolek and Burgund), and that in all cases priming involves attention, perception, memory, and categorization, as well as the specific processes associated with word and object recognition.

In the Preface, the editors describe the shift in perspective from viewing priming as a type of memory to one in which priming is seen as a natural by-product of perceptual and conceptual processing. This latter viewpoint is very much in line with the levels of processing framework put forward by Craik and Lockhart (1972). In that paper, Lockhart and I argued that the primary functions of the cognitive system are perceiving and understanding, and that episodic memory (explicit as well as implicit) should be viewed as a by-product of these primary processes. The term 'by-product' does not imply a lack of usefulness, however; both priming and episodic memories serve a crucial function in facilitating future processing and decision-making.

In a later paper describing some experiments in which an improvement in reading speed was observed when geometrically transformed texts were re-presented in the same perceptual format (Craik, 1991), I wrote:

> A slightly different way of describing the effects is to suggest that they represent a type of perceptual learning; that highly specific pattern-analyzing operations are brought into play to perceive and comprehend the text on the first reading, and that the execution of these operations modifies the perceptual system in a subtle, yet specific and possibly *permanent* way. One implication of this modification of the system is that carrying out the same sequence of operations on a subsequent occasion will be facilitated. It is not that 'activation' persists over time (as the 'priming' metaphor suggests) but simply that the underlying structures have been modified so that when the relevant processing operations are again required, they can be run off more fluently (Jacoby, 1982).

This suggestion again seems very congruent with the approach taken by the present authors. My own thinking in this area owes a great deal to the work and ideas of the late Paul Kolers (1975, 1976, 1979; Kolers and Roediger, 1984). Kolers would have been pleased with the findings and concepts in this volume, though less pleased, I fear, by the fact that his work is cited by only two of the present authors (Rueckl and Whittlesea)! His articles were prescient and are still very good value in my opinion.

A full understanding of priming and related effects will be reached only after considering results and concepts from several different approaches, such as the connectionist viewpoint (Rueckl), mathematical modeling (Wagenmakers and colleagues), visual pattern recognition (Marsolek and Burgund), and cognitive neuroscience (Marsolek). Findings from neuroimaging may prove particularly helpful in resolving puzzles that are insoluble from a cognitive standpoint. As one example relating to the debate about the existence of representations at different levels of specificity and abstraction, Marsolek and Burgund present evidence that different parts of the brain are associated with information at the two levels. Until the mapping rules between cognitive and neural processes are better understood, this type of evidence should perhaps be considered suggestive rather than definitive, but my point is that converging evidence from different approaches is bound to be helpful in arriving at a final model, couched presumably at several levels of description. Marsolek's related point that the time has come to replace the computer metaphor with the 'real' brain is persuasive, although all cognitive scientists are indebted to the computer model for such things as focusing our attention on the concept of information transmission. Completely satisfactory models of such concepts as repetition priming and episodic recollection will presumably involve descriptions at a variety of levels of scientific discourse—experiential, cognitive processes, brain processes, biochemical processes—with mapping rules between the levels carrying much of the theoretical burden.

The duration and specificity of long-term priming

In the early 1970s Kim Kirsner and I carried out some experiments on word recognition in which subjects listened to words spoken by either a male speaker or a female speaker (Craik and Kirsner, 1974). Words could occur for a second presentation at lags of 1–32 items, and repeated words could be spoken by the original speaker (MM or FF) or by the alternate speaker (MF or FM). We thought that we were exploring the limits of auditory sensory (or 'echoic') memory, which at that time was believed to last about two seconds, so we were quite surprised to find a slight but consistent same-voice advantage in recognition performance up to the longest lag used—32 items or roughly two minutes. This result clearly violated then current ideas of auditory sensory memory, so we concluded that the literal perceptual aspects of verbal stimuli persist in memory for much longer than theorists believed, that the information was perceptual and 'literal' rather than abstract-linguistic, and that there appeared to be 'little utility or validity in distinguishing between separate sensory and long-term stores, either on the basis of the persistence or the type of information stored' (Craik and Kirsner, 1974, p. 283). These results were confirmed and extended by Goldinger, Pisoni, and their colleagues (e.g., Palmeri *et al.*, 1993) and by other researchers cited by Goldinger and colleagues in the present volume.

Is it possible that this persistent usefulness of perceptual information is restricted to implicit memory? That is, participants may benefit from same-voice repetitions without being able to recollect the original speaker when the word is encountered again. In line with this possibility, Kolers (1976) found that when subjects re-read text passages in the same geometric transformation their reading speed was enhanced, even although they did not recognize the passages as old. This result did not hold for the Craik and Kirsner results, however. Participants were able to recall the original voice at much greater than chance levels *provided* that the word was recognized as old. Kolers' (1976) result suggests that at very long retention intervals (Kolers' subjects were re-tested one year later) some encoded information may still facilitate performance when there is insufficient information to produce conscious recollection. But this seems to be a matter of degree; there is no justification for concluding that the perceptual information resides in some separate privileged store labeled 'implicit memory'.

The preceding chapters provide compelling evidence that priming effects can be conceptual as well as perceptual. In these cases—for example, the evidence on morphological facilitation described by Feldman—the abstract-linguistic information is tolerant of substantial changes in surface form. There is therefore undeniable evidence for long-lasting perceptual and conceptual effects, but a related topic that receives relatively little attention is the extent to which one type of information modulates or constrains the other. In the Craik and Kirsner study, for instance, subjects were asked for a voice judgment even when they failed to recognize a repeated word, but voice recall was at chance in such cases. Geiselman and Bjork (1980) had subjects rehearse words either in a rote fashion or using elaborative encoding; they were also instructed to rehearse by mimicking a particular speaker's voice. In a later recognition test, words were presented either by that speaker or by a different speaker; the results showed a compatibility effect for rote-rehearsed words only. In this experiment at least it seems that the availability of well-encoded conceptual information eliminated either the availability or usefulness of the repeated surface form. In another demonstration, Read and Craik (1995) had subjects listen to short phrases spoken by different speakers. One of the phrases was spoken in a highly emotional tone. Seventeen days later the subjects were unexpectedly tested for memory of the voice that had spoken the emotional phrase. Recognition memory was good (66% compared to a chance level of 17%) but only when subjects heard the identical recording. Recognition of the speaker's voice dropped by a third when participants listened to a second recording made by the same voice actor trying to mimic his first recording exactly, and performance dropped to chance levels when participants attempted to recognize the original voice from a set of speakers reading a text passage. These results are in line with the REMI model proposed by Wagenmakers and colleagues, in the sense that reinstatement of encoded context plays a crucial part in priming and recognition memory.

It seems that priming effects can be extremely long-lasting; Kolers' (1976) demonstration of re-reading benefits after an interval of one year may be the most dramatic example. It seems also that the effects are rather specific, and may become more so at longer intervals (Read and Craik, 1995). Speculatively, the role of context and reinstatement may become ever more crucial as time passes. This pattern of effects is in line with an adaptive, functional approach that considers priming to be an illustration of perceptual learning; the cognitive system is 'attuned' by a pattern of stimulation to process that same pattern more readily on a subsequent occasion, provided that contextual information is also repeated exactly.

Specific or abstract representations?

One theme that runs through the whole book is whether words and other experienced events are represented in the cognitive system as individual instances, specific to their episode of occurrence, or as abstractions, comprising only the commonalities among the original events. Kinoshita attempts an interesting synthesis in this respect, arguing that visual word recognition in the lexical decision task relies on the same familiarity mechanism that partly underlies episodic recognition memory. There is general agreement that an extreme abstractionist point of view cannot be maintained; the preceding chapters describe a wealth of evidence showing that perceptual and surface features are retained by the cognitive system and affect subsequent behavior. But I have almost as much difficulty with the extreme specificity view. Whereas I have a great deal of sympathy with the proposition articulated by Whittlesea and others that 'knowledge is not retrieved, but constructed' I doubt if the principle is taken as literally by the cognitive system as it appears to be taken by some theorists. For example, are words meant to be represented only by the encoded records of the thousands or even millions of times that we have encountered them in the past? Does this mean that every time I read the word 'drink' my cognitive system swiftly computes the concept anew, hushing the rising clamour of voices (Glaswegian, Canadian, Australian...) that have spoken the word in all my previous drink-related experiences? It seems unlikely. Yet if *words* can be represented as lexical units abstracted, in part at least, from their initial contexts, it is not unreasonable to suggest that other commonly recurring concepts may also be so represented. Several authors in the preceding chapters debate whether representations are specific instances or abstractions. It seems unnecessary to opt for one or the other extreme position, and I have much more sympathy for those (including Bowers and Kouider, Luce, McLennan and Charles-Luce, and Lachs, McMichael and Pisoni) who advocate a mixed model in which abstract linguistic forms are represented along with specifics of their episodic occurrence. I return to this point later.

Some years ago John Morton reported intriguing findings showing that priming in perceptual identification tasks, both visual (Clarke and Morton, 1983) and auditory (Jackson and Morton, 1984), was facilitated by repeating words in the same modality, but that repetition of specific detail (orthography or speaker's voice) conveyed no further benefit. Other studies have shown that repetition of perceptual features is effective in enhancing performance, however (e.g., Craik and Kirsner, 1974; Palmeri *et al.*, 1993; Schacter and Church, 1992) and further cases showing that perceptual features play an important role in both implicit and explicit memory tasks are discussed in the chapters by Lachs and colleagues and by Luce, McLennan, and Charles-Luce. The resolution of this puzzle presumably involves the notion of interactions between encoding and retrieval processes. That is, specific retrieval tasks (and cognitive tasks generally) arguably require specific types of information to be effective. Performance on a particular task is enhanced to the extent that the relevant information is provided by the stimulus, context, or encoded representation, but performance is unaffected by the presence of information that is irrelevant to the task's informational requirements (Jacoby, 1983). An example from my own work is that a levels of processing manipulation has no effect on subsequent word-stem completion (an 'implicit memory' task) but has a large effect on exactly the same test stimuli given in a word-stem cued recall paradigm (an 'explicit memory' task). In my view this result (Craik *et al.*, 1994) reflects different task requirements rather than different memory systems in any sense (see also the chapter by Whittlesea).

A related point is that tasks, types of processing, and types of information often seem to interact. For example Goldinger (1996) showed that the strongest effects of voice repetition on the recognition of words were obtained in shallow processing conditions. Shallow processing may have emphasized the relative importance of the perceptual information in the transaction between the encoded record and recognition processes. A similar interaction occurs in associative repetition priming as discussed in the chapters by Uttl, Graf, and Consentino, and by Zeelenberg, Pecher, and Raaijmakers. In this case priming of new associations appears to depend on study-phase semantic processing (Graf and Schacter, 1985; Schacter and Graf, 1986). A third example from a somewhat different area is the finding that color after-effects (the McCollough effect) are found for meaningful words, but not for nonwords (Allen *et al.*, 1989). Apparently the utilization of perceptual features is supported or enhanced by the presence of semantic information. To my mind at least, these various demonstrations are better understood as interactions between types of information and task demands rather than as reflections of different cognitive systems.

Levels of representation

Rather than argue for specificity or abstraction or even for specificity *and* abstraction in the sense of two different modes of representation, my own predilection is to argue (following Craik and Lockhart, 1972) for a continuum of representations running from highly context-specific episodic instances to progressively more abstract context-free representations. Figure 15.1 shows the kind of thing I mean. Newly experienced episodes are represented as the end-points of a hierarchically organized system whose higher nodes represent the commonalities among groups of related episodes. Higher levels still represent abstracted

Hierarchical Model

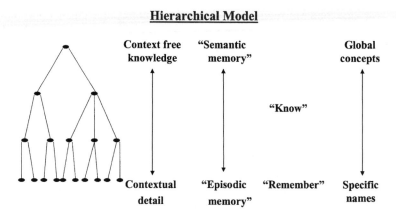

Figure 15.1 Hierarchical model of knowledge and memory. Reproduced from Craik and Grady (2000).

context-free knowledge. It is *possible* to label these higher levels 'semantic memory' and the lowest levels 'episodic memory' but I would argue that these terms refer to degrees of abstraction (see also Rueckl's chapter) rather than separate systems. It is also worth noting that such a hierarchical system of knowledge representations does not always operate in a bottom-up fashion, with general knowledge being abstracted from individual instances. Rather, the system *also* serves as the basis for interpreting new experiences; that is, new events are encoded in terms of existing knowledge. Finally, the same system comes into play again during retrieval; in this case the retrieval cue plus context are interpreted by higher levels of representation, and this interpreted cue-complex in the context of a 'set to retrieve' (Whittlesea) serves to evoke a representation of the original sought-for event.

Memory researchers have distinguished between 'remember' and 'know' judgments in recognition memory (e.g., Gardiner and Richardson-Klavehn, 2000). After recognizing a word subjects can say whether they 'remember' its occurrence—for example by recollecting some association they made at the time—or merely 'know' it was on the list. Some researchers have suggested that 'know' judgments reflect activations in semantic memory whereas 'remember' judgments reflect episodic memory. But 'know' judgments are still 'episodic' in the sense that the subject does indeed remember that the word was on the list and in the experiment, so it seems to me that 'know' judgments simply reflect a less specific form of episodic recollection.

This notion of a graded series of representations fits well with the ideas expressed by a number of the present authors, with Figure 14.1 from the chapter by Uttl, Graf, and Consentino coming close to my own Figure 15.1. The contributions by Lachs and colleagues and by Goldinger and colleagues also appear to endorse a similar view; they emphasize the retention of extra-linguistic as well as linguistic information in memory, although preferring to argue for a more instance-based model of knowledge rather than for abstract prototypes. This view also emerges from the connectionist viewpoint described lucidly by Rueckl. Bowers and Kouider allow that abstract priming may occur as a function of interactions among instances, but seem to lean somewhat to believing that abstract representations exist in their own right. Perhaps we will all have to wait for more definitive results emerging from the work on cognitive neuroscience described in Marsolek's chapter before the 'reality' of different types of representation, at different levels of scientific description, can be confirmed.

Whither implicit memory?

The present book is nominally about implicit memory, yet few of the authors—Roddy Roediger is one exception—grapple directly with the question of whether the concept remains a valuable one. Roediger votes 'no' on the issue, and Whittlesea also argues against the usefulness of the implicit/explicit dichotomy in memory theory. Indeed, the editors in their Preface also suggest that the multiple memory systems approach may not be the best way to understand the relations between episodic memory and priming. There can be no doubt that the memory systems viewpoint has been extremely helpful as a way to organize memory research and to provide a framework for understanding the results of that research (see for example Schacter and Tulving, 1994; Tulving and Schacter, 1990), but perhaps the time has come to focus on the representation of different types of encoded information and how these representations are utilized in the performance of cognitive tasks.

It makes more sense to me to talk about *knowledge systems* than about memory systems. Thus the hierarchical scheme shown in Figure 15.1 would actually refer to the organization of each of a large number of conceptual knowledge structures—each running from specific instances to generalized abstractions. One piece of evidence supporting such a view comes from semantic dementia patients who typically lose access to the specifics of a category of knowledge first, and then as the condition worsens, lose access to increasingly general types of information (Hodges, 2000; Warrington, 1975). I have suggested that a similar but less extreme set of changes may occur in normal aging, resulting in difficulties with naming and retrieval of specific contexts of occurrence (Craik, 2002).

By this view, various types of memory would be manifest by activating different levels of a knowledge structure. 'Episodic' would reflect activation of specific instances whereas 'semantic' would reflect activation of more abstract levels. Working memory may be conceived as continued attention to some aspects of activated knowledge, to a mixture of activated knowledge and recently perceived information, or occasionally to a mixture of knowledge representations. In all cases the information that is 'in working memory' is held in focal attention, as suggested by Cowan (1999) and others. Concepts such as the perceptual representational system, the word-form system, the articulatory loop, and the visuo-spatial sketchpad are not separate 'systems' by this view, but structures representing specific forms of knowledge and action, activated under relevant circumstances.

Finally, what about the implicit/explicit distinction? Is it still useful to regard implicit and explicit memory as separate systems or separate categories of learning and performance? I think I am in agreement with most contributors to this volume by answering this question in the negative. I align myself closely with Roediger and (reasonably!) closely with Whittlesea in this respect. As the work referred to by Roediger makes clear, the implicit/explicit distinction is not one between perceptual and conceptual representations;

implicit priming occurs for conceptual information and there is often explicit awareness of perceptual detail in episodic recollection. Rather, the distinction is more to do with the experiential awareness or lack of awareness that previous events and learning are playing a part in present perception and performance. In most cases such awareness is neither necessary nor helpful in performing sensori-motor and cognitive tasks; performance runs off efficiently, automatically, and unconsciously. Awareness appears to kick in when new solutions are required, new connections must be made, or when details of a previous episode are necessary to optimize the choice of future action. But, as argued by Whittlesea and others in this volume, such awareness need not involve different representational systems; implicit and explicit performances simply reflect two ways of accessing the same encoded knowledge base. 'Explicit versus implicit is a description of the outcome of this process, not a description of the knowledge on which it is based or the process that controls performance and creates awareness (Whittlesea, this volume, p. 239).' Different cognitive tasks require different types of previously encoded information, as Jacoby (1983) and others have shown. Thus, different aspects of the same encoded knowledge are drawn on at different times, depending on task demands and processing goals.

To return to one central question in conclusion—are commonalities among events and abstract concepts represented *as such* in the cognitive system, or are they constructed from encoded instances as claimed by some prominent theorists (e.g., Brooks, 1978; Logan, 1988)? This latter point of view is endorsed by Whittlesea who argues that episodic recollection occurs through a process of generation, inference, and attribution. Although I am not as thoroughgoing a constructivist as Whittlesea, I am comfortable with the idea that the 'levels of representation' sketched in Figure 15.1 represent the potential to construct different levels of specificity and abstraction in interaction with appropriate processes driven either by external stimulation or internal cogitation, as opposed to pre-formed representations of events and concepts waiting simply to be activated or retrieved. In a previous article (Craik, 1983) I asked the rhetorical question: 'Where is the percept when we are not perceiving?' The question does not make much sense; clearly percepts are not micro-representations waiting patiently for 'their' specific combination of input patterns to activate them. Rather, perceiving is a dynamic process that occurs on-line in a given time period, and reflects the interaction of incoming sense data with pre-wired and learned processes; this interaction in turn drives behavior and subjective awareness. It is thus perhaps equally meaningless to ask: 'Where is the memory trace when we are not remembering?' Again the various behavioral and experiential aspects of remembering occur only during memorial processing, and the hunt for the engram may prove as fruitless as the hunting of the Snark. To alter Lewis Carroll's mournful tale only slightly, those pursuing the memory trace may find 'in the midst of their laughter and glee' that the engram has 'softly and suddenly vanished away—for the Trace was a Boojum, you see'.

Acknowledgments

Preparation of this commentary was supported by a grant from the Natural Sciences and Engineering Research Council of Canada.

References

Allen, L. G., Siegel, S., Collins, J. C., and **MacQueen, G.** (1989). Color after effect contingent on text. *Perception and Psychophysics*, **46**, 105–13.

Brooks, L. R. (1978). Non-analytic concept formation and memory for instances. In *Cognition and categorization* (ed. E. H. Rosch and B. B. Lloyd), pp. 169–211. Hillsdale, NJ: Erlbaum.

Clarke, R. G. B. and **Morton, J.** (1983). Cross-modality facilitation in tachistoscopic word recognition. *Quarterly Journal of Experimental Psychology*, **35A**, 79–96.

Cowan, N. (1999). An embedded-processes model of working memory. In *Models of working memory* (ed. A. Miyake and P. Shah), pp. 62–101. Cambridge, UK: Cambridge University Press.

Craik, F. I. M. (1983). On the transfer of information from temporary to permanent memory. *Philosophical Transactions of the Royal Society*, **B302**, 341–59.

Craik, F. I. M. (1991). On the specificity of procedural memory. In *Memories, thoughts, and emotions* (ed. W. Kessen, A. Ortony, and F. Craik), pp. 183–97. Hillsdale, NJ: Lawrence Erlbaum Associates.

Craik, F. I. M. (2002). Human memory and aging. In *Psychology at the turn of the millennium* (ed. L. Bäckman and C. von Hofsten), pp. 261–80. Hove, UK: Psychology Press.

Craik, F. I. M. and **Grady, C. L.** (2000). Aging, memory, and frontal lobe functioning. In *Principles of frontal lobe function* (ed. D. T. Stuss and R. T. Knight). New York: Oxford University Press.

Craik, F. I. M. and **Kirsner, K.** (1974). The effect of speaker's voice on word recognition. *Quarterly Journal of Experimental Psychology*, **26**, 274–84.

Craik, F. I. M. and **Lockhart, R. S.** (1972). Levels or processing: A framework for memory research. *Journal of Verbal Learning and Verbal Behavior*, **11**, 671–84.

Craik, F. I. M., Moscovitch, M., and **McDowd, J. M.** (1994). Contributions of surface and conceptual information to performance on implicit and explicit memory tasks. *Journal of Experimental Psychology: Learning, Memory, and Cognition*, **20**, 865–75.

Gardiner, J. M. and **Richardson-Klavehn, A.** (2000). Remembering and knowing. In *The Oxford handbook of memory* (ed. E. Tulving and F. I. M. Craik), pp. 229–44. New York: Oxford University Press.

Geiselman, R. E. and **Bjork, R. A.** (1980). Primary versus secondary rehearsal in imagined voices: Differential effects on recognition. *Cognitive Psychology*, **12**, 188–205.

Goldinger, S. (1996). Words and voices: Episodic traces in spoken word identification and recognition memory. *Journal of Experimental Psychology: Learning, Memory, and Cognition*, **22**, 1166–83.

Graf, P. and **Schacter, D. L.** (1985). Implicit and explicit memory for new associations in normal and amnesic subjects. *Journal of Experimental psychology: Learning, Memory, and Cognition*, **11**, 501–18.

Hodges, J. R. (2000). Memory in the dementias. In *The Oxford handbook of memory* (ed. E. Tulving and F. I. M. Craik), pp. 441–59. New York: Oxford University Press.

Jackson, A. and **Morton, J.** (1986). Facilitation of auditory word recognition. *Memory and Cognition*, **12**, 568–74.

Jacoby, L. L. (1982). Knowing and remembering: Some parallels in the behavior of Korsakoff patients and normals. In *Human memory and amnesia* (ed. L. S. Cermak), pp. 97–122. Hillsdale, NJ: Lawrence Erlbaum Associates.

Jacoby, L. L. (1983). Remembering the data: Analyzing interactive processes in reading. *Journal of Verbal Learning and Verbal Behavior*, **22**, 485–508.

Kolers, P. A. (1975). Memorial consequences of automatized encoding. *Journal of Experimental Psychology: Human Learning and Memory*, **1**, 689–701.

Kolers, P. A. (1976). Reading a year later. *Journal of Experimental Psychology: Human Learning and Memory*, **2**, 554–65.

Kolers, P. A. (1979). A pattern-analyzing basis for recognition memory. In *Levels of processing and human memory* (ed. L. S. Cermak and F. I. M. Craik), pp. 363–84. Hillsdale, NJ: Lawrence Erlbaum Associates.

Kolers, P. A. and Roediger, H. L., III. (1984). Procedures of mind. *Journal of Verbal Learning and Verbal Behavior*, **23**, 425–49.

Logan, G. D. (1988). Toward an instance theory of automatization. *Psychological Review*, **95**, 492–527.

Palmeri, T. J., Goldinger, S. D., and Pisoni, D. B. (1993). Episodic encoding of voice attributes and recognition memory for spoken words. *Journal of Experimental Psychology: Learning, Memory, and Cognition*, **19**, 309–28.

Read, D. and Craik, F. I. M. (1995). Earwitness identification: Some influences on voice recognition. *JEP: Applied*, **1**, 6–18.

Schacter, D. L. and Church, B. A. (1992). Auditory priming: Implicit and explicit memory for words and voices. *Journal of Experimental Psychology: Learning, Memory, and Cognition*, **18**, 915–30.

Schacter, D. L. and Graf, P. (1986). Effects of elaborative processing on implicit and explicit memory for new associations. *Journal of Experimental Psychology: Learning, Memory, and Cognition*, **12**, 432–44.

Schacter, D. L. and Tulving, E. (1994). What are the memory systems of 1994? In *Memory systems 1994* (ed. D. L. Schacter and E. Tulving), pp. 1–38. Cambridge, MA: MIT Press.

Tulving, E. and Schacter, D. L. (1990). Priming and human memory systems. *Science*, **247**, 301–30.

Warrington, E. K. (1975). Selective impairment of semantic memory. *Quarterly Journal of Experimental Psychology*, **27**, 635–57.

INDEX